WORLD OF LANGUAGE

SILVER BURDETT & GINN

Marian Davies Toth   Nancy Nickell Ragno   Betty G. Gray

Contributing Author — Primary   Elfrieda Hiebert
Contributing Author — Vocabulary   Richard E. Hodges
Contributing Author — Poetry   Myra Cohn Livingston

Consulting Author — Thinking Skills   David N. Perkins

SILVER BURDETT & GINN
MORRISTOWN, NJ   NEEDHAM, MA
Atlanta, GA   Cincinnati, OH   Dallas, TX   Menlo Park, CA   Deerfield, IL

Acknowledgments

Cover: Allen Davis

Contributing Writers: Sandra Breuer, Judy Brim, Wendy Davis, Bernie Brodsky, Anne Maley, Marcia Miller, Gerry Tomlinson

Contributing artists: E. Albanese, Lori Bernero, Tom Bobroski, Lisa Bonforte, Paul Birling, Helen Davie, Bert Dodson, Susan David, Michele Epstein, Liane Fried, Dennis Hockerman, Robert Jackson, Pam Johnson, Lainie Johnson, John Killgrew, Gary Lippincott, Karen Loccisano, Richard Loehle, Peter McCaffrey, Diana Magnusen, Darcy May, Yoshi Miyake, Loughran O'Connor, Jordi Penalva, Brian Pinkney, David Rickman, Sandy Rabinowitz, Larry Raymond, Sally Schaedler, Pat Soper, Sandra Speidel, Deb Troyer, Gary Undercuffler.

Handwriting samples: Michele Epstein

Picture credits: All photographs by Silver Burdett & Ginn (SB&G) unless otherwise noted. **Introduction:** 5: Kamyar Samoul **Unit 1** 4: John Colwell/Grant Heilman Photography. 5: Animals Animals/© Charles Palek. 6: Grant Heilman/Grant Heilman Photography. 7: Earth Scenes/© Dr. Nigel Smith. 12: Grant Heilman/Grant Heilman Photography. 14: © David R. Frazier/Photo Researchers, Inc. 15: Larry Lefever/Grant Heilman Photography. 17: Thomas Zimmerman/FPG International. 20: Angel E. Allende. 42: Dan De Wilde for SB&G. 47: Jacket illustration by Lloyd Bloom from *Arthur, for the Very First Time* by Patricia Maclachlan, illustrated by Lloyd Bloom. Illustration copyright © 1980 by Lloyd Bloom. Reprinted by permission of Harper & Row, Publishers, Inc. **Unit 2** 60: Art Resource. 65: *Pete-Repete*, painted and carved on birch by Judy Kensley McKie, 1981. Courtesy Pritam & Eames Furniture Gallery, East Hampton, New York. 67: Photographed by Mark Sexton, courtesy of The Essex Institute, Salem, MA. 71: Glass vase by Louis C. Tiffany, at Smithsonian Institution, photographed by Aldo TuTino/Art Resource. 76: The Corning Museum of Glass, Corning, New York. 81: *t.* R. Duchaine/The Stock Market of NY. 87: Karl Kummels/Shostal Associates. 91: Robert Frerck/Odyssey Productions. 93: Larry Lefever/Grant Heilman Photography. 98: Dan De Wilde for SB&G. 102: Chris Jones/The Stock Market of NY. 103: *t. Model a Monster* by Colin Caket. Courtesy Bland Ford Press, Cassell plc, distributed in the US by Sterling Publishing Company, Inc., NY. **Unit 3** 133: Henley & Savage/The Stock Market of NY. 138: From the collection of the Museum of African American Art, Palmer C. Hayden collection. Gift of Miriam A. Hayden. 156: Dan De Wilde for SB&G. 161: Illustrations by Richard Powers from *American Tall Tales* by Adrienne Stoutenberg. Copyright © 1966 by The Viking Press, Inc. All rights reserved. Reprinted by permission of Viking Penguin, Inc. 183: *t.* Ernest Haas/Magnum; *b.* Mitch Epstein. 185: University Art Museum, University of Minnesota, Minneapolis/Purchase. 187: Hampton University Archival & Museum Collection, Hampton University, Hampton, Virginia. 192: ARS New York/ADAGP. Photo by Cathlyn Melloan/TSW-Click/Chicago. 198: *l.* Jim Pickerell; *r.* Courtesy of the Illinois State Historical Library. 202: Louise Nevelson, *Royal Tide 1,* 1960, wood painted gold, 96″ x 40″ x 8″. Private collection of Jean Lipman, photo courtesy of The Pace Gallery. 203: The State Historical Society of Wisconsin. 207: Courtesy of Hampton University Art Museum, Hampton, Virginia. 208: Courtesy of The State Historical Society of Wisconsin. 214: Dan De Wilde for SB&G. 218: Courtesy of Mr. August A. Busch, Jr. 219: *t.* Illustration by Donna Diamond from *Dorothea Lange: Life Through the Camera* by Milton Meltzer. Illustrations copyright © 1985 by Donna Diamond. All rights reserved. Reprinted by permission of Viking Penguin, Inc. **Unit 5** 233: NASA. 241: Ken Reagan/Camera 5. 246: Quilt, *Spacious Skies.* Charlotte Warr-Anderson, Kearns, Utah. Cotton with some polyester blends. 1985–1986. 72″ x 71½″. Collection of the Museum of American Folk Art; Museum of American Folk Art: The Scotchgard Collection of contemporary quilts (1986.14.2.) 257: Grace Moore. 268: Dan De Wilde for SB&G. 273: *t.* Photo by NASA from *To Space and Back* by Sally Ride and Susan Okie, courtesy William Morrow & Company, Inc./Publishers. **Unit 6** 282, 285: United States Department of the Interior, U.S. Geological Survey, David A. Johnston Cascades Volcano Observatory, Vancouver, Washington. 288: Steve Vidler/Four by Five. 289: *t.* W. Stoy/Bruce Coleman; *b.* Dennis Oda/Gamma Liaison. 296: Nicholas Devore III/Bruce Coleman. 298: Virginia Museum of Fine Arts, Richmond, Virginia. Giraudon/Art Resource. 302–306: United States Department of the Interior, U.S. Geological Survey, David A. Johnston Cascades Volcano Observatory, Vancouver, Washington. 309: Ed Cooper/Shostal Associates. 311: Renee Pauli/Shostal Associates. 313: Ed Cooper/Shostal Associates. 315: Stella Snead/Bruce Coleman. 316: Animals Animals/© E.R. Degginger. 317: Phil Degginger. 322: Dan De Wilde for SB&G. 327: Text Copyright © 1981 by Isaac Asimov, illustrations Copyright © 1981 by David Wool. 318: United States Department of the Interior, U.S. Geological Survey, David A. Johnston Cascades Volcano Observatory, Vancouver, Washington. **Unit 7** 340: Roy Morsch/The Stock Market of NY 342: James Ranklev/Shostal Associates. 349: Animals Animals/© John Chellman. 352: © The Metropolitan Museum of Art, bequest of Loula D. Lasker. New York City, 1961 (59.206). 372: Dan De Wilde for SB&G. 377: *t.* Jacket art from *A Visit to William Blake's Inn* by Nancy Willard, illustration copyright © 1981 by Alice Provensen and Martin Provensen, reproduced by permission of Harcourt Brace Jovanovich, Inc. **Unit 8** 389: Animals Animals/© G.L. Kogyman. 395: Bill Hurter/Leo deWys, Inc. 397: Animals Animals/© J.C. Stevenson. 404: Courtesy of Kennedy Galleries, Inc., New York. 414: Hans Pfletschinger/Peter Arnold, Inc. 415: *l.* © Toni Angermayer/Photo Researchers, Inc; *r.* Addison Geary/Stock, Boston. 417: *l.* Hans Reinhard/Bruce Coleman; *r.* Runk/Schoenberger/Grant Heilman Photography. 419: *l.* The Granger Collection; *r.* Owen Franken/Stock, Boston. 424: Dan De Wilde for SB&G. 428: C.C. Lockwood/Bruce Coleman. 429: *t.* Illustration from *Do Animals Dream?* by Joyce Pope. Copyright © 1986 by Marshall Editions, Ltd. All rights reserved. Reprinted by permission of Viking Penguin, Inc. **Dictionary** 457: *l.* Jim Alinder; *r.* Brown Brothers. 458: *l.* National Portrait Gallery, Smithsonian Institution, Washington, D.C.; *r.* State Preservation Board, Texas Capitol. Photo courtesy of the Archives Division, Texas State Library. 459: *l.* Fred Hirschmann; *r.* Greenwillow. 460: *l.* Ira Wyman for SB&G; *r. Lewis and Clark at Three Forks* (detail) by E.S. Paxson, completed 1912. Courtesy of the Montana Historical Society. 461: W.E. Ruth/Bruce Coleman; 462: *l.* Sam Sweezy/The Stock Market of NY; *r.* C.B. & D.W. Frith/Bruce Coleman. 463: David Stoecklein/West Stock, Inc. 465: *l.* William Ferguson; *r.* Copyright © 1973, Laura Ingalls Wilder Memorial Society. Every effort has been made to locate the original sources. If any errors have occurred the publisher can be notified and corrections will be made.

Acknowledgments continued on page 442

CONTENTS

INTRODUCTORY UNIT

UNIT 1

USING LANGUAGE TO NARRATE

UNIT 2

USING LANGUAGE TO INFORM

UNIT 3

USING LANGUAGE TO IMAGINE

UNIT THEME

Tall Tales

LITERATURE

''Sky-Bright Axe'' by Adrien Stoutenburg

UNIT 4

USING LANGUAGE TO PERSUADE

UNIT THEME

The Visual Arts

LITERATURE

"The Littlest Sculptor" by Joan Zeier

UNIT 5

USING LANGUAGE TO DESCRIBE

UNIT THEME

Lasting Impressions

LITERATURE

Zeely by Virginia Hamilton

UNIT 6

USING LANGUAGE TO RESEARCH

UNIT THEME

Volcanoes

LITERATURE

Volcano
by
Patricia Lauber

UNIT 7

USING LANGUAGE TO CREATE

UNIT THEME

Nature

LITERATURE

Poetry

x

UNIT 8

USING LANGUAGE TO CLASSIFY

PART ONE

LANGUAGE AWARENESS ♦ SENTENCES

UNIT THEME

Animal Habitats

PART TWO

A REASON FOR WRITING ♦ CLASSIFYING

LITERATURE

"Two of a Kind"
by
Ron Hirschi

WRITER'S REFERENCE BOOK

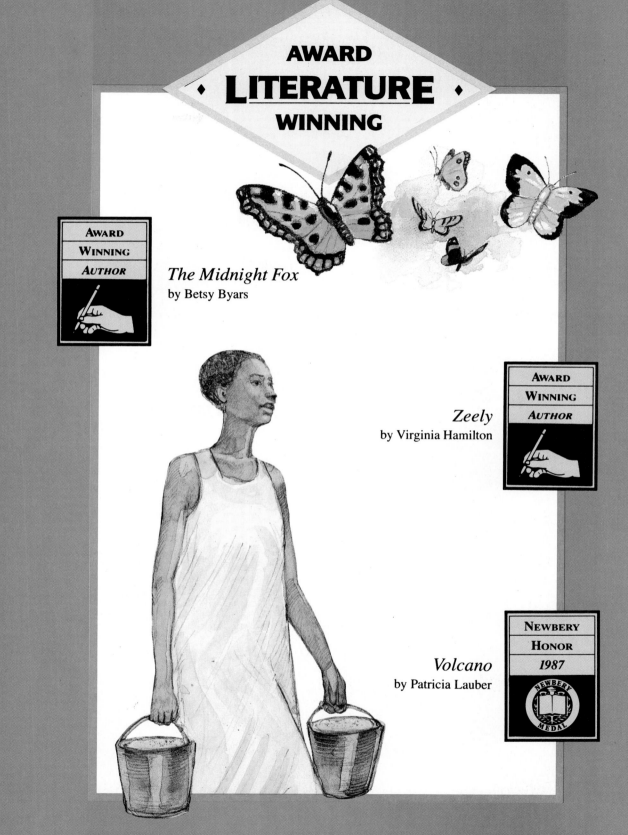

AWARD · LITERATURE · WINNING

The Midnight Fox
by Betsy Byars

Zeely
by Virginia Hamilton

Volcano
by Patricia Lauber

from

Zeel

by Virginia Ha

LITERATURE

from

The Midnight Fox

by Betsy Byars

In all his life, Tom had never spent longer, slower days than the first three days on his Aunt Millie's farm. He had fought going to the farm in the first place. He didn't get along with animals or enjoy the outdoors. He had only agreed to go, finally, so that his parents could take a summer trip to Europe.

Now Tom missed his parents and his friend Petie Burkis. Most of all, though, he missed doing his own, unplanned things every day. He felt completely useless on the farm, where everything had been well-planned without him. He was going to have a miserable summer, he feared, with nothing to look forward to but his daily trip to the mailbox. Then, everything changed. Here is Tom's story of what happened.

250

24

LITERATURE: Story

Introductory Unit

Literature in Your World

In the *World of Language* literature plays a key role. Why is it so important? What can literature mean for you in your world?

Literature unlocks your imagination. It opens your mind to the world of ideas. Through literature you can enter any time and any place. You can experience many different adventures, meet people you would never meet, share ideas with the greatest minds. Literature is indeed a key. It is a key to expanding your world. It is the key to enriching your world of language.

Writing in Your World

Writing begins with you. Writing is a way for you to connect with the world outside you. When you write, you write *to* someone. You write for your readers, and you write to be read. Writing is also a way for you to connect with your inner world, your world of thoughts, feelings, and dreams. Sometimes you write for others, and sometimes you write just for yourself.

Writing is creating, and you are the creator. Writing is thinking, and writing is discovering what you think. Writing is a way of finding out about your world, and writing is a way to change it! That is a powerful thought. Writing is powerful — a powerful tool in your world and in the wonderful world of language.

What Is a Writer?

A writer is anyone who writes. *You* are a writer. *You* are a writer whenever you jot down a message, write a letter, create a story, or outline a report. You do many kinds of writing, and you write for many reasons. Here are three kinds of writing. You will try them this year.

Writing to Inform ♦ Writing can help you get something done in the world. You might write a business letter, for example, to someone to let them know about a particular problem.

Writing to Create ♦ You can use your imagination to write a poem, a play, or a story.

Writing to Express Yourself ♦ You can use writing to express what you think or feel. Expressive writing is writing to explore your ideas, plans, and impressions. It is a kind of talking to yourself.

Writing for yourself is a very important kind of writing. It deserves a special place, for it will be special to you. A journal can be that ideal place.

Journal Writing

A journal is a writer's best friend. Carry one with you and you're always prepared to

- capture an idea by jotting it down
- practice and experiment with all kinds of writing
- think things through and explain things to yourself
- note what you think about books, movies, music
- record your impressions — your first day at school, a new friend, a painting, a puppy, for instance

A journal can be a special notebook or a section of another notebook. It can be a notebook you make yourself by stapling paper in a folder. Once you have your journal, you can begin to use it as other writers do. You will find many opportunities and ideas for journal writing throughout this book.

Introducing the Writing Process

Sometimes you want to write something, make it really good, polish it, and then share it with other people. What is the best way to go about doing this? Focus on the *process of writing*. Take time to think, plan, get ideas, make changes. Do not expect to write a perfect paper the first time. Take time to go through the writing process.

The writing process breaks writing into steps. For each step there are lots of *strategies* — ways of working — that you can learn. There are ways to get ideas and organize ideas. There are hints for how to get started and how to keep going. There are strategies for improving your writing and sharing it.

Think, Read, Speak, Listen, Write

At the end of each unit, you will use the writing process for writing something that you will publish, or share with others. You will be well-prepared for this, because first you will have a series of lessons to get you started.

- A **Thinking Skills** lesson will give you a strategy to use in reading and writing.
- A **Literature** lesson will provide you with a model for your writing.
- A **Speaking and Listening** lesson will show you how to use oral language correctly.
- **Writing** skills lessons will show you how to do the kinds of writing you will do in the Writing Process lessons.
- Two **Connection** lessons will show you how to apply the skills you learned in the unit directly to your writing.

Using the Writing Process

Write a Description

At the end of each unit, you will use the writing process for writing you will publish, or share with others. On the next four pages you will have a preview of the five stages of the writing process and will try each one. These stages are: *prewriting, writing, revising, proofreading,* and *publishing*.

Writers often start with prewriting and end by publishing. They may, however, go back and forth among the other stages or do two or more stages at once. As you become more familiar with the stages, you will feel more comfortable moving back and forth. With each stage there is an activity. When you have done all five activities, you will have written a description.

Read the Writer's Hint now. For your description your *purpose* is to describe an object so accurately your audience can "see" it; your *audience* is your classmates.

1 Prewriting ♦ Getting ready to write

Have you ever said, "I don't know what to write about" or "I don't have any ideas"? Welcome to the writers' club! Most writers feel that way before they start writing. How can you get the ideas you need? There are lots of ways. For example, you can brainstorm, draw an idea cluster, keep a journal, or do an interview.

PREWRITING IDEA

Using Your Senses: Sight

Choose an object to describe, something you can see in your classroom or outside through the window. Don't tell anyone what you choose.

Observe the object carefully for several minutes. What do you see? Take notes about your observations. Jot down words that describe size, shape, and color.

Write down everything you notice. First write down the main points — the things you probably notice first. Then look for small details. It is the little details that make your object unique.

Your notes will be your reminders of what you observed and thought. They can be just words if you wish.

2 Writing ♦ Putting your ideas on paper

You have decided what to write about. You have gathered some ideas. Now you are facing a blank page. It's time to start writing, but sometimes you don't know how to get started. Often, once you start, you don't know how to keep going.

The important thing is just to start writing. Don't worry if your ideas are out of order or if you make spelling errors. You will be able to improve your writing when you revise and proofread.

WRITING IDEA

Starting with a Question

Put your prewriting notes in front of you before you begin writing your description. How can you begin? You might begin with a question such as *Have you ever really looked at the oak tree outside our window?* After you start, use your notes to tell what the object looks like. Tell the main things you noticed and the interesting details. Do not try to include *everything* you jotted down, though. Pick and choose. Write on every other line to give yourself room to make changes later. Finally, add an ending sentence, such as *The oak tree is probably the oldest tree in our schoolyard.*

3 Revising ♦ Making changes to improve your writing

Reading to yourself is an important revising strategy. First think about your *purpose*. Did you stick to your purpose of describing an object? Or did you forget to describe and start telling a story? Also think about your *audience*. Were you writing for your classmates? Will they understand what you wrote?

Another revising strategy is sharing with a partner. Read your writing aloud. Ask your partner to make suggestions and ask questions. Think about your partner's suggestions. Then make the changes *you* feel are important.

REVISING IDEA

Read to Yourself and Read to a Partner

First read your description to yourself. Think about your purpose and audience. Did you really create a picture of what you are describing? Make changes to improve your description. You can cross out words and write in new words. You can draw arrows to show where to move words or sentences. Your writing may look very messy at this point. That is all right.

Next read your description to a partner. Ask, *"What part did you like the best? What would you like to know more about?"* Listen to the answers. Then make the changes you think will improve your description.

4 Proofreading ♦ Looking for and fixing errors

After you have made sure your writing says what you want it to say, proofread for correctness. Check capital letters and punctuation, indenting, and spelling. Then make a clean copy in your best handwriting. A correct copy is a courtesy to your reader.

PROOFREADING IDEA

One Thing at a Time

It's hard to look for every kind of error at once. Check for one thing at a time. First check indenting, then capitalization, then punctuation. Check your spelling last.

5 Publishing ♦ Sharing your writing with others

There are many ways to share your writing. You may read it aloud to others. You may record it with a tape recorder or post it on a bulletin board. One of the best parts of writing is hearing or seeing your audience's response.

PUBLISHING IDEA

A Guessing Game

Take turns reading your descriptions aloud to each other. For extra fun, play a guessing game. In place of the name of your object, say "thingamajig." For example,

Have you ever really looked at the thingamajig outside our window? See if you have described your object so well that your classmates can guess what it is.

USING LANGUAGE TO
NARRATE

PART ONE

Unit Theme *Farm Life*

Language Awareness Sentences

PART TWO

Literature *The Midnight Fox* by Betsy Byars

A Reason for Writing Narrating

Writing
IN YOUR JOURNAL

WRITER'S WARM-UP ◆ What do you know about farm life? Maybe you live on a farm. Perhaps you visited one once or saw a movie that took place on a farm. What animals live on farms? What special buildings do farms need? What jobs do people do on farms? Is there one special thing about farms that interests you? Write about farms in your journal. Tell about some aspect of farm life that you know about and like.

Choose an animal of the woods, fields, or farm. Without naming the animal, give some information about it. The first person to guess your animal tells about the next mystery animal.

1 Writing Sentences

When you exchange thoughts and ideas, you speak and write in sentences. A sentence goes somewhere and does something. It is complete when it finishes the thought it begins. A group of words that does not complete its thought is not a sentence. For example, *Does only part of the job* is not a sentence. *It does only part of the job* is a sentence.

Read each group of words below. The first group in each set is not a complete sentence. The second group of words is a sentence.

1. a. A fox.
   b. A fox ran into the forest.
2. a. Watched it.
   b. Mei Ling watched it.
3. a. About foxes on the farm.
   b. Luis wrote a report about foxes on the farm.

> **Summary** ◆ A **sentence** is a group of words that expresses a complete thought. When you write, make sure each of your sentences is complete. This will help your reader understand what you mean.

Guided Practice

Tell whether each group of words below is or is not a sentence.

1. Foxes look like small dogs.
2. Foxes have bushy tails and sharp snouts.
3. A fox and her pups.
4. Foxes live in dens.
5. Underground, among rocks, or in a hollow log.
6. A fox may appear suddenly.

Practice

A. Decide whether each group of words expresses a complete thought. Write *sentence* or *not a sentence*.

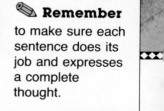

   7. An adult fox is about twenty-five inches long.
   8. Weighs about ten pounds.
   9. Living in family groups while young are growing.
  10. Foxes can be playful.
  11. Foxes have a keen sense of smell.
  12. Hunts mostly at night.
  13. Foxes communicate through growls and barks.
  14. Lives up to fourteen years.
  15. The red fox is common in the northern United States.
  16. Eats mice, birds, lizards, and rabbits.

B. Write the group of words in each pair that is a sentence.

  17. a. In late winter or early spring.
      b. A female fox gives birth to her pups.
  18. a. The male and female foxes bring food to the young.
      b. Leading enemies away from the den.
  19. a. The pups or cubs wrestle with each other.
      b. Jumps on insects and parents' tails.
  20. a. Showing the young how to stalk or chase prey.
      b. The adults bring live mice for the pups to pounce on.
  21. a. May wander far from the area in which they were born.
      b. The pups start to live on their own in late summer.

C. Add words to make each group of words a sentence.

  22. A sleek red fox _____.
  23. The cows in the pasture _____.
  24. _____ splashed across the shallow stream.
  25. The tall golden grass _____.
  26. _____ near the side of the farmhouse.

Apply • Think and Write

From Your Writing ♦ Read what you wrote for the Writer's Warm-up. Did you express yourself in complete sentences? Rewrite any incomplete sentences you find.

> ✎ **Remember**
> to make sure each sentence does its job and expresses a complete thought.

How many different ways can you think of to complete the sentence so that it tells something, asks something, or shows strong feeling: _____ *a severe thunderstorm* _____ (.) (?) (!)

2 Four Kinds of Sentences

There are four kinds of sentences. All begin with capital letters.

Four Kinds of Sentences	
Declarative A declarative sentence makes a statement. It ends with a period (.).	Rice is a popular food.
Interrogative An interrogative sentence asks a question. It ends with a question mark (**?**).	Are there many rice farmers in America?
Imperative An imperative sentence gives a command or makes a request. It ends with a period (.).	Begin harvesting the wheat tomorrow.
Exclamatory An exclamatory sentence expresses strong feeling. It ends with an exclamation mark (**!**).	How beautiful the waving wheat looks!

Remember to begin every sentence with a capital letter and end it with the correct punctuation mark.

Summary ◆ A **declarative sentence** makes a statement. An **interrogative sentence** asks a question. An **imperative sentence** gives a command or makes a request. An **exclamatory sentence** expresses strong feeling.

Guided Practice

Tell which kind of sentence each of the following is.

1. Rice is used in cereals.
2. What a day for plowing!
3. How much wheat will you plant?
4. Attach the plow to the tractor.

Practice

A. For each sentence below, write *declarative, interrogative, imperative,* or *exclamatory.*

5. Rice is the primary food for half the people of the world.
6. Is rice a grain?
7. Rice is often grown in flooded fields.
8. Plant the rice in the muddy ground.
9. What an incredible sight that rice field is!
10. Does a rice field need a constant supply of water?
11. Harvesting begins when the golden heads of rice bend down.
12. Leave the cut rice stalks in the sun to dry.

B. Write each sentence, using capital letters and end punctuation correctly.

13. wheat is a grasslike cereal grain
14. how tall those wheat plants are
15. do leaves grow from the stalk of a wheat plant
16. about 30,000 different kinds of wheat are grown
17. what a large number of varieties that is
18. is much wheat grown in the United States
19. wheat is ready for harvest when it is dry and hard
20. transfer the harvested wheat to the grain elevator

C. Rewrite each sentence. Change it to the kind named in parentheses ( ).

21. Is the soil plowed before wheat seeds are planted? (declarative)
22. Machines are used to plant the wheat. (interrogative)
23. Do you sometimes add nitrogen to the soil? (imperative)
24. The endless fields of golden wheat are beautiful. (exclamatory)

Apply ◆ Think and Write

Sentence Variety ◆ Pretend that you are about to enjoy a bowl of cereal made of rice or wheat. Using all four kinds of sentences, write about the cereal.

✎ **Remember** to use different kinds of sentences to express your ideas.

GETTING
STARTED

Play "Who-Does-What?" Begin a sentence with your first and last names. Use words that begin with your initials to finish the sentence. For example: *Carmen Ruiz collects rocks*.

3 Complete Subjects and Complete Predicates

Think about what a sentence needs in order to do its job of expressing a complete thought. It needs certain parts, just like a machine. Every sentence has two main parts. The complete subject names someone or something. The complete predicate tells what the subject is or does.

Read the sentences below. The part in blue is the complete subject. The part in green is the complete predicate.

1. **Insects** **can be harmful to farm plants.**
2. **Some insects** **help.**
3. **The potato beetle** **is a harmful insect.**
4. **Farmers in some areas** **lose their crops through insects.**

The complete subject may have only one word as in **1** above. The complete subjects in **2**, **3**, and **4** have more than one word. The complete predicate may also have one word or many words.

> **Summary** ◆ The **complete subject** is all the words in the subject part of a sentence. The subject part names someone or something. The **complete predicate** is all the words in the predicate part of a sentence. The predicate part tells what the subject is or does.

Guided Practice

Name each complete subject and complete predicate.

1. Insects are small animals.
2. All insects have six legs.
3. Millions of kinds of insects live throughout the world.
4. The bodies of dead insects enrich the soil.
5. Insects help many plants produce seeds through pollination.

Practice

A. Read each sentence. Then write the complete subject of each.

6. Many insects are helpful to farmers.
7. Bees pollinate farmers' crops.
8. The bees on our farm make delicious honey.
9. Predators are animals that eat other animals.
10. Some helpful insects are predators.
11. The ladybug eats several kinds of crop-destroying insects.
12. Other insects on the farm are parasites.
13. These insects live on or in the bodies of harmful insects.
14. A certain kind of wasp lays eggs in harmful caterpillars.
15. The young wasps feed on the caterpillars and kill them.

B. Write each sentence. Underline the complete subject once. Underline the complete predicate twice.

16. The corn earworm destroys corn crops.
17. The caterpillar of the cabbage butterfly damages cauliflower.
18. Wheat crops are hurt by maggots.
19. Gypsy moth caterpillars strip the leaves from many trees.
20. Harmful insects cause billions of dollars in crop damage.

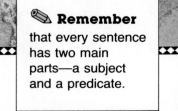

C. Add a complete subject or a complete predicate to each group of words below. Write the complete sentence.

EXAMPLE: _____ wrote a report about harmful insects.
ANSWER: Tom wrote a report about harmful insects.

21. _____ examined the damage insects caused to the crops.
22. The study of insects _____.
23. _____ have very few problems with insects.
24. _____ flew very close to my face.
25. A thick, furry caterpillar _____.

Apply • Think and Write

Telling a Story ◆ Imagine that you have spent a week on a farm. Write a story about your stay. Be sure to include your chores as well as any special events that occurred on the farm.

> ✎ **Remember**
> that every sentence has two main parts—a subject and a predicate.

GETTING
STARTED

What foods do you like in each category below?
dairy products   fruits   meats   vegetables
Use the names of those foods in the subjects of sentences.

4 Simple Subjects

Remember that the complete subject is all the words in the subject part of a sentence. The most important word in the complete subject is called the simple subject.

Read the sentences below. The complete subject of each sentence is shown in blue. The simple subject is underlined.

1. Livestock are farm animals.
2. Some farmers raise livestock.
3. The chickens on a farm provide eggs and meat.
4. Susie Thompson visited a nearby farm.
5. She fed the chickens.

Look at the sentences again. Notice that most of the time the simple subject is one word. Sometimes it is more than one word. In sentence **4** the simple subject is two words because it is a person's full name.

> **Summary** ◆ The **simple subject** is the main word in the complete subject. When you write, choose an exact word as a simple subject to make your meaning clear.

Guided Practice

A line has been drawn between the complete subject and the complete predicate of each sentence. Name the simple subject in each sentence.

1. Livestock | provide food and other valuable products.
2. Some specialized farms | raise only livestock.
3. The farmers on a specialized farm | may raise only one kind of animal.
4. Kevin Johnson | owns a cattle ranch.
5. The sprawling ranch | is over 10,000 acres in size.

Practice

A. Read each sentence below. A line has been drawn between the complete subject and the complete predicate. Write each complete subject. Draw a line under the simple subject.

    6. Many farmers in the United States | raise chickens.
    7. Chickens on a farm | may live in wire cages.
    8. A rooster | is an adult male chicken.
    9. A hen | is a mature female chicken.
    10. Over 240 eggs | may be laid by a hen in a year.
    11. Many farmers | buy pullets from other farms.
    12. A pullet | is a female chicken less than a year old.
    13. Some farms | raise chickens to produce meat.
    14. Special feed | makes chickens gain weight quickly.
    15. The age of a chicken | determines how it should be cooked.

B. Write the simple subject of each sentence.

    16. Cattle are very important farm animals.
    17. Many different meats come from cattle.
    18. The milk from cows is a very nutritious food.
    19. Some farmers milk their cows by hand.
    20. Most large farms use electric milking machines.

C. The sentences below are each missing a simple subject. Choose one of the following words to complete each sentence.

yogurt   step   truck   milk   technicians

    21. Cow's ＿＿ contains carbohydrates, fats, minerals, proteins, and vitamins.
    22. ＿＿ is one of many foods made from milk.
    23. A ＿＿ takes milk from the farm to the processing plant.
    24. Laboratory ＿＿ check the taste and appearance of milk.
    25. The final ＿＿ in the processing of milk is packaging.

Apply ◆ Think and Write

Restating Facts ◆ Write at least five sentences that state facts you learned in this lesson about livestock farming. Use your own words, and use a variety of simple subjects.

✎ **Remember**
to use precise simple subjects to make your meaning clear.

List animals whose names begin with the letters *a, b,* or *c.* Then tell in complete sentences what these animals do, did, or might do.

5 Simple Predicates

You have learned that the complete predicate is all the words in the predicate part of a sentence. The simple predicate is the most important word or words in this part. The simple predicate is the word or words that show action.

Bob's class was writing about various plants and animals that are found on farms. The students used exact action words to make the action seem real. Here are some of the sentences they wrote. The complete predicate of each sentence is shown in green. The simple predicate is underlined.

1. The rooster <u>crows.</u>
2. The Holstein cow <u>swished</u> its tail.
3. The wheat <u>is waving</u> rhythmically in the wind.
4. The horse <u>had trotted</u> toward me.

In sentences **1** and **2,** the simple predicate is one word. In sentences **3** and **4,** the simple predicate is more than one word.

> **Summary** ◆ The **simple predicate** is the main word or words in the complete predicate. When you write, use exact action words as simple predicates to make the action seem real.

Guided Practice

Here are some more sentences Bob's class wrote. A line has been drawn between the complete subject and the complete predicate. Name the simple predicate.

1. A ripe red apple | plopped to the ground.
2. My pony | snorted in disgust.
3. The bright yellow sunflowers | were bursting with seeds.
4. The lamb with the thick fleece | nuzzled my fingers.
5. My aunt's farmhand | had scattered feed for the hungry chickens.

Practice

A. Read each sentence below. A line has been drawn between the complete subject and the complete predicate. Write each complete predicate. Draw a line under the simple predicate.

6. Some farms | produce both crops and livestock.
7. They | are called mixed farms.
8. Mixed farms | grow crops and livestock for their region.
9. Cattle and peanuts | are produced on farms in the South.
10. A midwestern mixed farm | raises hogs, cattle, and grain.
11. Hogs | provide much meat for American consumption.
12. Belts and shoes | are made from hog's skin.
13. Hogs | wallow in mud on hot days.
14. Hogs | have a keen sense of smell.
15. A very young hog | is called a pig.

B. Write the simple predicate of each sentence.

16. A peanut plant grows about two and one-half feet high.
17. A peanut belongs to the pea family.
18. The peanuts themselves develop in pods underground.
19. George Washington Carver, an American botanist, made over 300 products from the peanut.
20. Manufacturers grind roasted peanuts for peanut butter.

C. The sentences are each missing a simple predicate. Choose one of the following simple predicates to complete each sentence.

sweetens   are located   stretch   thrive   is harvested

21. Pineapples _____ in Hawaii.
22. Many potato farms _____ in California, Idaho, and Maine.
23. A large tomato crop _____ in New Jersey each year.
24. The fresh scent of citrus fruits _____ the Florida breeze.
25. America's rich farmlands _____ from coast to coast.

Apply ♦ Think and Write

Dictionary of Knowledge ♦ George Washington Carver was an American botanist. Read about him in the Dictionary of Knowledge. Write some sentences about his discoveries.

✎ **Remember**
to use simple predicates that express action clearly.

GETTING STARTED

Think of commands that would be impossible to obey, such as "Drain all the water from the seas."

6 Subjects in Imperative Sentences

You have learned that the subject part of a sentence names someone or something. In a declarative sentence the subject usually comes first.

■ **Some farmers | face many problems.**

In the declarative sentence above, the complete subject is *Some farmers* and the simple subject is *farmers*.

In imperative sentences the simple subject is always the word *you*. However, the word *you* is not usually stated. We say that it is "understood." In each of the two imperative sentences below, the subject is *you* (understood).

■ *(You)* | **Turn on the water.**
■ *(You)* | **Turn on the irrigation system.**

Read the two imperative sentences above again. Notice that the second one gives more exact information and is easier to understand. Always make a command or request as clear as possible.

> **Summary** ◆ *You* (understood) is the subject of an imperative sentence. When you write an imperative sentence, make the command or request as clear as possible.

Guided Practice

Name the subject in each sentence below. Some of the sentences are imperative.

1. The layer of fertile soil is very thin.
2. Plow across the slope.
3. This soil does not have enough nutrients.
4. Apply the fertilizer.

Practice

A. Write each sentence. Underline the simple subject. Write (*You*) if the subject is understood.

EXAMPLE: Plant alfalfa in this field instead of corn.
ANSWER: (You) Plant alfalfa in this field instead of corn.

5. Erosion wears away soil and rock.
6. Rainwater washes away the soil on farms.
7. Plant grass between each row of corn.
8. Build terraces, or wide, flat rows, up that entire slope.
9. Wind can blow away topsoil.
10. Plant a row of trees for a windbreak.
11. Fields at plowing time are scattered with dead stalks and leaves from the previous crop.
12. Plow the field with the old plant matter.
13. Use this method of tilling for erosion control.
14. Conservation of the soil saves farmland from destruction.

B. Write each sentence. Write *declarative* or *imperative* to show the kind of sentence. Underline the simple subject in each declarative sentence. Write *(You)* for each imperative sentence.

15. Plants need seventeen nutrients for proper growth.
16. Analyze the nutrients in the soil.
17. Some fertilizers supply potassium to plants.
18. Farmers in very dry areas irrigate, or water, their crops.
19. Install a sprinkler irrigation system in the cornfield.
20. Turn on the water immediately.
21. Some animals harm farm crops.
22. Spray the crops with pesticide.
23. Mice are eating the grain in storage.
24. Bring in some foxes for control of the mice.

Apply ♦ Think and Write

Problems and Solutions ♦ Imagine that you own a farm. Write three declarative sentences and three imperative sentences. In each declarative sentence, state a problem on the farm. In each imperative sentence, provide a solution to the problem.

✎ **Remember**
to state your commands and requests clearly.

What animals come to mind when you read these words?

crawl	*prowl*	*slink*	*slither*	*wiggle*
writhe	*creep*	*wriggle*	*glide*	*skulk*

VOCABULARY ◆
Using the Thesaurus

The word *thesaurus* comes from a Greek word meaning "a treasure," and a thesaurus is truly a treasury of words. Like a dictionary, a **thesaurus** lists entry words in alphabetical order. A list of synonyms, or words with similar meanings, is given for each entry word. Antonyms, or words with opposite meanings, are also listed for many of the entry words. You will learn more about synonyms and antonyms in Unit 7.

A thesaurus is a valuable tool for writers. It helps them choose the best word to fit their meaning. You will find a thesaurus beginning on page 466 of this book. Study the thesaurus entry below for the word *tell*.

Part of Speech   **Definition**

Entry Word ──── **tell** (v)─to express in words; to say; to give an account of; to relate.

Example Sentence ── Tell me what you think of it.

advise—to give advice to; to counsel; to offer an opinion to. Would you advise me about what to get my mother for a birthday present?

communicate—to give news or information by speaking or writing; to telephone; to write. Have you communicated recently with your sister in New Mexico?

inform—to supply with facts, knowledge, or news; to tell. I was not informed of the change in plans until today.

Synonyms ──── *instruct*—to teach; to train; to give knowledge to; to give orders or directions to. I was instructed to hand out the drawing materials.

narrate—to tell the story of; to relate. He will narrate the well-known story, which has been set to music.

report—to tell of something seen, done, heard, or read; to state or announce. Allison reported the results of her science experiment to us.

Cross-reference ──── See also *say* (v).

Antonym ──── ANTONYM: listen

Building Your Vocabulary

Use the thesaurus entry on page 16 to answer these questions.

1. What word is opposite in meaning to *tell*?
2. What other word can you look up for more synonyms of *tell*?
3. What part of speech are *tell* and its synonyms?

Practice

A. Write each sentence. Complete it with a synonym for *tell*. Use a different synonym in each sentence.

1. Undersea telephone lines were put in so that the two countries could _____ .
2. Carl tried to _____ the child on how to use the computer.
3. _____ me about the animals that live in the tide pool.
4. The actor will _____ the story "Peter and the Wolf."
5. Did Ana _____ you to get up early because the trip would be long?

B. Use the Thesaurus to find the synonyms for *rough* that fit best in these sentences. Use a different synonym for each sentence.

6. A sea urchin has _____ spines covering its shell.
7. The landscape of the Nevada desert was rocky and _____ .
8. _____ sounds of machinery echoed through the factory.
9. The auto mechanic's hands were strong and _____ .
10. After the accident there were many _____ scraps of metal and glass lying about.

LANGUAGE CORNER ◆ Reversal Words

Some words say one thing when you read them forward and another thing when you read them backward. For example, *stab* read backward is *bats*.

Can you decode the following sentence? *Tap was net keels spools.*

How to Combine Sentences

Would a singer sing the same song more than once at a concert? Probably not, because most people would not want to hear the same thing twice. For a similar reason, you should avoid repeating words in your writing. One way to do this is by combining, or joining, sentences that repeat words. Read the examples below.

> **1.** Sheldon hiked ten miles through a rugged canyon. Marty hiked ten miles through a rugged canyon.
> **2.** Sheldon and Marty hiked ten miles through a rugged canyon.

In example **1**, both sentences tell about people who did the same thing. Example **2** was made by combining the two subjects, *Sheldon* and *Marty*, with the word *and*. The two sentences that share the same predicate are combined into one strong sentence.

You can also use the word *and* to combine two sentences that share the same subject. Which word is shared in the two sentences in example **3**?

> **3.** Leah wrote to the state park. Leah applied for a job.
> **4.** Leah wrote to the state park and applied for a job.

Read the two sentences in example **5**. The understood subject of both sentences is *you*. What word is added to combine the predicates in example **6** to make one strong sentence?

> **5.** Look at this picture. Tell me if these are moose or elk.
> **6.** Look at this picture and tell me if these are moose or elk.

The Grammar Game ◆ Match them up! Choose a sentence from the left to combine with a sentence from the right.

Put the cassette in the case.	Rick fixed the door handle.
Rick washed the car.	Her friend entered the race.
My cousin entered the race.	Give it to Marsha.

Working Together

As your group does activities **A** and **B**, you will avoid repeating words by using the word *and* to combine sentences.

A. Complete each pair of sentences with a group member's name. Then combine the sentences, using the word *and*. Can your group create its own sentences to combine? How many can you add?

1. _____ collects pine cones. _____ makes table decorations.
2. _____ designs puppets. _____ puts on shows for young children.
3. _____ builds model insects. _____ hangs them from the ceiling.
4. _____ loves wild birds. _____ feeds them every winter.
5. _____ enjoys music. _____ has a wonderful record collection.

B. Combine each pair of sentences. Make sure each group member writes at least one sentence. Then arrange the combined sentences into a paragraph.

6. A rooster crowed. A rooster woke me up.
7. The sun brought color to the morning sky. The clouds brought color to the morning sky.
8. Ducks quacked. Ducks waddled to the edge of the pond.
9. I yawned and stretched. I finally got out of bed.
10. Then the gray colt kicked up its heels. The gray colt trotted towards its mother.

WRITERS' CORNER • Stringy Sentences

Be careful not to use *and* or *and so* to string together too many sentences. Stringy sentences are hard to read and understand.

STRINGY: **We went to the movies last night, and everyone in town was there, and so we waited in line for over thirty minutes, and we were lucky to find seats together.**

IMPROVED: **We went to the movies last night, and everyone in town was there. We waited in line for over thirty minutes. We were lucky to find seats together.**

Read what you wrote for the Writer's Warm-up. Did you use any stringy sentences? If you did, can you improve them?

OXCART IN SUGAR CANE FIELD
painting by Angel E. Allende.

USING LANGUAGE TO

NARRATE

═══ PART TWO ═══

Literature *The Midnight Fox* by Betsy Byars

A Reason for Writing Narrating

CREATIVE
Writing

FINE ARTS ◆ This painting by Angel E. Allende shows an oxcart in a field of sugar cane. The oxcart is waiting there, but there are no workers. Where do you think the workers are? Have they gone home for the day? Are they eating lunch? Imagine that you are one of the workers who work in this field. Write an entry for this day in your journal. Tell about the work you did and what you did after work. Tell about the ox and how it helped you.

CRITICAL THINKING ◆
A Strategy for Narrating

AN OBSERVATION CHART

Telling a story is often called narrating. After this lesson, you will read part of a story called *The Midnight Fox*. You will see how its author, Betsy Byars, uses details to help the reader "see" what is happening. Later you will write a personal narrative—a story about an experience of your own.

In *The Midnight Fox* the storyteller, Tom, uses the words *I* and *me* to narrate an experience he had. Here is part of *The Midnight Fox* in which Tom tells about meeting a black fox. What details in these two sentences make the fox seem real?

> Her head was cocked to one side, her tail curled up, her front left foot raised. In all my life I never saw anything like that fox standing there with her pale golden eyes on me and this great black fur being blown by the wind.

A writer who observes carefully can include information that makes a story come to life. When you observe, you look for and pay special attention to details.

Learning the Strategy

You observe details all day long. For example, suppose you are in the park and see a great spot for flying your new kite. You want to be able to go there again. What details would help you remember where it was? Maybe you want to be a one-person band. What details would you need to imitate? Perhaps you are going to a World Series game. It is so exciting that you want to write a story about it for your school newspaper.

CRITICAL THINKING: Observing

Making an observation chart is a strategy that can help you remember details. For example, an observation chart about the World Series game could help you record details to use in the story you want to write. It might look like this.

Topic —

Subtopics —

— Details

	A World Series Game	
What I Saw	40,000 fans two home runs pennants	a sea of people the winners jumping up and down
What I Heard	people shouting The Star-Spangled Banner Take Me Out to the Ball Game	the crack of the bat hitting the ball
What I Felt	excited about being there thrilled when my team won	upset when my team struck out

Using the Strategy

A. Observe your left shoe. Then make an observation chart about it. Write "My Left Shoe" as the topic. Think of subtopics you like such as "How It Looks," "How It Feels," and "Where It Has Been." Record details for each heading. You might use your chart to help you tell someone a story about your shoe.

B. *The Midnight Fox* takes place on a farm. Before you read the story, think about what you know about farms. Organize your ideas in an observation chart. Write the topic, "Farms." Then decide on subtopics such as "What I Might See," "What I Might Hear," and "What I Might Feel." Record details for each subtopic. As you read *The Midnight Fox*, notice what Tom observes on the farm. Is the farm in the story like farms you have heard about or observed?

Applying the Strategy

♦ How did you decide which subtopics to include in your observation charts? Why might these headings be different the next time you make an observation chart?

♦ When might it be helpful to you to record observations in your journal?

LITERATURE

from

The Midnight Fox

by Betsy Byars

In all his life, Tom had never spent longer, slower days than the first three days on his Aunt Millie's farm. He had fought going to the farm in the first place. He didn't get along with animals or enjoy the outdoors. He had only agreed to go, finally, so that his parents could take a summer trip to Europe.

Now Tom missed his parents and his friend Petie Burkis. Most of all, though, he missed doing his own, unplanned things every day. He felt completely useless on the farm, where everything had been well-planned without him. He was going to have a miserable summer, he feared, with nothing to look forward to but his daily trip to the mailbox. Then, everything changed. Here is Tom's story of what happened.

The one highlight of my day was to go down to the mailbox for the mail. This was the only thing I did all day that was of any use. Then, too, the honking of the mail truck would give me the feeling that there was a letter of great importance waiting for me in the box. I could hardly hurry down the road fast enough. Anyone watching me from behind would probably have seen only a cloud of dust, my feet would pound so fast. So far, the only mail I had received was a post card from my mom with a picture of the Statue of Liberty on it telling me how excited and happy she was.

This Thursday morning when I went to the mailbox there was a letter to me from Petie Burkis and I was never so glad to see anything in my life. I ripped it open and completely destroyed the envelope I was in such a hurry. And I thought that when I was a hundred years old, sitting in a chair with a rug over my knees, and my mail was brought in on a silver tray, if there was a letter from Petie Burkis on that tray, I would snatch it up and rip it open just like this. I could hardly get it unfolded— Petie folds his letters up small—I was so excited.

Dear Tom,

There is nothing much happening here. I went to the playground Saturday after you left, and you know that steep bank by the swings? Well, I fell all the way down that. Here's the story—

BOY FALLS DOWN BANK
WHILE GIRL ONLOOKERS CHEER

Today Petie Burkis fell down the bank at Harley Playground. It is reported that some ill-mannered girls at the park for a picnic cheered and laughed at the sight of the young, demolished boy. The brave youngster left the park unaided.

Not much else happened. Do you get Chiller Theater? There was a real good movie on Saturday night about mushroom men.

Write me a letter,
Petie Burkis

I went in and gave the rest of the mail to Aunt Millie, who said, "Well, let's see what the government's sending us today," and then I got my box of stationery and went outside.

There was a very nice place over the hill by the creek. There were trees so big I couldn't get my arms around them, and soft grass and rocks to sit on. They were planning to let the cows into this field later on, and then it wouldn't be as nice, but now it was the best place on the farm.

Incidentally, anyone interested in butterflies would have gone crazy. There must have been a million in that one field. I had thought about there being a contest—a butterfly contest and hundreds of people would come from all over the country to catch butterflies. I had thought about it so much that I could almost see this real fat lady from Maine running all over the field with about a hundred butterfly nets and a fruit jar under her arm.

Anyway, I sat down and wrote Petie a letter.

Dear Petie,

I do not know whether we get Chiller Theater or not. Since there is no TV set here, it is very difficult to know what we could get if we had one.

My farm chores are feeding the pigs, feeding the chickens, weeding the flowers, getting the mail, things like that. I have a lot of time to myself and I am planning a movie about a planet that collides with Earth, and this planet and Earth become fused together, and the people of Earth are terrified of the planet, because it is very weird-looking and they have heard these terrible moanlike cries coming from the depths of it. That's all so far.

Write me a letter,
Tom

I had just finished writing this letter and was waiting for a minute to see if I would think of anything to add when I looked up and saw the black fox.

I did not believe it for a minute. It was like my eyes were playing a trick or something, because I was just sort of staring across this field, thinking about my letter, and then in the distance, where the grass was very green, I saw a fox leaping over the crest of the field. The grass moved and the fox sprang toward the movement, and then, seeing that it was just the wind that had caused the grass to move, she ran straight for the grove of trees where I was sitting.

It was so great that I wanted it to start over again, like you can turn movie film back and see yourself repeat some fine thing you have done, and I wanted to see the fox leaping over the grass again. In all my life I have never been so excited.

I did not move at all, but I could hear the paper in my hand shaking, and my heart seemed to have moved up in my body and got stuck in my throat.

The fox came straight toward the grove of trees. She wasn't afraid, and I knew she had not seen me against the tree. I stayed absolutely still even though I felt like jumping up and screaming, "Aunt Millie! Uncle Fred! Come see this. It's a fox, a *fox!*"

Her steps as she crossed the field were lighter and quicker than a cat's. As she came closer I could see that her black fur was tipped with white. It was as if it were midnight and the moon were shining on her fur, frosting it. The wind parted her fur as it changed directions. Suddenly she stopped. She was ten feet away now, and with the changing of the wind she had got my scent. She looked right at me.

I did not move for a moment and neither did she. Her head was cocked to one side, her tail curled up, her front left foot raised. In all my life I never saw anything like that fox standing there with her pale golden eyes on me and this great black fur being blown by the wind.

Suddenly her nose quivered. It was such a slight movement I almost didn't see it, and then her mouth opened and I could see the pink tip of her tongue. She turned. She still was not afraid, but with a bound that was lighter than the wind—it was as if she was being blown away over the field—she was gone.

Still I didn't move. I couldn't. I couldn't believe that I had really seen the fox.

I had seen foxes before in zoos, but I was always in such a great hurry to get on to the good stuff that I was saying stupid things like, "I want to see the go-rilllllas," and not once had I ever really looked at a fox. Still, I could never remember seeing a black fox, not even in a zoo.

Also, there was a great deal of difference between seeing an animal in the zoo in front of painted fake rocks and trees and seeing one natural and free in the woods. It was like seeing a kite on the floor and then, later, seeing one up in the sky where it was supposed to be, pulling at the wind.

I started to pick up my pencil and write as quickly as I could, "P.S. Today I saw a black fox." But I didn't. This was the most exciting thing that had happened to me, and "P.S. Today I saw a black fox" made it nothing. "So what else is happening?" Petie Burkis would probably write back. I folded my letter, put it in an envelope, and sat there.

I thought about this old newspaper that my dad had had in his desk drawer for years. It was orange and the headline was just one word, very big, the letters about twelve inches high. WAR! And I mean it was awesome to see that word like that, because you knew it was a word that was going to change your whole life, the whole world even. And everytime I would see that newspaper, even though I wasn't even born when it was printed, I couldn't say anything for a minute or two.

Well, this was the way I felt right then about the black fox. I thought about a newspaper with just one word for a headline, very big, very black letters, twelve inches high. FOX! And even that did not show how awesome it had really been to me.

Library Link ♦ *If you would like to read more about Tom and the fox, read* The Midnight Fox *by Betsy Byars*.

Reader's Response

Would you like to see the fox? Why or why not?

The Midnight Fox

◆ Responding to Literature

1. What animal would you like to see face to face? Tell where you would be and what you would do.

2. Tom and Petie made up headlines for exciting things that happened to them. What exciting thing might happen to you? Make up a headline. Tell the story that would go with the headline.

3. With a partner, discuss a sequel to this episode. Tell what might happen if Tom and the fox were to meet again. Together, share your ending with the class. As a class, decide which ending is the favorite.

◆ Writing to Learn

Think and Observe ◆ Select an animal that you know well. Take a few minutes to observe it carefully. Collect details in an observation chart like the one below.

	black fox
What I See	black fur tipped with white, pale golden eyes, pink tongue, quivering nose, cat-like steps
What I Hear	soft breathing, no other sound
What I Feel	afraid I will chase it off

Observation Chart

Write ◆ Compose a brief description of your animal. Include the details that you noted while you were observing.

Pretend that your classmates are first-graders. Tell them a joke or funny story. Remember, first-graders like drama. Exaggerate. Make funny faces. Can you make them laugh?

SPEAKING and LISTENING ◆
Telling an Anecdote

Tom is capturing Petie's interest with an anecdote. An anecdote is a short, interesting story about someone. You can use anecdotes to tell someone what happened in an amusing or dramatic fashion.

Keep your audience in mind. When telling an anecdote to adults, use words and a style different from those you use when speaking to children. Here are speaking and listening guides to help you.

Telling an Anecdote	1. Make sure to tell all of the important details and to tell them in order.
	2. Practice telling your story at least twice—the second time in front of a mirror. If possible, record your voice.
	3. Look at your audience. Be confident. Smile!
	4. Make sure everyone can hear you. Speak clearly.
	5. Be dramatic! Use your face, your voice, and your body to show how you feel. Use your voice to build suspense. Use sound words, such as *Bam*! *Crash*! *Zzzzzip*!
Being an Active Listener	1. Be polite. Show by your face that you are interested.
	2. As you listen to an anecdote, try to predict its ending.
	3. Keep the order of events straight in your mind.
	4. Listen to be prepared to ask questions.
	5. Listen and watch to see how the speaker dramatizes the story.

> **Summary** ◆ An **anecdote** is a short, interesting story about someone. When telling an anecdote, give all of the important details in the right order. Listen to an anecdote with interest.

Guided Practice

The sentence below is from *The Midnight Fox*.

I could hardly hurry down the road fast enough.

Say the sentence four times. Be dramatic and show these feelings.

1. amusement   **2.** fear   **3.** anger   **4.** excitement

Practice

A. Say these sentences from *The Midnight Fox* as if they were a part of an anecdote. Be dramatic. Say each in a way that shows how you feel.

    5. I want to see the go-rillllllas! (angry)
    6. I want to see the go-rillllllas! (pleading)
    7. The headline was just one word . . . .WAR! (amazed)
    8. The headline was just one word . . . .WAR! (nervous)
    9. Today I saw a black fox. (matter-of-fact)
    10. Today I saw a black fox. (overjoyed)

B. Tell an anecdote to a partner. Before you tell it, jot down notes to make sure you tell all of the details in order. Try to build suspense. When you tell your story, stop just before the end and ask your listener what might happen next.

Apply ♦ Think and Write

Dictionary of Knowledge ♦ Anecdotes are often used in speeches to amuse the audience or to make a point. Read the entry about speechmaking techniques in the Dictionary of Knowledge. Then write an anecdote you might use to begin or end a speech.

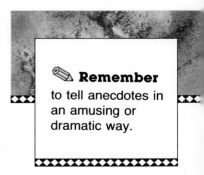

✎ **Remember**
to tell anecdotes in an amusing or dramatic way.

Create a chain story. Take turns building a story by adding one sentence at a time. Start with this sentence: *It all began when my dog chased a squirrel.*

WRITING ♦
Character, Setting, and Plot

No two stories are exactly alike. Yet most stories contain the same three parts: character, setting, and plot. The parts of a story are explained below.

The Parts of a Story
1. You need one or more characters—people, animals, or imaginary creatures. Create characters to interest your readers.
2. Put your characters in a setting—a time and a place. The setting is a background for the characters and the action.
3. Add a plot—action and events. A plot has a beginning, a middle, and an end. It usually tells events in time order, or the order in which they happened.
4. Remember to add an interesting title.

Here are some examples of the parts of a story.

A character: Uncle Giorgio; Rumpelstiltskin; Wilbur
A setting: (time) a March morning; sunrise; June 21, 1865
(place) a fox's den; an empty house; the Alamo
A plot: (beginning) The main character faces a problem.
(middle) Action, suspense, and excitement build.
(end) The character solves the problem.

Summary ♦ The three main parts of a story are **character**, **setting**, and **plot**. They work together to capture a reader's interest.

Guided Practice

Tell whether each of these is an example of character, setting, or plot.

1. The road was dusty.
2. Tom was often lonely.
3. The fox ran toward him.
4. It was a lazy, hazy day.
5. The fox stopped just ten feet away.

Practice

A. Read these sentences about *The Midnight Fox*. Write *character*, *setting*, or *plot* to show what each one illustrates.

   6. There must have been a million butterflies in the field!
   7. I have a lot of time to myself and am planning a movie.
   8. I was so excited that I could hardly unfold the letter!
   9. It was a fox, and she was running straight toward me.
   10. There were big trees and soft grass and rocks to sit on.

B. Answer these questions about a book you recently read.

   11. What is the title of the book, and who is the main character?
   12. Where does the story take place?
   13. What problem does the main character face?
   14. What is the most important event in the story?
   15. How does the story end?

C. Make up three story parts of your own. Follow the example below.

Characters: Alicia, a ten-year-old
Felipe, her four-year-old brother
Setting: A farm in Kansas
A stormy summer afternoon
Plot: Felipe is afraid of storms.
Alicia helps him to be brave.

Apply ◆ Think and Write

A Problem and Solution ◆ Put yourself in this plot: You are trapped on a planet in outer space. How will you escape? What will you do? Write a solution.

✎ **Remember**
to make character, setting, and plot work together when you write a story.

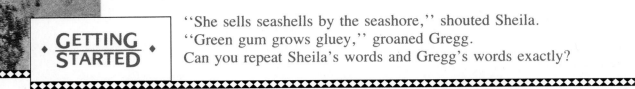

GETTING STARTED

"She sells seashells by the seashore," shouted Sheila.
"Green gum grows gluey," groaned Gregg.
Can you repeat Sheila's words and Gregg's words exactly?

WRITING ◆
Quotations

When you repeat someone's exact words, the repeated words are a <u>quotation</u>. When you write, quotation marks (" ") help identify and set off a quotation. Here are two ways to write a quotation.

■ **Mike commented, "Today I saw a frog with red markings."**
■ **"I've never heard of a frog with red markings," said Amy.**

The first word of a quotation begins with a capital letter. A comma separates the quotation from the words that tell who spoke.

If a quotation is a question, it ends with a question mark.

■ **"Did you do anything special today?" asked Uncle Bill.**

An **interjection** is a word that expresses feeling or emotion. It is usually followed by an exclamation mark. The two quotations below express strong feelings. The first quotation contains an interjection.

■ **"Wow!" yelled Mike.   "That's great!" cried Amy.**

Sometimes a quotation is divided into two parts. If the two parts make one sentence, use commas to separate the quotation from the words that tell who spoke.

■ **"Aunt Jane," said Mike, "let me help you."**

If a divided quotation is two separate sentences, use a period after the words that tell who spoke. Begin the second sentence with a capital letter.

■ **"Dave is outside," Mike whispered. "He's my best friend."**

Don't overuse the word *said*. Use a variety of verbs. You might try *replied*, *snickered*, *wailed*, *begged*, or *added*.

> **Summary** ◆ Use **quotation marks** (" ") to show the exact words of a speaker.

Guided Practice

Read these quotations that might have been said by the characters of *The Midnight Fox*. Tell where quotation marks should be added.

1. Tom grumbled, I'm not used to things here on the farm.
2. I'm afraid, complained Tom, that I'm a little bored.
3. May I drive the tractor? asked Tom.
4. Gracious! replied Uncle Fred. You're just a kid.

Practice

A. Write each sentence. Place quotation marks where they belong.

5. Did you bring the stale bread? asked Tommy.
6. Of course, Jeffrey answered. It's in this bag.
7. Let's go down to the lake, Susie urged.
8. Wait! Jeffrey shouted. I'm not running there!
9. Susie yelled, It's not far from here.
10. I know, replied Jeffrey, but I don't want to scare them.
11. Look, exclaimed Tommy. There they are!
12. Oh! whispered Susie. I count six of them.
13. Yes, said Jeffrey. There are six baby ducks.
14. Look how they follow the mother duck, added Tommy.

B. Write the sentences correctly. Add the necessary punctuation. Use capital letters where they are needed.

15. Give me some bread to feed them pleaded Susie
16. Wait a minute answered Jeffrey let me open the bag
17. Wow said Tommy look at them eat
18. If you ask me added Susie they look like they're starving

C. 19–23. Suppose you were discussing the ducks with Susie. Write five quotations from your conversation. Be sure to include all the necessary punctuation marks and capital letters.

Apply ◆ Think and Write

Writing Conversation ◆ Look at the conversation "balloons" of a comic strip. Rewrite one of the cartoon conversations, using quotation marks. Use lively verbs to tell how the characters speak.

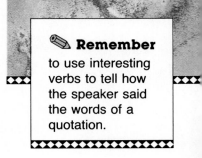

✎ **Remember**
to use interesting verbs to tell how the speaker said the words of a quotation.

Focus on the Narrator

Every story has a narrator. When you read a story or when you write one, you must ask yourself these questions: Who is telling this story? Is the story being told by one of the characters? Or is it being told by the author? The answers to these questions are important. You need to know the story's **point of view**.

Nearly all stories are in the first-person or third-person point of view. Notice how these points of view differ.

First Person
The story is told by a character in the story who refers to himself or herself as *I* or *me*.
I stared at the black fox.

Third Person
The story is told by the writer, who refers to the main character as *he* or *she*.
He stared at the black fox.

A writer chooses point of view carefully, for that choice shapes the story. In *The Midnight Fox*, which you read earlier, Betsy Byars writes in the first person. She wants to have Tom tell his own story. We see events unfold through Tom's point of view. We share his thoughts, his feelings, his observations.

First-person point of view makes us feel that we are on the scene with the main character. We really get to know that character. The drawback of this point of view is that it is limiting. The writer can tell us *only* the main character's thoughts. If an event occurs where the main character is not present, the first-person narrator cannot report it directly.

The Writer's Voice ◆ The key words for identifying first-person point of view are *I* and *me*. The key words for identifying third-person point of view are *he* and *she*. However, the words *he* and *she* (as well as *they* and *them*) also appear in first-person narration. Why?

Working Together

Point of view can be either first person or third person. Remember this as you work with your group on activities **A** and **B**.

In Your Group

♦ Encourage others to share their ideas.

♦ Help the group reach agreement.

♦ Show appreciation for everyone's contribution.

♦ Record the group's ideas.

A. Each sentence is written in the first-person point of view. Change each one into third person.

    EXAMPLE: I remembered having seen foxes in zoos.
    ANSWER: He remembered having seen foxes in zoos.

    1. So far I had received just a post card from my mom.
    2. When I went to the mailbox, there was a letter for me.
    3. I was in such a hurry that I ripped open the envelope.
    4. I thought about being a hundred years old.
    5. Would they bring me my mail on a silver tray?

B. Have your group pretend to be the black fox in *The Midnight Fox*. The fox will be a first-person narrator. Write a short report of your (the fox's) meeting with Tom. Follow the events in Betsy Byars's story, but add details of your own. Try to have everyone contribute ideas. Make the fox seem as real as possible.

THESAURUS CORNER ◆ Word Choice

Rewrite the paragraph below. Change it to first-person point of view. Use the Thesaurus and Thesaurus Index to replace each word in dark type with a better word.

Sarah spent an **inflammatory** summer on a ranch in New Mexico. Although the scenery was **pretty**, her greatest **hilarity** came from learning about ranch life. She had to **do** certain duties, just as the ranch hands did. Daily life was **neat**, and her **spirit** for ranch life increased week by week. She learned to **trap** stray cattle, a task that required **heroism**. She found some **unique** rocks in the foothills. With so much for her to do, the summer flew by **hastily**.

Writing a Personal Narrative

A story is often called a narrative. A person's own story is a personal narrative. The point of view of a personal narrative is first person. The writer uses the words *I* and *me*.

In *The Midnight Fox*, Tom narrates his exciting adventure with a black fox. No one else can tell the story exactly the way Tom does. First-person point of view helps us see through Tom's eyes. It helps us share his thoughts and feelings.

Know Your Purpose and Audience

You may never have met a black fox. However, you have probably had some experience with an animal. In this lesson you will write a personal narrative. Your purpose will be to tell about an experience you had with an animal.

Your audience will be your classmates. Later, you and your classmates can read your personal narratives to each other. You can also display your narratives on a story net.

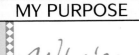

MY PURPOSE

MY AUDIENCE

1 Prewriting

Prewriting is getting ready to write. First choose a topic for your personal narrative. Then gather ideas about your topic.

Choose Your Topic ◆ Perhaps you were riding your bike and saw a deer. Maybe you found a lost cat or watched a seal at an aquarium. Make a list of animals and circle your choice.

Think About It

Close your eyes and try to visualize animals you have met. Try saying "animal, animal, animal" to yourself until a picture comes to mind. Then look at your list. Which animal did you see most clearly? Which was the most memorable? That is your choice.

Talk About It

Discuss animal encounters with your classmates. Recall times when you were at a zoo, a park, or in a woods. You might have seen a horse pulling a carriage on a city street, even. Make a list of places where you might have seen animals.

Topic Ideas

a deer near bushes
a lost cat
a seal at the aquarium
a giraffe at the zoo
a robin in a nest

Choose Your Strategy ♦ Here are two strategies that could help you remember details about your animal. Read both. Then decide which strategy you will use.

PREWRITING IDEAS

CHOICE ONE

A Conversation

One way to recall details is to have a conversation with a partner. Tell each other a story about your experience with an animal. Be sure that you tell the complete story about what happened. After your conversation, jot down the details you told.

Model

riding my bike home
saw a deer near bushes
Deer: big, beautiful,
smooth hide, tan,
stared at me
Me: excited, held my
breath

CHOICE TWO

An Observation Chart

An observation chart is another way to gather details. First, visualize the animal. Let your experience with it run like a movie in your mind. What did you see? What did you hear? How did you feel? Write the details.

Model

Meeting a Deer	
What I Saw	a doe, sleek hide, huge eyes, still as a statue
What I Heard	a faint rustling, then silence
What I Felt	surprised, excited, as if in a dream

2 Writing

Place your conversation notes or observation chart in front of you. Then begin to write your personal narrative. Here are ways to begin.

- Did I ever tell you about the time I found a _____?
- I couldn't believe my eyes when I saw the _____.
- "Be careful of stray animals," Mom told me, but _____.

Remember that a story includes characters, a plot, and a setting. In your narrative, you and the animal will be characters. The plot will be what happened. The setting will be where it happened. Use *I* and *me* for first-person point of view.

The main thing is to keep writing till you finish your story. Don't worry about mistakes. You can correct them later.

Sample First Draft ◆

I couldn't believe my eyes! I had taken a new shortcut, and suddenly I found a deer munching leafs.
It had a smooth, tan hide and was taller than my bike. It was eating from the tall bushes next to the parking lot. I rode my bike closer. The deer looked up.
I said, "hello, you beautiful creature."
I expected the deer to bolt, but it didn't it just stared at me with its Large brown eyes. Quietly, I got off my bike and placed it on the ground. When I looked up, the deer was gone.

3 Revising

Revising is making changes to improve your writing. How can you know if you need to make changes? Here is a strategy that may help you decide.

REVISING IDEA

FIRST   Read to Yourself

Review your purpose. Did you write a personal narrative about an experience with an animal? Think about your audience. Will they see what you saw? Hear what you heard? Feel what you felt? Decide which part of your story you like best.

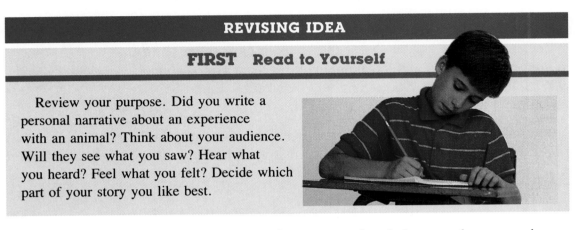

Focus: Have you used first-person point of view to make your readers see your story through your eyes?

THEN   Share with a Partner

Ask a classmate to be your first audience. Read your narrative aloud and ask for honest opinions. Below are some guidelines that may help you both.

The Writer

Guidelines: Read aloud to your partner slowly and clearly. Listen to your partner, then make the changes *you* think are important.

Sample questions:
- Did you understand what happened?
- **Focus question:** Did you understand how I felt about the experience?

The Writer's Partner

Guidelines: Be honest. Say what you really think. Be kind. Make your comments politely.

Sample responses:
- What did you do when _____?
- How did you feel when _____?

Revising Model ◆ Look at this sample that is being revised. The marks show the changes the writer wants to make.

Revising Marks

cross out	-----
add	∧
move	⟳

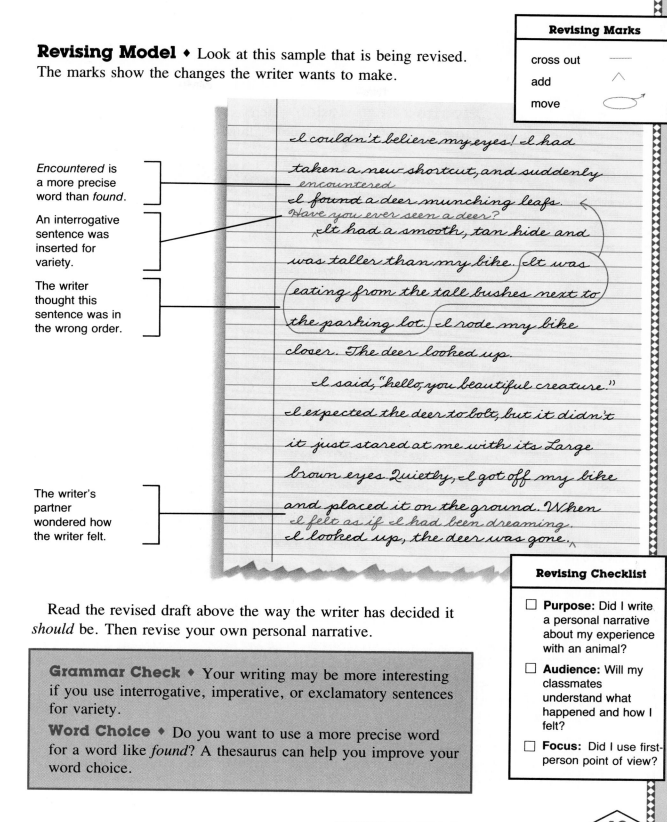

Encountered is a more precise word than *found*.

An interrogative sentence was inserted for variety.

The writer thought this sentence was in the wrong order.

The writer's partner wondered how the writer felt.

I couldn't believe my eyes! I had taken a new shortcut, and suddenly
encountered
~~I found~~ a deer munching leafs.
~~Have you ever seen a deer?~~
It had a smooth, tan hide and was taller than my bike. It was eating from the tall bushes next to the parking lot. I rode my bike closer. The deer looked up.

I said, "hello, you beautiful creature."
I expected the deer to bolt, but it didn't it just stared at me with its Large brown eyes. Quietly, I got off my bike and placed it on the ground. When
I felt as if I had been dreaming.
I looked up, the deer was gone.

Read the revised draft above the way the writer has decided it *should* be. Then revise your own personal narrative.

Grammar Check ◆ Your writing may be more interesting if you use interrogative, imperative, or exclamatory sentences for variety.

Word Choice ◆ Do you want to use a more precise word for a word like *found*? A thesaurus can help you improve your word choice.

Revising Checklist

☐ **Purpose:** Did I write a personal narrative about my experience with an animal?

☐ **Audience:** Will my classmates understand what happened and how I felt?

☐ **Focus:** Did I use first-person point of view?

4 Proofreading

Proofreading is looking for and fixing errors.

Proofreading Model ♦ Here is the sample draft of the narrative. Notice that red proofreading marks have been added.

¶ I couldn't believe my eyes! I had taken a new shortcut, and suddenly

encountered

I found a deer munching leafs. *leaves*

Have you ever seen a deer?

It had a smooth, tan hide and was taller than my bike. It was eating from the tall bushes next to the parking lot. I rode my bike closer. The deer looked up.

I said, "hello, you beautiful creature."

I expected the deer to bolt, but it didn't. it just stared at me with its Large brown eyes. Quietly, I got off my bike and placed it on the ground. When

I felt as if I had been dreaming.

I looked up, the deer was gone.

PROOFREADING IDEA

Spelling Check

To catch spelling errors, try reading through a window. Cut a small rectangle in the middle of a piece of paper. Read one word at a time as you move the window along your paper.

Now proofread your personal narrative, add a title, and make a neat copy.

5 Publishing

Publishing is sharing your writing with others. Try one of the ideas below for sharing your personal narrative.

Meeting a Deer

I couldn't believe my eyes! I had taken a new shortcut, and suddenly I encountered a deer munching leaves. It was eating from the tall bushes next to the parking lot.

Have you ever seen a deer? It had a smooth, tan hide and was taller than my bike. I rode my bike closer. The deer looked up.

I said, "Hello, you beautiful creature." I expected the deer to bolt, but it didn't. It just stared at me with its large brown eyes. Quietly, I got off my bike and placed it on the ground. When I looked up, the deer was gone. I felt as if I had been dreaming.

PUBLISHING IDEAS

Share Aloud

Draw pictures of the animals featured in your personal narratives. Mount them on a bulletin board. Read your personal narratives aloud. Ask your classmates to identify the picture that matches your story.

Share in Writing

Arrange netting across one wall. Mount your narratives on the story net. Place small pieces of paper and paper clips near the netting. Invite readers to write comments and clip their notes to the narratives.

Writing Across the Curriculum   Science

In this unit you wrote about a personal encounter with an animal. Scientists do that, too. Scientists first learn about an animal by observing it. Then they are able to write about what they saw. You can use an observation chart when you are studying about an animal in a class.

Writing to Learn

Think and Observe ◆ Find information about an animal that interests you in your science book. Make an observation chart about the animal based on the information you read. Record details about the animal's color, size, or shape. Record other information such as number of legs, body covering, or special abilities.

Observation Chart

Write ◆ Use the information from your chart to write about the animal. Tell whether you would like to see one someday, or if you would like one for a pet.

Writing in Your Journal

In the Writer's Warm-up you wrote about an aspect of farm life that interested you. Throughout this unit you've learned a lot more about foxes and other animals. You've also learned about how farms work. Browse back through the pages. What did you learn that you didn't know about before? Choose an aspect of farm life you learned about in this unit and write about it in your journal.

BOOKS TO ENJOY

Read More About It

The Summer of the Swans *by Betsy Byars*
Betsy Byars has given us many stories just as good as
The Midnight Fox. In this book, Sarah tells us about
her feelings for her retarded brother, Peter.

Newbery Award

Arthur, For the Very First Time
by Patricia MacLachlan
Arthur learns a lot about handling grownups the
summer he spends on a farm. His Great Aunt Elda and
his Great Uncle Wrisby seem to live in a scattered way.

Sounder *by William Armstrong*
The dog Sounder had the neck and shoulders of a
bulldog and the melodious bay of a hound. The boy
loved the dog almost as much as he loved his father.
When the sheriff's shotgun wounds Sounder, the dog
crawls off and bays no more.

Newbery Award

Book Report Idea   Postcard

Did you ever read a story that
took you right along for the ride?
The next time you give a book
report, give it as though you were
along for the ride.

Create a Giant Postcard ◆ On
one side, draw a picture of a scene
from the story. On the other side,
tell about the story as though you
were there. Address the postcard to
other readers, and be sure to tell
why you liked the "trip."

> I will never forget
> the day I woke up
> on the beach of a
> desert island. How
> had I gotten there?
> Who were these
> strange, mean-
> looking people
> coming toward me?
> Read about my
> adventures in *The
> First Two Lives of
> Lukas-Kasha* by
> Lloyd Alexander.

> The Fifth ⋆
> Central Sch
> 234 Main
> Grand Bri

UNIT REVIEW

Unit 1

Sentences   Pages 6–15

A. Write each sentence. Then write *declarative, interrogative, imperative,* or *exclamatory* to show what kind of sentence it is.

1. Give me that book.
2. How cold it is today!
3. Will I see you at the party?
4. John rarely watches television.
5. Lucy is going to the gym.
6. Is Frank catching a cold?
7. That girl can really run!
8. Please help me with this problem.
9. Harriet is my second cousin.
10. Did Linda paint that picture?

B. Write each sentence. Underline the complete subject once. Underline the complete predicate twice.

11. Charles is taking voice lessons.
12. The girl in the television commercial wore a green dress.
13. My father likes mystery stories.
14. The boy next door won a prize.
15. Diana Sims works here after school.
16. The tall, blond man is my uncle.
17. The white cat had kittens.
18. Our history class wrote a play about the Revolutionary War.
19. The voters elected a new mayor.
20. Paul and I played golf on Friday.

C. Write the simple subject of each sentence. Write (*You*) if the subject is understood.

21. My visit to the city was wonderful.
22. Follow these directions carefully.
23. The tiny bird chirped merrily.
24. Take me to the zoo with you.
25. Nancy is a marvelous storyteller.
26. That portrait is by Rembrandt.
27. Bring the coleslaw to the picnic.
28. Carry this heavy package, please.
29. A shiny new bicycle sped past us.

D. Write the simple predicate of each sentence.

30. We are going to a movie.
31. Cynthia has won the last two races.
32. Four dogs were running in the yard.
33. The puppy barked at the stranger.
34. A leaf fluttered to the ground.
35. Lifeguards have saved many lives on this beach.
36. An elderly man was humming a tune.
37. The river will overflow its banks.
38. The library closes in five minutes.

Thesaurus   pages 16–17

E. Read the thesaurus entry. Then answer each question.

enormous (adj)—larger than normal in size or force. The <u>enormous</u> cat approached the house.
gigantic—huge in size
mammoth—huge in size and bulk
ANTONYMS: tiny, puny

39. What are two synonyms for *enormous?*
40. What are two antonyms for *enormous?*

Character, Setting, and Plot
pages 32–33

F. Read the following paragraph. Then write answers to the questions.

Mark Twain's *The Adventures of Tom Sawyer* is about a young boy growing up in a small town. Tom's Aunt Polly assigns him the chore of "whitewashing" a fence—painting it white. Tom hates this chore. Even so, he makes a start at it. Another boy comes along and teases Tom for having to do the job. Tom manages to convince his friend that whitewashing a fence is an honor and a privilege. The other boy asks if he can do some of the work. Tom pretends to be unwilling but lets his friend do the whitewashing. Other boys come along. Each of them gets the "privilege" of whitewashing the fence. By the end of the day, the job is done. Tom has performed almost none of the work himself. Even more, he has been able to persuade his friends to pay for the privilege. He is richer after the chore is finished than when it began.

41. Where does the story take place?
42. Who is the main character of the story?
43. Who are the other characters?
44. How does the story begin?
45. What happens in the middle of the story?
46. How does the story end?
47. What do you learn about the main character?
48. What do you learn about the other characters?

Quotations   *pages 34–35*

G. Write each sentence correctly. Add quotation marks where they belong. Add capital letters and punctuation marks where they are needed.

49. Wow Joe exclaimed that is certainly a surprise
50. Aunt Betty asked what did you do in school today
51. Look out Perry yelled here they come again
52. I understand said Mrs. Torres what you are trying to say
53. I think I know the answer Stu said thoughtfully
54. Why not Bernice suggested bring your little brother to the picnic
55. Golly Shirley said that was fun
56. My mother warned wipe your feet before you come into the house
57. We all know said Faith how the movie ends
58. If you try Mr. Bacon urged I know you will do a good job
59. Can someone please help me carry these books asked Frank
60. Donna whispered this place frightens me
61. Watch out yelled Melvin that tree is about to fall
62. I know said Kathy that this path is the shortest way home
63. It's much faster than the main road agreed her brother Ernie
64. Look cried Kathy there's a blue jay
65. Is that a woodpecker up in that tree asked Ernie
66. I believe it is answered his big sister

Unit **1** Challenge

Sports Chain

The clue to this sports puzzle is a chain of letters. The last two letters of each subject are the first two letters of the verb in the following sentence. Also, the last two letters of the subject in the last sentence are the first two letters of the verb in the first sentence. (Hint: Remember that *You* is the understood subject of an imperative sentence.)

1. The crowd's noise _ _ _ _ _ _ _ the golfers.
2. The new snow _ _ _ _ skiers to the slopes.
3. My brother _ _ _ _ me a new pair of sneakers.
4. _ _ _ _ _ the scoreboard.
5. Joan _ _ _ _ _ _ the other racers.
6. The coach _ _ _ _ _ _ _ _ my question sharply.
7. The umpire _ _ _ _ _ _ _ the lineup.
8. The tennis star _ _ _ _ _ _ _ _ the serve.
9. The visiting team _ _ _ _ _ _ _ this morning.
10. The team captain's plan _ _ _ _ _ _ us.

Secret Messages

Here is a system for sending secret messages. First a sentence is broken into five-letter groups.

Pat arrives by train on Monday.
Patar / rives / bytra / inonM / onday.

Then each group is written backward without punctuation or capitalization.

ratap sevir artyb mnoni yadno

Write the secret message hidden in the four lines below. (Hint: Each line is a sentence.) Be sure to insert punctuation and capital letters.

vahew nuofe tehtd usaer xober
utiaw ylitn eesuo itahw tinis
oynac htegu otere thgin
tonod allet enoyn

Unit 1 Extra Practice

1 Writing Sentences

p. 4

A. Write *sentence* or *not a sentence* for each group of words below.

1. Writing began with pictures.
2. On rocks and on the walls of caves.
3. Ancient people recorded many things.
4. Drew pictures of people and animals.
5. Three thousand years ago in the Middle East.
6. Scratched lines on wet clay.
7. This writing is called cuneiform.
8. During that time in Egypt, only certain people were allowed to write.
9. Drawn on papyrus or carved on stone.
10. Chinese writing began as a kind of picture writing.
11. Scratched on bone, bronze, or stone.
12. Changed very little in the last 3,000 years.
13. Today the Chinese write on paper with a brush and ink.
14. More than 40,000 separate signs are used in Chinese.
15. These signs are sometimes called pictographs.
16. Different pictographs for new words.
17. A difficult task for Chinese students.
18. The sign for *sun* behind the sign for *tree*.
19. This combination means ''east.''

B. Write the group of words in each pair that is a sentence.

20. **a.** Sitting in the library.
    b. Jana worked on her report every day.
21. **a.** She needed more pictures for her report.
    b. The librarian at the main desk.
22. **a.** After reading Jana's first draft.
    b. Over the weekend she made some changes.
23. **a.** Saw an A+ the top of her paper.
    b. Jana got an A+ on her report.
24. **a.** Jana's teacher put the report on the bulletin board.
    b. With slight changes and using more pictures.

2 Four Kinds of Sentences   *p. 6*

A. Write each sentence. Then write *declarative* or *interrogative* to show what kind of sentence it is.

1. Many foods of today were first found in the New World.
2. Potatoes come from Peru.
3. Chocolate was a favorite food of the Aztecs in Mexico.
4. How many kinds of squash did Native Americans grow?
5. Wild rice is a special kind of plant.
6. Does anyone know the origin of the hot dog?
7. Yams were brought to America from Africa.
8. What kind of corn is used to make hominy?
9. Alligator pear is another name for avocado.
10. Where were peanuts first grown?
11. Spanish explorers brought peanuts to Africa and Spain in the sixteenth century.
12. Did you know that the peanut is a member of the pea family?
13. Tomatoes were once thought to be poisonous.
14. Are the tomato and the potato related?
15. French gardeners grew potatoes for their blossoms.
16. When did people begin to eat vegetables that were found in the New World?
17. Corn and beans were eaten by the Pilgrims.
18. Peppers are called chilies by the people of Mexico.
19. What would pizza taste like without tomatoes?

B. Write each declarative and interrogative sentence. Begin the sentence correctly. Use correct punctuation at the end.

20. how many Native American foods can you name
21. peppers, corn, and tomatoes were first grown in America
22. bananas are native to South America
23. are pineapples originally from Hawaii
24. what did Europeans eat for Christmas dinner before 1492
25. the turkey should be our national bird
26. is anything more American than pumpkin pie
27. when were jack-o'-lanterns first made
28. the colonists brought apples to America
29. did they bring blueberries, too
30. was Thomas Jefferson the first president to eat a tomato

C. Write each sentence. Then write *imperative* or *exclamatory* to show what kind of sentence it is.

31. Look at that strange mask.
32. What a great disguise that is!
33. You really fooled me!
34. Put your costume on quickly.
35. Please tie my shoes for me.
36. How dark it is outside!
37. Please help me fix this crown.
38. You look great in that helmet!
39. Try some of this yellow paint on your mask.
40. I can hardly wait for Alan's party to begin!
41. Meet me there at five o'clock.
42. Watch out for the tub of apples in the basement.
43. What a weird noise that is!
44. Don't be afraid to go down those stairs.
45. That is the most terrifying sound I have ever heard!
46. Let Paula go ahead of you then.
47. Absolutely nothing frightens her!
48. How strange everything looks down here!
49. Please wait for me to catch up with you.
50. Be careful in the dark.
51. How scary this is!

D. Write each imperative and exclamatory sentence. Begin each sentence correctly. Use a period or an exclamation mark at the end.

52. that sounded just like an owl screeching
53. please be careful over there
54. sit down next to me on the bench
55. there's a cat peering in that window
56. reach into this bowl
57. something cold and slimy is in there
58. how awful it feels
59. please say what this is
60. turn the lights on
61. please look in the bowl
62. what a relief it is to see cold spaghetti
63. don't scare us again like that
64. how exciting this party is

3 Complete Subjects and Complete Predicates

A. Write each sentence. Underline the complete subject once. Underline the complete predicate twice.

1. Caves may have been the first human dwellings.
2. Simple mud houses were a later development.
3. Castles of stone and iron kept off attackers.
4. A houseboat provides shelter and transportation.
5. The White House is a home as well as a national monument.
6. Cave dwellers painted animal pictures on the walls of caves.
7. Snow houses can be quite warm.
8. The Pueblos of New Mexico built homes of clay.
9. Settlers in Nebraska built sod houses.
10. People in ancient Egypt lived in mud and brick houses.
11. Tribes of wandering shepherds made tents of skin.
12. Tepees sheltered Native Americans on the Great Plains.
13. Glass houses make good use of solar energy.
14. The dwelling place of the future may be a space station.
15. Stone cottages with tile roofs are common in Ireland.
16. Woven grass kept the rain out of Hawaiian homes long ago.
17. A tree house is a temporary dwelling.
18. Some people like to live in log houses.

B. Add a complete subject or a complete predicate to each group of words below. Write the complete sentence.

EXAMPLE: _____ were made of wood.
ANSWER: The stairs were made of wood.

19. The carpenter _____ .
20. _____ is on the top floor.
21. _____ has just been painted.
22. The old brick house _____ .
23. _____ lives in a twelve-story building.
24. Two new apartment houses _____ .
25. _____ lived in a cottage in the woods.
26. _____ stood on a rocky island.
27. A log cabin _____ .
28. Our neighbors _____ .

54 Extra Practice

4 Simple Subjects

p. 10

A. Read each sentence below. A line has been drawn between the complete subject and the complete predicate. Write the complete subject. Draw a line under the simple subject.

1. School | is very exciting this year.
2. Every school in town | has a computer.
3. My English class | goes to the computer lab twice a week.
4. Luís Ramos | used the computer today.
5. He | made this design.
6. Our whole class | was surprised.
7. A strange machine | sat on the desk.
8. The first lesson on the computer | was easy.
9. Leroy Johnson | showed us what to do.
10. Computers | can solve problems quickly.
11. Scientists | use special computers for difficult problems.
12. Ordinary people | can use computers easily.
13. Every computer | has a memory.
14. Information | is stored in the memory.
15. The computer's memory | contains instructions.
16. The instructions | are in a special language.
17. The words in this language | look like English.
18. Some meanings | are different, though.
19. Special commands | tell the computer when to count.
20. A touch of the finger | stops the machine.

B. Write the simple subject of each sentence.

21. This button turns on the machine.
22. An arrow on the screen lights up.
23. The keys on the right make the arrow move.
24. A student types letters on the keyboard.
25. Words appear on the screen.
26. Emma's friends in the class want to work with the computer.
27. The class uses the computer for writing.
28. Some programs will correct misspelled words.
29. Two students draw pictures with the computer.
30. The computer in Mrs. Walker's class can talk.
31. Sarah Easton hopes to have a computer of her own.
32. My brother uses a computer in his college classes.

5 Simple Predicates

p. 12

A. Read each sentence below. A line has been drawn between the complete subject and the complete predicate. Write each complete predicate. Draw a line under the simple predicate.

1. Balls | bounce.
2. The Aztecs | played ringball.
3. The pitcher, a left-hander, | was throwing mostly fastballs.
4. The soccer ball in the garage | had lost most of its air.
5. The game of golf | was invented in Scotland.
6. The surprised umpire | lost his glasses.
7. Sally Jo, a champion rodeo rider, | practices every day for six hours.
8. The player in the red shirt | has made three fouls in just the first half of the game.
9. The winner of last year's prize | is playing again this year.
10. Many different sports | are played today.
11. Some sports | develop skills for daily use.
12. Soccer | is growing more popular than ever.
13. Baseball | requires speed and practice.
14. Water sports | teach confidence to sailors and swimmers.
15. A swim on a hot day | cools the body.
16. The ability to float | has saved many lives.
17. Practice with jacks | makes fingers nimble.
18. Exercise in the open air | helps your heart and lungs.
19. Sports | have proved useful in many ways.

B. Write the simple predicate of each sentence.

20. Our team has made another touchdown.
21. The quarterback had called a new play.
22. The new shortstop threw the ball to second.
23. She was trying for a double play.
24. Ellen, our best hitter, has broken her wrist.
25. Julio scored several goals a game.
26. The great goalie prevented the other team from scoring.
27. The large chestnut horse cleared the first fence easily.
28. Marcy Jackson, a new young rider, won the blue ribbon.
29. Lee likes water sports.
30. He competes in swimming races.

6 Subjects in Imperative Sentences

p. 14

A. Write each sentence. Underline the simple subject. Write (*You*) if the subject is understood.

EXAMPLE: Start feeding in September.
ANSWER: (You) Start feeding in September.

1. A large red bird flew to the feeder.
2. Watch the birds from the window.
3. Fill the bird feeder every day.
4. The nuthatch walks down the side of the tree.
5. Mix peanut butter and oatmeal together.
6. Birds with short, stubby beaks crack seeds.
7. Throw stale bread covered with bacon grease on the ground.
8. One interesting hobby is bird-watching.
9. Birds of all kinds can be seen in the park.
10. Borrow a pair of field glasses.
11. Look for finches in the pine trees.
12. Your own backyard is a good place for bird-watching.
13. Robins look for worms in the ground.
14. A thrush in a nearby park brightens the day with song.
15. Get some books about birds from the library.
16. Ask the librarian for more information about birds.
17. Set up a bird-feeding station near the kitchen window.

B. Write each sentence. Then write *declarative* or *imperative* to show what kind of sentence it is. Underline the simple subject in each declarative sentence. Write (*You*) for each imperative sentence.

18. Different birds eat different kinds of food.
19. Supply a variety of foods.
20. The bright red cardinal likes sunflower seeds.
21. Mix fats with peanut butter.
22. Keep the squirrels away.
23. Hummingbirds will sip nectar and sugar water.
24. Put the food on the ground.
25. Some birds eat only from the ground.
26. A hungry jay will drive away other birds.

UNIT TWO

USING LANGUAGE TO
INFORM

=== **PART ONE** ===

Unit Theme   *Handicrafts*

Language Awareness   Nouns

=== **PART TWO** ===

Literature   "Handicrafts" by Patricia Fent Ross

A Reason for Writing   Informing

Writing
IN YOUR JOURNAL

WRITER'S WARM-UP ◆ What do you know about handicrafts? Have you ever worked with clay to make a mug or a bowl? Perhaps you have woven a simple potholder or a place mat. Maybe you have carved a toy boat from soap or wood. You may have visited a crafts demonstration at a museum or a hobby shop. You might own a handmade object that you got as a gift. Write in your journal about handicrafts. Tell what you like about them and what makes them special.

Think of words that name things you might bring to school. The things might be ordinary, like a pencil, or unusual, like a centipede.

1 Writing with Nouns

In order to speak and write, we have to use naming words. Without such words, we would have blank spaces in our communication. We would say

■ The _____ shaped the _____ with his _____ .

instead of

■ The <u>man</u> shaped the <u>clay</u> with his <u>hands</u>.

Man, *clay*, and *hands* are nouns—words that name. A noun can name a person, a place, or a thing. We can see or touch all of these. A noun can also name an idea, something we cannot see or touch.

Examples of Nouns			
Persons	Freddie	potter	weaver
Places	town	beach	Japan
Things	plate	chair	blanket
Ideas	honesty	skill	beauty

Summary ◆ A **noun** names a person, place, thing, or idea. Use nouns to give information when you speak and write.

Guided Practice

Each sentence below has three nouns. Read the sentences. Name the nouns.

1. Ralph is reading a book about handicrafts.
2. Potters in ancient Greece made vases.
3. Such objects were valued for their usefulness and beauty.
4. Handicrafters use tools in their trades.

Practice

A. Write the nouns you find in each sentence.

5. Yoshi is learning about making cloth.
6. Her mother owns a loom.
7. Her sister will use dye to add colors.
8. In America, weavers have produced beautiful objects.
9. Their skill has earned great respect.
10. Blankets woven by the Navajo now hang in museums.
11. The warmth of the colors brightens many homes.
12. Yoshi has studied the work of the weavers of the Southwest.
13. These workers still practice their craft.
14. Their products are national treasures.

B. Use the nouns below to complete the paragraph. Write the completed paragraph.

cloth	Yoshi	Native American	blanket	airplane
loom	Arizona	reservation	color	sister

(**15.** ____) and her (**16.** ____) traveled on an (**17.** ____) to (**18.** ____). They visited a vast (**19.** ____). There they saw a (**20.** ____) weaving a (**21.** ____) on her (**22.** ____). The (**23.** ____) of the (**24.** ____) was beautiful.

C. Use the model below to write five sentences of your own. Notice how using different nouns gives a totally different meaning to each sentence.

25–29. The ____ made a ____ for the ____ .

Apply • Think and Write

From Your Writing ♦ Read what you wrote for the Writer's Warm-up. List the nouns you used in four categories: persons, places, things, and ideas.

✎ **Remember** that nouns help to create a clear word picture for your reader.

GETTING
◆ STARTED ◆

Follow the examples below to play "To Have or Have Not."
I would like to have two hamsters.
I would not like to have forty-seven snakes.

2 Singular and Plural Nouns

Nouns can name one thing or more than one thing. In other words, nouns can be singular or plural. Most nouns add an ending in the plural. Some nouns change their spelling. A few nouns are the same in the singular and the plural.

Here are the singular and plural forms of some nouns.

Singular	Plural
girl tiger mirror	girls tigers mirrors
bush lunch dress tax	bushes lunches dresses taxes
lady baby country	ladies babies countries
boy valley turkey	boys valleys turkeys
leaf wolf knife	leaves wolves knives
foot tooth man	feet teeth men
salmon deer moose	salmon deer moose

Summary ◆ A **singular noun** names one person, place, thing, or idea. A **plural noun** names more than one person, place, thing, or idea. When you write, pay special attention to the spelling of plural nouns.

Guided Practice

Tell whether each of these nouns is singular or plural.

1. dogs
2. monkey
3. tooth
4. village
5. men
6. country
7. feet
8. tool
9. leaves
10. dishes
11. cousin
12. kites

Practice

A. Write the underlined noun in each sentence. Then write *singular* if the noun is singular. Write *plural* if it is plural.

13. Items made of baked clay are called pottery.
14. There are different methods of making pottery.
15. Some pottery is made in factories.
16. A potter led us on a guided tour.
17. Our class visited such a place.
18. We examined wheels used by potters.
19. We watched several men packing the finished items.
20. These people put the bowls and vases into boxes.
21. One vase had a red strawberry painted on it.
22. Another was formed in the shape of a shoe.
23. My fondest wish is to become a potter.
24. I would make beautiful bowls.
25. I would decorate each one with a picture.
26. Butterflies are my favorite decorations.

B. Write the plural of each of these nouns.

27.	hand	**32.**	church	**37.**	life
28.	city	**33.**	foot	**38.**	salmon
29.	tray	**34.**	deer	**39.**	tooth
30.	man	**35.**	ostrich	**40.**	army
31.	cherry	**36.**	donkey	**41.**	brush

C. Write four sentences of your own, using the plural forms of the words below.

42. box
43. leaf
44. woman
45. moose

Apply • Think and Write

Dictionary of Knowledge • Read about pottery in the Dictionary of Knowledge. Then write several sentences about the art of making pottery. Use plural nouns in your writing.

✏️ **Remember**
to check your spelling of plural nouns as you proofread your work.

◆ GETTING ◆
STARTED

If he went to an island, Marty Torres could take a melon and a turtle. Cindy Evans could take a cat and eggs. Figure out what you could take to an island.

3 Common and Proper Nouns

What is the difference between these two sentences?

A <u>girl</u> visited a <u>museum</u> in a <u>city</u>.
<u>Linda</u> visited the <u>American Craft Museum</u> in <u>New York</u>.

The first sentence uses general naming words to refer to a person, a thing, and a place. The second sentence names a particular person, a particular thing, and a particular place. The words *girl*, *museum*, and *city* are common nouns. The proper noun *Linda* names a particular person. The proper noun *American Craft Museum* names a particular thing. The proper noun *New York* names a particular place. Notice that a proper noun can be more than one word.

When you speak and write, you sometimes want to be as specific as possible. You might use the proper noun *Baltimore* instead of the common noun *city*. You might use *Aunt Lucy* instead of *relative*, and *Walters Art Gallery* instead of *gallery*.

> **Summary** ◆ A **common noun** is the general name for a person, place, or thing. A **proper noun** names a particular person, place, or thing. Use proper nouns to make your writing more specific.

Guided Practice

Tell whether the underlined nouns are common or proper.

1. <u>Ms. Ashe</u> showed us <u>pictures</u> of handmade <u>furniture</u>.
2. <u>Linda</u> admired a beautiful <u>table</u> made in <u>Italy</u>.
3. The <u>antique</u> was sold to a <u>collector</u> in <u>Chicago</u>.
4. He gave the <u>piece</u> to the <u>Art Institute of Chicago</u> on <u>Michigan Boulevard</u>.
5. <u>Nathan</u> saw a <u>collection</u> of handmade <u>items</u> in the <u>Cranfield Library</u>.

Practice

A. Write each underlined noun. Then write *common* or *proper* to show what kind of noun it is.

    6. Woodworkers are people who make things from wood.
    7. My uncle, David Johnson, makes furniture.
    8. Uncle David designs and assembles cabinets and desks.
    9. He lives near New Orleans in Louisiana.
    10. The Mississippi River is not far from his home.
    11. Mrs. Baxter told Karen about the materials she uses.
    12. Oak is a hardwood, and pine is a softwood.
    13. Mayor Jesse Roe gave handmade shelves to the Scott School.
    14. My cousin in Georgia carves her initials in her work.
    15. Kristen made a checkerboard, a birdhouse, and a bookcase.

B. Write the sentences. Draw one line under the common nouns. Draw two lines under the proper nouns.

    16. Much furniture is made by machines.
    17. Some woodworkers, such as John Dunnigan, make tables by hand.
    18. Judy Kensley McKie has created an unusual table.
    19. This piece features two carved animals.
    20. Museums and galleries in places such as Los Angeles display furniture.
    21. Gary and Sue took a bus to the Metropolitan Museum of Art in New York City.
    22. Gary enjoyed the ride through the Lincoln Tunnel.
    23. In Manhattan, skyscrapers soared into the sky.
    24. The museum had an exhibit of furniture.
    25. The displays included many handmade items.

"Pete & Repete"—painted and carved on birch by Judy Kensley McKie, 1981. Courtesy Pritam & Eames Furniture Gallery, East Hampton, New York

C. 26–28. Write three sentences about wooden toys or other objects. Use at least one proper noun in each sentence.

Apply • Think and Write

Planning a Trip ✦ Be an armchair traveler. Write about a museum you would like to visit. Include the names of people you would like to take along.

✎ **Remember**
that you can use both common and proper nouns to give information.

What is the difference between *turkey* and *Turkey*? Between *china* and *China*? Think of other words whose meanings change when the words are capitalized.

4 Capitalizing Proper Nouns

When you write a proper noun, always begin it with a capital letter. Many proper nouns consist of more than one word. In that case, capitalize each important word.

The chart below gives some rules and examples for capitalizing proper nouns.

Capitalizing Proper Nouns	
Rule	**Examples**
1. Capitalize the names of people and pets.	Pedro Garcia, Ms. Adams, Fido, the Franklins, Americans
2. Capitalize every important word in the names of particular places and things.	New England, Madison Avenue, Museum of Modern Art, Texas, San Diego, Statue of Liberty, Gulf of Mexico, Holland Tunnel
3. Capitalize the names of months, days, and holidays.	January, May, Thursday, Fourth of July, Labor Day

Summary ◆ When you write, use capital letters to begin the important words in proper nouns.

Guided Practice

Name the proper nouns in each sentence below. Tell which letters should be capitalized.

1. Last july, several students traveled with roland washington to chicago, illinois.
2. The students visited the sears tower on wacker drive.
3. At the art institute of chicago, the group saw fine needlework done by americans.

Practice

A. Write each sentence. Capitalize the proper nouns.

4. I hope uncle joe is making a quilt for my birthday in october.

5. He is a georgian, and he lives near stone mountain.

6. On friday, manuel cruz showed the davises a book about handicrafters.

7. The whole family liked the sampler by sarah stone of salem, massachusetts.

8. The needlework that catherine wheeler did is beautiful.

9. A fine coverlet was embroidered by prudence geer punderson.

10. She lived in preston, connecticut.

11. The coverlet is owned by the connecticut historical society.

12. Have you seen this linen sampler by patty coggeshall?

13. Needleworkers such as mary comstock have left a rich heritage for americans.

B. Write a proper noun for each common noun below. Then use the proper noun in a sentence.

14. lake   **17.** mountain   **20.** street

15. state   **18.** country   **21.** bridge

16. pet   **19.** holiday   **22.** month

Sampler by Mary Hollingsworth, 1665. Courtesy of the Essex Institute, Salem, Massachusetts

C. 23–28. Write three common nouns and three proper nouns for the animal in the picture.

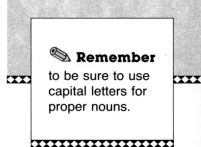

Apply • Think and Write

A Proper-Noun Sampler ♦ Imagine that you are going to embroider onto a sampler some sentences about your friends. Write the sentences. Include your friends' full names.

> ✎ **Remember**
> to be sure to use capital letters for proper nouns.

Follow this example to answer the questions that follow:
reminder: meet Mr. Lopez, 672 Main St.
What other adults might you meet? Where else might you meet them?

5 Abbreviations

In the following message, the letters in red are abbreviations, or shortened forms of words. The letters in blue are initials, or the first letters of names.

■ **Ms. M. G.** Dolan: departs for Mexico, 8:00 **P.M.** , **Mon.** , **Jan.** 2

Most abbreviations may be used only in special types of writing, such as messages and lists. Only titles with names (*Mr.*, *Ms.*, *Mrs.*, *Sr.*, *Jr.*, *Dr.*) and *A.M.* and *P.M.* may be used in sentences. Initials may be used in any writing. Here are some abbreviations.

Abbreviation	Explanation	Abbreviation	Explanation
Mr.	Mister (a man)	St.	Street
Ms.	a woman	Ave.	Avenue
Mrs.	a married woman	Blvd.	Boulevard
Sr.	Senior (older)	Dr.	Drive
Jr.	Junior (younger)	Rd.	Road
Dr.	Doctor	Rte.	Route
A.M.	before noon	P.M.	after noon

Mon.	Tues.	Wed.	Thurs.	Fri.	Sat.	Sun.

Jan.	Feb.	Mar.	Apr.	Aug.	Sept.	Oct.	Nov.	Dec.

Summary ♦ An **abbreviation** is a shortened form of a word. Many abbreviations begin with a capital letter and end with a period. An **initial** is the first letter of a name. It is written with a capital letter and followed by a period.

Guided Practice

Explain the abbreviations and initials in each group of words.

1. Dr. Felicia S. Iglesias
2. 427 Jackson Blvd.
3. 3:15 P.M., Tues., Aug. 19
4. Rte. 15 and Drexler Rd.

Practice

A. Each group of words below is written incorrectly. Write each group correctly, using capital letters and periods.

5. mr Juan d Blanco
6. 57 Westmont ave
7. dr Susan r Clayton

8. ms Lien Chang
9. 10:30 am, mon, mar 9
10. mr d j Warren, jr

B. The messages below contain initials and abbreviations written incorrectly. Write each message. Correct all mistakes.

11. 10:30 am: dental appointment with dr Davis
12. band practice: wed at 3:15 pm
13. mrs Clement: called jan 16
14. speaker about Mexican Handicrafts: ms Carmen f Acuna
15. location: Central Library on Kent dr
16. Central Library entrance: between Culver blvd and Elm st
17. mon, oct 29, 5:30 pm: meet m l

C. You know that some abbreviations can be used in sentences. Find the words that can be abbreviated in the sentences below. Write the sentences with the abbreviation.

18. Mister Harvey took us to the Mexican Gallery of Art.
19. We went on a guided tour led by Doctor Roberto Sanchez.
20. The tour began at 10:30 before noon.
21. Jonathan Marks, Junior, enjoyed the handicrafts exhibit.

Apply ◆ Think and Write

Giving Information ◆ You are taking a trip. Copy the travel agency form, and fill it out. Use abbreviations where possible.

World Travel Agency

Name _____

Street _____

City _____ State _____ Zip _____

Destination _____ Departure date _____

> ✎ **Remember**
> to use abbreviations and initials when they are appropriate.

Have fun with sentences that show relationships. You might say, "Fluffy is Teena's brother's daughter's cat." Then a partner can try to explain, "Fluffy belongs to the daughter of the brother of Teena." Try it.

6 Possessive Nouns

You have learned that a noun names a person, a place, a thing, or an idea. The underlined word in each sentence below is a possessive noun. The possessive form of a noun shows that the person or thing named owns something.

1. The girl's mother is a potter.
2. The vases' colors are vibrant and beautiful.
3. I admire those women's creations.

In sentence **1** the possessive noun is singular. In sentences **2** and **3** the possessive nouns are plural.

The chart below lists the rules for forming possessive nouns. You write an apostrophe and *s* or only an apostrophe.

To form the possessive of	Add	Examples
a singular noun	's	girl's aunt, James's smile
a plural noun ending in -s	'	vases' colors, boys' hats
a plural noun not ending in -s	's	women's creations, moose's hoofs, men's jobs

Summary ◆ A **possessive noun** shows ownership. When you write, be careful to form possessive nouns correctly.

Guided Practice

Name the possessive noun in each sentence below. Tell whether it is singular or plural.

1. The weavers' craft requires much skill.
2. Sara's aunts make handwoven rugs.
3. Her aunts' rugs have pictures on them.

Practice

A. Write the sentences. Draw one line under each possessive noun that is singular. Draw two lines under each possessive noun that is plural.

4. Thomas's uncle Nathan is a glassblower.
5. Many glassblowers' works are on display in the Chen Gallery.
6. Karen Chen, the gallery's owner, shook Nathan's hand.
7. Ms. Chen's greeting was warm and friendly.
8. She led him to the exhibitors' displays.
9. She said, ''Your elegant vases show an artist's touch.''
10. The man's smile lit up the gallery.
11. Then she took him to a room with children's handicrafts.
12. The young handicrafters' rag-doll exhibit was popular.
13. The youngsters' wonderful dolls received much praise.

B. Write the possessive form of each noun below.

14. calf	18. guests	22. people
15. cousin	19. women	23. canaries
16. exhibitor	20. deer	24. mouse
17. potters	21. weavers	25. coaches

C. Write each sentence. Choose the possessive noun in parentheses ( ) that correctly completes the sentence.

26. With my (mothers', mother's) help, I am learning to knit.
27. A (knitters', knitter's) basic stitches are the knit and the purl.
28. My two (brothers, brothers') sweaters were hard to make.
29. Knitted goods are sold at (men's, mens') clothing stores.
30. My (family's, families') preference is for handmade sweaters.

Apply · Think and Write

Craft Sale Information · Imagine that you and your friends went to a sidewalk craft sale. Write several sentences telling about the things people were buying and selling. Use singular and plural possessive nouns in your writing.

> ✎ **Remember**
> that possessive nouns show that something belongs to someone.

What do you think the underlined words in the following sentences mean? *The clay pots were thrown on a potter's wheel. A smooth, shiny coating of glaze was then put on the crockery.*

VOCABULARY ♦
Context Clues

When you read, you often come across unfamiliar words. Sometimes the **context**, or the words that surround an unknown word, will give you clues to the word's meaning. Such clues are called **context clues**. These clues can help you understand an unknown word when you are not able to use a dictionary.

The chart below gives examples of different kinds of context clues.

Kinds of Clues	Example
A *synonym*, or word with almost the same meaning	Most textiles, or *cloths*, were originally woven on a loom.
A *definition* of the new word	Weaving is *the art of making fabric out of thread.*
Further information about the new word's meaning	A satin weave is *very smooth, soft, and shiny.*

Building Your Vocabulary

Determine the meaning of each underlined word in the sentences below.

1. A dowel held the two pieces of wood together. This wooden pin is used in place of a metal screw or nail.
2. The woman pared the wood with a chisel. Thin shavings of the wood fell to the floor.
3. Pottery is baked in a kiln, which dries out any moisture and produces a hardened product.

Practice

A. Write *definition*, *further information*, or *synonym* to name the context clue given for each underlined word.

1. Twine, which is a strong cord, is made by weaving together several strands of string.
2. Strands of hair can be woven to form plaits, or braids.
3. Wood slats can be woven together to form a trellis, which vines can grow on.
4. Cotton is often spun, or twisted, into thread.
5. Yarn—that is, spun thread—is often used for weaving.

B. A *nonsense word* is a made-up word that doesn't mean anything. Below are several nonsense words. Use context to guess their meanings. Then write the meanings.

6. James is in dirple because he came in late.
7. Doris gets up every morning at six and trushes for two miles at a fast pace.
8. His favorite dessert is triffium. He especially likes chocolate or vanilla triffium sundaes.
9. We squaked so loud that we woke our neighbors. It was the funniest program we had ever watched.
10. Dad asked me to buy a sursip, or four quarts, of milk.

C. 11–15. Make up five nonsense words of your own. Then use them in sentences that show their meanings. See if your classmates can guess the meanings of your words.

LANGUAGE CORNER • Alliteration

Can you say quickly three times "Sheep shun sunshine?" Tongue twisters like this use **alliteration**, the repeated use of beginning sounds.

Create some tongue twisters for your classmates to try.

How to Revise Sentences with Nouns

You have been using nouns in sentences to name persons, places, and things. The nouns you choose can make a difference in your writing. Exact nouns can give a reader important details and information. For example, which of the sentences below gives you more information?

1. The mechanic asked Tanya for a tool.
2. The mechanic asked Tanya for a wrench.

Both sentences tell us what the mechanic asked for. Sentence **2**, however, tells us exactly what the mechanic wanted. The noun *wrench* is more exact than the general, or vague, noun *tool*. Some other exact nouns for *tool* are *pliers, saw, chisel*, and *hammer*. Asking for a specific tool can make a difference if you must pound in a nail or turn off the water in a hurry.

Look for chances to use exact nouns in your writing. They can make the difference between a vague sentence and a specific one.

The Grammar Game ✦ Check your noun knowledge from A to Z! As quickly as you can, think of exact nouns for each word or group of words below.

athlete	furniture	laborer	sport
bird	game	machine	store
body of water	hobby	noise	tree
career	home	occasion	vegetable
dog	insect	place	world
event	jewelry	relative	zoo animal

Compare lists with a classmate. Did you write any of the same exact nouns?

Working Together

Work as a group on activities **A** and **B**. Choose exact nouns to add details and information to your writing.

A. Draw this "Word Wheel." Each group member should choose an exact noun to add information to each spoke of the wheel. Then draw the wheel again, this time writing general nouns in each spoke.

food *animal*
method of transportation *musical instrument*
entertainer *occupation*
building *item of clothing*

B. How well do you know your group members? Each of you should complete the paragraph by using the most exact nouns. (Don't let anyone see what you wrote!) Then mix up the papers and have the group figure out who wrote each one.

I almost never leave my house without my _____ . I'm most comfortable wearing _____ and _____ . I could eat _____ seven days a week. I love to go to _____ . I hope to work as a _____ someday. I think the person who invented the _____ is the greatest of them all.

WRITERS' CORNER ♦ Fuzzy Sentences

Don't get lazy when you speak or write! Avoid using too many vague nouns in your sentences. Fuzzy, unclear sentences are dull and confusing to read. Can you tell what is happening in the fuzzy sentence below?

FUZZY: **Bring me that thing so I can finish these things and go to the thing.**

IMPROVED: **Bring me that pan so I can finish these dishes and go to the movies.**

Read what you wrote for the Writer's Warm-up. Did you use any fuzzy sentences? If you did, can you improve them?

LEADED GLASS WINDOW
design by Louis C. Tiffany
The Corning Museum of Glass, Corning, New York.

UNIT TWO

USING LANGUAGE TO

INFORM

PART TWO

Literature "Handicrafts" by Patricia Fent Ross
A Reason for Writing Informing

CREATIVE
Writing

FINE ARTS ◆ Have you ever seen stained glass windows? Look at the window at the left. What do you see in the design? What story does the window tell? Is the story about a magic kingdom? Does the story take place hundreds of years ago? Look at and through that window. Write the story that the window wants to tell.

CRITICAL THINKING ◆
A Strategy for Informing

AN ORDER CIRCLE

When you write to inform, you give important facts about a topic. Sometimes you give step-by-step directions for how to do something. After this lesson, you will read an article called "Handicrafts." In it the author gives directions for making pictures with yarn. Later you will write a how-to article about something you can do well.

"Handicrafts" is more than a how-to article. It also gives general information about Mexican villagers' crafts.

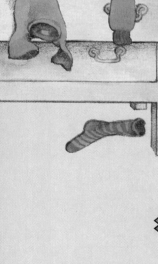

> One of the reasons the villagers still work at their crafts is that
> . . . Mexicans have a great respect for tradition . . . . A more
> important reason is that they love beauty, and they like to
> create things that are beautiful.

The author gives two reasons why the villagers work at their crafts. A less important reason is first, a more important reason second. Putting information in order helps readers understand and remember it.

◆ Learning the Strategy

There are many times when putting things in order is important. Suppose you decided to organize your dresser drawers. You might put your clothes in the drawers according to color. What is another way? Imagine you are describing to someone a beautiful lake where you went camping. In what order would you give the details? Suppose you have to write a report about the life of Christopher Columbus. In what order would you organize the facts? Do you think there might be another good way?

An order circle, like the one shown below, can help you. Inside the circle write what you want to put in order. On the arrows write some kinds of order. Decide which kind of order works best for what you plan to organize.

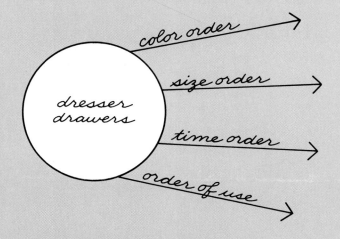

Using the Strategy

A. Use an order circle to help organize your desk. What kinds of order could you use? Which would work best? Write *my desk* inside an order circle. Write some kinds of order on the arrows. Decide which kind of order would work best. Is there another order that might work better?

B. In "Handicrafts" the author tells how to make yarn pictures. In what kind of order might the steps be given? Write *making yarn pictures* inside an order circle. Write some kinds of order on the arrows. Decide which kind of order the author will use to present the steps. Then read to find out if you were right.

Applying the Strategy

♦ How did you decide how to organize your desk? How many possible ways do you think there are?
♦ When have you had to put things in order during the past week? What kind of order did you use?

LITERATURE

Handicrafts

from Mexico

By Patricia Fent Ross

In the small villages of Mexico, people make by hand many of the things they use. Sometimes they make their own furniture. They weave beautifully designed bags and blankets. And they make their own sandals, hats, and baskets. Village craft workers make gaily decorated dishes and cooking vessels, and lovely lacquered trays, bowls, and boxes. All over the country there are craft villages, where almost everyone works at the same craft. In one village, for example, most of the workers are potters. In another village, most of them are weavers. Craft workers sell what they make to people from neighboring villages or to tourists.

One of the reasons the villagers still work at their crafts is that people in villages have always made things by hand. Mexicans have a great respect for tradition. They respect and love the customs, the way of living, and the crafts handed down to them by their ancestors.

A more important reason is that they love beauty, and they like to create things that are beautiful. Even useful things can be made beautiful. A cooking pot is just as useful when it is plain and dull. But when it is painted a pretty color and decorated with odd little animals or a neat design, it is beautiful too. A beautiful pot gives pleasure to the people who use it. And the beans they cook in it taste better. Although each region has its traditional colors and designs, no two objects are ever made exactly alike. The decoration is changed just a little to make each blanket or bowl or lacquered gourd a special work of art.

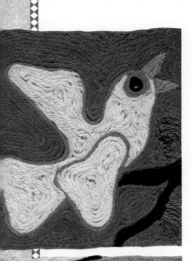

Colorful pictures "painted" with yarn are one of the village crafts sold in marketplaces in modern Mexico. These Mexican yarn paintings may picture animals and flowers, historical designs, or any other subjects that interest the artists. Here are the directions for making a yarn painting of your own design.

How to Make a Yarn Painting

You will need	
pencil	paper
chalk	white glue
six-inch by six-inch cardboard	yarn

The first step in making a yarn painting is to plan your design carefully. Sketch a simple design on a piece of paper. Plan which colors of yarn you will use.

Next, use chalk to lightly copy your sketch onto the cardboard square. The chalk can be rubbed off later if it is not completely covered by yarn.

Begin outlining your design with a dark color of yarn. Cover a small part of your outline with beads of glue. It takes only a small amount, so be careful not to use too much. Lightly press a piece of yarn onto the glue. Continue outlining your design in this way.

When your outline is complete, fill in the rest of the design with a lighter color of yarn. Continue putting glue on small sections and covering them with yarn. Applying the yarn in one direction might improve the appearance of your finished painting. You might choose to apply the yarn up and down, side to side, or round and round until your outline is filled.

Last, you may wish to glue a small loop of yarn to the back of the painting. Then you can hang it up for others to enjoy.

Library Link ◆ *If you would like to learn more about the country of Mexico, read* Mexico, *in the American Neighbors series, by Patricia Fent Ross.*

◆ Reader's Response

What handicraft would you like to know how to make? Tell why.

Handicrafts

Responding to Literature

1. Hundreds of years ago, potters fashioned bowls on wheels that they turned by hand. Many artists make bowls in the same way today. Those artists could use machines to do their work. Why do you think they prefer to work in the old ways?

2. Many people have respect for tradition. Cooking and stuffing a Thanksgiving turkey is an example of a tradition that many American families enjoy. Tell about your favorite tradition. What makes it special to you?

3. You know that a weaver is a person who weaves fabric or rugs. A weaver uses tools such as yarn and a loom. Many people use tools in their work. What tools do these workers use?

   carpenter   **auto mechanic**   **chef**   **journalist**

Writing to Learn

Think and Order ♦ An order circle helps you decide how something should be arranged. Plan information to tell how to do something. Make an order circle like the one below. Choose the order you will use to present your information.

(your subject)

time order
order of importance
space order
alphabetical order

Order Circle

Write ♦ Use the order you chose. Write your information in that order.

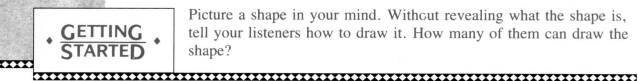

◆ **GETTING** ◆
STARTED

Picture a shape in your mind. Without revealing what the shape is, tell your listeners how to draw it. How many of them can draw the shape?

SPEAKING and LISTENING ◆
Directions

In the past, people learned the handicrafts of their ancestors by listening and watching. They followed the directions of their elders as they learned to make pottery, to weave, and to decorate tools and everyday objects. Knowing how to give and how to follow directions is just as important today as it was then. We still give oral directions to teach someone else what we know. We listen to directions to find out how to do something new. We observe, too, although we now often turn to ''how-to'' books or television programs.

Here are some guidelines to help you give and follow oral directions. These same guidelines might well have been followed by your ancestors as they learned and taught their handicrafts to their children.

Giving Directions	1. Look directly at your listeners and speak clearly. 2. Tell what materials, if any, are needed. 3. Explain every step in its correct order, giving details so that your listeners can picture each step. 4. Use gestures, drawings, or objects to help you. 5. Ask if there are any questions.
Following Directions	1. Look directly at the speaker and listen closely. 2. Show that you understand; for example, nod your head. 3. Picture each step in your mind. 4. Repeat the directions to yourself or to the speaker. 5. Ask the speaker to explain anything you do not understand.

Summary ◆ Give complete directions and explain the steps in order. Listen closely to directions to picture each step and to remember the steps in order.

Guided Practice

The pictures on this page show how to make a yarn doll. Study the pictures. Then take turns giving and listening to directions on how to make it.

Practice

A. Work with a partner. Choose one of the ideas below. Take turns giving clear and complete directions. Make notes for yourself if you wish. As a listener, picture each step in your mind. Ask questions about anything you do not understand.

1. Explain how to mix paints to make different colors.
2. Tell how to make a colorful bookmark.
3. Tell how to check a book out of the library.
4. Explain the safe way to use swings on the playground.
5. Explain how to use the telephone.

B. With a partner, take turns giving and following directions. Choose one of the ideas below, and give step-by-step directions for that task. To find out whether your directions are clear and complete, ask your partner to do *only* what you say.

6. how to sharpen a pencil
7. how to zip a jacket
8. how to draw an automobile
9. how make a paper-bag book cover
10. how to find a word in a dictionary

Apply ◆ Think and Write

Dictionary of Knowledge ◆ Have you ever heard of Ursa Major? Look it up in the Dictionary of Knowledge. Write a set of directions telling how to locate and recognize Ursa Major in the night sky. Then you will be able to tell someone else how to locate this constellation.

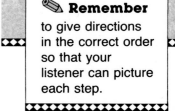

✎ **Remember**
to give directions in the correct order so that your listener can picture each step.

GETTING
STARTED

Play "What's the Big Idea?" Choose a picture in this book and tell its main idea in a sentence. Whoever finds the picture first and gives two details about it gives the next main idea.

WRITING ◆
A Paragraph

You already know that a paragraph is a group of sentences about one topic or about one main idea within that topic. You already know, too, that the first word of a paragraph is indented, or moved in. Do you know *why* you need to write in paragraphs? There are several good reasons—reasons for your reader and reasons for you, the writer.

Let us consider your reader first. Pick up a book and find a page without pictures. Now imagine that page without paragraphs. Would you want to read it? You would probably look at it and think, "Give me a break!" That is exactly what a new paragraph gives the reader—a mental break.

More importantly, though, paragraphs signal major ideas. A new paragraph tells the reader, "You have just come to the end of one main idea. Now the author is going to discuss another."

What does writing paragraphs do for you, the writer? As you write a paragraph, you have to focus on your main idea. All of the sentences in the paragraph must relate to the main idea. The paragraph gives you writing power, because it helps to make your meaning clear. Notice how the paragraph below focuses your attention on its main idea.

One of the reasons the villagers still work at their crafts is that people in villages have always made things by hand. Mexicans have a great respect for tradition. They respect and love the customs, the way of living, and the crafts handed down to them by their ancestors.

Summary ◆ A **paragraph** is a group of sentences that tell about one main idea. When you write a paragraph, indent the first word.

Guided Practice

Some of the sentences below belong together in a paragraph. Others do not. Tell which sentences belong in the paragraph.

1. The history of handicrafts is as old as history itself.
2. Handicrafts can help disabled people develop stronger muscles.
3. The first handicrafts developed as people made useful objects.
4. Hobbies are not necessarily the same thing as handicrafts.
5. Basketry, weaving, and pottery were among the first handicrafts.

Practice

A. Decide which sentences below belong in a paragraph about making quilts. For each sentence, write *yes* or *no*.

6. Three layers of fabric are used to make a quilt.
7. Quilts are a popular item in antique stores.
8. People appreciate the warmth of a fine down quilt.
9. Pieces of cloth can be sewn together to make a quilt top.
10. The quilter needs thread, scissors, and special needles.

B. Decide which three sentences below tell about the main idea. Then use the main idea and the three sentences to write a paragraph. Start with the main idea.

MAIN IDEA: Papier-mâché craft is inexpensive and fun.

11. Working in stained glass is an expensive handicraft.
12. This material is made from paper, water, and paste.
13. Professional jewelry designers work with papier-mâché.
14. Papier-mâché is used like clay to model almost anything.
15. Jewelry, masks, and puppets are just a few things you can make from papier-mâché.

Apply ◆ Think and Write

An Informative Photo ◆ Write a paragraph about the photograph on this page. It shows a jewelry maker at work. Think of a main idea first and use it to decide what you will say.

> ✎ **Remember** that a paragraph focuses on a single main idea.

List some main ideas about your classroom, such as *Our classroom is a creative place.* Take turns giving details that explain one of those main ideas.

WRITING ◆ Topic Sentence and Supporting Sentences

Every paragraph has a main idea. Some paragraphs put that main idea into words. If a paragraph puts that idea into words, it is stated in a topic sentence. The topic sentence often comes first, since it is helpful to let the reader know the topic of the paragraph right away. The other sentences in the paragraph are supporting sentences. They support the main idea by telling more about it or by giving details about it. Here is an example. Notice that the supporting sentences are arranged in a logical order.

Topic sentence

Supporting sentences

All over Mexico there are craft villages. Almost everyone works at the same craft. In one village, for example, most of the people may be potters. In another they may be weavers, and in still another they may be jewelry makers.

A topic sentence does not have to come first. Often it comes last. Then the supporting sentences lead up to the main idea, as in this example.

Supporting sentences

Topic sentence

In one Mexican village most of the people are potters. In another they are weavers. In still another they are jewelry makers. Such villages are common. All over Mexico there are craft villages.

When the purpose of your writing is to give information, you may wish to begin or end a paragraph with a topic sentence. It helps both you and your reader focus on the most important idea.

> **Summary** ◆ The **topic sentence** states the main idea of a paragraph. **Supporting sentences** develop the main idea. Topic sentences are especially useful in informative writing.

Guided Practice

Put these sentences in order, starting with the topic sentence. Then arrange the supporting sentences in a logical order.

1. There may be many that look alike.
2. Pottery is made by craftspeople and in factories.
3. Inexpensive mugs, for example, are generally mass-produced.
4. Some pieces of pottery have become valuable.
5. A potter, however, is more likely to make a one-of-a-kind piece considered a work of art.

Practice

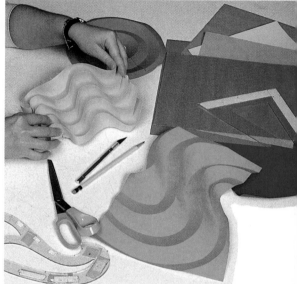

A. Use the sentences below to write a paragraph. Find the topic sentence and write it first. Then complete the paragraph by writing the supporting sentences. Write them in an order that makes sense.

6. By folding and curving the paper, you get a new effect.
7. Paper sculpture is fun to try.
8. The curved paper looks three-dimensional.
9. Begin by folding and curving a flat piece of paper.

B. Write two supporting sentences for each topic sentence below.

10. You can make many beautiful things from seashells.
11. Papier-mâché can be used instead of clay.

C. Write a topic sentence and two or more supporting sentences for each of these topics.

12. a handicraft you would like to try
13. why people enjoy handicrafts

Apply ◆ Think and Write

A Paragraph ◆ Will everything be made by machines in the future? Write a paragraph that tells about handicrafts in the year 2500. Begin or end your paragraph with a topic sentence.

✎ Remember
to state the main idea of your paragraph in a topic sentence.

I was an early American statesman and scientist. Find my name.
Benjamin Franklin   Franklin, Benjamin   Benjamin, Franklin
I was the third American president. Find my name.
Jefferson, Thomas   Thomas Jefferson   Thomas, Jefferson

WRITING ◆
Using Commas

A comma can tell a reader where to pause. Correctly placed commas help to make your meaning clear.

> Please buy paper towels, tuna salad, and limes.
> Please buy paper, towels, tuna, salad, and limes.

Four different uses for commas are shown below.

When to Use a Comma	Examples
1. To separate words in a series of three or more items (No comma is used after the last item.)	Beth gathered, sorted, and polished the stones.
2. To set off *yes, no,* or *well* at the beginning of a sentence	Yes, I have seen rock art. No, I haven't tried it myself.
3. To set off the name of someone directly spoken to	José, gather some small rocks. I think, Lou, we have enough.
4. To separate a last name from a first name when the last name is written first	Jackson, Lou Kwan, Beth Laredo, José

Summary ◆ Use commas for the purposes shown in the chart. Commas used correctly make your meaning clear and your writing easier to understand.

Guided Practice

Tell where commas belong in these sentences.

1. Who borrowed the book on wood handicrafts Mr. O'Dowd?
2. Well the name on the card says "Dixon Cara."
3. I found the book to be interesting informative and detailed.

Practice

A. Write each item below, using commas where they are needed.

4. frosty cool and refreshing
5. apples lemons and melons
6. cutting pasting and painting
7. Mrs. Kliban Ms. Bannerji and my cousin
8. Schofield Patrick

B. Write the sentences. Use commas where they are needed.

9. Ancient Greek mosaics decorated walls floors and ceilings.
10. Josh some Greek mosaics are over two thousand years old.
11. How did the Greeks get the stones to stick Molly?
12. Well they didn't have the modern efficient and long-lasting glue that we have.
13. They usually used cement or plaster Roger.
14. Yes but we don't have those supplies in school.
15. No Evan but Mr. O'Dowd says that white glue will work fine.
16. What can we use for a suitable firm and sturdy background?
17. We could use heavy cardboard plastic trays or a piece of slate.
18. Let's get our supplies roll up our sleeves and begin.

C. Write sentences with commas to answer the questions below.

EXAMPLE: Can you follow directions well?
ANSWER: Yes, I can follow directions well.

19. What four foods do you consider healthful?
20. How does your name look if you write your last name first?
21. What are the names of three people you admire?

Apply ◆ Think and Write

A Chart ◆ Pretend that your class will take part in a handicrafts show. Make a chart that lists at least eight students in your class. List their full names, last name first. Beside each name, write the handicraft that person will work on for the show.

> ✎ **Remember**
> that commas help to make your meaning clear.

Focus on Sequence

You have probably heard the expression "First things first." That is excellent advice to follow whenever you write directions or explain something in time order. In fact, you might add "Second things second, third things third," and so on. When it comes to directions or time order, **sequence** is very important.

Sequence comes from a Latin word meaning "to follow." The numbers *1, 2, 3, 4* follow each other in a numerical sequence. The letters *A, B, C, D* follow each other in an alphabetical sequence. In a set of directions or in a time-order paragraph, the steps follow each other in a chronological, or time, sequence.

- FIRST: The first time-order step may use the word *first.*
- SECOND: Sometimes the words *second, third,* and so on, are used. More often the writer switches to *then* or *next.*
- THEN: The words *then, next,* and *after that* are all-purpose time-order words. They may appear more than once in an explanation.
- FINALLY: The words *finally* and *last* are common in conclusions.

Sequence is often based on chronology, but not always. Sometimes it is based on order of importance, as in the article "Handicrafts," which you read earlier. That article is developed with reasons, not chronological steps. In "Handicrafts" the order is from the least important to the most important reason.

- *One of the reasons...*
- *A more important reason...*

The Writer's Voice ◆ Words like *first, then,* and *finally* show chronological order. What are some other words and expressions that show chronological order? (Think about dates and hours.)

Why is it so important to get the sequence correct in writing directions?

Working Together

When you write, you must arrange ideas in a logical order. The sequence may or may not be chronological. Work with your group or activities **A** and **B**.

A. Arrange the sentences below in a logical order. Look for time-order words that provide clues.

1. Each rider covered seventy miles on seven horses.
2. After ten miles he switched to a fresh horse at a pony express station and kept riding.
3. While he rested, other riders galloped on with the mail.
4. Pony express riders rode their horses at breakneck speed between St. Joseph, Missouri, and San Francisco, California.
5. The exhausted rider then rested for the return trip.
6. First a rider raced at full gallop for ten miles.

B. Discuss possible topics for a paragraph. Decide on one of the topics. Then make a list of at least five points to be covered in the paragraph. Arrange the points in a logical order. This can be chronological order or order of importance. Be ready to present the paragraph plan in class and to explain it.

In Your Group

- Contribute ideas to the discussion.
- Invite others to talk.
- Help the group reach agreement.
- Keep a list of people's ideas.

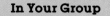

THESAURUS CORNER · Word Choice

Twelve of the main entry words in the Thesaurus are nouns. Write them down. Then write a good paragraph based on one of the nouns. For instance, you might write on a funny *accident* or a *story* from last summer. In your paragraph, try to use at least three synonyms for the noun you have chosen. Make sure your sentences are in a logical order.

WRITING PROCESS

INFORMING

Writing a How-to Article

A how-to article, as its title suggests, explains how to do something. An example in "Handicrafts" was the part that told how to make yarn pictures. If you followed the directions, you could make a yarn picture yourself.

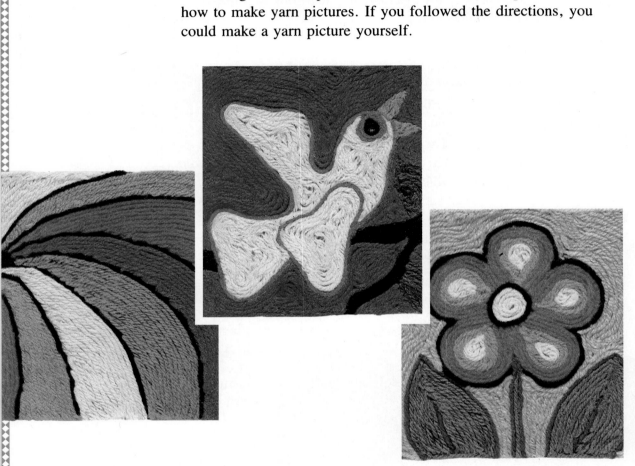

Know Your Purpose and Audience

In this lesson you will write a how-to article. Your purpose will be to explain how to do something.

Your audience will be your classmates. Later you can share your article with an oral presentation or a comic strip.

1 Prewriting

To get ready to write, first choose your topic. That is, decide what you will explain how to do. Then gather ideas about your topic.

Choose Your Topic ◆ Make a list of things you can do well. Then look over your list. Which topic would be most fun to write about? Circle your choice.

Think About It	Talk About It
You can do many things. Which would you choose for your topic? Think about which idea would be the most fun to explain. Which could you explain most clearly? Which would your classmates find most interesting? Circle your favorite.	Work with a group of three or four. Discuss things you know how to do. Take turns saying, ''I know how to do _____.'' Then make your list. Help others by reminding them of things you know they can do well.

Topic Ideas

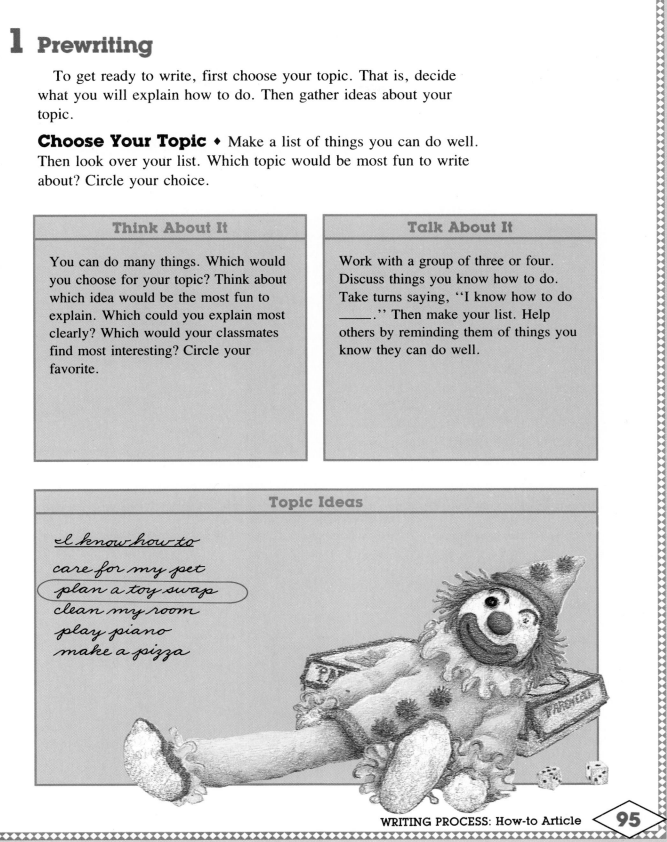

I know how to
care for my pet
plan a toy swap
clean my room
play piano
make a pizza

Choose Your Strategy ◆ Here are two strategies that can help you gather ideas for your how-to article. Read both. Then decide which strategy you will use.

PREWRITING IDEAS

CHOICE ONE

An Order Circle

Write your topic inside an order circle. Write some kinds of order on arrows. How will you arrange your how-to directions? Look at your order circle and decide which kind of order will work best.

You might try a kind of order named below. Time order tells what to do first, next, and last. Order of use tells what materials to use first, next, and last. Order of importance starts with the most important step, and ends with the least. Space order tells what happens in one place, then another.

Model

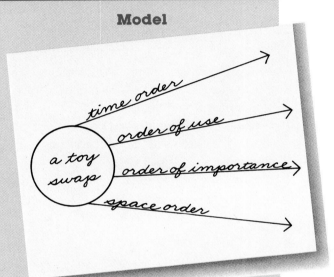

CHOICE TWO

A Clock Graph

Work with a partner to make a clock graph. Draw a large clock shape. Then explain your activity to your partner. Ask your partner to write the steps around the clock graph as you talk. What if you tell a step out of order? Help your partner write it in the right place on the graph. When you are sure the steps are in the right order, number them.

Model

1. Check with parents.
2. Look through old toys.
3. Set aside toys to swap.
4. Make posters.
5. Put toys out on swap day.

2 Writing

Look over your order wheel or clock graph. Then begin to write your how-to article. Here are some ways you might start.

• Would you like to learn how to _____?

• _____ can be a lot of fun to do.

Now write the directions in the order you have chosen to use. For clarity, use order words like *first*, *next*, *then*, and *last*.

Sample First Draft ♦

Planning a toy swap can be fun. Look through your old toys games and activitys. Set aside the ones you'll offer in the swap. Next make posters to advertise the swap. Decorate the posters with drawings of things you plan to swap. Hang up the posters around your Neighborhood. Finally, on the day of the swap, put your toys and games on a table. Soon you'll have a pile of "new" toys and games to play with. First get your parents permission make sure that they don't object to your swapping your toys and games.

3 Revising

Now you have written your how-to article. Would you like to improve it? This idea for revising may help you.

REVISING IDEA

FIRST Read to Yourself

As you read, review your purpose. Did you write a how-to article? Did you explain how to do something? Consider your audience. Would your classmates be able to follow the steps?

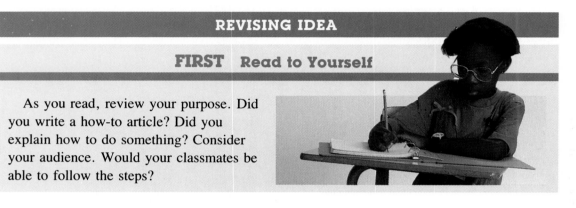

Focus: Is the order of directions clear? Put a caret (^) where you want to add order words like *first*, *next*, *then,* and *last.*

THEN Share with a Partner

Ask a partner to read your article aloud to you. Listen for parts you would like to improve. These guidelines may help you.

The Writer

Guidelines: Listen as if you were hearing your writing for the first time. Ask for your partner's ideas.

Sample questions:
- Did I give enough information?
- Could you follow my directions?
- **Focus question:** Is the order of the steps clear?

The Writer's Partner

Guidelines: Read the article aloud clearly. Then give honest, helpful suggestions.

Sample responses:
- Could you explain more about _____ ?
- I think this step should come before _____ .

Revising Model ♦ Look at this sample how-to article that is being revised. The marks show changes the writer wants to make.

The writer's partner suggested specific directions here.

Exact nouns *toys* and *games* replaced the vague noun *things*.

Arrange is a more precise word than *put*.

This important step should be stated first.

> Planning a toy swap can be fun. Look
> through your old toys games and activitys.
> Set aside the ones you'll offer in the swap.
> Next make posters to advertise the swap.
> ~~Write the date, time, and place on each poster.~~
> Decorate the posters with drawings of
> ∧ *toys and games*
> ~~things~~ you plan to swap. Hang up
> the posters around your Neighborhood.
>   Finally, on the day of the swap,
> *arrange*
> ~~put~~ your toys and games on a table.
> Soon you'll have a pile of "new" toys and
> games to play with. First get your
> parents permission make sure that
> they don't object to your swapping
> your toys and games.

Read the above how-to article the way the writer thinks it *should* be. Then revise your own how-to article.

Grammar Check ♦ Exact nouns make your meaning clearer.

Word Choice ♦ Do you ever want a more precise word for a word like *put*? A thesaurus can help you find the word.

Revising Checklist

☐ **Purpose:** Did my article explain how to do something?

☐ **Audience:** Would my classmates be able to follow the steps?

☐ **Focus:** Did I use words like *first*, *next*, and *last* to make the order clear?

4 Proofreading

Proofread your how-to article and correct any mistakes you find.

Proofreading Model ♦ Here is the draft of the how-to article about a toy swap. Red proofreading changes have been added.

Proofreading Marks

capital letter	=
small letter	/
indent paragraph	¶
check spelling	⬭

Planning a toy swap can be fun. Look
through your old toys games, and ⬭activitys⬭.
⟶ *activities*
Set aside the ones you'll offer in the swap.
¶ Next make posters to advertise the swap.
Write the date, time, and place on each poster.
Decorate the posters with drawings of
toys and games
things you plan to swap. Hang up
the posters around your Neighborhood.
    Finally, on the day of the swap,
arrange
put your toys and games on a table.
Soon you'll have a pile of "new" toys and
games to play with. ⬭First get your
parents'
⬭parents⬭ permission. make sure that
they don't object to your swapping
your toys and games.

Proofreading Checklist

- ☐ Did I spell words correctly?
- ☐ Did I indent paragraphs?
- ☐ Did I use capital letters correctly?
- ☐ Did I use correct marks at the end of sentences?
- ☐ Did I use my best handwriting?

PROOFREADING IDEA

Handwriting Check

Check your handwriting for poorly formed letters. Do some letters look like others? Handwriting charts in your classroom or spelling book can help you correct bad handwriting habits.

Now proofread your how-to article, add a title, and make a neat copy.

5 Publishing

Try one of these ways of sharing your how-to article.

A Toy Swap

Planning a toy swap can be fun. First, get your parents' permission. Make sure that they don't object to your swapping your toys and games. Look through your old toys, games, and activities. Set aside the ones you'll offer in the swap.

Next make posters to advertise the swap. Write the date, time, and place on each poster. Decorate the posters with drawings of toys and games you plan to swap. Hang up the posters around your neighborhood.

Finally, on the day of the swap, arrange your toys and games on a table. Soon you'll have a pile of "new" toys and games to play with.

PUBLISHING IDEAS

Share Aloud

Read your article to a small group of classmates. Use a visual aid, such as a chart of steps or a clock graph. If you can, demonstrate the activity. Ask members of your audience to tell what part of your activity they would enjoy most.

Share in Writing

Draw comic-strip instructions for your activity. Show one step in each frame. Display your comic strip beside your how-to article. Ask classmates to suggest a title for the comic strip.

CURRICULUM
◆CONNECTION◆

Writing Across the Curriculum   Art

Recently you wrote a how-to article. You used an order circle to help you choose the best order for your information. Another way to present information is by setting up an exhibit. When you visit a museum or an art gallery, you may notice that the items are arranged in a certain order. The arrangement helps you see important things about the art. It helps you compare and contrast different pieces. An order circle can be a tool for determining how to arrange an art exhibit.

Writing to Learn

Think and Plan ◆ Imagine that you have been asked to arrange an exhibit of pottery, furniture, and quilts in your school auditorium. These items come from every state in the country. Some items are very old, others are new. Use an order circle to help you decide how to organize your art exhibit.

Order Circle

Write ◆ Draw a plan that shows how you would arrange your exhibit. Add labels and explain why you have chosen this arrangement.

Writing in Your Journal

In the Writer's Warm-up, you wrote about crafts. Then you read about weaving, pottery, and furniture making. What other crafts have you read about? In your journal, write about an interesting craft. Tell why you might like to master it.

BOOKS TO ENJOY

◆ Read More About It

The Weaver's Gift *by Kathryn Lasky*
Spend a year with Carolyn and Milton Frye on their sheep farm. The Fryes raise sheep and shear them each year. Carolyn cleans the wool and spins it into yarn. Then she weaves the yarn into blankets.

Model a Monster *by Colin Caket*
Learn how to model your favorite prehistoric animals. The step-by-step directions in this book are easy to follow. The author includes facts about the dinosaurs you will make.

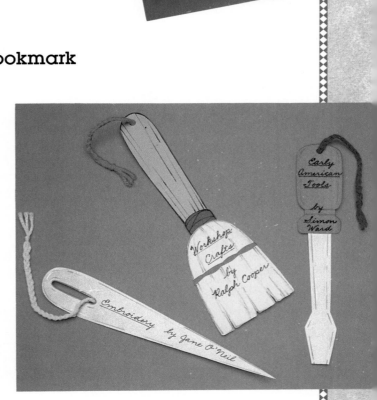

◆ Book Report Idea Bookmark

A handmade bookmark can tell about a book while it marks a page. Share a book in a new and useful way.

Create a Bookmark ◆ Begin with a strip of oaktag, assorted markers, and some colored yarn. Cut the oaktag into a long shape suggested by the book you read. Fasten a tail of yarn to one end. Write the book's title and the author's name on the front of the bookmark. To catch the interest of possible readers, copy a short, interesting passage from the book on the back. Share the bookmarks by hanging them from their tails in a book-review display.

UNIT REVIEW

Unit 2

Nouns *pages 60–65*

A. Write the plural form of each noun.

1. pet	**14.** sheep
2. ox	**15.** goose
3. wife	**16.** monkey
4. pie	**17.** berry
5. deer	**18.** man
6. foot	**19.** hat
7. city	**20.** boy
8. penny	**21.** wish
9. shelf	**22.** box
10. woman	**23.** glass
11. dress	**24.** leaf
12. country	**25.** tooth
13. village	**26.** lady

B. Read each noun. If it is a common noun, write *common*. If it is a proper noun, write *proper*.

27. Pittsburgh	**38.** Thanksgiving
28. theater	**39.** polar bear
29. month	**40.** Abraham Lincoln
30. February	**41.** marching band
31. trees	**42.** public library
32. Lake Erie	**43.** Pacific Ocean
33. ostrich	**44.** encyclopedia
34. Bronx Zoo	**45.** Samuel Houston
35. Mars	**46.** train station
36. Delaware	**47.** soccer field
37. mayor	**48.** Davis Boulevard

Capital Letters and Periods
pages 66–69

C. Write each sentence. Capitalize the proper nouns.

49. The chongs went to san fransisco last october.

50. They visited their relatives on geary boulevard.

51. Mrs. chong and her daughter rose had a picnic in golden gate park.

52. Her son lee fed the animals at the zoo.

53. The entire family ate lunch at a restaurant on union square.

54. Then they went to the san francisco museum of modern art.

55. Lee chong admired a painting by john sloan.

56. Later the chongs rode on a cable car down to fisherman's wharf.

57. They gazed across san francisco bay toward alcatraz island.

58. At the end of the week, the chongs returned to boston, massachusetts.

D. Write the sentences. Abbreviate the underlined words.

59. Harold Walker, <u>Junior</u>, is running for mayor.

60. <u>Doctor</u> Jeanne Klein is my aunt.

61. She lives on Jackson <u>Boulevard</u>.

62. Her birthday is <u>October</u> 29.

63. Our music teacher is <u>Mister</u> Brody.

64. The big game will take place on <u>Friday</u> afternoon.

65. The band will march up Washington <u>Street</u>.

66. On <u>Saturday</u>, everybody will rest.

Apostrophes   *pages 70–71*

E. Write the possessive form of each noun.

67. girls   **72.** friend
68. child   **73.** people
69. Sally   **74.** building
70. men   **75.** Charles
71. mice   **76.** deer

Paragraphs   *pages 86–87*

F. Decide which sentences below belong in a paragraph about stamp collecting. For each sentence, write *yes* or *no*.

77. People of all ages collect stamps.
78. Some people prefer to collect rare coins.
79. A stamp album will protect your stamps from damage.
80. Stamps from foreign countries are often interesting.
81. The cost of mailing a letter keeps increasing.

Topic Sentence and Supporting Sentences   *pages 88–89*

G. Use the sentences below to write a paragraph. Find the topic sentence and write it first. Then complete the paragraph by writing the supporting sentences in an order that makes sense.

82. First, purchase a model plane kit.
83. Let the glue dry.
84. Building a model plane can be fun.
85. Glue the plane parts together.
86. Finally, paint the assembled plane.
87. Gather the parts of the plane.

Commas   *pages 90–91*

H. Write the sentences. Add commas where they are needed.

88. The kittens romped quarreled and finally went to sleep.
89. Bonnie Jared and Ellen are bringing the food.
90. No that is an incorrect answer.
91. Her name is listed in the book's index as *Bloomer Amelia*.
92. Tom give me the pencil.
93. Yes she is my sister.
94. We studied rested then studied some more.
95. Look in the phone book under *Sanchez Pedro*.
96. Well I am certainly disappointed in you!
97. Fred meet my uncle and aunt.
98. The small dog barked wagged its tail and ran up to greet me.
99. Sidney Rowe I am surprised at you!
100. We need butter eggs and two cups of flour for this recipe.
101. No Henrietta that is not a portrait of my father.
102. Mr. Phelan Ms. Boggs and I are rehearsing for the play.
103. Will you please tell me Perry what you have done all day.
104. The Nolans the Chens and the Goldbergs were all at the picnic.
105. No madam I am not the person who rang your doorbell.
106. Bradley have you seen my pet lizard?
107. Everyone knows that the American flag is red white and blue.

CUMULATIVE REVIEW

Unit 1: Sentences *pages 6–15*

A. Write the declarative, interrogative, imperative, and exclamatory sentences. Begin each sentence correctly. Use correct punctuation at the end.

1. what a lovely dress
2. is that a robin on the windowsill
3. bring your cousin to the party
4. how exciting this movie is
5. here is my drawing
6. will you give me your advice
7. tell me what you think
8. what a rainy day this is
9. when will it stop raining
10. tomorrow is supposed to be sunny and warm
11. do you know my music teacher
12. the supermarket is located next to the bank
13. please bring me that book
14. she is my best friend
15. why can't you sit still
16. the dog sniffed the tree
17. turn off that television set
18. did you see an enormous turtle crawl by here
19. your turtle is over there
20. what a huge creature he is
21. how much does it cost to feed him
22. his food is not that expensive
23. he eats mostly leafy vegetables
24. does he have a name
25. his name is Max

B. Write the complete subject of each sentence. Underline the simple subject. Write (*You*) if the subject is understood.

26. The kitten in the middle is mine.
27. The boys are brushing their teeth.
28. Look at that beautiful rainbow!
29. That bunch of purple grapes looks delicious.
30. Ask me a question.
31. The timid puppy hid behind a tree.
32. Put your notebook on the desk.
33. The best players on the team are Ben and Gerry.
34. Take off those dirty shoes.
35. The huge, black bear slept soundly.
36. Three students in my class received perfect scores on the test.
37. The big toe on my left foot aches.
38. The prices in that store are high.

C. Write the complete predicate of each sentence. Underline the simple predicate.

39. I am studying for my math test.
40. The boys ran up and down the hall.
41. Kelvin is going with us.
42. Mia has done all her chores.
43. The roses look beautiful!
44. Ms. Romano was driving her new car.
45. We have learned our parts for the class play.
46. Susie threw the basketball to her friend.
47. Tom loves mystery stories.
48. Our team has won the tennis match.
49. Jeremy and Terri will visit their grandparents next week.
50. Debbie worked hard on her project.

Unit 2: Nouns   *pages 60–65*

D. Write each sentence. Underline the nouns in each sentence.

51. Our class visited a museum of art.
52. There is a beautiful fountain near the entrance to the building.
53. Joan admired a painting by Vincent van Gogh.
54. Mr. Watts led us to a group of statues by Michelangelo.
55. Steve and Liza stood gazing for minutes at a mural by Diego Rivera.
56. A room near the entrance displays prints by many famous artists.
57. A large case made of glass holds a collection of old coins.
58. Tina bought several postcards with pictures of famous works of art.
59. After several hours the students returned to school.
60. Jennie, Sam, Tony, and Melissa wanted to go again.

E. Write the plural form of each noun.

61. mouse
62. woman
63. deer
64. glass
65. child
66. inch
67. foot
68. life
69. baby
70. holiday

F. Write *common* or *proper* for each noun.

71. cow
72. Houston
73. bicycle
74. envelope
75. Ms. Wong
76. country
77. Ben Franklin
78. Great Salt Lake
79. tennis court
80. Pennsylvania

Unit 2: Capital Letters and Periods   *pages 66–69*

G. Write each sentence. Capitalize the proper nouns.

81. I read a biography of thomas jefferson.
82. He was a great american.
83. This statesman wrote the declaration of independence.
84. He was born on april 13, 1743, in albemarle county, virginia.
85. In 1772 he married martha wayles skelton, the daughter of a lawyer.
86. In 1801, jefferson was elected president of the united states.
87. One of his greatest achievements was the louisiana purchase.
88. This land deal with france doubled the size of the united states.
89. In 1826, jefferson died at monticello, his virginia home.

H. Write the sentences. Abbreviate the underlined words.

90. <u>Mister</u> Russo is a wonderful dancer.
91. We went fishing on <u>Sunday</u> morning.
92. Please finish the work by <u>April</u> 15.
93. <u>Doctor</u> Harper is my dentist.
94. Her office is located on <u>Route</u> 27.

Unit 2: Apostrophes   *pages 70–71*

I. Write the possessive form of each noun.

95. women
96. singer
97. Otis
98. books
99. sheep
100. brother
101. foxes
102. cows
103. tiger
104. actresses

Story Ad-Libs

Complete this science-fiction story with the kinds of nouns named in ( ). Then write an exciting ending of your own.

On June 6, 2989, an earthling named (proper) set out for a vacation on the planet (proper). For the trip she borrowed her (possessive) spacemobile and packed a (common) and a (common). She also brought her (possessive) (common).

When she got to the other planet, she was surprised to find that the houses were made of (common). She decided to stay at the (proper), which was very near (proper).

At dinner that night she met (proper), who was the (common) of (proper). He warned her not to go to (proper) because there was a dangerous (common) there...

A Noun Scramble

Unscramble each set of letters. (Hint: The unscrambled words contain capital letters.)

1. a state: untcosailohra
2. a city: ooaannnist
3. a holiday: oerdmiyamla
4. a language: iesnhce
5. a club: mcnknecaearienlubl
6. a continent: rhmaotirenac
7. a dog breed: aengtdare
8. a month: emrsbetep
9. a body of water: ntliatoacneca
10. a newspaper: rkwoytnmseie

Unit 2 Extra Practice

1 Writing with Nouns

p. 60

A. Write the following sentences. Underline all the nouns in each sentence.

1. The class studied life in ancient Greece.
2. The students saw statues in a museum.
3. Ancient Greeks studied mathematics and music.
4. This report is about their houses and their cities.
5. The Greeks liked sunshine.
6. Ancient Greeks lived in plain and simple houses.
7. The warm weather made the garden a popular place.
8. Families worked and played under the trees.
9. Many people lived in cities.
10. Towns were planned with great thoughtfulness.
11. The adults met their friends at the open markets.
12. Temples and theaters were also important buildings.
13. Tim showed a picture of a theater to the class.
14. Wide streets led into town.
15. Walls surrounded the city for safety.

B. Write the following sentences. Complete each sentence with one of the nouns below. Use the noun that best fits the sentence.

chairs   clothes   beds   writers   windows
nails   house   comforts   tables   heat

16. Many _____ have left descriptions of ancient Greece.
17. The Greeks enjoyed many of the _____ of life.
18. Each room in a Greek _____ had a different use.
19. Some rooms contained _____ for sleeping.
20. Some clothing was hung on _____ in the walls.
21. Other _____ were stored in chests.
22. Greeks did not sit on _____ to eat their meals.
23. Instead, their _____ were placed beside couches.
24. Their _____ was supplied by charcoal stoves.
25. The _____ were left open for fresh air.

2 Singular and Plural Nouns

A. Write whether each of these nouns is singular or plural.

  1. wish **3.** monkeys **5.** dash **7.** knives **9.** women
  2. toy   **4.** box   **6.** feet **8.** rake   **10.** kite

B. Write the underlined noun in each sentence. Then write *singular* if the noun is singular. Write *plural* if it is plural.

  11. The smallest muscle is in the ear.
  12. The tallest women are over seven feet tall.
  13. One cat had a litter of thirteen kittens.
  14. What is the largest ruby in the world?
  15. Are the most expensive dresses from Paris?
  16. What holidays are celebrated by the most people?
  17. These sheep have the longest horns in the world.
  18. What country has the greatest number of wolves?
  19. The largest flag in the world is in the United States.
  20. This mouse weighs less than an ounce.

C. Write the plural of each of these nouns.

  21. ax   **26.** goose
  22. army   **27.** village
  23. glass   **28.** ostrich
  24. moose **29.** shelf
  25. turkey **30.** bat

3 Common and Proper Nouns
p. 64

A. In each sentence below, the nouns are underlined. Write each noun. Then write *common* or *proper* to show what kind of noun it is.

  1. Death Valley is the lowest, hottest desert in America.
  2. Sequoia National Park is not far from this desert.
  3. The General Sherman Tree is the largest tree in the state.
  4. Many beautiful churches and missions are found between Carmel and San Luis Obispo.
  5. Father Junipero Serra built chapels at the missions.

B. Write each sentence. Draw one line under the common nouns.
Draw two lines under the proper nouns.

6. Grapes for raisins are grown in the valleys.
7. People seeking gold hurried to Sutter's Creek.
8. Now tourists visit Sutter's Mill on the creek.
9. Another favorite attraction is Yosemite National Park.
10. Many movies are made in Hollywood.
11. Giant redwood trees grow in Muir Woods National Monument.
12. The highest peak in the Sierra Nevada is Mount Whitney.
13. Lake Tahoe is a beautiful place for a vacation.
14. Disneyland charms adults as well as children.
15. The Sacramento is the longest river in California.
16. The Golden Gate Bridge is a famous landmark.
17. Fisherman's Wharf is a popular area in San Francisco.
18. Many seals live on the rocks along the coast.
19. San Diego is a large city near Mexico.

4 Capitalizing Proper Nouns   *p. 66*

A. Write each sentence. Capitalize the proper nouns.

1. The town of plymouth is in massachusetts.
2. Many people visit the town each november.
3. They remember the first thanksgiving.
4. Actors dress up as pilgrims for the dinner.
5. Some visitors cross main street to look at plymouth rock.
6. It is on the shore at the edge of cape cod bay.
7. At a little store alicia and laura bought postcards.
8. On the way home they visited the thornton burgess museum.
9. They saw some glass plates with pictures of peter rabbit and joe otter.

B. Write a proper noun for each common noun below.

10. state	15. city
11. lake	16. bridge
12. president	17. river
13. school	18. street
14. holiday	19. pet

C. Capitalize the proper nouns in each sentence below.

20. The harrisons flew to florida last week.
21. The park hotel is in everglades national park.
22. On friday we'll drive to key west on the gulf of mexico.
23. The audubon house is on whitehead street.
24. They will visit disney world in orlando.
25. The whole family will fly back to logan airport in boston.

5 Abbreviations   *p. 68*

A. Each message below contains initials or an abbreviation written incorrectly. Write each message. Make the abbreviation or initials correct.

1. The students in mrs Gelardi's class have a bulletin board.
2. They collect their messages at 9 am every day.
3. Oliver Mayo, jr, sent Akiko a note.
4. Meet me at the Garden st door after school.
5. One message says, ''Hear dr Giddings speak today.''
6. Public debate will start at 4 pm in the auditorium.
7. Writer m a cruz will speak to the science fiction book club.
8. Winter vacation begins on dec 21.
9. We have invited ms Ling's class to our play.
10. They will take a field trip on apr 3.

B. Each sentence or message below contains a word that can be abbreviated. Write the sentence or message using the correct abbreviation.

11. The following messages have been left for Doctor Romero.
12. Martha Potts cannot be here Monday night.
13. She would like an appointment for January 11 instead.
14. The patient at 15 Valley Road called.
15. Please telephone Mister Chang immediately.
16. George Young, Senior, called yesterday.
17. The hospital on Central Boulevard has room for him.
18. You have a conference this Saturday at the medical school.
19. You can get there quickly on Route 3.
20. Please fill out this form before February 1.

C. Explain the initials and abbreviations in the messages below.

21. Meet T. J. at 126 Brewer St.
22. Club meeting Fri., 3 P.M.
23. R. L. to dentist Thurs.
24. Nov. 19: Adam's birthday
25. Call Mr. Warshawsky
26. B. K.'s home: 11 Elm Dr.

6 Possessive Nouns

p. 70

A. Write the sentences. Draw one line under each possessive noun that is singular. Draw two lines under each possessive noun that is plural.

1. Martina's grandmother came to visit.
2. Her stories always kept the children's interest.
3. The stories' last words were always proverbs.
4. The fox's tail will show no matter how hard he tries to hide it.
5. Fools' names, like their faces, are often seen in public places.
6. You cannot hold two cows' tails at once.
7. The chicken hawk's prayer does not catch the chicken.
8. People's purses will never be bare
If they know when to buy, to spend, and to spare.
9. Beware of a wolf in sheep's clothing.
10. A friend's frown is better than a fool's smile.
11. Poor folks' wisdom goes for little.
12. In a fiddler's house all are dancers.
13. Merchants' goods are bought and sold.

B. Write the possessive form of each noun given.

14. flower
15. officers
16. tribe
17. men
18. hotel
19. neighbors
20. niece
21. coaches
22. chimpanzee
23. actors
24. leader
25. navy
26. carpenters
27. canary
28. wife
29. nephew
30. man
31. worker
32. lions
33. mouse
34. child
35. puppy

UNIT THREE

USING LANGUAGE TO
IMAGINE

=== PART ONE ===

Unit Theme *Tall Tales*

Language Awareness Verbs

=== PART TWO ===

Literature "Sky-Bright Axe" by Adrien Stoutenburg

A Reason for Writing Imagining

Writing
IN YOUR JOURNAL

WRITER'S WARM-UP ✦ What do you know about the world of American tall tales? Perhaps you have heard or read stories about some tall-tale characters, such as Paul Bunyan or Pecos Bill. Some of the wild and woolly characters of America's past have even starred in cartoons or films you may have seen. Why do people find tall tales funny? What parts of tall tales may be based on facts? Write in your journal. Tell what you already know about tall tales.

1 Writing with Action Verbs

You have learned that you need both a subject and a predicate to form a complete sentence. You have also learned to identify the simple predicate—the main word or words in the predicate. The simple predicate is often an action verb. An action verb tells what the subject of the sentence does.

Read the sentences below. The underlined word in each sentence is an action verb.

Pecos Bill <u>rides</u> the wild stallion.
The stallion <u>snorts</u>.
It <u>rears</u> and <u>bucks</u>.
The horse <u>flies</u> like the wind.

The verb *rides* tells what Pecos Bill does. The verbs *snorts*, *rears*, *bucks*, and *flies* tell what the wild stallion does. Here are some more verbs that can be used to tell about a horse's actions.

■ twist   leap   whinny   gallop   halt

What action verbs can you add to this list?

> **Summary** ♦ An **action verb** shows action. When you write, use vivid action verbs that make the action clear.

Guided Practice

Name the action verb in each sentence.

1. People read tall tales.
2. Tall tales spark readers' imaginations.
3. Sometimes readers laugh at these adventures.
4. Many tales told of Pecos Bill, the world's greatest cowboy.
5. Pecos Bill romped throughout the West.

Practice

A. The sentences below tell about Pecos Bill. Write the action verb you find in each sentence.

  6. Today people tell tales about Pecos Bill.
  7. One day he fell from his family's covered wagon.
  8. A coyote found him.
  9. For years, Bill lived among the coyotes.
 10. He learned the coyote's ways.
 11. He howled like a coyote.
 12. As an adult, he started the biggest ranch in the West.
 13. During a drought he dug the Rio Grande for water.
 14. He named his horse Widow Maker.

B. Write the sentences. Use an action verb to complete each sentence.

EXAMPLE: Pecos Bill _____ the ranchers how to tame horses.

 ANSWER: Pecos Bill teaches the ranchers how to tame horses.

 15. The rancher _____ her dark brown horse.
 16. She _____ a rope on the fence post.
 17. The cattle _____ across the pasture.
 18. The ranchers _____ in the scorching heat.
 19. They _____ for hours without a drink of water.
 20. The ranchers _____ lunch at twelve noon.
 21. Dark billowy clouds _____ in the distance.
 22. All of the ranchers _____ for rain.
 23. Everyone _____ a low rumble of thunder.
 24. A horse _____ its tail.
 25. Some giant raindrops _____ on the ground.
 26. Lightning _____ brilliantly.
 27. A blast of thunder _____ loudly.

Apply ♦ Think and Write

From Your Writing ♦ Read what you wrote for the Writer's Warm-up. List the action verbs you used. If some of the verbs were not exact, replace them with more exact verbs.

✎ **Remember**
to use lively verbs that appeal to a reader's imagination.

GETTING STARTED

Tell something you do. Tell why you are able to do it.

EXAMPLE: *I play basketball.*

I am in good physical condition.

2 Linking Verbs

A verb can show action by telling what the subject does.

■ **Slue Foot Sue rides a huge catfish.**

A verb can also show being, as in the sentences below.

1. She is a brave woman.
2. This catfish was the biggest in the West.

In sentence **1** the verb *is* links, or connects, the subject *she* with the word *woman*. In sentence **2** the verb *was* connects the subject *catfish* with the word *biggest*. Both *is* and *was* are forms of *be*, the most common linking verb.

Using the Forms of *Be*		
Use *am/was*	with *I*	I am/I was
Use *is/was*	with *she*, *he*, *it*, and singular nouns	She is Slue Foot Sue was
Use *are/were*	with *we*, *you*, *they*, and plural nouns	They are The ranchers were

Other linking verbs are *seem, feel, taste, smell,* and *look*.

Summary ◆ A **linking verb** shows being. A linking verb connects the subject with a word or words in the predicate.

Guided Practice

Name the linking verb in each sentence. Name the words in the subject and the predicate that the linking verb connects.

1. My favorite dish is catfish.

2. You seem surprised by that.

3. Catfish taste delicious.

4. It was a fine meal.

Practice

A. Write each sentence. Underline the linking verb. Use an arrow to connect the words that the linking verb links.

EXAMPLE: Slue Foot Sue was a special friend of Pecos Bill.

ANSWER: Slue Foot Sue <u>was</u> a special friend of Pecos Bill.

5. Sue seemed afraid of nothing.
6. Sue was ready for anything.
7. "Sue is a good match for me," said Pecos Bill.
8. The catfish were her servants.
9. She looked extremely graceful.
10. "You are light on your feet," said Bill.
11. Sue felt embarrassed by that remark.
12. "I am sorry," Bill apologized.
13. Her smile felt warm like the sun.
14. They were friends forever.

B. Write the sentences. Choose the correct form of *be* to complete each sentence.

15. Tena ____ a reader of tall tales. (is, are)
16. Tales about heroes ____ her favorites. (is, are)
17. Tena ____ a rancher's daughter. (is, are)
18. Horses ____ her childhood friends. (was, were)
19. I ____ an eager listener when she tells stories. (am, are)

C. 20–24. Write five sentences with linking verbs. Use forms of *be* and other linking verbs. Use these models.

She <u>is</u> the best roper on this ranch.
The freshly mown hay <u>smells</u> sweet.

Apply ♦ Think and Write

Dictionary of Knowledge ♦ Slue Foot Sue and Pecos Bill were not real people. Read about Daniel Boone, a real-life hero, in the Dictionary of Knowledge. Using a variety of linking verbs, write a paragraph about this frontiersman.

> ✎ **Remember**
> that linking verbs relate the subject to an idea in the predicate.

3 Main Verbs and Helping Verbs

In each of the following sentences, the simple predicate is more than one word.

> Sophia is writing a report on Slue Foot Sue.
> She has read several books about Sue and Pecos Bill.
> We will hear her report tomorrow.

In these sentences, *is*, *has*, and *will* are **helping verbs**. They work with the main verbs *writing*, *read*, and *hear*. The **main verb** is the most important verb in the predicate. The chart shows you how to use helping verbs with main verbs.

Using Helping Verbs	
When you use the helping verb *am, is, are, was,* or *were*, the main verb often ends in *-ing*.	I am reading. You are reading. They were reading.
When you use the helping verb *has, have,* or *had*, the main verb often ends in *-ed*.	He has finished. We have finished. They had finished.
When you use the helping verb *will*, the main verb is unchanged.	She will present a report. You will present a report. I will present a report.

Summary ◆ A helping verb works with the main verb.

Guided Practice

Tell whether the underlined word in each sentence is a main verb or a helping verb.

1. The wedding day was approaching fast.
2. Slue Foot Sue had wanted to ride Bill's horse, Widow Maker.
3. The guests will see Sue ride Widow Maker on that day.

Practice

A. Write each sentence. Draw one line under the main verb. Draw two lines under the helping verb.

   4. Sophia will tell us about Slue Foot Sue's wedding day.
   5. Pecos Bill had courted Sue for many months.
   6. On their wedding day she was staring at Widow Maker with great curiosity.
   7. Widow Maker had pranced up and down the corral.
   8. Sue was approaching the horse.
   9. The guests were watching Sue closely.
   10. Sue has mounted Widow Maker.
   11. Will Slue Foot Sue ride Widow Maker?
   12. The horse is bucking fiercely.
   13. Sue is bouncing up and down on Widow Maker.
   14. Widow Maker has thrown her.
   15. Sue has bounced all the way to the moon!
   16. Will Pecos Bill save Slue Foot Sue?

B. Write the sentences. Use the helping verbs *am, are, has, have,* and *will* to complete the sentences.

   17. Pecos Bill ____ rescued Sue with his lasso.
   18. The cowhands ____ cheering wildly.
   19. Bill and Sue ____ found true love.
   20. They ____ live happily ever after.
   21. I ____ enjoying the tales about Slue Foot Sue.

C. 22–26. Write five sentences using these helping verbs with the correct forms of these main verbs.

   Helping verbs: are, was, has, had, will
   Main verbs: ride, rope, bounce, buck, study
   EXAMPLE: Slue Foot Sue <u>will</u> <u>ride</u> tomorrow.

Apply ◆ Think and Write

Personal Tall Tales ◆ Write some "whoppers," or tall tales, about yourself. Use main verbs and helping verbs in your sentences. For example: *Someday I <u>will</u> <u>jump</u> to the moon.*

> ✎ **Remember**
> to choose helping verbs carefully to express action clearly.

A glort is a creature with special powers. Tell what it does to several different things. For example: *A glort moves skyscrapers.*

4 Verbs with Direct Objects

Like a verb, a direct object is part of the complete predicate. A direct object comes after an action verb and is often a noun. It answers the question *whom* or *what*.

In the sentences below, the underlined nouns are direct objects.

Railroad workers tell tales about John Henry.   (tell what?)

They sing songs about the steel-driving man.   (sing what?)

The railroad workers cheered John Henry.   (cheered whom?)

If you want to find the direct object in a sentence, ask "whom?" or "what?" after the verb.

In the sentences below, the underlined nouns are direct objects. They receive the action of the verbs *hammered* and *remembered*. What question does each direct object below answer?

John Henry hammered huge spikes.

People remembered the steel-driving man.

> **Summary** ◆ The **direct object** receives the action of the verb. Direct objects answer the questions *whom* or *what*.

Guided Practice

Read these sentences about John Henry. Name the action verb and the direct object in each sentence.

1. John Henry dug a tunnel through a mountain.
2. He used a twelve-pound hammer.
3. He drove steel for many hours without a break.
4. The other railroad workers admired John.
5. People still praise his work in song and story.

Practice

A. Write each sentence. Draw one line under the action verb. Draw two lines under the direct object.

6. A black cloud covered the moon.
7. Thunder pounded the earth like a hammer.
8. The thunder announced the birth of a great hero.
9. As a baby, John Henry ate food in huge quantities.
10. His parents put his meals on seven tables.
11. As a child, he picked cotton.
12. When grown up, he married Polly Ann.
13. She helped her husband with his railroad work.
14. His hammer drove spikes deep into the rock.
15. Later he used two hammers at the same time.

B. Write the direct object of each sentence. Then write *what* or *whom* to show what question the direct object answers.

16. One day a man brought a special drill to the boss.
17. Steam powered the new machine.
18. The machine did not scare John Henry.
19. He did more work than the steam drill.
20. The race with the drill killed this amazing worker.

C. Choose for each sentence a direct object from the following list of nouns. Write each sentence.

work   death   sound   **John Henry**

21. John Henry did the ____ of ten men.
22. The railroad tunnel workers mourned his ____ .
23. No one forgot ____ .
24. Railroad workers still hear the ____ of his pounding hammer.

Apply ◆ Think and Write

Objects in Action ◆ Write a verb riddle about an object. Tell what the object does. Use a direct object in your riddle. Then ask a classmate to read and solve your riddle. For example: *It hides the sun. It brings the rain. What is it?* (a cloud)

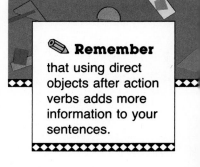

✎ **Remember**
that using direct objects after action verbs adds more information to your sentences.

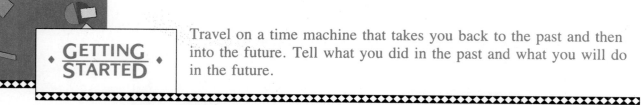

♦ GETTING
STARTED ♦

Travel on a time machine that takes you back to the past and then into the future. Tell what you did in the past and what you will do in the future.

5 Tenses of Verbs

The form of a verb shows when the action takes place.

> **1.** Mr. Scott <u>directs</u> the play.
> **2.** The class <u>learned</u> the script.
> **3.** Lois Chu <u>will perform</u> the role of Molly Pitcher.

In sentence **1** the verb is in the present tense: *directs*. In sentence **2** the verb is in the past tense: *learned*. In sentence **3** the verb is in the future tense: *will perform*.

A verb in the **present tense** shows action that happens now.

■ They <u>work</u>.   She <u>studies</u>.   We <u>stop</u>.

A verb in the **past tense** shows action that already happened.

■ They <u>worked</u>.   She <u>studied</u>.   We <u>stopped</u>.

A verb in the **future tense** shows action that will happen. The future tense is usually formed with the helping verb *will* or *shall*.

■ They <u>will work</u>.   She <u>will study</u>.   We <u>will stop</u>.

Sometimes the spelling of a verb changes when you write its form in the present or past tense. Notice how *study* changes to *studies* and *studied*. The verb *stop* changes to *stopped*.

> **Summary** ♦ The tense of a verb shows the time of the action.

Guided Practice

The verbs in the sentences are underlined. Tell whether each verb is in the present, past, or future tense.

1. The stage crew <u>carried</u> the props to the stage.
2. Rosa and Carl <u>paint</u> a cardboard cannon.
3. The actors <u>will perform</u> the play tonight.

Practice

A. Write the verb in each sentence. Then write *present*, *past*, or *future* to show what tense it is.

4. In her costume, Lois Chu resembles Molly Pitcher.
5. Lois will make a fine heroine.
6. Songs and stories about Molly created an American legend.
7. Molly Pitcher worked as a servant in Carlisle, Pennsylvania.
8. She married John Casper Hays, a barber.
9. Just before the Revolutionary War, he joined the army.
10. Molly traveled with her husband to the battlefields.
11. Our play about the battle of Monmouth will thrill you.
12. The soldiers fight bravely.
13. Molly helps them during the battle.

B. Each underlined verb below is in the present tense. Write each sentence. Change the verb to the tense shown in parentheses ( ).

EXAMPLE: Molly Pitcher <u>earns</u> her nickname in a battle. (past)
ANSWER: Molly Pitcher earned her nickname in a battle.

14. Molly <u>carries</u> pitchers of water to the soldiers in battle. (past)
15. She <u>pours</u> the water quickly. (past)
16. The water <u>relieves</u> the soldiers' thirst. (past)
17. Molly's husband <u>drops</u> to the ground from heatstroke. (past)
18. Molly <u>fills</u> his place during the battle. (past)
19. The legend of Molly Pitcher <u>lives</u> forever. (future)
20. Americans <u>remember</u> her always. (future)

C. 21–23. Write three sentences, one for each of the following verbs: *perform*, *act*, *rehearse*. Write one sentence in the past tense, one in the present tense, and one in the future tense.

Apply ◆ Think and Write

Imagining Fame ◆ Write sentences telling how you might become an American legend. Tell what you have done, what you are doing, and what you will do to make yourself famous.

> ✎ **Remember**
> to use appropriate verb tenses to tell when the action takes place.

GETTING
STARTED

Picture yourself in Colonial days, during the time of the Revolutionary War. Take turns telling what one child does. Then take turns telling what ten children do.

6 Using the Present Tense

When you studied linking verbs, you learned that certain forms of *be* are used with certain subjects.

I **am** an admirer of Tempe Wick.
Historians **are** unsure of the facts about her and her horse.

A subject and verb are said to agree when the correct form of the verb is used. For example, *am* agrees with the subject *I*. *Are* agrees with the subject *historians*.

Action verbs must also agree with their subjects. This means you have to know when to use *-s* or *-es* in the present tense.

Using the Present Tense

With a singular noun, use *-s* or *-es*.
  Carl listens to the Tempe Wick story. Carl studies it.
With a plural noun, do not use *-s* or *-es*.
  People listen to the Tempe Wick story. People study it.
With *she*, *he*, or *it*, use *-s* or *-es*.
  She admires Tempe Wick. She teaches the legend.
With *I*, *you*, *we*, or *they*, do not use *-s* or *-es*.
  We admire Tempe Wick. We teach the legend.

Summary ◆ A verb in the present tense needs to agree with the subject of the sentence. When you are proofreading, check for agreement between each subject and its verb.

Guided Practice

Name the form of the verb in parentheses ( ) that correctly completes each sentence.

1. We (know, knows) Tempe Wick was a real person.
2. Her house still (stand, stands).
3. Tourists (visit, visits) Tempe Wick's house.

Practice

A. Write each sentence. Use the correct form of the verb in parentheses ( ).

4. People (remember, remembers) Tempe Wick for her courage.
5. Her story (take, takes) place during the Revolutionary War.
6. The Wick house (stand, stands) near Morristown, New Jersey.
7. Historians (tell, tells) about soldiers rebelling against George Washington.
8. Carl (know, knows) that the soldiers got little food.
9. When Tempe Wick heard a cannon shot, she thought, ''I (sense, senses) trouble.''
10. Her horse, Bonny, (play, plays) an important part in the legend.
11. People (believe, believes) the soldiers wanted the horse.
12. We (think, thinks) Tempe Wick resisted them.
13. The legend (teach, teaches) the meaning of courage.

B. Write each sentence. Use the correct present-tense form of the verb in parentheses ( ).

14. The story of Betsy Ross _____ as another American legend. (survive)
15. The story _____ she sewed the first American flag. (say)
16. According to legend, George Washington _____ her. (visit)
17. He _____ her to make a flag with a certain design. (ask)
18. She _____ the flag with stars and stripes. (sew)
19. Historians _____ the story may not be true. (think)
20. Still, people _____ about her because of this legend. (write)

C. 21–23. Write three sentences in the present tense. At least one of your subjects should be singular, and at least one should be plural.

Apply ♦ Think and Write

A Present-Day Legend ♦ Write at least five sentences about a real person who you think could become a legend. Use present-tense verbs.

✎ **Remember**
that subjects and verbs need to agree.

7 Using Irregular Verbs

You have learned that the past tense of most verbs is formed by adding *-ed*. Verbs that do not follow this rule are called **irregular verbs.**

The forms of some common irregular verbs appear below. The **past participle** is the form used with the helping verb *has*, *have*, or *had*.

Present	Past	Past Participle
come	came	(has, have, had) come
do	did	(has, have, had) done
eat	ate	(has, have, had) eaten
fall	fell	(has, have, had) fallen
fly	flew	(has, have, had) flown
give	gave	(has, have, had) given
go	went	(has, have, had) gone
grow	grew	(has, have, had) grown
ride	rode	(has, have, had) ridden
run	ran	(has, have, had) run
see	saw	(has, have, had) seen
take	took	(has, have, had) taken
wear	wore	(has, have, had) worn
write	wrote	(has, have, had) written

Summary ◆ Irregular verbs do not form the past and past participle by adding *-ed*. When you write, use forms of irregular verbs carefully.

Guided Practice

Name the past and past participle of each verb. Use the helping verb *has* with each past participle.

1. give   **2.** run   **3.** come   **4.** do   **5.** see

Practice

A. Write each sentence. Use the past tense of the verb in parentheses ( ).

6. Authors (write) tall tales about animals as well as people.
7. Some legendary animals (eat) enormous amounts of food.
8. Others (do) amazing stunts.
9. Some (ride) with the speed of the wind.
10. Other imaginary animals (grow) to an enormous size.
11. Writers told about horses that (fly).
12. I never (see) a flying horse myself.
13. Pecos Bill (give) his horse the name Widow Maker.
14. This horse (run) like streaked lightning.
15. Still, Widow Maker (come) when Bill called to him.

B. Write each sentence. Use the past participle of the verb in parentheses ( ).

16. I have (ride) horses for a long time.
17. I have (fall) off a few horses before.
18. Widow Maker had (take) food from Bill's hand.
19. Widow Maker had (do) anything that Bill asked.
20. This horse had never (wear) a saddle until Bill tamed him.
21. I have (go) to many rodeos.
22. I have (see) many fine horses.
23. No horse like Widow Maker has ever (run) in them.

C. 24–33. Write two sentences for each verb below. In the first sentence for each verb, use the past form. In the second sentence, use the past participle.

fly   see   fall   ride   write

Apply ◆ Think and Write

An Imaginary Meeting ◆ Imagine that you are an animal—perhaps one with special powers. You, the animal, are seeing you, the person, for the first time. Write five sentences about this meeting. Use some of the irregular verbs listed on page 128.

> ✎ **Remember**
> to check the
> past forms of
> any irregular verbs
> you use.

8 Using Irregular Verbs

Some irregular verbs follow a pattern in forming the past and past participle. Three common patterns are shown below.

Some verbs have the same past and past participle.

Present	Past	Past Participle
bring	brought	(has, have, had) brought
catch	caught	(has, have, had) caught
find	found	(has, have, had) found
say	said	(has, have, had) said
think	thought	(has, have, had) thought

Some form the past participle by adding -n to the past.

Present	Past	Past Participle
break	broke	(has, have, had) broken
choose	chose	(has, have, had) chosen
freeze	froze	(has, have, had) frozen
speak	spoke	(has, have, had) spoken

Some change one vowel in the past and in the past participle.

Present	Past	Past Participle
drink	drank	(has, have, had) drunk
ring	rang	(has, have, had) rung
sing	sang	(has, have, had) sung
swim	swam	(has, have, had) swum

Summary ◆ Some irregular verbs follow a pattern in the way they are formed. When you write, use forms of irregular verbs carefully.

Guided Practice

Name the past and the past participle of each verb.

1. sing   **2.** choose   **3.** break   **4.** say   **5.** swim

Practice

A. Write each sentence. Use the past or the past participle of the verb in parentheses ( ).

6. People everywhere have (find) tall tales enjoyable.
7. Some people say it got so cold in Michigan that the flames in lanterns (freeze).
8. Folks just (break) off the lantern flames to put them out.
9. People who have (choose) to live in cold places enjoy such tales.
10. In some places, tales tell about people who have (catch) gigantic fish.
11. Anglers (bring) in fish that amazed everyone.
12. Some people (think) these ''fish stories'' were true.
13. Even so, such fish have (swim) only in imaginary rivers.
14. On Cape Cod they (sing) songs about the ''hoss-mackerel.''
15. Bowleg Bill had almost (break) this huge fish by riding it like a wild horse.
16. I (choose) to believe this story.
17. In North Dakota the dinner bell once (ring) for Paul Bunyan's loggers.
18. The men (drink) a whole lake filled with pea soup.
19. People in Colorado (speak) of the slide-rock bolter.
20. They have (say) this animal zoomed around scooping up tourists.
21. In Oklahoma, storytellers have (speak) of giant grasshoppers eating cows.
22. I had (think) such insects existed only in books.

B. How many past-tense forms of verbs from this lesson could you use to complete the sentence below? Write as many sentences as you can.

I _____ some fish this week.

Apply ◆ Think and Write

Active Animals ◆ Write a verb riddle about an animal. Use verbs from this lesson to tell what it did. Exchange riddles with a classmate. Try to guess each other's riddles.

✎ **Remember**
to check the
past forms of
any irregular verbs
you use.

Make up questions that begin with *Mother, may I*. Make up statements that begin with *Father, I can*.

9 Using Troublesome Verb Pairs

Some pairs of verbs are often confused. You can avoid mistakes if you know the meanings of these verbs.

People often confuse the verbs *can* and *may*.

Can you tell me about Paul Bunyan?
May I borrow your collection of Paul Bunyan tales?

Use *can* when you mean "to be able." Use *may* when you ask or give permission.

People also confuse the verbs *sit* and *set*.

Sit beside me and tell me about Davy Crockett.
Set the book about Davy Crockett on the table.

Use *sit* when you mean "to rest." Use *set* when you mean "to put or place something."

> **Summary** ◆ Use the verb *can* when you mean "to be able to do something." Use the verb *may* when you ask or give permission. Use the verb *sit* when you mean "to rest." Use the verb *set* when you mean "to put or place something."

Guided Practice

Name the verb in parentheses ( ) that correctly completes each sentence.

1. I could (sit, set) for hours sharing tall tales.
2. (Can, May) I tell you about Annie Christmas now?
3. (Can, May) you describe her to me?
4. Did you (sit, set) the statue on Ms. Van's desk?
5. (Can, May) we read stories aloud now?

Practice

A. Write each sentence. Use the correct verb in parentheses ( ).

6. (Can, May) we talk about the folk hero named Tomacito?
7. The hunters tell tiny Tomacito, ''You (can, may) not go buffalo hunting with us.''
8. Tomacito does not want to (sit, set) at home.
9. He thinks, ''I (can, may) hunt buffalo as well as anyone.''
10. When does Tomacito (sit, set) a plan in place to join the hunters?
11. Pat (can, may) tell how the buffalo swallows Tomacito.
12. Does Tomacito (sit, set) in the belly of the buffalo?
13. (Can, May) I tell how he escapes and returns to his village?
14. The other hunters cheer and (sit, set) Tomacito on their shoulders.
15. Afterwards, he is content to (sit, set) in his mother's kitchen.

B. Write the sentences. Use *can*, *may*, *sit*, or *set* to complete each sentence.

16. _____ the class have a tall-tale party?
17. We _____ dress up as our favorite characters.
18. We will _____ in a circle and talk about heroines and heroes.
19. _____ Kristen come as Pocahontas, the Indian princess?
20. _____ with us, Kristen, and tell us about her.
21. I will _____ this book about Pocahontas on the desk.
22. I _____ say that Pocahontas was a real person.
23. _____ I tell you how Pocahontas saved Captain John Smith?
24. No historian _____ be certain that the story is true.
25. _____ the painting of Pocahontas by the door.

Apply ◆ Think and Write

Posing Questions ◆ Write four questions, using the verbs *can*, *may*, *sit*, and *set*. Trade papers and then write sentences that answer your classmate's questions.

> ✎ **Remember**
> to use the verbs *can*, *may*, *sit*, and *set* correctly, according to their meanings.

Contrary people say the opposite of what they mean. If they mean *happy*, they say *unhappy*. Make these words contrary: *equal*, *obey*, *honest*, *lock*, *behave*.

VOCABULARY ♦
Prefixes

Many words have two parts—a base word and a prefix. A **base word** is the simplest form of a word. It has no letters added to its beginning or end. In the word *unwrap*, *wrap* is the base word.

The letters *un* in *unwrap* are a prefix. A **prefix** is a word part added to the beginning of a word. The prefix changes the meaning of the word.

Here are some examples of prefixes and their meanings.

Prefix	Meaning	Example
dis-	opposite of	disagree
mis-	wrong, wrongly	misjudge
pre-	before	prejudge
re-	again, back	rebuild
un-	not, opposite of	uncover

Building Your Vocabulary

In each sentence, find the word that starts with a prefix. Name the prefix.

1. Many tall tales were retold over the years.
2. Few people dislike these amusing, exaggerated stories.
3. Paul Bunyan is a fictional character who grew to an unbelievable size.
4. Paul was a misfit, but everyone liked him.
5. Paul had a blue ox named Babe, who was the size of a prehistoric dinosaur.

Practice

A. Add the prefix *dis-*, *mis-*, *pre-*, *re-*, or *un-* to the underlined base word in each sentence below. Notice how the meaning of the sentence changes when you add the prefix.

1. Denise and Dorothy <u>agreed</u> about which movie to see.
2. Miguel <u>understood</u> the teacher's instructions.
3. Follow the recipe instructions and <u>heat</u> the oven.
4. The hummingbird <u>appeared</u> each afternoon at three o'clock.
5. Ernie was <u>able</u> to cut the wood with the dull saw.
6. Dinosaurs lived in <u>historic</u> times.
7. Mary <u>read</u> the directions and turned left instead of right.
8. Roger was told never to <u>use</u> his father's computer.

B. Write a word for each definition. Use the prefixes and base words below to form the words.

PREFIXES: dis- mis- pre- un- re-
BASE WORDS: trust pay behave cover place think

9. to give money before
10. to act badly
11. to lose
12. to give money back
13. to take the top off something
14. to put back in place
15. to lack confidence in
16. to go over again in one's mind

C. Write the meaning of the underlined word in each sentence.

17. If *consider* means "to think about," <u>reconsider</u> means ____ .
18. If *guide* means "to steer," <u>misguide</u> means ____ .
19. If *allow* means "to permit," <u>disallow</u> means ____ .
20. If *pleasant* means "enjoyable," <u>unpleasant</u> means ____ .
21. If *arrange* means "to make plans," <u>prearrange</u> means ____ .

LANGUAGE CORNER ◆ Word History

Did you know that *an apron* was once *a napron*? Can you figure out what caused the change? Here are two clues: *an umpire* was once *a numpire* and *an adder* (a kind of snake) was once *a nadder*.

GRAMMAR
◆CONNECTION◆
WRITING

How to Revise Sentences with Verbs

You know about verbs and how they work in sentences. Your choice of verbs can make a difference in your writing. A carefully chosen verb will make a sentence clear and interesting. Read the sentences below. What differences do you find?

1. The Blue Ox ate the trees off the mountainside.
2. The Blue Ox devoured the trees off the mountainside.
3. The Blue Ox nibbled the trees off the mountainside.

The only difference among these sentences is the verb. Sentence **1** is a perfectly fine sentence. The choice of verbs in the other sentences, however, enlivens them and paints different pictures. The verb in sentence **2** probably makes you picture a very hungry ox, and sentence **3** tells about an ox just having a snack.

How does changing the verb in these sentences change the picture?

4. Alice knocked on the door of the creature's house.
5. Alice tapped on the door of the creature's house.
6. Alice pounded on the door of the creature's house.

The Grammar Game ◆ Check your verb power! Write exact verbs for each word below. Give yourself one point for each exact verb. Add a bonus point for every word with three or more exact verbs.

talk	throw	break	laugh	ask
cut	like	put	drink	

Working Together

See how you can enliven your writing by using exact verbs. Work with your group on activities **A** and **B**.

In Your Group

♦ Contribute your ideas.

♦ Remind each other to listen carefully.

♦ Record the group's ideas.

♦ Show appreciation for people's ideas.

A. Take turns writing these sentences about imaginary creatures. Replace each underlined verb with a more exact verb.

1. The gowrow <u>called</u> from its dark cave.
2. The hoopajuba <u>ate</u> a mudworm and <u>drank</u> leaf juice.
3. The unhappy squonk <u>cries</u> all the time.
4. Milamo birds <u>jump</u> into giant worm holes to <u>get</u> food.

B. Complete these newspaper headlines with exact verbs of the group's choice. Then, using different verbs, rewrite the headlines to change their meanings.

5. CITY COUNCIL ____
6. PRESIDENT ____ TO TEXAS
7. FIREFIGHTERS ____ BLAZE
8. APRIL FOOL'S TRICK ____
9. TIGERS ____ BIG GAME
10. TEACHER ____ MILLIONS
11. HOSPITAL WORKERS ____
12. FLOOD ____ TOWN
13. GIRAFFE ____
14. BANK TELLER ____ BOSS

WRITERS' CORNER ♦ Exact Meaning

Think about what you want to say when you choose your verbs. A little difference in the meaning of words can make a big difference in your writing.

VAGUE: **Marty ran to the finish line and broke the school record. While going to the locker room, however, he hurt his ankle.**

EXACT: **Marty sprinted to the finish line and smashed the school record. While skipping to the locker room, however, he twisted his ankle.**

Read what you wrote for the Writer's Warm-up. Could you improve your writing by choosing more exact verbs?

HIS HAMMER IN HIS HAND
painting by Palmer C. Hayden From the collection of the Museum of African American Art, Palmer C. Hayden Collection,
Gift of Miriam A. Hayden.

USING LANGUAGE
TO
IMAGINE

=== **PART TWO** ===

Literature   "Sky-Bright Axe" by Adrien Stoutenburg
A Reason for Writing Imagining

CREATIVE
Writing

FINE ARTS ♦ John Henry is an American folk hero. He used just his hammer and his muscles to race a steam-driven hammer. John Henry became a hero because he was very strong and he worked hard. Imagine that you will become famous someday. What will make you famous? Write a speech accepting an award. Tell what award you have won and what you did to deserve it.

CREATIVE THINKING ◆
A Strategy for Imagining

ANSWERING "WHAT IF?"

Imagining can be a way of pretending or making believe. One kind of imaginary tale is a tall tale. A tall tale is a story that stretches the truth. It sounds like a true story. Yet everything in it is bigger, or better, or just plain sillier than in real life. After this lesson, you will read the tall tale "Sky-Bright Axe." Later you will write your own tall tale.

The hero of "Sky-Bright Axe" is Paul Bunyan, a giant lumberjack. Now, what if Paul wanted pancakes for breakfast? How big would the pancake griddle have to be?

Paul . . . decided that he had to do something about making a big enough griddle. He went down to the plow works . . . and said, "I want you fellows here to make me a griddle so big I won't be able to see across it on a foggy day."

Authors of tall tales often answer "what if" questions. The passage above is one of many possible answers to the question "What if Paul Bunyan wanted pancakes for breakfast?" Can you think of other answers?

◆ Learning the Strategy

Asking "what if" is a way of supposing or imagining a situation. When you answer a "what if" question, you imagine possible results. For example, what if you left your homework at home? What might be the consequences? What if you woke up and found that you were twenty feet tall? How would your life change? What if humans don't find a way to stop pollution? What might the earth's future be like? "What if" questions come up all the time. How can you think through possible answers?

Sometimes a series of follow-up questions can help. For example, what if you left your homework at home? One follow-up question might be "What would I tell the teacher?" Another might be "What would the teacher do?" Can you think of others? The chart below shows some follow-up questions and answers to the question "What if I woke up and found that I was twenty feet tall?" What other follow-up questions and answers could there be?

What if I woke up and found that I was twenty feet tall?	
How would I feel?	surprised, confused
What would I do?	try to find out why I grew wonder if I was dreaming
What problems would I have?	clothes wouldn't fit furniture too small people would be afraid of me

Using the Strategy

A. Write "What if I traded places with my teacher?" Consider the "what if" question. Then write two or three good follow-up questions and answer them. You might like to ask your teacher what he or she thinks would happen!

B. What about that enormous pancake griddle Paul Bunyan orders? After it is made, can it be moved? Write "What if Paul Bunyan tries to move the giant pancake griddle?" Write some good follow-up questions and answer them. Then read "Sky-Bright Axe" to see if the author used any of your ideas.

Applying the Strategy

- How did you decide on follow-up questions for **A** or **B** above?
- When might you ask and answer "what if" questions in your daily life?

LITERATURE

from

Sky-Bright Axe

by Adrien Stoutenburg

Some people say that Paul Bunyan, who was over fifty feet tall, could chop down a hundred trees just by swinging his sky-bright axe in a wide circle. In those days, a lot of trees had to be cut down and turned into lumber for building houses and ships. The work was called logging, and people say that Paul Bunyan was the best logger who ever lived.

Logging was lonely work for Paul, though, until he found Babe the Blue Ox. Babe was as long as Paul was tall. Together, they made a mighty logging team.

Paul and the Blue Ox logged all over the northern timber country, from Maine to Michigan, Wisconsin, and Minnesota. Paul hired many men to help him. These lumberjacks liked working for Paul Bunyan, because he was always good to them and made sure that they had plenty of food.

The lumber crews liked pancakes best, but they would gobble up and slurp down the pancakes so fast that the camp cooks couldn't keep up with them, even when the cooks got up twenty-six hours before daylight. The main problem was that the griddles the cooks used for frying the pancakes were too small.

The winter that Paul was logging on the Big Onion River in Michigan, he decided that he had to do something about making a big enough griddle. He went down to the plow works at Moline, Illinois, and said, "I want you fellows here to make me a griddle so big I won't be able to see across it on a foggy day."

The men set to work. When they were finished, they had

built a griddle so huge there was no train or wagon large enough to carry it.

"Let me think what to do," said Paul. "We'll have to turn the griddle up on end, like a silver dollar, and roll it up to Michigan." He hitched the Blue Ox to the upturned griddle, and away they went. It wasn't any job at all for Babe and Paul, though they had to hike a couple of hundred miles. A few miles from the Big Onion lumber camp, Paul unhitched Babe and let the griddle roll on by itself. When it stopped rolling, it started to spin as a penny does when it's ready to fall. It spun around and around and dug a deep hole in the ground before it flopped down like a cover over the hole.

The lumberjacks cheered and rushed off to haul a few acres of trees into the hole for a fire. The cook and a hundred and one helpers mixed tons of batter. When everything was ready, with the flames under the griddle blazing like a forest fire, Paul picked out a crew of men who could stand the heat better than others. He had them strap fat, juicy slabs of bacon on their feet.

"You men skate around on that griddle and that'll keep it well-greased," he told them.

The men skated until the griddle shone with bacon fat. White batter came pouring out onto the griddle and soon the smell of crisp, brown, steaming pancakes was drifting across the whole state. There were tons of pancakes—with plenty left over for Babe, who could eat a carload in one gulp.

There wasn't much Paul couldn't do, especially with Babe's help. But there was one job that seemed almost too hard even for him. That was in Wisconsin, on the St. Croix River. The logging road there was so crooked, it couldn't find its own way through the timber. It would start out in one direction, then turn around and go every which way until it grew so snarled up it didn't know its beginning from its end. The teamsters hauling logs over it would start home for camp and meet themselves coming back.

Maybe even Babe couldn't pull the kinks and curves out of a road as crooked as that one, Paul thought, but there was nothing to do but try.

He gave Babe several extra pats as he put the Blue Ox's pulling harness on. Then he hitched Babe to the end of the road and stood back.

Babe lowered his head and pushed his hoofs into the earth. His muscles stood out like rows of blue hills. He strained forward, pulling at the road. He stretched so hard that his hind legs spraddled out until his belly nearly scraped the ground. The road just lay there, stubborn as could be.

"You can do it, my big beautiful Babe!" Paul said.

Babe tried again. He strained so hard that his eyes nearly turned pink. He sweated so that water poured from the tips of his horns. He grunted and pulled, and his legs sank into the ground like mighty blue posts.

There was a snap, and then a loud C-R-A-C-K! Paul saw the first kink come out of the road, and he cheered. The road kept fighting back, flopping around and trying to hold on to its crooked twists and turns, but it was no match for Babe. At last, the road gave a kind of shiver and then lay still. Babe pulled it straighter than a railroad tie.

Paul Bunyan and Babe moved on to forests all across America. The pair eventually reached Alaska. People say that you can find them logging there still.

Library Link ♦ *If you would like to read more about tall-tale heroes, read* American Tall Tales *by Adrien Stoutenburg.*

◆ Reader's Response

After reading about Paul Bunyan, do you think you would like to read more tall tales? Explain why or why not.

Sky-Bright Axe

◆ Responding to Literature

1. Which part of the story made you smile the most? Why?

2. Spin a yarn. Tell a tale. Retell your favorite part of the story to a partner. Since it is now your tale, make it even more outlandish. Listen to your partner's tale. Try to outdo your partner. See who can spin the tallest tale. If you like, you may enlist others and act out your tale.

3. What are the characteristics of a tall tale? Write a definition with a partner. Then share your definition with another pair of partners. Work on your definition until all of you agree with what it says.

◆ Writing to Learn

Think and Suppose ◆ Write a "what if" story about Babe the Blue Ox or Paul. Start by writing three "what if" questions. Then choose one question to explore with follow-up questions.

What if Babe began to drink the Mississippi? What if a bee stung Babe? What if Paul rode a bicycle?	What if a bee stung Babe? How big would the bee be? — two feet long How high would Babe jump? — ten miles What would happen when he landed? — dig a giant hole

What-if Chart

Write ◆ Write answers to your follow-up questions. Then take notes on what your new story will be.

Describe Paul Bunyan's pancake griddle in your own words. Exaggerate! Make it even bigger than the griddle you read about in "Sky-Bright Axe."

SPEAKING and LISTENING ◆
Exaggeration

Tall tales are an American tradition. From frontier times on, Americans have had fun swapping stories to see who could tell the tallest tale, the biggest whopper.

Here is how you can swap stories. First tell your tale with a straight face, as if it were absolutely true. Then your listener can try to top your tall tale with a taller one—also told with a straight face, of course. Since a tall tale is told as if it were true, you need to be alert for exaggeration, or the stretching of the truth. You will need to listen very carefully. Otherwise, you might miss the humor and the fun.

Whenever you are telling tall tales or listening to them, use the following guidelines. The guidelines will help you use and listen for exaggeration.

Telling a Tall Tale	1. Tell a tall tale with a straight face. Resist the urge to laugh or grin as you tell it. 2. Show emotion, however, if the story calls for it. Use your voice, face, and body for drama. 3. Speak clearly and distinctly. Having to repeat part of your tale detracts from its humor.
Being an Active Listener	1. Be ready to listen. Pay close attention. 2. Listen for exaggeration. Ask yourself, "Could this really happen? Could this be true?" 3. To enjoy its humor, picture the exaggerated situation in your mind.

Summary ◆ When telling a tall tale, be sure to use exaggeration. When listening to one, try to picture mentally the exaggerated details.

Guided Practice

Tell what is exaggerated in this selection from the Paul Bunyan tale. Then practice reading it aloud with expression.

That same winter, men's words froze in front of their mouths and hung stiff in the air. Brimstone Bill, who was a great talker, was frozen in by a solid wall of words all turned to ice. Paul had to chip the ice from around Bill's shoulders, tie a rope to him, and have Babe pull him out.

Practice

A. With a partner, take turns reading these sentences aloud. Have your partner tell what the exaggeration is. Remember to read the sentences with feeling.

   1. "I want you fellows here to make me a griddle so big I won't be able to see across it on a foggy day."
   2. When they were finished, they had built a griddle so huge there was no train or wagon large enough to carry it.
   3. There were tons of pancakes—with plenty left over for Babe, who could eat a carload in one gulp.
   4. The logging road there was so crooked, it couldn't find its own way through the timber.
   5. The teamsters hauling logs over it would start home for camp and meet themselves coming back.

B. Have a tall-tale swapping contest. For each situation below, make up a tall tale by adding exaggeration. Then have a partner top your tale by adding more exaggeration.

   6. It is the seventh game of the World Series. The game is tied in the ninth inning. It is your turn at bat.
   7. Four mountain climbers are trapped in a snowstorm near the peak of Mount Everest. Only you can save them.

Apply ◆ Think and Write

Dictionary of Knowledge ◆ Davy Crockett was a real hero who is now a folk hero as well. Read about him. Then write a tall tale about him by exaggerating what you read.

✎ **Remember**
that exaggeration is what makes a tall tale humorous.

Here are two comparisons: *The old car moved like a snail. The ocean waves are hammers pounding the shore.* Create new comparisons that begin with *The old car* and *The ocean waves.*

WRITING ◆
Similes and Metaphors

To compare one thing to another, writers often use short comparisons called similes. A simile uses the word *like* or *as* to make a comparison. Here are two examples. In each one the road is compared to something else.

1. The crooked road twisted and turned <u>like</u> a pretzel.
2. Babe pulled it as straight <u>as</u> a railroad tie.

In sentence **1** the road is compared to a pretzel, and in **2** it is compared to a railroad tie. Notice how those comparisons help us picture what the writer wants us to ''see.''

Writers also use another kind of comparison, called a metaphor. A metaphor makes a comparison without using the word *like* or *as.* Instead a metaphor says that one thing <u>is</u> another.

1. The road <u>is</u> a pretzel, with its twists and turns.
2. Babe's legs <u>were</u> mighty blue posts.

Similes and metaphors can make your writing more vivid. The key is to be creative. Avoid old, worn-out comparisons, such as ''sweet as sugar.'' Instead, try for unusual comparisons. Create your own!

> **Summary** ◆ A **simile** uses the word *like* or *as* to compare two things. A **metaphor** compares two things by saying one thing *is* the other. Use similes and metaphors to make your writing vivid.

Guided Practice

Tell what is being compared in each sentence. Then tell whether the comparison is a simile or a metaphor.

1. Big trees fell like toothpicks when Paul Bunyan swung his axe.
2. Babe was a two-ton bundle of blue dynamite.
3. Babe's hoofbeats were thunder resounding through the hills.

Practice

A. Write what is being compared in each sentence. Then write *simile* or *metaphor* to identify the type of comparison.

4. The forest was as quiet as a falling leaf.
5. Paul's voice was a cannon breaking the silence.
6. His words were blocks of ice in the frigid air.
7. Frozen words shattered like glass.
8. Icy syllables splattered in the forest like hailstones.

B. Complete each sentence to make a simile.

9. Paul Bunyan was as strong as ____ .
10. Babe's iron shoes were like ____ .
11. Paul's laughter was as merry as ____ .
12. Paul's mind worked fast like ____ .
13. Babe was as blue as ____ .

C. Complete each sentence to make a metaphor.

14. Babe's blazing eyes were ____ .
15. When Paul made up his mind, he was ____ .
16. The sun was ____ over the deep woods.
17. To Paul, making a giant pancake was just ____ .
18. The wind whistling through the trees was ____ .

Apply ♦ Think and Write

Imagining Likenesses ♦ Write a simile and a metaphor about yourself. Choose something to compare yourself with, such as an animal or object. Think about ways in which you and the thing you chose are alike. Then write your simile and metaphor.

✎ **Remember**
to use similes and metaphors to make your writing vivid.

Focus on Tall Tales

A **tall tale** is pure fun. It tells of events that never happened and never could. It takes the truth and s–t–r–e–t–c–h–e–s it past all belief. Outlandish and chock-full of exaggeration, these tales are preposterous but never dull!

Tall tales have a hero — but not just any hero. He or she is usually a larger-than-life figure, such as Paul Bunyan. Bunyan, like other heroes of tall tales, is the biggest, strongest, roughest, toughest character around. His deeds are breath-taking. He will tackle any problem, no matter how large or difficult. (He will solve it, too!)

> The teamsters hauling logs over [the crooked road] would start home for camp and meet themselves coming back.
>   Maybe even Babe [Paul Bunyan's blue ox] couldn't pull the kinks out of a road as crooked as that one, Paul thought, but there was nothing to do but try.

The humor in a tall tale stems from both exaggeration and surprise. The storyteller starts slowly, as if in dead earnest. He or she seems to be trying to remember all the facts. The story sounds believable. Then suddenly — *surprise*! An outrageous exaggeration startles us. We realize that this is not just an ordinary tale, but a tall tale.

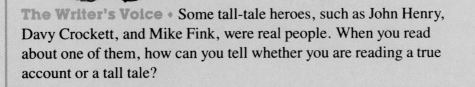

The Writer's Voice ◆ Some tall-tale heroes, such as John Henry, Davy Crockett, and Mike Fink, were real people. When you read about one of them, how can you tell whether you are reading a true account or a tall tale?

Working Together

Use your imagination and your sense of humor as you work with your group on activities **A**, **B**, and **C**.

A. Create a tall-tale hero. Have your group decide on each of your hero's characteristics, using the list below. Choose someone from the group to record what you decide.

   1. Your hero's name
   2. Your hero's appearance and clothes
   3. Your hero's larger-than-life abilities
   4. Your hero's amazing deeds, even from childhood

B. Your group now has a hero (from activity **A**). What gigantic problems will he or she solve? What amazing feats will he or she accomplish? Brainstorm ideas with your group. You might choose a local lake, river, mountain, or other feature, and then explain how your hero created it.

C. Choose one of the tall-tale problems your group discussed in activity **B**. Work with your group to write a tall tale in which your hero solves the problem. Remember that a tall tale is outlandish!

THESAURUS CORNER • Word Choice

Look up the verb *do* in the Thesaurus. Then write three sentences telling what your group's tall-tale hero is able to do. Use a different synonym for *do* in each sentence. Be sure that each synonym fits the meaning of the sentence.

Writing a Tall Tale

"Sky-Bright Axe" introduces one of the most famous tall-tale characters of all time, Paul Bunyan. Paul and his companion Babe the Blue Ox are exaggerated characters. They are bigger than life. Their humorous adventures appeal to a reader's imagination.

In a tall tale, a writer stretches the truth about character, plot, or setting. The writer exaggerates the details. A tall tale gets "taller" each time it is repeated.

Know Your Purpose and Audience

In this lesson you will write a tall tale. Your purpose will be to s-t-r-e-t-c-h the truth. Tell the biggest, funniest, strangest tall tale you can imagine.

Your audience will be your classmates. Try to make them smile. Later you and your classmates will share your tall tales during a folkfest. You can put them together in a "Tall Book of Tall Tales."

MY PURPOSE

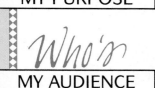

MY AUDIENCE

1 Prewriting

Get ready to write. First choose a topic. Then gather details that will make your tall tale different and special.

Choose Your Topic ◆ Begin to think about stretching the truth. Start with one statement, then try to exaggerate that statement. Look at the ideas below for help.

Think About It

Recall tall tales that you know. Instead of being a large man, Paul Bunyan was as tall as the trees. Pecos Bill lassoed a tornado. What feat could you exaggerate to start your story? What if you were as tall as a tree? What could you do then?

Talk About It

With a partner, play a game of "I used to ___ but now ___." First make an ordinary statement and then finish it with an exaggeration. Look at the Topic Ideas box below for ideas. When your partner smiles, you have found your topic.

Topic Ideas

I used to collect fireflies to light the back porch, but now I collect stars and light the whole state.

I used to have a dog that lapped water from his dish, but now I have a dog that drinks the Pacific Ocean when he is thirsty.

Choose Your Strategy ◆ Here are two strategies that can help you gather details for your tall tale. Read both. Then decide which strategy you will use.

PREWRITING IDEAS

CHOICE ONE

A Comic Strip   Model

Plan the plot of your tall tale by drawing a comic strip. In each frame of the strip, sketch a different story event. Arrange the events in the order that they will occur in the story. Write a caption for each sketch.

I USED TO CATCH FIREFLIES TO LIGHT OUR PORCH.

MILLIONS OF STARS DANCED ABOVE ME.

I DECIDED I'D CAPTURE A STAR TO LIGHT THE PORCH.

IT LIT UP ALL OF TEXAS!

CHOICE TWO

Answering "What If?"   Model

Write a "what if" question about your topic. Then begin to tell your story to a partner. Have your partner ask you follow-up questions. List the questions. Then write your answers. Make your answers as imaginative as you can.

What if I decided to capture a star?

How would you get there?

How would the star act when you tried to catch it?

What would happen when you got it?

In a rented rocket

Hard to catch; as jumpy as a nervous bullfrog

It would light the state!

2 Writing

Look at your comic strip or your "what if" answers. Then begin to write your tall tale. You may want to begin with your "I used to ____ but now ____." statement. You might also begin with a question or an exclamation. Here are some example sentences.

♦ Do you want to know how I catch stars?
♦ Don't call the police! I'm off to steal a star.

As you write, tell story events in order. Include similes and metaphors that will make your readers smile.

Sample First Draft ♦

I used to catch fireflies to light my porch, but now I catch stars. One night I looked up. The sky sparkled like a sea full of dimonds. Millions of stars shone like tiny beautiful lanterns could one of those stars light my porch?

The next day I made a big net. I rented a Rocket from the space center. When the first evening star twinkled, I went.

Catching stars was hard. Finally I caught a brilliant star that lit up every porch in Texas! They jumped like nervous bullfrogs when I got close.

3 Revising

Would you like to improve your tall tale? Here is one idea for revising that may help you.

REVISING IDEA

FIRST   Read to Yourself

As you read, review your purpose and audience. Did you tell a tall tale? Will your audience understand it? Read your story from beginning to end. Mark unclear parts with a wavy line〰. Later go back and try to improve those parts.

Focus: A tall tale makes things bigger than life. A tall tale uses humor. Will your audience smile at your exaggerations?

THEN   Share with a Partner

Ask your partner to read your tall tale aloud as you listen. Note any parts you would like to improve. Encourage your partner to make helpful comments. Here are some guidelines.

The Writer

Guidelines: Be the audience for your own story. Listen carefully as your partner reads to you.

Sample questions:
• Were any parts of my story hard to read?
• **Focus question:** Can I add any funny exaggerations?

The Writer's Partner

Guidelines: Read the writer's story aloud with humor and feeling. Help the writer enjoy his or her own story.

Sample responses:
• This part would read more smoothly if you ＿＿＿.
• Maybe you could exaggerate this part by saying ＿＿＿.

Revising Model ♦ Look at this sample tall tale that is being revised. The marks show changes the writer wants to make.

Revising Marks

cross out ——

add ∧

move ⟋

I used to catch fireflies to light my porch, but now I catch stars. One night I looked up. The sky sparkled like a sea full of dimonds. Millions of stars shone like tiny ~~beautiful~~ dazzling lanterns

Dazzling is a stronger adjective than *beautiful*.

could one of those stars light my porch? The next day I made a big net ∧ from a telephone pole and a fence. I rented a Rocket from the space center.

The writer's partner suggested adding an exaggeration here.

When the first evening star twinkled, I went. blasted off

Blasted off is more vivid than the verb *went*.

Catching stars was hard. Finally I caught a brilliant star that lit up every porch in Texas! They jumped like nervous bullfrogs when I got close.

This simile was moved to make the comparison clearer.

Read the tall tale above the way the writer thinks it *should* be. Then revise your own tall tale.

Grammar Check ♦ Vivid verbs can make your writing more lively and interesting to read.

Word Choice ♦ Do you want a stronger word for a word like *beautiful*? A thesaurus can help you improve your word choice.

Revising Checklist

☐ **Purpose:** Did I write a tall tale?

☐ **Audience:** Will my classmates understand my tall tale?

☐ **Focus:** Did I use humorous exaggerations in my tall tale?

4 Proofreading

Proofreading can help you find and correct any errors.

Proofreading Model ♦ Here is the tall tale about star-catching. The new red marks are proofreading marks.

Proofreading Marks

capital letter =

small letter /

indent paragraph ¶

check spelling ⬭

I used to catch fireflies to light my porch, but now I catch stars. One night I looked up. The sky sparkled like a sea full of ⬭dimonds⬭ *diamonds*. Millions of stars shone like tiny beautiful *dazzling* lanterns; could one of those stars light my porch? The next day I made a big net. *from a telephone pole and a fence.* I rented a Rocket from the space center. When the first evening star twinkled, *blasted off* I went.

¶ Catching stars was hard. Finally I caught a brilliant star that lit up every porch in Texas! They jumped like nervous bullfrogs when I got close.

Proofreading Checklist

☐ Did I spell words correctly?

☐ Did I indent paragraphs?

☐ Did I use capital letters correctly?

☐ Did I use correct marks at the end of sentences?

☐ Did I use my best handwriting?

PROOFREADING IDEA

Trading with a Partner

Ask a classmate to proofread your work and put a check next to lines that contain a mistake. Then find and correct the errors in those lines. Help your partner in the same way.

After proofreading, add a title, and make a neat copy of your tall tale.

5 Publishing

To share your tall tale with an audience, try one of the ideas below.

Catching Stars

I used to catch fireflies to light my porch, but now I catch stars. One night I looked up. The sky sparkled like a sea full of diamonds. Millions of stars shone like tiny dazzling lanterns. Could one of those stars light my porch?

The next day I made a net from a telephone pole and a fence. I rented a rocket from the space center. When the first evening star twinkled, I blasted off.

Catching stars was hard. They jumped like nervous bullfrogs when I got close. Finally I caught a brilliant star that lit up every porch in Texas!

PUBLISHING IDEAS

Share Aloud

Hold a class folkfest. Groups of listeners will sit in small circles. Wear a costume. You can dress like a character in your tale. Tell your tall tale. Ask each listener to tell you one exaggeration he or she heard in your story.

Share in Writing

Illustrate and gather all the stories into a book with tall pages. Call it "The Tall Book of Tall Tales." Put it in the library. Ask readers to write their own "I used to _____ but now I _____." statements on blank pages at the back.

CURRICULUM ◆CONNECTION◆

Writing Across the Curriculum
Mathematics

In this unit you wrote a tall tale. Asking and answering some "what if" questions may have helped you plan your tale. Mathematicians also use the skill of asking and trying to answer "what if" questions.

Writing to Learn

Think and Suppose ◆ Suppose that logs are floating slowly down a winding river. Paul Bunyan and Babe the Blue Ox decide to straighten the river. As they do so, the logs start to travel faster. What if the first shipment downstream takes 180 days, the second 144 days, and the third 108 days? How long will the next one take? (Hint: Look for a pattern in the numbers.)

What-if Chart

Write ◆ There is more than one way to solve this problem. Explain how *you* arrived at your answer. Then explain how you think Paul and Babe may have straightened out the river.

Writing in Your Journal

In the Writer's Warm-up you wrote about a familiar tall tale. Throughout this unit you learned about different characters in tall tales. Browse through the unit again. Choose the character you think was the cleverest. In your journal explain why you think so.

BOOKS TO ENJOY

Read More About It

American Tall Tales *by Adrien Stoutenburg*
If you enjoyed "Sky-Bright Axe," you'll enjoy some of the other tall tales the author has collected. Marvel at Mike Fink, the river roarer. Meet Stormalong, the salty sailor. Each character in this collection is an American folk hero.

John Henry, The Steel Driving Man
by C.J. Naden
John Henry was a steelworker. His greatest feat was a race against a steam drill. His strength and determination have made him an American legend.

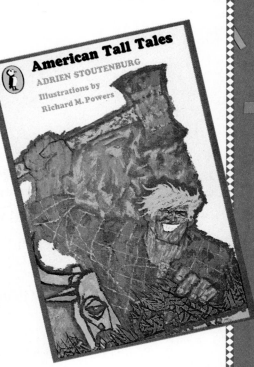

Book Report Idea   Book Collage

The next time you give a book report, make a collage to recall its main ideas, important characters, or memorable scenes.

Create a Book Collage
Look through old magazines for pictures that remind you of your book. You won't find a picture of the main character, but you may find a picture of something that character liked to do. Cut out a variety of pictures and words. Combine the words and pictures in a collage. Be sure to give the title and author.

Casey Jones was the legendary driver of the Cannonball Express. He was smart, strong, brave, and proud to be a railroad man.

UNIT REVIEW

Unit 3

Verbs *pages 116–133*

A. Write the action verb from each sentence.

1. The rabbit sniffed the carrot.
2. The black cat curled its tail.
3. The snake hissed.
4. The panther leaped to the ground.
5. This book discusses many animals.
6. I read it yesterday.
7. Darryl borrowed it from me.
8. We share books all the time.
9. Some books educate their readers.
10. Other books entertain us.

B. Write the verb from each sentence. Then write whether it is an *action verb* or a *linking verb*.

11. Janice returned the records to the library.
12. You are almost ten minutes late.
13. Cecilia was the star of the play.
14. The dog growled at the new letter carrier.
15. This orange tastes bitter.
16. The earthquake shook the ground.
17. The horse galloped along the track.
18. This jacket feels damp.
19. Betty won first prize.
20. Mark seems especially happy today.
21. Yoni sampled her brother's cookies.
22. They were delicious!

C. Write whether each underlined verb is a *main verb* or a *helping verb*.

23. Susan <u>is</u> planning to visit her aunt's house.
24. Jenny will <u>go</u> with her.
25. They have <u>thought</u> about this trip for many months.
26. Aunt Margaret will <u>take</u> the girls on a tour of New York City.
27. Jenny <u>has</u> lived in Florida all her life.
28. She is <u>buying</u> a warm sweater for the trip.
29. Susan <u>has</u> stayed in New York several times.
30. She has <u>toured</u> the Museum of Modern Art twice.
31. The class <u>was</u> asking Susan about her most recent trip.
32. She <u>will</u> tell us about her next trip upon her return.

D. Write the direct object of each sentence.

33. Jamie bought a new wristwatch.
34. Sally plays the piano beautifully.
35. I met Carl at the fair.
36. The squirrel gripped the nut between its paws.
37. Our class wrote a poem together.
38. John baked a tasty spinach pie.
39. Rosemary brought her tame skunk to school today.
40. Harold told Lynn about his new baby sister.
41. The cat guarded its kittens.
42. The small boy dragged the rusty old wagon up the hill.

E. Write the verb in each sentence. Then write *present*, *past*, or *future* to show what tense it is.

43. Ms. Ruiz will speak at the dinner.
44. Liu gave her old toys to her baby brother.
45. I talk to my best friend every day of the week.
46. Our class learned about reptiles today.
47. Mr. Ward shops at the supermarket around the corner.
48. I never shall understand this problem!
49. Yolanda jumped over the rope.
50. The class will go to the science museum on Friday.
51. The movers struggle with the large sofa.
52. Carol stayed at our house last weekend.

F. Write the correct present-tense form of the verb in parentheses ( ).

53. My friend Stu (live) next door.
54. My brother and I (visit) him often.
55. Stu (play) piano in a rock band.
56. He even (write) his own songs.
57. Everyone (enjoy) Stu's music.
58. We (attend) all of his concerts.

G. Write the past tense and past participle of each verb. Use the helping verb *has* with each past participle.

59. catch	**64.** eat
60. say	**65.** speak
61. bring	**66.** freeze
62. swim	**67.** ring
63. choose	**68.** think

H. Write the verb in parentheses ( ) that correctly completes each sentence.

69. (Can, May) I read your newspaper this morning?
70. (Set, Sit) the candle on the table near the window.
71. I (can, may) see Venus in the sky!
72. Ron (sets, sits) down at the table.

Prefixes   *pages 134–135*

I. Read each definition. Write a word that has the same meaning by adding the prefix *dis-*, *mis-*, *pre-*, *re-*, or *un-* to the underlined word.

73. opposite of <u>lucky</u>
74. to <u>judge</u> wrongly
75. to fail to <u>agree</u>
76. to <u>work</u> again
77. to <u>test</u> before
78. to <u>build</u> again
79. opposite of <u>approval</u>
80. opposite of <u>happy</u>
81. to <u>place</u> wrongly
82. to <u>view</u> before

Proofreading

J. Proofread each sentence. Then write each sentence correctly.

83. Carls mother asked him a question.
84. Where are you going?" she asked.
85. "I'm going to the game" he replied.
86. Mr. Wu drove Carl to taylor park.
87. Jane, Fran, and, Alex came, too.
88. the soccer game was very exciting.
89. Fran scored the winning Goal.
90. "Did we win?" asked Fran?
91. "Carl answered, "We sure did!"

LANGUAGE PUZZLERS

Unit 3 Challenge

Hidden Verbs

Look at how the past-tense forms of ten verbs are hidden in this puzzle. Write the present-tense form of each hidden verb.

Hide the past-tense form of each verb below in a similar puzzle. Ask a classmate to solve your puzzle.

d	e	i	r	r	u	h
e	e	a	d	b	c	o
g	d	c	e	e	f	p
n	t	r	i	e	d	p
a	g	d	l	d	h	e
h	o	p	e	d	e	d
c	i	c	r	i	e	d
x	j	k	l	m	r	n
e	m	p	t	i	e	d

trap   **qualify**   **open**   **attend**   **shop**
trot   **worry**   **mop**   **apply**   **use**

Claim-to-fame Matchup

Match each famous person or thing with the correct claim to fame. (Hint: The answer to what each did is the past tense of a verb in the list below.)

Santa María   **Florence Nightingale**   **Orville Wright**
Liberty Bell   **Paul Bunyan**

1. I ＿＿ the first airplane. My name is ＿＿.
2. I ＿＿ in 1776 to announce the signing of the Declaration of Independence. I am the ＿＿.
3. I ＿＿ to be a giant. My name is ＿＿.
4. I ＿＿ Christopher Columbus to America. I am a ship called the ＿＿.
5. I ＿＿ the first nurse's uniform. My name is ＿＿.

wear   **grow**   **fly**   **bring**   **ring**

Unit 3 Extra Practice

1 Writing with Action Verbs
p. 116

A. Each sentence below contains an action verb. Write each sentence and underline the verb.

1. Two scientists traveled to Nepal.
2. They studied the habits of tigers in the wild.
3. They watched the tigers for months.
4. They learned many interesting facts.
5. Their article describes the life of a tiger.
6. The tigers make their home in a large valley.
7. Tall, thick grass covers much of the ground.
8. Rivers run through the valley.
9. In hot weather the tigers cool themselves in the water.
10. The tigers hunt various kinds of deer.
11. They hide in the tall grasses.
12. Tigers live alone, not in groups.
13. Young tigers learn from their mothers for two years.
14. Each tiger controls its own territory.
15. It roams long distances inside this area.

B. Write the sentences. Use an action verb to complete each sentence.

EXAMPLE: Angelo _____ a tiny kitten.
ANSWER: Angelo found a tiny kitten.

16. It _____ outside the front door in the rain.
17. Angelo _____ it with a towel.
18. He _____ the kitten to his mother.
19. Then they _____ it something to eat and drink.
20. The kitten _____ its paws carefully.
21. It _____ straight into Angelo's room.
22. With a loud ''meow,'' it _____ onto the bed.
23. It _____ down right in the middle of the pillow.
24. Angelo _____ its sleek, soft head.
25. The kitten _____ happily before it fell asleep.
26. Angelo _____ his friends about his new pet.

2 Linking Verbs

p. 118

A. Write the linking verb in each sentence. Write and underline the words in the subject and the predicate that the linking verb connects.

1. Hawaiian winters are mild.
2. Sunny days seem endless.
3. My aunt is a hula teacher.
4. The breeze feels delightful.
5. Hawaii is warm all year.
6. Surfing looks dangerous.
7. Pineapples taste wonderful.
8. A coconut smells sweet.
9. Orchids look fragile.
10. Kim was a fine surfer.

B. Write each sentence. Underline the linking verb. Use an arrow to connect the two words that the verb links.

EXAMPLE: Some waves are very large.

ANSWER: Some waves are very large.

11. December was too cold.
12. Every year the winter seems longer.
13. Hawaii was our destination.
14. The sun feels warm on our faces.
15. Fresh coconuts taste creamy.
16. Even the cabdrivers look happy.
17. Tanaka is a fire-walker.
18. Honolulu is the capital of Hawaii.
19. Liliuokalani was the last queen of Hawaii.
20. The volcanoes were quiet during our stay.

C. Write the sentences. Choose the correct form of *be* in parentheses ( ) to complete each sentence.

21. Palm trees _____ heavy with fruit. (was, were)
22. I _____ glad we spent our vacation there. (is, am)
23. Fresh pineapple _____ new to me. (was, were)
24. You _____ right about the beaches. (was, were)
25. Coral reefs _____ homes for many fish. (is, are)
26. Feather cloaks _____ the badges of royalty. (was, were)
27. They _____ still bright today. (is, are)
28. We _____ eager to try the outrigger canoes. (was, were)
29. Haleakala _____ a very large volcano. (is, are)
30. It _____ inactive today. (is, are)

3 Main Verbs and Helping Verbs *p. 120*

A. Write each sentence. Draw one line under the main verb.
Draw two lines under the helping verb.

   1. Kay and Nick are practicing for a contest.
   2. They have danced together for two years.
   3. Someday they will become professional dancers.
   4. This contest has attracted many talented people.
   5. The winners will appear with a professional company.
   6. Each dancer is performing twice.
   7. They all have worked very hard for this chance.
   8. They will exercise for two hours every morning.
   9. Kay has stretched her leg muscles.
  10. Nick was bending forward and backward.
  11. The musicians had practiced, too.
  12. Soon everyone will compete.

B. Write whether the underlined word in each sentence is a main
verb or a helping verb.

  13. They will present the fourth annual ballet competition.
  14. Dancers have arrived from all over the world.
  15. The town was preparing to house and feed everyone.
  16. The judges are arriving today.
  17. This contest has provided much excitement.

C. Write the sentences. Use the helping verb *are*, *have*, or *will* to
complete each sentence.

  18. Kay and Nick ____ performing today.
  19. They ____ prepared two dances.
  20. In one, Kay ____ wear special shoes.
  21. In them she ____ stand on the tips of her toes.
  22. The two young dancers ____ feeling very nervous.
  23. The judges ____ watching carefully.
  24. Both dancers ____ turned in circles around the stage.
  25. They each ____ balanced on one foot, with their arms
         gracefully and proudly raised.
  26. Now they ____ bowing to the audience.
  27. The judges ____ make their decision soon.

4 Verbs with Direct Objects

p. 122

A. Write the action verb and the direct object in each sentence.

1. Clouds absorb much energy from the earth.
2. Large air masses cause changes in the weather.
3. Weather information helps gardeners.
4. Air holds more moisture on a hot day.
5. A weather vane shows the direction of the wind.
6. An anemometer measures its speed.
7. Barometers measure the pressure of the atmosphere.
8. Low pressure usually brings rainy weather.
9. High pressure systems blow clouds away.

B. Write each sentence. Draw one line under the action verb. Draw two lines under the direct object.

10. Weather satellites take pictures of the clouds.
11. During tornadoes, people seek shelter.
12. A meteorologist studies weather.
13. The hurricane damaged the coastline.
14. Tornadoes cause the most damage of any storm.
15. Sometimes a powerful thunderstorm scares my dog.
16. Huge cumulonimbus clouds bring thunderstorms.
17. Bodies of water affect the weather of the nearby land.
18. Weather follows regular patterns in most cases.

C. Write the direct object of each sentence. Then write *what* or *whom* to show what question the direct object answers.

19. The meteorologist predicted a huge snowstorm.
20. The first flakes hit the ground at six o'clock.
21. The snow almost covered my window by midnight.
22. The mayor warned the motorists about the blizzard.
23. High winds caused drifts four feet high.
24. I called my sister over to my window.
25. My sister Rita brought an extra blanket for warmth.
26. Three feet of snow covered our driveway.
27. The superintendent closed the schools.
28. We invited our friends for lunch.
29. Then we took our sleds to the park.

5 Tenses of Verbs

A. The verbs in the sentences below are underlined. Write whether each verb is in the present, past, or future tense.

1. Noreen <u>wanted</u> a job as a firefighter.
2. Next month the fire department <u>will offer</u> the test.
3. Noreen <u>asks</u> for an application at the station.
4. She <u>worked</u> hard before the test.
5. She <u>will study</u> at the fire academy for six weeks.

B. Write the verb in each sentence. Then write *present*, *past*, or *future* to show what tense it is in.

6. The men and women prepare for the test.
7. They jogged eight miles every day.
8. They carried sandbag dummies up and down the stairs.
9. Some of them also lift weights.
10. For strength, Noreen eats only healthful foods.
11. They will drag eighty pounds of hose.
12. They will climb a ladder to a second-story window.
13. They will run up five flights of stairs.
14. The test lasts just over four minutes.
15. Noreen finished it in less than three minutes.

C. Each underlined verb below is in the present tense. Write each sentence. Change the verb to the tense shown in parentheses ( ).

EXAMPLE: The firefighters <u>wear</u> leather hats. (future)
ANSWER: The firefighters will wear leather hats.

16. Day shifts <u>last</u> nine hours. (future)
17. Noreen <u>stays</u> at the firehouse all day. (past)
18. The fire alarm <u>interrupts</u> dinner. (past)
19. The engines <u>race</u> to the fire. (future)
20. The firefighters <u>need</u> air masks. (future)
21. They <u>enter</u> the burning building. (past)
22. Noreen <u>pulls</u> the hose up the stairs. (past)
23. Gallons of water <u>pour</u> out of the hose. (past)
24. Noreen <u>struggles</u> with the heavy hose. (past)
25. After work the firefighters <u>rest</u> at home. (future)
26. The firefighters <u>protect</u> people's lives. (past)

6 Using the Present Tense

p. 126

A. Write each sentence. Use the correct form of the verb in parentheses ( ).

1. Maureen (work, works) as a marine biologist.
2. She (study, studies) sea life.
3. She (supply, supplies) facts about sea turtles.
4. Sea turtles (lay, lays) their eggs in the sand.
5. Shorebirds (eat, eats) the turtle eggs.
6. Humans also (hunt, hunts) turtles for food.
7. The narwhal (have, has) a tusk like a unicorn's horn.
8. The elephant seal (get, gets) its name from its large nose.
9. During the mating season its nose (fill, fills) with air.
10. The male seals (roar, roars) their readiness to fight.
11. They (like, likes) a diet of penguins and fish.
12. After eating, a leopard seal (sleep, sleeps) on land.
13. Often it (lie, lies) underwater.
14. Only its nostrils (show, shows) above the water.
15. The walrus (live, lives) in a small family group.
16. Its tusks (serve, serves) as a powerful weapon.
17. A walrus mother (swim, swims) with her infant on her back.
18. It (use, uses) its bristly mustache for hunting fish.

B. Write each sentence. Use the correct present-tense form of the verb in parentheses ( ).

19. Our boat _____ in an hour. (leave)
20. I _____ an otter family over there. (see)
21. Sea urchins _____ a tasty meal for otters. (provide)
22. Like their land relatives, sea otters _____ a lot. (play)
23. While napping, they _____ their eyes with their paws. (cover)
24. A sea otter _____ a rock to open shellfish. (use)
25. It _____ on squid and fish, too. (feed)
26. A thick coat _____ the otter warm. (keep)
27. Their webbed feet _____ them swim easily. (help)
28. The animal _____ to the ocean floor. (dive)
29. Humpback whales _____ playfully at the surface. (feed)
30. The blue-fin tuna also _____ out of the water. (jump)
31. Dolphins _____ the waves in pods of twenty or more. (ride)
32. A sea gull _____ close to the water. (fly)

7 Using Irregular Verbs

p. 128

A. Write each sentence. Use the past tense of the verb in parentheses ( ).

1. Hooray! Our tickets finally (come).
2. Our family (fly) to Cairo with a tour group.
3. Our group (see) the three pyramids at Giza.
4. We (do) a great deal of walking that day.
5. Ken (wear) out two pairs of sneakers on the trip.
6. We (take) a trip up the Nile on our way to Alexandria.
7. Cotton (grow) on the Nile banks in ancient times, too.
8. Rain (fall) unexpectedly when we were in Alexandria.
9. Marta (write) postcards from her high-rise hotel.
10. My parents (give) a farewell gift to our tour guide.

B. Write each sentence. Use the past participle of the verb in parentheses ( ).

11. Our passports had already (come).
12. Sami had (eat) Egyptian food many times.
13. I had (do) all the packing for the trip.
14. Jim had never (fall) off a camel before.
15. Ellie has (run) a mile at dawn every day.
16. She had (go) to the train with us.
17. Mom and Dad have (take) the last camels to the hotel.
18. I have (see) twenty souvenir stands in three days.
19. Dust, wind, and rain have (wear) away the temple steps.
20. The pilot has (fly) this route many times before.

C. Write the past tense or past participle of each verb in parentheses ( ).

21. The storm had (grow) worse by midnight.
22. Several inches of snow (fall) before morning.
23. I (take) the dog for a walk during the storm.
24. By noon, more than a foot of snow had (fall).
25. We had never (see) such a storm.
26. The mound of snow on the car (grow) huge.
27. Luckily, I had (take) my bicycle inside the house.
28. After the storm we (ride) our sleds on the big hill.

D. Write the past and past participle of each verb. Use the helping verb *has* with each past participle.

29. see   **31.** give   **33.** write   **35.** do   **37.** eat
30. ride   **32.** wear   **34.** grow   **36.** go   **38.** fall

8 Using Irregular Verbs

p. 130

A. Write the past tense and past participle of each verb.

1. find   **3.** think   **5.** break   **7.** choose   **9.** sing
2. drink   **4.** bring   **6.** swim   **8.** speak   **10.** catch

B. Write each sentence. Use the past or the past participle of the verb in parentheses ( ).

11. Ronnie (say) that he could hardly wait for summer.
12. The lake (freeze), but he dreamed of warm weather.
13. He had (speak) to Gary about the vacation program.
14. Everyone (think) it would be fun to do again.
15. They had (swim) every day at the community center.
16. Cheryl complained that she had (freeze) in the cold water.
17. No one had (catch) a cold, though.
18. A bell always (ring) to call the campers.
19. All the campers (bring) bag lunches with them.
20. They (drink) juice with their sandwiches.
21. After lunch they had (break) into different groups.
22. Some of the campers (sing) in a chorus.
23. Some (choose) colored glass for their crafts projects.
24. One day Gary had (bring) fishing poles for everyone.
25. He had (say) that they were going on a trip.
26. Darryl had (choose) the seat next to Leona.
27. Everyone had (sing) loudly during the bus ride.
28. At the park they (swim) in the lake.
29. Then they (find) a place to go fishing.
30. No one (speak) while they baited their hooks.
31. Suzanne had (think) she would be bored.
32. She was surprised when she (catch) so many fish.
33. At sundown Ronnie had (ring) the bell for taps.
34. After they had (drink) some cocoa, everyone went home.

9 Using Troublesome Verb Pairs   *p. 132*

A.   Write each sentence. Use the correct verb in parentheses ( ).

   1.   Did you (sit, set) the paper plates on the table?
   2.   Is there anyone who (can, may) blow up these balloons?
   3.   Where will everyone (sit, set) during the show?
   4.   (Can, May) I taste the popcorn now?
   5.   In which room (can, may) Eva practice her juggling act?
   6.   Yes, you (can, may) bring a friend to the party.
   7.   The extra guests will (sit, set) on the floor.
   8.   (Can, May) we eat before the magic show begins?
   9.   Magic Marla (sit, set) a covered basket on the table.
   10.   A good magician (can, may) fool the audience every time.
   11.   Magic Marla asked Leroy to (sit, set) in the Chair of Invisibility.
   12.   How did she (sit, set) it down again?
   13.   (Can, May) you figure out how it's done?
   14.   A good juggler (can, may) juggle five objects at a time.
   15.   The juggler's dog likes to (sit, set) and beg.

B.   Write the sentences. Use *can*, *may*, *sit*, or *set* to complete each sentence.

   16.   You _____ begin eating right after the show.
   17.   Where should we _____ for the refreshments?
   18.   Nicky, _____ you reach the jar of pickles?
   19.   Please don't _____ a place for me at that table.
   20.   Who _____ reach the pitcher of juice?
   21.   If you _____ it on the edge, it will fall off.
   22.   Jody and his mother _____ together at a table.
   23.   Nothing has been _____ on the table.
   24.   _____ we have some napkins?
   25.   Jody _____ some on the table.
   26.   _____ you reach those tomatoes?
   27.   Be careful when you _____ the bowl down.
   28.   You _____ leave the table when you're finished.
   29.   Let's _____ in the living room and tell jokes.
   30.   _____ I borrow that deck of cards for a card trick?
   31.   If you _____ here, you'll be able to see her better.
   32.   _____ you show us another card trick?

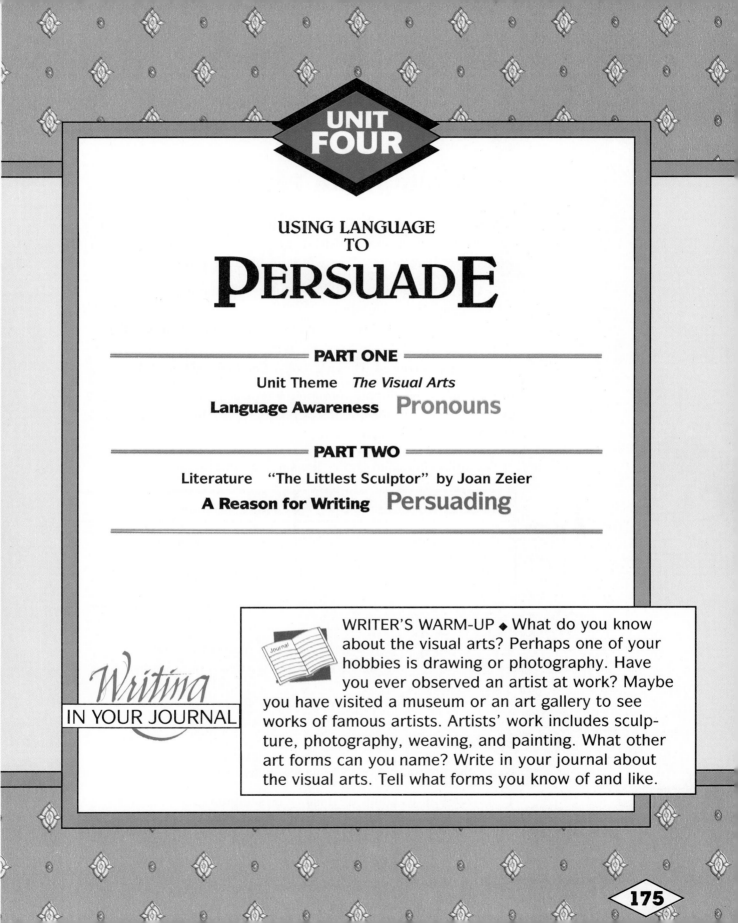

USING LANGUAGE
TO
PERSUADE

PART ONE

Unit Theme   *The Visual Arts*

Language Awareness   Pronouns

PART TWO

Literature   "The Littlest Sculptor" by Joan Zeier

A Reason for Writing   Persuading

Writing
IN YOUR JOURNAL

WRITER'S WARM-UP ◆ What do you know about the visual arts? Perhaps one of your hobbies is drawing or photography. Have you ever observed an artist at work? Maybe you have visited a museum or an art gallery to see works of famous artists. Artists' work includes sculpture, photography, weaving, and painting. What other art forms can you name? Write in your journal about the visual arts. Tell what forms you know of and like.

In the following sentence, change the underlined words to nouns: *The principal brought it to them.* Can you think of nouns that make the sentence humorous? Frightening? Exciting?

1 Writing with Pronouns

When you speak and write, you can avoid repeating the same noun by using a pronoun instead. Look at the sentences below. The words in red are nouns. The words in blue are pronouns.

1. The book about art was helpful. It contained several chapters on sculpture.
2. The class enjoyed the photographs . Students used them for ideas.
3. Lisa borrowed Deven's book. She took his book home.

In sentence **1** the singular pronoun *it* replaces the noun *book*. In **2** the plural pronoun *them* replaces *photographs*. In **3** the singular pronoun *his* replaces *Deven's*.

The following chart shows the singular and plural pronouns.

Singular Pronouns	Plural Pronouns
I, me, my, mine you, your, yours she, he, it, her, him, hers, his, its	we, us, our, ours you, your, yours they, them, their, theirs

Summary ◆ A **pronoun** takes the place of a noun or nouns. When you write, use pronouns to avoid repeating the same nouns.

Guided Practice

Name the pronoun in each sentence below.

1. Deven told us about the history of sculpture.
2. Did you see the African sculpture at the museum?
3. The special masks held our attention for a long time.

Practice

A. Write each sentence. Underline the pronoun.

   4. Today I learned that sculpture is an ancient art.
   5. It was practiced by the ancient Greeks.
   6. Which pieces of sculpture on display are theirs?
   7. Usually they carved statues from marble.
   8. Sculpture has left us a record of human history.
   9. Africans' wooden statues show their beliefs.
   10. Later we saw Italian sculpture by Bernini.
   11. His works are dramatic and realistic.
   12. Is this book about Bernini yours?
   13. That statue shows great detail in its facial features.

B. Rewrite each sentence using pronouns in place of the underlined words.

   EXAMPLE: Peter is studying African sculpture.
   ANSWER: He is studying African sculpture.

   14. Several of Peter's ancestors were sculptors.
   15. In Africa, sculptors made statues of bronze.
   16. The large collection of statues was very impressive.
   17. Peter spent much of Peter's time in the museum.
   18. The museum contained exciting exhibits for Peter to see.

C. 19–23. Write five sentences of your own. Use these pronouns in your sentences: *she, him, mine, your,* and *their*.

Apply ◆ Think and Write

From Your Writing ◆ Read what you wrote for the Writer's Warm-up. If necessary, replace some of the nouns with pronouns to avoid repetition.

> ✎ **Remember**
> to use pronouns to avoid repeating the same nouns.

You and your friends have spent a busy weekend at the state fair or a block party. Tell what everyone did. Do not mention anyone's name. Use pronouns instead.

2 Subject Pronouns

Certain pronouns can take the place of a noun used as the subject of a sentence. In the sentences below, the subjects are underlined. Each subject is a noun or a subject pronoun. In sentence **1b**, the pronoun *she* replaces the noun *Louise Nevelson*. In sentence **2b**, the pronoun *they* replaces the noun *sculptures*.

> **1.** a. Louise Nevelson is a well-known artist.
>   b. She is a famous sculptor.
> **2.** a. The sculptures created by Nevelson are often boxlike.
>   b. They are usually made out of wood.

The word or group of words that a pronoun replaces is called the antecedent. The name *Louise Nevelson* in sentence **1a** is the antecedent of the pronoun *she* in sentence **1b**.

The subject pronouns are below. *I* is always capitalized.

Subject Pronouns		
Singular	**Used for**	**Plural**
I	talking about yourself	we
you	talking to someone	you
she, he, it	talking about someone or something	they

Summary ◆ The **subject pronouns** are *I, you, she, he, it, we,* and *they.* When you write, you can use these pronouns to replace nouns that are the subjects of your sentences.

Guided Practice

Name the subject pronoun in each sentence.

1. I once visited the Mount Rushmore National Memorial.
2. It is a huge piece of sculpture carved in a mountain.
3. Have you ever been there?

Practice

A. Write the subject pronoun in each sentence.

4. I enjoyed the visit to Mount Rushmore.
5. It is in the Black Hills of South Dakota.
6. We saw carvings of the faces of four American Presidents.
7. They are Washington, Jefferson, Lincoln, and T. Roosevelt.
8. While there, I watched a film about Gutzon Borglum.
9. He was the American sculptor of the memorial.
10. Did you know that workers carved with dynamite?
11. After fourteen years of work, they finished the memorial.

B. Write each sentence. Use a subject pronoun in place of the underlined word or words.

12. Tanya and Billy will visit Mount Rushmore in July.
13. Tanya is very excited about the trip.
14. Yesterday Harold gave Tanya a picture of Mount Rushmore.
15. The picture is magnificent.
16. Mountain goats can be seen walking near the faces.

C. Write each pair of sentences using the correct subject pronoun in each blank. Underline the word or words each pronoun replaces.

17. Tanya and Billy studied the life of Gutzon Borglum.
    _____ discovered some interesting facts.
18. Borglum spent several years in London and Paris.
    In 1901 _____ settled in New York City.
19. Auguste Rodin was a sculptor from France.
    _____ influenced the work of Borglum.
20. Tanya said something that was surprising.
    _____ said that Borglum's son Lincoln was also a sculptor.
21. In fact, Gutzon and Lincoln Borglum shared a big project.
    _____ carved the Mount Rushmore National Memorial.

Apply ◆ Think and Write

Creative Writing ◆ Pretend you are a sculptor. Tell what kind of sculpture you would make. Use a variety of subject pronouns in your sentences.

✎ **Remember**
that you can use subject pronouns to replace nouns in the subject of a sentence.

Tell a story about taking pictures. Begin with this sentence: *Yesterday, Rita took pictures of us.* Use some of these pronouns to complete the story: *me, you, him, her, it, us, them.*

3 Object Pronouns

You have learned that certain pronouns can replace nouns used as the subject of a sentence. Other pronouns can replace nouns used as direct objects. Remember that a direct object follows an action verb. In the sentences below, the direct objects are underlined.

1. a. Marta received a <u>camera</u> for her birthday.
   b. She took <u>it</u> out of the box.
2. a. Marta snapped <u>pictures</u> with the camera.
   b. She will show <u>them</u> to us.

In sentence **1b** the pronoun *it* replaces the noun *camera*. In sentence **2b** the pronoun *them* replaces the noun *pictures*. Pronouns that replace nouns used as direct objects are called object pronouns. The following chart lists them.

Object Pronouns		
Singular	**Used for**	**Plural**
me	talking about yourself	us
you	talking to someone	you
him, her, it	talking about someone or something	them

Summary ♦ The **object pronouns** are *me, you, him, her, it, us,* and *them.* When you write, you can use these pronouns to stand for nouns used as direct objects.

Guided Practice

Name the object pronoun in each sentence.

1. Marta surprised us with a new instant camera.
2. Bryan and Anthony carefully examined it.
3. Marta told them about the features of the camera.

Practice

A. Write the second sentence of each pair. Underline the object pronoun.

   4. The first cameras were developed early in the nineteenth century. Today, many people use them.
   5. A camera captures a picture on film. After the film is developed, we see it.
   6. In 1888 George Eastman introduced a practical, inexpensive camera. This invention made him famous.
   7. Today professional photographers may work for a magazine. I admire them.
   8. Photographer Margaret Bourke-White worked for *Life* magazine. The magazine sent her to cover the events of World War II.

B. Write each sentence. Use an object pronoun in place of the underlined words.

   9. People everywhere admired <u>Margaret Bourke-White</u>.
   10. She recorded <u>events</u> for future generations.
   11. Wherever there was action, she captured <u>the episode</u>.
   12. Soldiers, sailors, and air force pilots welcomed <u>Margaret</u>.
   13. Margaret often accompanied <u>a pilot</u> on a dangerous mission.

C. Write the sentences. Complete each sentence with the singular (S) or plural (P) object pronoun you use to talk about yourself.

   14. Tell ___(P)___ more about Margaret Bourke-White.
   15. Let ___(S)___ see her photographs.
   16. This photograph especially pleases ___(S)___ .
   17. Paco told ___(P)___ that she also wrote books.
   18. Margaret Bourke-White's talents impress ___(S)___ .

Apply ◆ Think and Write

Dictionary of Knowledge ◆ Read about the life and work of photographer Ansel Adams. Write a paragraph about his life and artistic achievements. Use object pronouns in your sentences.

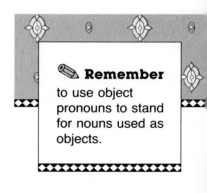

> ✎ **Remember**
> to use object pronouns to stand for nouns used as objects.

GETTING STARTED

Tell who's got the football. Don't name the team. Don't name the players. *The football is ———— . It's ———— football.*

4 Possessive Pronouns

You have learned that possessive nouns show ownership. Pronouns can show ownership, too. In the sentences below, the possessive words are underlined.

1. a. Ruth's father is a photographer.
   b. Her father is a photographer.
2. a. Mr. Irwin's darkroom is better equipped than Ruth's.
   b. His darkroom is better equipped than hers.

In sentence **1b** the pronoun *her* replaces the possessive noun *Ruth's*. In sentence **2b** the pronouns *his* and *hers* replace the possessive nouns *Mr. Irwin's* and *Ruth's*.

Pronouns that show ownership are called possessive pronouns. Some possessive pronouns are used before nouns: *Is that your camera?* Other possessive pronouns are used alone: *That camera is mine.* The possessive pronoun *his* can be used both ways.

Used Before Nouns	Used Alone
my, your, his, her its, our, their	mine, yours, his, hers ours, theirs

Summary ◆ A **possessive pronoun** shows ownership. You can use possessive pronouns to replace possessive nouns.

Guided Practice

Name the possessive pronoun in each sentence.

1. Ruth got her new camera last week.
2. She enjoys using its zoom lens.
3. The book of photographs is theirs.
4. Please bring your camera along.

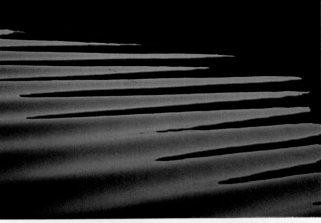
Gentle Ripples by Ernst Haas

Practice

A. Write each sentence. Use the pronoun in parentheses ( ) that correctly completes the sentence.

5. Photographers practice (their, theirs) art in different ways.
6. Is this photo album (you, yours)?
7. A photo essay uses pictures to tell (it, its) story.
8. Dorothea Lange is known for (her, hers) pictures of people.
9. This report about Lange is (my, mine).

B. Write the sentences. Use possessive pronouns in place of the underlined words.

10. Which photographs in this book are Dorothea Lange's?
11. This book has her picture on the book's cover.
12. Has Leon written Leon's report about her yet?
13. Is this collection of photos Pat and Lee's?
14. I like Olivia Parker's and Mitch Epstein's photos.
15. Have you ever seen pictures as interesting as Parker's and Epstein's?
16. Ernst Haas's photographs have breathtaking colors.
17. That deep blue picture of rippling water is Haas's.
18. Portraits by Richard Avedon show celebrities' personalities.
19. Avedon's photos show the latest fashions.

photograph by Mitch Epstein

C. 20–24. Write five sentences of your own. Use these pronouns in your sentences: *my, mine, our, ours, theirs.*

Apply ♦ Think and Write

A Friendly Letter ♦ Imagine you have explored your grandparents' attic. Write a brief letter to a friend telling about the things you found. Use possessive pronouns in your letter.

> ✎ **Remember**
> that possessive pronouns show ownership.

You and a classmate are working together on a large watercolor painting. Write sentences that tell how the two of you work on the painting. Do not use your classmate's name. Use pronouns.

5 Using Pronouns

Read the following sentences.

1. My sister and **I** are inviting **you** to our house.
2. **You** can help Lita and **me.**
3. **We** have new watercolor paints.
4. **She** and **I** are painting animals.

The words in red are subject pronouns. They are the subjects of sentences. The words in blue are object pronouns. They are used after action verbs.

Notice that when you name yourself and someone else, you always name yourself last: *my sister and I, Lita and me,* and *she and I.*

Summary ♦ Use a subject pronoun as the subject of a sentence. Use an object pronoun after an action verb.

Guided Practice

Name the pronoun in parentheses ( ) that correctly completes each sentence.

1. Kristen and (I, me) are learning to use watercolors.
2. Mr. Wong is teaching her and (I, me).
3. (He, Him) and Ms. Gomez teach proper technique.
4. You will see her and (we, us) at the art exhibit.
5. (She, Her) and other art teachers will show their paintings.

Practice

A. Write each sentence. Use the word or words in parentheses ( ) that correctly complete each sentence.

  6. (Me and Kristen, Kristen and I) spend much time painting.
  7. Right now (she, her) and I like the same kinds of paintings.
  8. Mr. Wong, our art teacher, encourages (she and I, her and me).
  9. (He, Him) and the other art teachers are talented artists.
  10. Why don't you visit (he and I, him and me) in art class?

B. Write each sentence. Use the pronoun in parentheses ( ) that correctly completes the sentence. Then write whether the pronoun you used is a subject or an object pronoun.

  11. Cindy and (she, her) went to the art class.
  12. Sue and (I, me) studied paintings by two artists.
  13. The works of Georgia O'Keeffe and Grant Wood impressed Sue and (I, me).
  14. You and (she, her) would enjoy O'Keeffe's paintings of flowers and rocks.
  15. Wood's painting titled *American Gothic* might surprise Pat and (she, her).

Oriental Poppies by Georgia O'Keeffe. University Art Museum, University of Minnesota, Minneapolis

C. Write the sentence. Use *I* or *me* to complete each sentence.

  16. Velma and _____ are interested in modern art.
  17. Our parents took Velma and _____ to an art exhibit.
  18. The exhibit of Picasso's paintings thrilled her and _____ .
  19. She and _____ discovered Picasso's cubist paintings.
  20. The cubist style of painting puzzled Velma and _____ .

Apply ◆ Think and Write

A Newspaper Article ◆ Pretend you and your class have visited an art museum. Write a school newspaper article about your class trip. Use subject and object pronouns in your sentences.

✎ **Remember**
to choose carefully the subject and object pronouns you use.

You can send a telegram, but it must not be longer than three words. You want to say, "I am doing well." How can you shorten the message to three words?

6 Contractions

You have learned that the subject pronouns are *I, you, she, he, it, we,* and *they.* These pronouns can be combined with the verbs *am, is, are, has, have, had, will, shall,* and *would.* The combined forms are called contractions. You can write *she will,* for example, as the contraction *she'll.*

In the following sentences, the contractions are underlined.

1. It's a fine day for painting.
2. I think I'll take my easel to the lake.
3. He'd like to come with me.
4. We're going to paint together.

Notice that in each contraction, an apostrophe (') shows where a letter or letters have been left out.

Pronoun + Verb	= Contraction
pronoun + am	= I'm
pronoun + are	= you're, we're, they're
pronoun + is or has	= he's, she's, it's
pronoun + have	= I've, we've, you've, they've
pronoun + had or would	= I'd, you'd, he'd, she'd, we'd, they'd
pronoun + shall or will	= I'll, we'll
pronoun + will	= you'll, he'll, she'll, they'll

Summary ♦ A **contraction** is a shortened form of two words. When you write a contraction, use an apostrophe to show where a letter or letters have been left out.

Guided Practice

Name the contraction for each pair of words.

1. I am   2. you have   3. it is   4. she will   5. we are

Practice

A. Write the contraction for each pair of words.

6. you have	**11.** we have	**16.** he had
7. they are	**12.** it would	**17.** you will
8. it has	**13.** they will	**18.** she would
9. we shall	**14.** you are	**19.** I will
10. I am	**15.** she has	**20.** he is

B. Write the contraction in each sentence. Then write the words from which the contraction is formed.

The Old Waterworks, n.d. Aaron Douglas. Oil on canvas, 18" × 15". Hampton University Museum Collection.

21. We're going to see an art show by great artists.
22. We've already seen some of Romare Bearden's work.
23. He's a well-known painter.
24. You'll really enjoy Augusta Savage's sculptures.
25. I'd like to see more murals by Aaron Douglas.
26. I'm told he painted a portrait of Marian Anderson.
27. Perhaps you've heard of the painter Jacob Lawrence.
28. I've seen several of his works.
29. Becky says she's got a copy of a painting by Norma Morgan.
30. Wait until you've seen the sculpture by Elizabeth Catlett.

C. For each pair of words below, first write its contraction. Then write a sentence using that contraction.

31. I have	**33.** we are	**35.** you had
32. she would	**34.** it is	

Apply ◆ Think and Write

An Advertisement ◆ Pretend you own an art supply store and will have a one-day sale. Write an ad to persuade shoppers to come to the sale. Use some contractions in your ad.

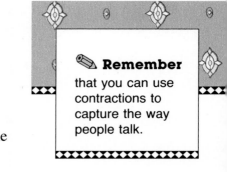

✎ **Remember**
that you can use contractions to capture the way people talk.

GETTING STARTED

Can you "translate" these sentences? *Wood yew cell hymn a hoarse? Eye wood.* Make up sentences that use words of this kind.

VOCABULARY •
Homophones

Study the following sentences.

> To me, two bears are two too many.
> The maid, a bore, made the boar sleepy.
> The bare bear buries his head in the berries.

The underlined words above are homophones. **Homophones** are words that sound alike but have different meanings and spellings.

English has many homophones. Sometimes these homophones cause trouble in writing. The pronouns *their*, *its*, and *your* are often confused with the contractions *they're*, *it's*, and *you're*. These homophones are underlined in the sentences below. Notice how they are used.

> They're walking their pet rabbit.
> It's strange to see its bushy tail on the sidewalk.
> You're funny with your whiskers and floppy ears, rabbit!

Building Your Vocabulary

Find the homophones below and tell their meanings.

1. Ned knew there were two new animals at the zoo; Nan did, too.
2. Nellie thinks that two gnus are good news.
3. Norma thinks they're funny with their big, oxlike heads.

Correct the homophone errors in the sentences below.

1. The truck driver saw that it was time to brake for lunch.
2. Ducks like to fly in fowl weather.
3. *Lettuce Flea* is a book about an escape from a terrible storm.
4. After he fell in the bucket of water, he looked very pail.

Practice

A. Write the rhyme below. Use the correct form of all homophones.

The animals entered a bakery shop—
A dear, a bare, and a hoarse.
In order two by the things that they liked,
They kneaded sum cash, of coarse.
The dear longed four "doenuts," at least to oar three;
The bare dreamed of buries, dipped in sweet honey.
The hoarse wished for oatmeal cookies with hey
(Witch the baker thought funny, serving cookies this weigh).
They soon left, I'm sorry two tell ewe,
And the baker maid nary a sail,
But he had a grate laugh, and his wife, to.
And that is the end of this tail.

B. Use the words below to complete the sentences.

their   **they're**   **your**   **you're**   **its**   **it's**

1. "_____ sure of _____ answer?" Ted's teacher asked.
2. "_____ that nasty rabbit that always gets _____ paws on our lettuce!" exclaimed the gardener.
3. Leave them alone, _____ having the time of _____ lives.

LANGUAGE CORNER ⋅ Portmanteau Words

A **portmanteau** (pôrt maṅ tō) word is made from two words that have been blended into one. For example, *flurry,* as in "snow flurry," is a blend of the words *flutter* and *hurry.*

What blends can you make out of these words?

breakfast + lunch = ?
splash + surge = ?
smoke + fog = ?
squirm + wiggle = ?

How to Revise Sentences with Pronouns

In this unit you have been learning how to use pronouns in sentences. You know that pronouns are used to replace nouns. You can use pronouns instead of repeating the same noun too often. Would you expect to read or hear a sentence like the one below?

> **1.** Mr. Craig says Mr. Craig met Mr. Craig's wife at an exhibit of Mr. Craig's and Mrs. Craig's favorite artist's work.

Sentence **1** is a very confusing and awkward sentence! The noun *Craig* is used five times in this sentence. Now read sentence **2** to see how pronouns can make an improvement.

> **2.** Mr. Craig says he met his wife at an exhibit of their favorite artist's work.

The pronouns in sentence **2** make it much smoother to read and easier to understand. Look for chances to use pronouns to improve your writing.

The Grammar Game ◆ Check your pronoun progress! Replace the underlined words with subject, object, and possessive pronouns. Some of the words could be replaced by more than one pronoun. Give yourself one point for each pronoun. (A score of 20 is excellent!)

the poet's limericks	for Sandy and me
about the nurses	as the storm raged
Joe's neighbors	if Mike objects
when Nellie arrives	to Peg's and my friend
written by Ed and Todd	Mrs. Karlan's house
if the bricks are heavy	laughed at the clown
about the mayor	after David and I talked
the girls' soccer team	at the river's edge

Working Together

Work as a group on activities **A** and **B**, using pronouns instead of repeating the same nouns too often.

In Your Group

♦ Pay attention to each person's ideas.

♦ Don't interrupt each other.

♦ Encourage others to talk.

♦ Help the group reach agreement.

A. Write these familiar song lines, using pronouns to complete them. If you aren't sure of the correct pronoun, use one that makes sense. Can your group add more lines to this list?

1. Oh say, can ____ see, by the dawn's early light?
2. ____ come from Alabama with ____ banjo on ____ knee.
3. Merrily ____ roll along, roll along, roll along.
4. Oh, give ____ a home where the buffalo roam.
5. ____ left ____ heart in San Francisco.
6. Daisy, Daisy, give ____ ____ answer, do.
7. ____'ll be coming 'round the mountain when ____ comes.
8. ____'s a small world after all; ____'s a small, small world.

B. Write the paragraph below, using pronouns in place of nouns wherever possible. Be sure your group agrees that the new paragraph makes sense!

Joan and Joan's brother have a business called Hands for Hire. Joan and Joan's brother work hard every summer. People hire Joan and Joan's brother to wash cars, pull weeds, and care for pets. Joan says Joan's favorite job is gardening, because gardening is relaxing and Joan loves flowers. Joan's brother says Joan's brother's favorite job is walking dogs and playing with the dogs. Joan's brother enjoys the exercise.

WRITERS' CORNER ◆ Fuzzy Sentences

Sometimes replacing too many nouns with pronouns can make your writing fuzzy. Can you tell *who* was excited in the fuzzy sentence below?

FUZZY: **Mark wrote Juan a letter. He was very excited.**
IMPROVED: **Mark wrote Juan a letter. Mark was very excited.**

Read what you wrote for the Writer's Warm-up. Did you write any fuzzy sentences? Can you improve them by replacing any pronouns?

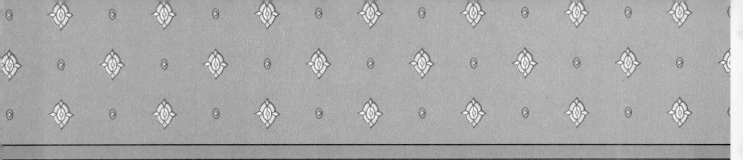

FLAMINGO
stabile by Alexander Calder
at Federal Center, Chicago © ARS New York/ADAGP.

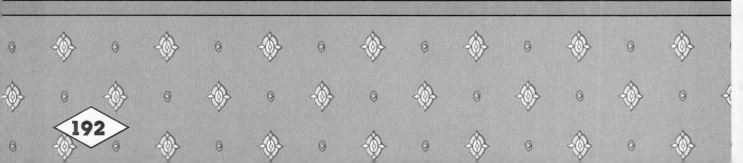

USING LANGUAGE
TO

PERSUADE

PART TWO

Literature "The Littlest Sculptor" by Joan Zeier

A Reason for Writing Persuading

CREATIVE

Writing

FINE ARTS ◆ The giant sculpture by Alexander Calder is called "Flamingo." In what ways does the sculpture resemble a flamingo? Does the sculpture resemble any other bird? Write an arts review of the sculpture. Explain how the various shapes of the sculpture resemble a bird.

CREATIVE THINKING ◆
A Strategy for Persuading

A THOUGHT BALLOON

Persuading means getting someone to believe or to do something. After this lesson, you will read part of ''The Littlest Sculptor.'' It is about Vinnie Ream, who wanted to sculpt President Lincoln. It tells how she tried to persuade him to pose for her. Later you will write a persuasive letter.

President Lincoln did not want to pose for Vinnie. The passage below shows how she tried to change his mind.

> ''Miss Ream,'' he sighed. ''I would like to oblige you, but as you know, we are in the midst of a horrible war. How could I possibly take the time to pose for a sculpture now? . . .''
>
> ''I work quickly,'' she said . . . . ''If I were to bring my clay here and work for three hours every afternoon, I could complete most of the project while you are at your desk.''

Vinnie listened carefully to the President's reasons. She put herself in his place. She tried to see things from his point of view. It was during the Civil War, and she understood how important his work was. She thought he might agree to pose if he did not have to stop working. Do you think he agreed?

Learning the Strategy

It is often helpful to understand another person's point of view. Suppose you meet someone who has moved to America from another country. Could you understand that person's feelings about being in a new land? How? Suppose you find a science fiction book for a friend with the chickenpox. Would that please your friend? How do you know? Suppose you are watching the Academy Awards on television. An actress wins. What is she thinking as she walks up to the stage? How can you guess?

One way to understand another person's point of view is to imagine what *you* might think. Have you ever received an award? Can you guess how you would feel if you did? Making a thought balloon is another way to help imagine someone else's point of view. Think of that actress on her way to the stage. The thought balloon below shows what she might be thinking. What ideas could you add to this thought balloon?

Could I be dreaming? I hope I don't trip! I'd better smile for the cameras. Who's that waving at me?

actress

Using the Strategy

A. Imagine that the principal of your school drops in for a visit right this minute. Look around the classroom. Try to see it through the principal's eyes. Then make a thought balloon for your principal.

B. Reread the passage from "The Littlest Sculptor" on page 194. What do you imagine President Lincoln thought after Vinnie spoke? Make a thought balloon for President Lincoln. As you read "The Littlest Sculptor," decide if President Lincoln felt the way you thought he would.

Applying the Strategy

♦ How did you decide what your principal would think?
♦ When might knowing someone else's point of view help you?

LITERATURE

from

The Littlest Sculptor
by Joan T. Zeier

''They tell me that you'd like to sculpt a statue of me—is that correct?''

The deep, gentle voice helped calm Vinnie's nerves. Asking a favor of the President of the United States was no casual matter, especially for a seventeen-year-old girl.

''Yes, sir,'' she replied, her dark eyes meeting his. ''I wouldn't have dared to ask you, but my teacher, Mr. Mills, says I am ready. I plan to sculpt you in a creditable manner.''

President Lincoln smiled. ''Painters, sculptors—they've all

LITERATURE: Nonfiction

tried to make the best of this homely face, but I'm afraid there's not much hope. What did you have in mind, Miss Ream? A bust?"

Vinnie opened her mouth to say yes, but before she could speak, the President hurried on, a shade of apology in his voice. "Of course—I shouldn't have asked. A full-length pose would be much too strenuous a project for a young woman your size."

Vinnie flushed. She realized that she looked like a child, with her shoulder-length black ringlets and her tiny frame. "Small does not mean weak, sir," she replied indignantly. "I was born in the wilderness of Wisconsin. I've driven teams of horses and carried water. Many times I've put my shoulder to a wheel mired in mud. Molding a full-length clay figure would not tax my strength at all—and that is what I intend to do!"

The President's eyes twinkled at her show of spirit. "My apologies, madam. Had I known your background, I wouldn't have underestimated you. I, too, am from the West, so I understand the hardships of frontier life."

But his smile faded as he rubbed his beard with bony fingers, in thought. "Miss Ream," he sighed. "I would like to oblige you, but as you know, we are in the midst of a horrible war. How could I possibly take the time to pose for a sculpture now? I scarcely have a minute to myself."

Vinnie glanced around and noted the size of his office. "I work quickly," she said. Her voice was soft but confident as she pointed to the corner near the windows. "If I were to bring my clay here and work for three hours every afternoon, I could complete most of the project while you are at your desk."

The President seemed to consider her idea seriously. He got up, shook Vinnie's hand warmly, and looked down upon her from his great height. "I've heard from Mr. Clark Mills that you are a talented young woman, and I have found you charming and intelligent as well. I cannot make my decision immediately, but you will hear from me soon."

The very next day Vinnie received a note from the President.

My dear Miss Ream,

I have considered your request and invite you to come to my office next Monday afternoon at two o'clock. You may bring whatever supplies are necessary to begin your work. However, owing to limitations of time and space, I can only agree to the modeling of a bust.

Yours,

A. Lincoln

Vinnie proudly showed the invitation to Mr. Mills, who was delighted with her success. "What luck! He's turned down some very famous artists, you know. Your enthusiasm must have won him over."

During the next few months, Vinnie Ream observed and sculpted President Lincoln in his office. She was just finishing her bust of President Lincoln when he was shot to death on April 14, 1865. Sadly, Vinnie left the completed bust of the President in the White House.

As the nation mourned President Lincoln, Congress voted to honor him by commissioning a full-length sculpture. There was a contest to select the artist, and Vinnie Ream won. In 1871 her magnificent marble statue of President Abraham Lincoln was placed in the Capitol rotunda. Vinnie Ream's personal memory of a great President still stands in the rotunda today.

Library Link ♦ *To learn more about Vinnie Ream, read "The Littlest Sculptor" in the February 1986 issue of* Cricket *magazine.*

Reader's Response

If you had been President Lincoln, would you have honored Vinnie Ream's request? Why or why not?

The Littlest Sculptor

Responding to Literature

1. Mr. Mills thought Vinnie's enthusiasm must have won the argument for her. Why, do you think, did the President accept Vinnie's request? Was it her enthusiasm, her talent, or another quality that most impressed President Lincoln? Explain.

2. If you were to sculpt a bust of a famous person, whom would you choose? Why? What reasons would you give the person for wanting to do this?

3. Vinnie Ream has a place in history as a sculptor of Lincoln. What would you like to do to earn a place in history? Draw a picture of yourself achieving your dream. Then write a headline for your accomplishment. Add the headline to your picture.

Writing to Learn

Think and Imagine ◆ Imagine the President's point of view when he heard Miss Vinnie Ream's request. Draw two thought balloons. In the first balloon, write the request that Vinnie made of the President. In the other balloon, write President Lincoln's thoughts.

Thought Balloon

Write ◆ Use the notes from the thought balloons to write a short conversation between the President and Vinnie.

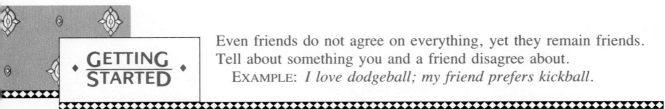

Even friends do not agree on everything, yet they remain friends. Tell about something you and a friend disagree about.

EXAMPLE: *I love dodgeball; my friend prefers kickball.*

SPEAKING and LISTENING •
Expressing Opinions

Melissa: This painting is exciting. I love the bold lines and wild splashes of color. It's wonderful!

James: Are you kidding? I can't even tell what it is. How could anyone like it? That's not art!

Melissa: Well, I like it, and it's great art. You have no taste. You're ignorant!

Melissa and James are allowing their difference of opinion to turn into a heated argument. How can they express their opinions without destroying their friendship? Here are some guidelines to help you share opinions.

Expressing Your Opinion	1. State your opinion clearly, but do not be a know-it-all. Use phrases such as *in my opinion* or *I believe.*
	2. Give facts or reasons to support your opinion.
	3. Respect the opinions of others. When you make fun of people's opinions, you insult them and make them angry. Then they will not listen to anything you say.
	    This: Could you give me an example of what you mean?
	Not this: What a dumb idea! That's a stupid remark!
	4. When you want to persuade others to agree with you, start by stating all the points on which you do agree.
	    This: I like that artist's use of color, too.
	Not this: You like modern art; I hate it.

Being a Critical Listener	1. Listen for proof of the speaker's opinion. Does the speaker give facts or reasons to support it? 2. Evaluate the speaker. Does the speaker know the facts? 3. Try to keep an open mind if you disagree with the speaker.

Summary • Both speakers and listeners need to respect each other's opinions. Find points on which you both agree. Be courteous when you disagree.

Guided Practice

Read each sentence. If it follows the guidelines for speaking and listening, say *yes*. If it does not, say *no*.

1. Anyone who likes modern art ought to have an eye exam!
2. I feel that the camera can capture real life more accurately than an artist can.
3. In my opinion, modern art is not beautiful.

Practice

A. Take turns reading the sentences aloud with a partner. If a sentence follows the guidelines for speaking and listening, say *yes*. If it does not, say *no*.

4. It seems to me that today's artists should study the work of the nineteenth-century masters.
5. Your ideas are old-fashioned; they belong in a museum!
6. Others may disagree, but I think that a photograph can be more realistic than a painting.
7. How could you say such a thing and mean it?
8. I may not agree, but you do have a good point.
9. You are right. Picasso was one of the world's greatest artists, but I prefer the Old Dutch masters.
10. You may be right. Could you give me an example?
11. I'll prove that I'm right and you're wrong!

B. Practice sharing opinions with your classmates. Decide on a topic, such as whether homework is valuable for students. Use the guidelines in this lesson.

Apply ◆ Think and Write

Expressions Chart ◆ Make a chart like the one below.

Expressions to Avoid	Expressions to Use
Your idea is really dumb.	I'll consider what you just said.

✎ Remember
to show respect for the opinions of others.

On the left, list other expressions that cause people to quarrel, not discuss. On the right, list expressions that encourage people to discuss, not quarrel.

Think of an advertising slogan you hear on radio or television. Do you feel the slogan is based on facts?

WRITING ◆
Fact and Opinion

Every day you hear and read messages that try to persuade you. Advertisements and speeches try to persuade you to do something or think a certain way. How can you tell whether to believe them? To decide this, you must be able to tell facts from opinions.

Sometimes, on the other hand, *you* want to persuade others to share your opinion. You want to convince them. To do this, you need to back up your opinion with facts.

What is the difference between a fact and an opinion? A <u>fact</u> is true information. It can be checked or proved to be true. An <u>opinion</u> is what a person *thinks* about something. It is not always easy to tell facts from opinions. An opinion may be stated very positively. It may sound like a fact, even though it is just someone's opinion. Here are three ways to check a statement to see if it is really a fact.

Use what you already know ◆ Think, "Do I know from my own knowledge or experience that the statement is true?"

Experiment ◆ Test the "fact" yourself to find out if it is true.

Investigate ◆ Read about the fact. Check the fact in reference books. Ask an expert about it.

Royal Tide I by Louise Nevelson. Photograph courtesy of The Pace Gallery

Facts:	**1.**	Clay is a soft, moldable material.
	2.	Congress awarded Vinnie Ream $30,000 for a statue.
	3.	Louise Nevelson, the sculptor, was born in Russia.
Opinions:	**1.**	Louise Nevelson's walls are her best sculptures.
	2.	The finest statues are made of white marble.
	3.	No sculptor will ever surpass Michelangelo.

Summary ◆ A **fact** is true information that can be checked. An **opinion** is what someone *thinks* is true. When you want to persuade other people, use facts to show how you arrived at your opinion.

Guided Practice

Tell whether each statement is a fact or an opinion.

1. You would have enjoyed meeting the sculptor Vinnie Ream.
2. Vinnie Ream's last sculpting session with Lincoln was on April 14, 1865.
3. On the evening of April 14, 1865, Lincoln was shot by John Wilkes Booth.

Practice

A. Write *fact* or *opinion* for each statement below.

4. Vinnie Ream was born in the wilderness of Wisconsin.
5. The wilderness is not the best home for an artist.
6. Congress voted to have a sculpture made of Lincoln.
7. Every sculptor dreamed of being chosen to do the work.
8. Vinnie Ream was selected to be the sculptor.
9. Ream's statue of Lincoln stands in the Capitol.

B. Decide how you could check each fact below. Write *already know it*, *test it*, or *read about it* for each statement.

10. Paris is a large city in France.
11. Auguste Rodin was born in Paris, France.
12. A bronze statue will sound hollow when you tap it.
13. The statue called "The Thinker" was sculpted by Rodin.

C. Write two sentences for each word below. In the first sentence express an opinion. In the second sentence, state a fact.

14–15. photograph   16–17. city   18–19. wood

Apply ◆ Think and Write

An Art Review ◆ Here is your chance to be an art critic. Write your opinion of the sculpture shown on the opposite page. Remember to give reasons for your opinion.

✎ **Remember**
to give facts or reasons to support your opinions.

◆ GETTING ◆
STARTED

State a fantastic or a real opinion, such as "We should paint the room pink" or "We should have homework every day." Then give a reason for that opinion.

WRITING ◆
A Persuasive Paragraph

How did Vinnie Ream persuade Abraham Lincoln to let her sculpt him? She gave him convincing reasons. When you want to persuade someone to agree with you, you need to do the same thing. You need to give reasons to prove you are right. You need to state them clearly. You need to focus on what matters to the people you are trying to persuade. What you need is a plan.

Read the paragraph below. It is a persuasive paragraph with a plan. Think about the reasons the writer presented. Notice, too, how the reasons are organized. Which reason is presented first?

Topic sentence gives opinion

Reasons, with most important reason first

Last sentence repeats opinion

I think the students in Jefferson School should volunteer to help clean up the park. It is, after all, our park. Most of us live near it. We would play in the park if it were clean. But it is littered with bottles, cans, and old newspapers. The trash is not only dirty and ugly; it is dangerous. How would you like to run to catch a softball and trip on a broken bottle someone tossed aside? Imagine a clean park, a park without litter—a safe place to play. That could be our park. Let's volunteer to help make the park clean.

Notice that the writer states an opinion in the topic sentence of the paragraph. Then the writer, wanting to persuade the readers, gives reasons for the opinion. In this paragraph the most important reason is given first and other reasons follow. Sometimes a writer chooses to build up to the most important reason and gives it last. What does the writer do in the last sentence of this paragraph?

Summary ◆ A **persuasive paragraph** gives the writer's opinion and reasons to support it. Reasons are often listed in the order of importance.

Guided Practice

State a topic sentence that gives an opinion about each of these questions.

1. Should school be held in the summer?
2. What TV program is worth watching?
3. Is reading comic books a waste of time?

Practice

A. Write a topic sentence that gives an opinion about each of these questions.

4. How much homework should students your age have?
5. Should students your age get an allowance?
6. How old should you be to deliver newspapers?
7. What time should students your age go to bed?
8. Is it better to be the oldest or the youngest child in a family?
9. What television program is boring?
10. What sport is the most interesting?
11. Which season is the most enjoyable?
12. Who is the best popular singer?
13. What is the greatest invention of all time?

B. Choose one of the topic sentences you wrote for **Practice A.** Write a persuasive paragraph to convince your classmates that you are right. Give at least four reasons that will convince them. Remember to give the most important reason first.

Apply ♦ Think and Write

Dictionary of Knowledge ♦ Sayings such as ''Haste makes waste'' are called proverbs. Read about proverbs in the Dictionary of Knowledge, and choose one to write about. Write a paragraph to persuade your reader that the saying is true, or that it is sometimes not true.

✎ Remember
to support an opinion with reasons that are important to your readers.

The abbreviations of state names are the answers to these challenging riddles. Which state abbreviation

says "hello"?   is never out?

has nothing in it?   means the same as *I*?

WRITING ♦
A Business Letter

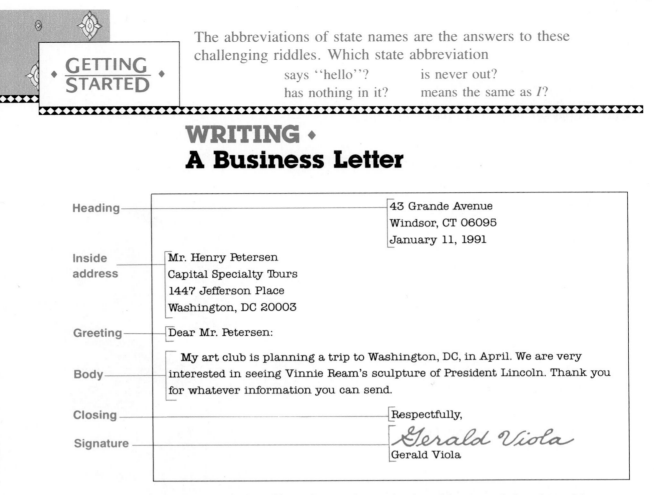

Heading

43 Grande Avenue
Windsor, CT 06095
January 11, 1991

Inside address

Mr. Henry Petersen
Capital Specialty Tours
1447 Jefferson Place
Washington, DC 20003

Greeting

Dear Mr. Petersen:

Body

My art club is planning a trip to Washington, DC, in April. We are very interested in seeing Vinnie Ream's sculpture of President Lincoln. Thank you for whatever information you can send.

Closing

Respectfully,

Signature

Gerald Viola
Gerald Viola

Six Parts of a Business Letter

1. The **heading** shows the writer's address and the date. Use a comma between the city and state and between the date and year.
2. The **inside address** gives the name and address of the person and company to whom the letter is written.
3. The **greeting** is formal. If you do not have a name, use a greeting such as *Dear Sir or Madam*. End the greeting with a colon.
4. The **body** states the purpose of the letter. It may be short.
5. The **closing** is formal. Another formal closing is *Sincerely*.
6. The **signature** gives the writer's name. If the letter is typed or word-processed, the name goes four lines below the closing.

See pages 487 and 489 for information about friendly letters and about addressing envelopes.

Summary ♦ A **business letter** has six parts: the heading, inside address, greeting, body, closing, and signature.

Guided Practice

Name the following parts of a business letter.

1. Dear Art Director:

2. Deborah Wells

3. Sincerely,

4. Public Art Society
10 Madison Street
Washington, DC 20203

Practice

A. Write the name of each part of a business letter.

> **5.** I am interested in learning more about the programs offered by the museum. Please send me your latest brochure.
>
> **6.** Yours truly,
>
> **7.** 312 Brook Lane
> Meredith, NH 03253
> November 8, 1991

B. Write the answers to these questions about a business letter.

> **8.** Which part gives the writer's address?
> **9.** What greeting could you use if you have no specific name?
> **10.** What punctuation ends the greeting?
> **11.** What punctuation ends the closing?

C. Write these items as if they were parts of business letters. Punctuate and capitalize them correctly.

> **12.** 487 blue hills road
> **13.** hartford ct 06103
> **14.** march 4 1991
> **15.** silver inn
> **16.** 18 georgia avenue
> **17.** silver spring md 20910
> **18.** dear manager
> **19.** with best regards
> **20.** april 2 1990
> **21.** dear ms. taylor

Apply ◆ Think and Write

A Letter of Request ◆ Pretend your club was planning a trip to Washington, DC. What would you need to know? Think of some information that would be helpful. Write a business letter with a message that asks for facts or advice.

> ✎ **Remember**
> that the purpose of a business letter should be clear and the message brief.

Focus on Persuasive Words

There will be times when you will want to persuade a person or a group of persons. When you want to persuade someone to agree with you, the words you choose are very important. Words that mean almost the same thing can cause quite different feelings in the listener or reader. Some words suggest pleasant feelings; other words suggest unpleasant feelings.

Here are some statements about "The Littlest Sculptor," which you read earlier in the unit. Compare the underlined words in each pair of sentences. These words mean basically the same thing in each sentence, but notice the different feelings they suggest.

1. **Vinnie said that molding a <u>full-length</u> clay <u>figure</u> would not <u>tax</u> her <u>strength</u> at all.**
2. **Vinnie said that molding a <u>big</u> clay <u>dummy</u> would not <u>hurt</u> her <u>muscles</u> at all.**
3. **Although Lincoln would sometimes <u>smile</u> and <u>chuckle</u>, Vinnie wanted to portray his <u>sadness</u> and <u>concern</u>.**
4. **Although Lincoln would sometimes <u>smirk</u> and <u>chortle</u>, Vinnie wanted to portray his <u>misery</u> and <u>anxiety</u>.**

You can see how the underlined words in sentences **2** and **4** affect meaning. A "big clay dummy" does not have the force and impressiveness of a "full-length clay figure." A man with a "smile and chuckle" tends to be likable, while a man with a "smirk and chortle" probably is not very likable.

The Writer's Voice ◆ Some words with basically the same meanings suggest different feelings. In each of the following groups of words, which word suggests the *best*, or *most favorable*, impression?

1. molder, carver, sculptor   **3.** smart, brainy, intelligent
2. boastful, confident, arrogant   **4.** young, childish, babyish

Working Together

A writer needs to consider the effects of certain words on the reader when deciding which words to use. Keep this in mind as your group does activities **A** and **B**.

A. Discuss these sentences about "The Littlest Sculptor." Pay special attention to the underlined words. Write each one on paper. Label the underlined word with a plus sign (+) if it suggests good feelings. Label it with a minus sign (−) if it does not.

1. Lincoln speaks in a deep, gentle voice that calms Vinnie.
2. His smile fades as he rubs his beard with bony fingers.
3. The war has dragged on for four years, with much suffering.
4. Lincoln, apparently impressed, shakes Vinnie's hand warmly.
5. The final days of the war were filled with sorrow and turmoil.

B. In "The Littlest Sculptor," Vinnie and President Lincoln get along well together. They use the right words with each other. Choose three or four of the direct quotations and suggest some different, *in*appropriate words that they might have used.

In Your Group

- Make sure group members understand the directions.
- Record the group's ideas.
- Show appreciation for others' ideas.
- Agree or disagree in a pleasant way.

THESAURUS CORNER • Word Choice

The five words in dark type suggest the wrong feelings for the content of the paragraph. Rewrite the paragraph. Choose five words from the Thesaurus that are more appropriate. Use the Thesaurus Index when necessary. Change all *Vinnies* and *Lincolns* to pronouns after their first appearance.

Vinnie **interrogated** President Lincoln about doing a statue of Lincoln. Vinnie's teacher, Mr. Mills, had **exclaimed** that Vinnie was talented enough to **construct** a **pretty** statue. Although Vinnie was only seventeen, Vinnie **thought** that Vinnie could sculpt an excellent likeness of the President, one that would please Lincoln.

Writing a Persuasive Letter

What do you do when you have a strong opinion? Probably you try to persuade other people to agree with you. To persuade them, you give facts and reasons to support your opinion.

In ''The Littlest Sculptor,'' you read about Vinnie Ream, who persuaded President Lincoln. Vinnie stated her opinion that she could work without disturbing him. She gave facts and reasons to support her opinion. Vinnie succeeded in persuading Lincoln to agree with her.

Know Your Purpose and Audience

In this lesson you will write a letter. Your purpose will be to write persuasively on a topic that you care about.

Your audience will be the person you choose to write to. Later, you can mail or deliver your letter. You and your classmates might also produce a radio show to share your opinions.

What's
MY PURPOSE

Who's
MY AUDIENCE

1 Prewriting

First you will need to choose a topic. Then you will want to gather ideas about your topic.

Choose Your Topic ♦ Perhaps you would like to have more books in the library. Maybe you feel your town needs a leash law for dogs. Make a list of topics, then circle your favorite.

Think About It	Talk About It
Look at your list. Which do you feel most strongly about? Which do you know most about? Cross out your least favorite, then pick one. Now decide whom you would like to persuade. It might be your principal or the mayor. Write that person's name.	Work with a small group of classmates. Discuss improvements that you think can be made in your school or community. Brainstorm a list of possible topics. You will get ideas from the class list.

Topic Ideas

we need more books in
    the library
we need a leash law
our park needs new flowers
people should not litter

Choose Your Strategy ♦ Here are two strategies for gathering ideas. Read both. Then use the strategy you think will be more helpful in planning your letter.

PREWRITING IDEAS

CHOICE ONE

An Opinion Ladder

A good persuasive strategy is to save your most important fact or reason for last. Make an "opinion ladder." Write your opinion at the bottom. Write your supporting arguments in reverse order of importance. Put the least important at the bottom, the most important at the top.

Model

4. *Unleashed dogs cause accidents.*

3. *Many dogs get hit by cars.*

2. *Too many dogs get lost.*

1. *Dogs can harm neighbors' lawns.*

My opinion: We need a leash law.

CHOICE TWO

A Thought Balloon

In order to persuade someone, it helps if you understand his or her point of view. Make a thought balloon for the person you are writing to. In it, write what you believe that person thinks about your topic.

Then think of ways to answer these concerns. For example, "Three families on our block have complained about stray dogs." or "People would obey the leash law if they knew that the law can protect their dogs as well as themselves."

Model

Most dogs don't bother anyone. People would not obey a leash law.

Mayor Steiner

2 Writing

Look over your opinion ladder or your thought balloon. Then begin to write your persuasive letter. Begin with a topic sentence that lets your reader know your opinion. Here are some ways to begin.

- ◆ I believe that _____.
- ◆ It is my opinion that _____.

Add facts and reasons that support your opinion. Include persuasive words and polite language. When you have finished the body, add the other parts of a business letter. Add a heading, an inside address, a greeting, a closing, and your signature. As you write, don't worry about errors. You can fix them later.

Sample First Draft ◆

Dear Mayor Steiner:
Unleashed dogs often run away from their owners and get lost. Dogs dash into bisy streets. They get hit by cars. I believe our city should have a leash law. Some dogs scare bike riders and cause serious acidents. You have said that people would not obey a leash law. I believe they would.
Im sure youll agree that our City wants a leash law.

respectfully,

Roberto Gomez

3 Revising

Now that you have written your letter, you may want to improve it. Here is an idea for revising that may help you.

REVISING IDEA

FIRST Read to Yourself

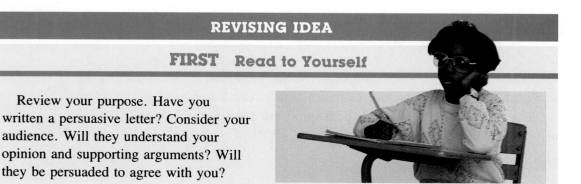

Review your purpose. Have you written a persuasive letter? Consider your audience. Will they understand your opinion and supporting arguments? Will they be persuaded to agree with you?

Focus: Have you used the most persuasive words you can think of? Circle any words you may want to change.

THEN Share with a Partner

Ask a partner to pretend to be the person receiving your letter. Ask him or her to read the letter silently. How does your partner react to the letter? Below are some guidelines that may help you both.

The Writer

Guidelines: Listen to your partner's comments. Then make the changes you think are important.

Sample questions:
- Did I persuade you? Why or why not?
- Are there other facts or reasons I should include?
- **Focus question:** What is a more persuasive word for _____?

The Writer's Partner

Guidelines: Say what you really think, but say it politely.

Sample responses:
- I still don't agree that _____.
- Another argument may be _____.
- A persuasive word you might use is _____.

Revising Model ♦ Here is a persuasive letter that is being revised. The revising marks show the writer's changes.

Revising Marks

cross out ——

add ∧

move ⟋

The pronoun *they* replaced the repeated noun *dogs*.

The writer wanted to put the topic sentence first.

The writer added this detail to answer the mayor's concern.

The writer's partner suggested that *needs* is a more persuasive word than *wants*.

Dear Mayor Steiner:

Unleashed dogs often run away from their owners and get lost. ~~Dogs~~ They dash into bisy streets. They get hit by cars. I believe our city should have a leash law. Some dogs scare bike riders and cause serious acidents. You have said that people would not obey a leash law. I believe they would. if they knew that the law would protect their dogs.

Im sure youll agree that our ~~City~~ needs wants a leash law.

respectfully,

Roberto Gomez

Roberto Gomez

Read the letter above as the writer has decided it *should* be. Then revise your own persuasive letter.

Grammar Check ♦ Replacing some nouns with pronouns can make your writing less repetitive.

Word Choice ♦ Do you want a more persuasive word for a word like *wants*? A thesaurus can help you find these words.

Revising Checklist

☐ **Purpose:** Did I write a persuasive letter?

☐ **Audience:** Will my reasons persuade the person I wrote to?

☐ **Focus:** Did I use persuasive words?

4 Proofreading

Proofread your letter to find spelling, capitalization, and punctuation errors. A correct letter will be more persuasive.

Proofreading Model ◆ Here is the sample letter to the mayor. Notice that red proofreading marks have now been added.

Dear Mayor Steiner:

¶ Unleashed dogs often run away from their owners and get lost. Dogs dash into *bisy* streets. They get hit by cars. I believe our city should have a leash law. Some dogs scare bike riders and cause serious *acidents*. You have said that people would not obey a leash law. I believe they would. *if they knew that the law would protect their dogs.*

Im sure youll agree that our City wants a leash law.

respectfully,

Roberto Gomez

Roberto Gomez

PROOFREADING IDEA

One Thing at a Time

When you are looking for more than one kind of error, you may miss mistakes. Pay attention to just one thing at a time. Read your paper once for spelling errors. Read it again for capitalization and punctuation.

Now proofread your persuasive letter. Check the heading, greeting, closing, and signature. Be sure to put commas and capital letters in the right places. Then make a neat copy.

5 Publishing

Now it's time to share your persuasive letter. Try one of the ideas below.

26 Clearview Lane
Safety Harbor, FL 33572
June 23, 1991

Mayor Mildred Steiner
10 City Hall Plaza
Safety Harbor, FL 33572

Dear Mayor Steiner:
I believe our city should have a leash law. Unleashed dogs often run away from their owners and get lost. They dash into busy streets. They get hit by cars. Some dogs scare bike riders and cause serious accidents.

You have said that people would not obey a leash law. I believe they would if they knew that the law would protect their dogs.

I'm sure you'll agree that our city needs a leash law.

Respectfully,
Roberto Gomez
Roberto Gomez

PUBLISHING IDEAS	
Share Aloud	**Share in Writing**
Produce a radio talk show. Take turns being the host. Have guests read their letters "over the air." Encourage listeners to "call in" to agree or disagree.	Mail or deliver your letter. Be sure to address the envelope correctly. Perhaps you will get a letter back!

CURRICULUM ◆CONNECTION◆

Writing Across the Curriculum

Social Studies

During this unit you read about Vinnie Ream. Her sculpture of President Lincoln shows the sadness he felt for his war-torn country. The paintings and photographs in social studies texts can enrich your study of history. Look carefully. You can often imagine the thoughts and feelings of the people they show.

Writing to Learn

Think and Imagine ◆ Look at the picture below. It shows people who have left their homeland to come to America. Write a thought balloon for one of the people in the picture.

Thought Balloon

Courtesy of Mr. August A. Busch, Jr.

Write ◆ Think about the picture and your thought balloon. Write about what it might feel like to emigrate to another country.

Writing in Your Journal

In the Writer's Warm-up you wrote about the visual arts. Throughout the unit you saw how the arts can help us remember people. Someday, a photograph, portrait, or other form of art might help people remember *you*. In your journal describe how you would like to be remembered.

Read More About It

Dorothea Lange: Life Through the Camera
by Milton Meltzer
Dorothea Lange (1895–1965) worked very hard to become a professional photographer. She used her camera to capture scenes of American life. Read this biography of a pioneering artist.

Snap! *by Miriam Cooper*
You can be a photographer, too. All you need to begin is a camera, some film, and the desire to take pictures. This book will help you understand how cameras work and how to plan good pictures.

WOMEN
OF OUR TIME
DOROTHEA LANGE
LIFE THROUGH THE CAMERA

BY MILTON MELTZER
ILLUSTRATIONS BY DONNA DIAMOND
PHOTOGRAPHS BY DOROTHEA LANGE

Book Report Idea   Model a Book

Visual book reports can persuade readers to try a new book. The next time you share a book, choose a character or object that represents the book you have read. Make a simple sculpture or model of it.

Create a Sculpture ◆ Use clay, plaster, wire, papier-mâché, or any other sculpting material you like to use. Create a model or sculpture of a main character or important idea that represents your book. When your model is finished, write a brief book report on a card. Place the card next to your model for display.

Matthew Brady was a pioneer in photography. He and his helpers traveled with heavy, old-fashioned camera equipment to take pictures of the Civil War.

UNIT REVIEW

Unit 4

Pronouns *pages 176–185*

A. Write the pronoun in each sentence. Then write whether it is a *subject pronoun* or an *object pronoun.*

1. Sandy and I like Chinese food.
2. Bill told her about a new restaurant called Hunan Village.
3. It is located on Mott Street.
4. We ate there last night.
5. They make a delicious dish of asparagus and beef.
6. The chef cooks it with seven spices.
7. He prepares many terrific dishes.
8. Sandy wants to try them all!
9. Andrea told us about a fine Indian restaurant.
10. Last week we had dinner there.
11. You ought to try the restaurant.
12. Sandy spoke with the waiter and gave him a good tip.
13. She recommends the restaurant.
14. Tell me about Mexican food.
15. It uses many spices, right?
16. Connie gave me a recipe for Mexican-style chicken.
17. Grandma cooked it with two different kinds of chili peppers.
18. We enjoyed the delicious chicken.
19. I soon became very thirsty.
20. Connie would be happy to give you the recipe.

B. Write each sentence. Use the pronoun in parentheses ( ) that correctly completes the sentence.

21. Will you lend me (your, yours) record album?
22. I accidently broke (my, mine).
23. (Her, Hers) is one of the best voices I have heard.
24. (My, Mine) sister likes many rock singers.
25. Come to (my, mine) house this afternoon.
26. We will play one of (her, hers) records.
27. That group blends (their, theirs) voices beautifully.
28. (Their, Theirs) is a difficult type of singing.
29. (They, Them) do it very well.
30. There is always music in (our, ours) home.
31. Few families are more musical than (our, ours).
32. (My, Mine) mother loves to sing.
33. We often sing along with (her, hers) after dinner.
34. (My, Mine) oldest brother plays in a jazz band.
35. He works hard at (him, his) music.
36. Will you tell me about (your, yours) musical talents?
37. What about that sister of (your, yours) who plays the trumpet?
38. Beth told me about (her, hers) uncle Stanley.
39. We saw (him, his) play a concert in our town.
40. (Him, His) dream is to appear at Carnegie Hall some day.

Contractions *pages 186–187*

C. Write the contraction for each pair of words.

41. we are
42. I am
43. she is
44. you will
45. they had
46. you are
47. we will
48. it is
49. I have
50. they have
51. he will
52. it has
53. he would
54. she had
55. I will
56. we had
57. you have
58. they are

Homophones *pages 188–189*

D. Write the sentences. Use the homophones in parentheses ( ) that correctly complete the sentences.

59. (Its, It's) a beautiful day down by the (sea, see) today.
60. (Would, Wood) you like to (sale, sail) my boat with me?
61. (Meat, Meet) me on the dock at (ate, eight) o'clock.
62. You might (knot, not) have time (to, too) eat breakfast.
63. I have saved a delicious golden (pair, pear) (four, for) you.
64. I (ate, eight) (two, too) of these juicy fruits earlier.
65. (Their, They're) perfectly ripe, and I got them on (sail, sale)!
66. Did you (know, no) (hour, our) uncle Leonard?
67. He always (war, wore) a (blew, blue) fishing cap.
68. (Won, One) day it (blew, blue) away and landed on a fish's head!

Fact and Opinion *pages 202–203*

E. Write *fact* or *opinion* for each of the following statements.

69. John Adams was the second President of the United States.
70. John Quincy Adams was the son of John Adams.
71. John Quincy Adams was not as good a President as his father was.
72. The Declaration of Independence was written in 1776.
73. Mathematics is an easy subject.
74. Jupiter is the largest planet in the solar system.
75. *Heidi* is a wonderful movie.
76. My mother is certainly a brilliant lawyer.
77. Not all snakes are poisonous.
78. That brand of soap isn't very good.
79. Austin is the capital of Texas.

F. Write an opinion that goes with each fact below.

80. Blueberries grow on bushes.
81. Nearly all birds can fly.
82. New York is a very large city.
83. A baseball field has four bases.

Business Letters *pages 206–207*

G. Write the following items as if they were parts of business letters. Capitalize and punctuate them correctly.

84. dear madam
85. yours truly
86. dear ms coe
87. sincerely
88. sirs
89. atlanta ga 30305
90. dear sir or madam
91. 425 willow avenue
92. may 31 1990
93. fran's fruit mart

UNIT 1: Sentences   *page 6–15*

A. Write the declarative, interrogative, imperative, and exclamatory sentences. Begin each sentence correctly. Use correct punctuation at the end.

1. what a beautiful sunset
2. a lone bird flew high in the sky
3. can you see the distant mountains from here
4. hand me the binoculars
5. will you go with me to the museum
6. the special showing of the film ends tomorrow
7. how slow you are
8. is your sister ready to go yet
9. the sun sets early in January
10. did Bobbie bring the picnic basket
11. my mother's hobby is archery
12. she has won many contests
13. watch the wren feed its young
14. how funny it is
15. turn up the electric fan
16. have you done your chores for today
17. her cousin is my best friend
18. come over here
19. shall we join the others now
20. his brother plays for a professional basketball team
21. what a great story this is
22. please set the table
23. where did I leave my jacket
24. look out below
25. the lazy cat snoozed on the couch

B. Write each sentence. Underline the complete subject once. Underline the complete predicate twice.

26. I can do a triple somersault.
27. The timid kitten stayed close to its mother.
28. That blue ceramic bowl was made by my mother.
29. Thousands of tiny ants crawled on the sand.
30. The girl in the front seat of the car hummed a tune.
31. An owl in the huge oak tree hooted.
32. Ms. Ryan is a karate expert.
33. The White House is the home of our President.
34. My father's brother is my uncle.
35. A pile of dirty dishes was stacked in the sink.
36. We just missed the bus.
37. Sam is learning to speak Spanish.
38. The runners in the race grew tired.
39. Gloria plays the piano beautifully.
40. Ned's least favorite food is liver.

C. Write the simple subject of each sentence. Write (*You*) if the subject is understood.

41. Mary is my cousin.
42. Bring your record with you.
43. The frightened squirrel fled.
44. Take a picture of our team.
45. A huge blizzard is heading our way.
46. Lend me your field glasses.
47. Send the package by express mail.
48. The herd of elephants stampeded.
49. Watch my bike for me.
50. The man in that car is my father.

D. Write the simple predicate of each of the following sentences.

51. I am writing my essay for American history.
52. Mrs. Diaz has returned from her trip to Mexico.
53. The moon hid behind a cloud.
54. Roger will sing at the music festival.
55. The girls have learned their lines for the school play.
56. The wind blew through the trees.
57. The little man was whistling an old tune.
58. Two cats are howling outside my bedroom window.
59. The small black horse had outrun its rivals.
60. We will harvest the corn crop soon.

Unit 2: Nouns   *pages 60–65*

E. Write the plural form of each noun.

61. horse
62. chicken
63. story
64. turkey
65. box
66. mouse
67. moose
68. bench
69. shelf
70. radish

F. Write *common* or *proper* for each of the following nouns.

71. city
72. Dallas
73. museum
74. Dr. Woods
75. doctor
76. water buffalo
77. Broadway
78. South Carolina
79. spaceship
80. Amazon River

Unit 2: Capital Letters and Periods   *pages 66–69*

G. Write each sentence. Capitalize the proper nouns.

81. My family visited relatives in new orleans, louisiana.
82. The mississippi river flows through this city.
83. We toured the site of the battle of new orleans.
84. General andrew jackson defeated the british there in 1815.
85. My mother and I visited the delgado museum of art.
86. My aunt lives on tulane avenue.
87. We listened to a lively jazz band at preservation hall.

H. Write the sentences. Abbreviate the underlined words.

88. Will you meet me on Pelham <u>Avenue</u>?
89. That car belongs to <u>Doctor</u> Simpson.
90. It snowed on <u>Tuesday</u> morning.
91. Grand <u>Drive</u> is a one-way street.
92. Alan Thomas, <u>Senior</u>, is my father.

Unit 2: Apostrophes   *pages 70–71*

I. Write the possessive form of each noun.

93. tree
94. mice
95. Ms. Peters
96. children
97. schools
98. men
99. citizens
100. dragon
101. princess
102. buses

J. Write the verb from each sentence. Then write whether it is an *action verb* or a *linking verb*.

103. Harold writes funny stories.
104. Sheila is a tremendous athlete.
105. Snow covered the ground.
106. The wind feels cold.
107. You look angry.
108. Mr. Larsen collects rare books.
109. We examined some lovely pictures.
110. This apple tastes sour.
111. Roger hops on one foot.
112. The dog seemed frightened.
113. This milk smells bad.
114. Barbara sniffed the flowers.

K. Write each sentence. Draw one line under the main verb. Draw two lines under the helping verb.

115. Valerie is studying insects.
116. The rain has stopped.
117. The plane will arrive late.
118. The puppies are playing.
119. Lewis had read the book already.
120. We shall go to the opera next Thursday.
121. Donald was visiting his uncle.
122. The actors have rehearsed all afternoon.
123. Mr. Brooks will announce the contest's outcome.
124. I am painting a portrait of my grandfather.
125. Claudia has lost her keys.
126. The boys were raking the leaves.
127. The leaves had fallen overnight.

L. Write the direct object of each sentence. Then write *what* or *whom* to show what question the direct object answers.

128. I invited Miguel to my house.
129. We ate a delicious dinner.
130. The baby chicks made soft sounds.
131. Tornados frighten me.
132. Suzy helps her sister with the housework.
133. Rico wraps the gift neatly.
134. Ann saw Louise at the playground after lunch.
135. Tina bought a camera yesterday.
136. I found a dollar in the park.
137. The fine weather pleased the picnickers.
138. Dave will deliver the newspapers.
139. This photograph shows my entire family.
140. Jeb threw the ball in the air.

M. Write the verb in each sentence. Then write *present*, *past*, or *future* to show what tense it is.

141. Dorothy sings well.
142. The ferocious lion growled loudly.
143. Ms. Tanaka will present the award.
144. Sean told us about his trip.
145. I shall solve the mystery eventually.
146. Marie has twin brothers.
147. The duck waddled toward the pond.
148. The rain will fall for hours.
149. The doctor examines the patient.
150. The student in the front row raised his hand.
151. Jodi will train her new puppy.
152. The kangaroo hops across a field.

N. Write the past-tense form of each verb.

153. eat	**163.** take
154. run	**164.** walk
155. go	**165.** fly
156. grow	**166.** jump
157. do	**167.** see
158. fall	**168.** ride
159. try	**169.** carry
160. buy	**170.** think
161. sing	**171.** meet
162. bake	**172.** greet

O. Write the verb in parentheses ( ) that correctly completes each sentence.

173. (Can, May) you do a cartwheel?
174. You (can, may) go to the party.
175. Florence (sets, sits) next to me.
176. (Set, Sit) the books on the desk.

Unit 4: Pronouns *pages 176–185*

P. Write the pronoun in each sentence. Then write whether it is a *subject pronoun* or an *object pronoun*.

177. Ms. Reed told them the good news.
178. I eat fresh fruit for dessert.
179. Hand me the chalkboard eraser.
180. It has fallen onto the floor.
181. The zany clown entertained us.
182. Laura's uncle invited her to Ohio.
183. She is leaving home on Saturday.
184. Adventure stories can take you to faraway places.
185. You would like Mr. Watie.
186. He is a terrific teacher.
187. We finally found the missing cat.
188. Dan discovered it behind a bush.
189. Mr. and Mrs. Taylor thanked him.
190. They were worried about the cat.

Q. Write each sentence. Use the pronoun in parentheses ( ) that correctly completes the sentence.

191. (We, Us) are rehearsing the play.
192. The director has chosen Alan and (I, me) for the two main roles.
193. (Her, She) picked Alan for the part of the lion.
194. Alan thanked (her, she).
195. Imagine (he, him) in that role!
196. Alan and (me, I) have always wanted to act in a play.
197. The audience gave (us, we) a standing ovation.
198. (Them, They) must have enjoyed the play.

R. Write each sentence. Underline the possessive pronoun.

199. That kite is mine.
200. Your father called last night.
201. Their kitten is only six days old.
202. Al took his baby brother to the zoo.
203. The best model plane was ours.
204. The cat licked its fur.
205. My bicycle is starting to rust.
206. Hers is the newer bicycle.

Unit 4: Contractions
pages 186–187

S. Write the contraction for each pair of words.

207. I shall	**213.** he would
208. she is	**214.** you have
209. it has	**215.** I am
210. you will	**216.** we are
211. he had	**217.** they will
212. they are	**218.** she has

A Pronoun Acrostic

In an acrostic the first letters of the lines spell a word. Write a pronoun acrostic like the one below. Each line must begin with a subject pronoun and end with an object pronoun. (Hint: Try *wit*, *this*, *with*, or *sit* as your acrostic word, or use *hit* for a baseball acrostic.)

She and I saw you and him.
He knew her, and I knew you.
You and she introduced me.

Pronoun Gymnastics

Figure out the six pronouns from the clues below.

1. Take the monkey out of *shape* and add a vowel. You have a subject.
2. Drop the *h* from sixty minutes. You have a possessive.
3. Add a *t* to the bottom edge of a skirt to form this object.
4. Take an ear out of the twelve months and add two vowels. This one can be a subject or an object.
5. Drop the *m* from *gloom* and turn the rest into a house made of ice. Now remove the house's glue and this subject will stand alone.
6. Drop the first four letters from the small animal that hops. You have a subject or an object.

Unit 4 Extra Practice

1 Writing with Pronouns

p. 176

A. Write each sentence. Underline the pronoun.

> **EXAMPLE:** Vote for your favorite movie star.
> **ANSWER:** Vote for <u>your</u> favorite movie star.

1. We watched a silent movie.
2. Michael had borrowed it from the library.
3. Mr. Oppenheim asked me to turn out the lights.
4. Could you see the screen easily?
5. Was Charlie Chaplin your first choice?
6. In this film a young woman helps him.
7. The Little Fellow becomes her friend.
8. They walk down the road together.
9. The Marx Brothers—Groucho, Harpo, Chico, and Zeppo—always make us laugh.
10. Their act is usually the same.
11. Chico and Harpo often get them into trouble.
12. Chico outsmarts his brother Groucho.
13. We love to hear Harpo play the harp.
14. Our favorite Marx Brothers film is *A Night at the Opera*.
15. Harold Lloyd films are my mother's favorites.

B. Write both sentences in each pair. Underline the pronoun in sentence **b**. Underline the noun or nouns in sentence **a** that the pronoun replaces.

16. **a.** Marla decided to make a movie.
    b. She would be the producer and director.
17. **a.** Carlos and Rana heard about the movie.
    b. Marla wanted them to be the stars.
18. **a.** Marla filmed Carlos's special stunts.
    b. His best stunt was tightrope walking.
19. **a.** Rana's scene also had a special effect.
    b. Her finest scene featured a disappearing act.
20. **a.** Marla showed the movie to her family.
    b. Marla's brother and sister enjoyed it very much.

2 Subject Pronouns
p. 178

A. Write each sentence. Underline the subject pronoun.

1. Yesterday I studied several maps of Canada.
2. It is the second largest country in the world.
3. Did you know that Canada has ten provinces?
4. We went to the province of Quebec.
5. It was settled by the French in the early 1600s.
6. Today they speak both French and English there.
7. You can see signs written in both languages.
8. I heard German and Italian spoken in Ontario.
9. We traveled 4,280 miles on the Trans-Canada Highway.
10. In Nova Scotia I talked to a Scottish Canadian dancer.
11. She danced a lively Highland fling.

B. Write each sentence. Use a subject pronoun in place of the underlined word or words.

12. Jeannette Clery speaks both French and English.
13. After the dance competition, Maureen and Patrick had tea.
14. Nova Scotia was a new home for many Scottish people.
15. The Scots and the Irish settled in eastern Canada.
16. James MacGregor Anderson played the bagpipes.

C. Write the sentences. Complete each sentence with the singular (S) or the plural (P) subject pronoun that you use to talk about yourself.

17. (P) liked Winnipeg.
18. (S) sailed to Halifax.
19. (P) skied in Montreal.
20. (S) saw a caribou.

3 Object Pronouns
p. 180

A. Write the object pronoun in each sentence.

1. Ramona told us about South America.
2. Sal asked her to talk about the countries there.
3. Ramona described them well.
4. Peru particularly interested me.
5. Ramona described it as mountainous.

B. Write the second sentence of each pair. Underline the object pronoun.

   6. Copper ore comes from Chile. Mining companies sell it around the world.
   7. Many farmers in Ecuador grow bananas. Merchants buy them after the harvest.
   8. Señora Torres exports coffee. Brazilian coffee growers supply her with coffee.
   9. Manfred visited an oil well in Venezuela. A relative invited him there.
   10. Sam worked on a cattle ranch in Argentina last year. Sam may take you along next year.

C. Write each sentence. Use an object pronoun in place of the underlined words.

   11. Puerto Rico welcomed Christopher Columbus in 1493.
   12. Columbus claimed the island for Spain.
   13. Columbus's crew tasted the fruits and vegetables.
   14. Later they told Queen Isabella about the strange foods.
   15. The Spaniards did not like the corn.

D. Write the sentences. Complete each sentence with the singular (S) or the plural (P) object pronoun you use to talk about yourself.

   16. A guide told (P).   **19.** The captain knew (P).
   17. Felipe invited (S).   **20.** A friend asked (S).
   18. Carlos helped (S).   **21.** Sonia saw (P).

4 Possessive Pronouns
                                                                    p. 182

A. Write the possessive pronoun in each sentence.

   1. Cleaning up is our job today.
   2. My brother is washing the dishes.
   3. The easiest chore is mine.
   4. I will clean your room.
   5. Yours is the neatest room.
   6. Molly's room is messier than his room.

B. Write each sentence. Use the pronoun in parentheses ( ) that correctly completes the sentence.

7. Chim and Cam want to clean (their, theirs) bookcase.
8. Ming Chin has offered (her, hers) help.
9. Please bring (your, yours) ladder.
10. (My, Mine) is too short to reach the top shelves.
11. (Our, Ours) first step is to take everything out.
12. The books about snakes are (your, yours).
13. Which books are (their, theirs)?
14. Where is (my, mine) car magazine?
15. Cam says the mystery stories are (her, hers).

C. Write each sentence. Use a possessive pronoun in place of the underlined word or words.

16. Eddie helped Eddie's sister bathe the dog.
17. They put Eddie and Doris's dog in the tub.
18. The dog has the dog's own shampoo.
19. Doris decided to use Doris's instead.
20. Doris said that drying the dog was Doris's job.
21. The towel she used was Eddie's.
22. Eddie trimmed the pet's nails.

5 Using Pronouns

p. 184

A. Write each sentence. Use the word or words in parentheses ( ) that correctly complete the sentence.

1. (I and Dora, Dora and I) would like to thank you for the tour of your bakery.
2. You helped (she, her) and me with our project.
3. (She, Her) and I enjoyed meeting your helpers.
4. You and (they, them) explained everything so clearly.
5. We especially liked watching you and (they, them).
6. Dora's brother asked her and (I, me) about our report.
7. I told (he, him) about your bakery.
8. (He, Him) and Teresa tasted the rolls you made.
9. Our friends and (we, us) would like to visit again.
10. Would you show (we, us) how to make bread?

B. Write each sentence. Use the pronoun in parentheses ( ) that correctly completes the sentence. Then write whether the pronoun you used is a subject or an object pronoun.

11. Luis and (I, me) wrote to the Tiny Toy Company.
12. (He, Him) and I asked for some information.
13. The president of the company answered (he, him) and me.
14. She thanked Luis and (I, me) for our letter.
15. She told (we, us) about the company.
16. (She, Her) and the vice-president invited our parents and us to visit the company.
17. Our parents and (we, us) accepted the invitation.
18. The president showed (they, them) and us the factory.
19. We thanked (she, her) and the vice-president.
20. Then (they, them) and we said good-by.

6 Contractions

p. 186

A. Write the contraction for each pair of words.

1. we will   **5.** you are   **9.** I am   **13.** they have
2. it is   **6.** I will   **10.** it has   **14.** we are
3. I would   **7.** she has   **11.** I had   **15.** you would
4. we shall   **8.** you have   **12.** he is   **16.** they are

B. Write the contraction in each sentence. Then write the words from which the contraction is formed.

17. I'm going camping in a Tennessee mountain range.
18. It's called the Great Smoky Mountains.
19. The mountains look smoky because they're covered with a blue-gray haze.
20. After camping we'll go to Oak Ridge.
21. We've always wanted to visit the American Museum of Science and Energy in Oak Ridge.
22. We're also planning a trip to Memphis.
23. I'd like to visit Nashville, too.
24. They've named it the country-music capital of the world.
25. You've probably heard of the Grand Ole Opry House.
26. Uncle Sy said he'll take us there for a concert.

UNIT FIVE

USING LANGUAGE TO
DESCRIBE

Writing
IN YOUR JOURNAL

WRITER'S WARM-UP ◆ What lasting impressions have you experienced? Have you had a memorable experience that is still as vivid today as the day it happened? You may have a special friend who told you something you'll never forget. Perhaps you can picture a place you once visited as vividly as if you were there right now. Why do you think some experiences remain so sharp in our memories? Write in your journal. Tell about a lasting impression you have. Tell why you think it is so vivid to you.

Imagine that you are on a space flight orbiting the Earth. What words would you use to describe how the Earth looks from space?

1 Writing with Adjectives

When we write, we often need words that add important details. Such words are adjectives. An adjective tells something about a noun or a pronoun. An adjective often answers the question ''What kind?'' or ''How many?''

Notice the difference between the following two sentences.

- **Astronauts put on helmets.**
- **Five <u>confident</u> astronauts put on <u>the</u> <u>strong</u> and <u>shiny</u> helmets.**

The second sentence is much more vivid than the first. The adjectives in the second sentence are underlined. They add interesting details. *Confident, strong*, and *shiny* help readers see the astronauts and the helmets. They tell *what kind*. The adjective *five* tells *how many*.

Notice that the word *the* is also underlined. *A, an*, and *the* are a special kind of adjective called an **article.** Use *a* before a word that begins with a consonant sound. Use *an* before a word that begins with a vowel sound.

- <u>a</u> rocket   <u>an</u> immense rocket   <u>an</u> astronaut   <u>a</u> brave astronaut

> **Summary** ◆ An **adjective** describes a noun or a pronoun. Use adjectives to add details to your writing.

Guided Practice

Name the adjectives in these sentences. Include articles.

1. Sally Ride is a true pioneer.
2. She was the first woman from the United States to fly in space.
3. Sally Ride was a dedicated and exceptional student.
4. Sally's favorite subject in school was science.
5. She never dreamed she would become a famous astronaut.

Practice

A. The sentences below tell about Sally Ride's flight in the space shuttle *Challenger*. Write the adjectives in each sentence. Include articles.

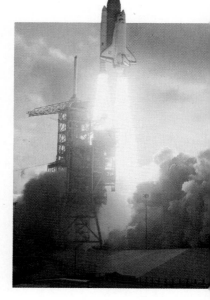

    6. At dawn on June 18, 1983, the gleaming *Challenger* waited.

    7. Soon Sally Ride and four other astronauts would zoom into space.

    8. The powerful shuttle roared into the clear sky above Florida.

    9. A trail of bright hot flame followed the speedy *Challenger*.

    10. The powerful force of gravity pressed on the five astronauts.

    11. The uncomfortable feeling lasted for a few minutes.

    12. When sufficient altitude was achieved, a smooth and peaceful ride followed.

    13. Sally Ride enjoyed the new and startling feeling of weightlessness.

    14. Cheerful astronauts floated about the cabin.

    15. The astronauts performed many important experiments.

B. Write each group of words. Use the correct article.

    16. (a, an) orbiting space shuttle

    17. (a, an) spectacular view

    18. (a, an) open cargo bay

    19. (a, an) broken satellite

    20. (a, an) successful mission

C. Write each sentence. Use an adjective to complete it.

    21. The _____ space voyage neared its end.

    22. The spacecraft glided toward the _____ ground below.

    23. The space shuttle made a _____ landing.

    24. The astronauts walked across the _____ runway.

    25. They took one final look at the _____ space shuttle.

Apply ◆ Think and Write

From Your Writing ◆ Read what you wrote for the Writer's Warm-up. Try to make your writing more vivid by changing some of the adjectives.

✎ **Remember**
to use adjectives
to make
your writing
colorful
and interesting.

◆ GETTING ◆
STARTED

Change one adjective to another by changing one letter in the word. Use both of the adjectives in sentences. For example: *The road was bumpy. The gravy was lumpy.*

2 Adjectives After Linking Verbs

Adjectives often come before the nouns they describe.

■ The **fascinating** books are by Laura Ingalls Wilder.

Adjectives can also follow the nouns or pronouns they describe.

The characters are memorable.

Charles Ingalls was brave.

He felt secure and relaxed in the wilderness.

In the sentences above, the adjectives *memorable*, *brave*, *secure*, and *relaxed* are predicate adjectives. A predicate adjective describes the subject of the sentence. Sometimes the subject is a noun like *characters*. Sometimes it is a pronoun like *he*.

A linking verb connects a predicate adjective with the subject. The most commonly used linking verbs are forms of the verb *be*: *am*, *is*, *are*, *was*, and *were*. Some other linking verbs are *seem*, *look*, *feel*, *taste*, *smell*, and *become*.

> **Summary** ◆ An adjective that follows a linking verb describes the subject of a sentence. Use predicate adjectives to add details to your writing.

Guided Practice

Name the predicate adjectives in the sentences. Tell which noun or pronoun in the subject each adjective describes.

1. The Ingalls were comfortable in their home in Wisconsin.
2. However, the woods became crowded.
3. Charles Ingalls was anxious and restless.

Practice

A. Write each sentence about Laura Ingalls Wilder's book, *Little House on the Prairie*. Draw one line under each predicate adjective. (Several sentences have more than one.) Draw two lines under the noun or pronoun it describes.

EXAMPLE: Charles Ingalls was sensitive to his family's needs.

ANSWER: <u><u>Charles Ingalls</u></u> was <u>sensitive</u> to his family's needs.

4. The morning was cold and quiet for the Ingalls' departure.
5. The sky was pale in the east.
6. The frozen lake seemed empty and still.
7. Laura felt better after spotting a little log house.
8. The westward journey seemed endless.
9. The land became black after sundown.
10. The stars seemed close in the dark sky.
11. The Ingalls' campfire looked tiny.
12. Their new log cabin was solid and sturdy.
13. Pa Ingalls was proud of his house on the prairie.

B. Write sentences for each pair of adjectives and nouns. Use a linking verb, and use the adjective as a predicate adjective.

EXAMPLE: industrious Pa Ingalls

ANSWER: Pa Ingalls was industrious.

14. long logs
15. hard work
16. helpful neighbor
17. snug house
18. warm campfire

19. delicious supper
20. strong wind
21. vast sky
22. bright moon
23. fresh air

C. 24–28. Use the model below to write five sentences of your own.

<u>(Noun)</u> <u>(linking verb)</u> <u>(predicate adjective)</u>.

Apply ♦ Think and Write

Dictionary of Knowledge ♦ Read about the author Laura Ingalls Wilder and her life on the prairie. Write some sentences about her. Use predicate adjectives in each of your sentences.

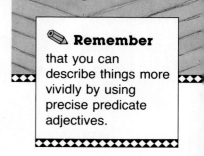

✏️ **Remember**
that you can describe things more vividly by using precise predicate adjectives.

Choose two persons, places, or things. Compare the nouns in each pair, using as many *-er* words as you can. For example: *Arizona is bigger (warmer, drier) than Vermont.*

3 Adjectives That Compare

Adjectives describe nouns. One way they describe is by comparing persons, places, or things. When you want to compare two nouns, use the *-er* form of the adjective. In the sentence below, two folk heroes are compared.

■ **John Henry was <u>stronger</u> than Casey Jones.**

When you want to compare three or more nouns, use the *-est* form of the adjective. In the sentence below, John Henry is compared with all the persons in a group.

■ **John Henry was the <u>strongest</u> of all the railroad workers.**

When you write, you sometimes have to change the spelling of an adjective to add *-er* or *-est*.

Drop final e:	brav<u>e</u>	braver	bravest
Change final y to i:	heav<u>y</u>	heavier	heaviest
Double final consonant:	hot<u> </u>	hotter	hottest

> **Summary** ◆ When you speak and write, use the *-er* form of an adjective to compare two persons, places, or things. Use the *-est* form of an adjective to compare three or more persons, places, or things.

Guided Practice

Tell which word in parentheses ( ) correctly completes each sentence.

1. Digging a railroad tunnel is (harder, hardest) than other work.
2. John Henry was the (faster, fastest) worker on the railroad.
3. Casey Jones was the (braver, bravest) of all engineers.
4. Casey's Cannonball Express was (faster, fastest) than the local train.

Practice

A. Write each sentence. Use the form of the adjective shown in parentheses ( ).

    5. Railroad steel drivers were (strong + -er) than other workers.

    6. Sheep-nose hammers were the (fine + -est) tools available.

    7. The (heavy + -est) spikes were hammered in place.

    8. Even the (long + -est) tunnels were drilled by hand.

    9. Automatic steam drills were used in (late + -er) times.

   10. John Henry's two hammers were the (large + -est) of all.

   11. His arms were (big + -er) than tree trunks.

   12. His (fierce + -est) duel was against the steam drill.

   13. John Henry's hammers were (speedy + -er) than the steam drill.

   14. He dug (deep + -er) holes than the steam drill but died doing it.

B. Write each sentence. Use the correct form of the adjective in parentheses ( ).

   15. Casey Jones's Cannonball Express was the (swift) train of all.

   16. A freight train that was (big) than a monster blocked the track.

   17. Casey's grip on the brakes was (firm) than a wrench.

   18. His locomotive slammed into the freight train with the (loud) bang of all.

   19. The death of Casey Jones may be the (sad) tale I know.

C. 20–24. Write five pairs of sentences that use adjectives to compare. Use the model below for each pair.

   The (noun) is (adjective) than the (noun).
   The (noun) is the (adjective) of all.

Apply ◆ Think and Write

Descriptive Comparisons ◆ Think of two characters you know through stories and songs. Write several sentences comparing the two characters.

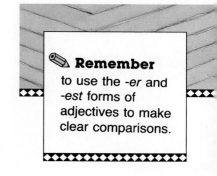

✎ Remember
to use the *-er* and *-est* forms of adjectives to make clear comparisons.

4 Using *more* and *most* with Adjectives

Some adjectives do not use the *-er* or *-est* form to compare.

One syllable: calm   calmer   calmest
Two or more syllables: inspiring   more inspiring   most inspiring

Many adjectives of two or more syllables use *more* or *most* to make comparisons. *More* is used with an adjective to compare two persons, places, or things. *Most* is used with an adjective to compare three or more persons, places, or things.

Luisa is a <u>more powerful</u> speaker than you are.
Dr. Martin Luther King, Jr., was the <u>most powerful</u> speaker of all.

Never use *more* before the *-er* form of an adjective.

Wrong: Dr. King was more braver than I.
Right: Dr. King was braver than I.

Never use *most* before the *-est* form of an adjective.

Wrong: Dr. King was the most bravest person I know.
Right: Dr. King was the bravest person I know.

Notice how the adjectives *good* and *bad* show comparison.

a <u>good</u> speech   a <u>better</u> speech   the <u>best</u> speech
a <u>bad</u> situation   a <u>worse</u> situation   the <u>worst</u> situation

> **Summary** ◆ When you make comparisons, you must often use *more* and *most* with adjectives of two or more syllables.

Guided Practice

For each adjective below, name the two forms used to compare.

1. tall   **2.** sincere   **3.** good   **4.** admirable   **5.** serious

Practice

A. Write each sentence. Use the correct form of the adjective in parentheses ( ).

6. Martin Luther King, Jr., was (smart) than his classmates.
7. His grades were the (impressive) of all.
8. When he entered Morehouse College, he was (young) than most of his classmates.
9. His decision to be a minister was the (wise) one of all.
10. Dr. King was the (courageous) leader in the struggle for equal rights.
11. Dr. King's pleas for justice are some of the (great) speeches of his time.
12. His (memorable) speech proclaimed "I have a dream."
13. His deeds were even (honorable) than his words.
14. The Nobel Peace Prize was his (important) honor.
15. Dr. Martin Luther King, Jr., was one of the (inspiring) of all leaders.

B. Write the sentences about the essay contest on Dr. Martin Luther King, Jr. Use the correct form of *good* or *bad* to complete each sentence.

16. This year's essays were (good) than last year's.
17. Liu's essay was the (good) of all.
18. Finishing second was the (bad) disappointment for me.
19. It felt like nothing (bad) than that could ever happen.
20. My next essay will be (good) than this one.

C. Write four sentences that compare persons, places, or things. Use the following adjectives in your sentences.

21. sincere **22.** honest **23.** truthful **24.** brave

Apply ◆ Think and Write

Descriptive Comparisons ◆ Write sentences comparing two famous people of the twentieth century. One might be Dr. Martin Luther King, Jr. Use a variety of adjectives, including several that need *more* or *most*, to make comparisons.

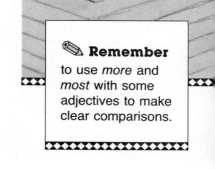

✎ **Remember** to use *more* and *most* with some adjectives to make clear comparisons.

Penny is penniless, homeless, jobless, shoeless, sleepless, *and* restless. *How many other words ending in* -less *can you think of to describe Penny?*

VOCABULARY ◆
Adjective Suffixes

You have already learned that a prefix—a word part added to the beginning of a word—changes a word's meaning. For example, *un-* can be added to *happy* to form *unhappy*.

A word part can also be added to the end of a word. For example, *-less* can be added to *luck* to form *luckless*. A word part added to the end of a word is called a **suffix**. A suffix also changes the meaning of a word.

Remember that a base word is the simplest form of a word. Many adjectives are formed by adding a suffix to a base word. Here are some common suffixes and their meanings.

Suffix	Meaning	Example
-able	worthy of, able to be	honorable, likable
-ful	full of, having qualities of	helpful, beautiful
-less	without	tasteless, colorless
-y	having, being like	funny, fuzzy

Notice how the spellings change when suffixes are added to base words like these: like, likable; beauty, beautiful; fun, funny.

Building Your Vocabulary

Your family is having a picnic. You are having a wonderful time. Suddenly, however, you notice a huge band of dark clouds quickly covering the sky. Tell more about your picnic. Use adjectives made from the words below.

storm	wind	harm	power	rain
cloud	help	scare	enjoy	care

Practice

A. Write each sentence. Add one of the suffixes below to the word in parentheses ( ) to complete the sentence.

-able   -ful   -less   -y

1. That shirt is too expensive; it is not (afford).
2. The cobblestone road was long and (bump).
3. Maria was well liked because she was very (thought).
4. The ride by wagon was quite (uncomfort).
5. It was a (cloud) and (star) night.
6. Steven bakes (wonder) chocolate chip cookies.
7. The cat crouched (motion) under the bush.
8. The young soldier was (fear) in the face of danger.

B. *Joyful* means "full of joy." *Joyless* means "without joy." Use *-ful* and *-less* to form adjectives from the words in parentheses.

9. Thad was (help) to the (help) bird with the broken wing.
10. A (power) bear grabbed the (power) salmon.
11. Airline mechanics must do (care), not (care), work.
12. The garter snake is (harm), but the rattlesnake is (harm).

C. Write a word for each definition. Use the suffixes below.

-able   -ful   -less   -y

13. without life
14. full of peace
15. being like a mouse
16. having scales
17. able to break
18. without worth

LANGUAGE CORNER ◆ Acronyms

Have you ever been scuba diving? *Scuba* is an **acronym**, a word made from the first letters of *self-contained underwater breathing apparatus. Soth* might be an acronym for *students opposed to homework.* Make some acronyms of your own.

Self
  Contained
    Underwater
      Breathing
        Apparatus

How to Expand Sentences with Adjectives

You have been using adjectives to write more colorful and interesting sentences. Adjectives can make a difference in your writing. The ones you choose can add details that will help readers create clear pictures in their minds. Which sentence below gives you a better description of what Dale delivers?

■ **1.** **Dale delivers dinners and desserts.**
■ **2.** **Dale delivers delicious dinners and delightful desserts.**

Both sentences tell us what Dale delivers, but sentence **2** gives us much more than the facts. Sentence **2** includes adjectives that describe the nouns *dinners* and *desserts*. The adjectives *delicious* and *delightful* make Dale's meals sound very inviting.

Different adjectives could give an entirely different picture. Would you order a meal from Dale if he served the food described in sentence **3**?

■ **3.** **Dale delivers dreadful dinners and drab desserts.**

The Grammar Game ♦ Get active with adjectives! Choose a noun and write three adjectives that describe it. Try to include adjectives that appeal to different senses. Then choose another noun and start again. Can you write adjectives for all of the nouns below?

tiger	dream	machine	explorer	castle
idea	skateboard	mountain	fire	flag
dancer	sweater	tower	planet	elephant
ocean	house	boots	winter	bridge

Working Together

As you do activities **A** and **B** with your group, use adjectives to add interesting details to your writing.

In Your Group
◆ Use people's names during discussion.
◆ Help keep everyone on the topic.
◆ Record all ideas and suggestions.
◆ Agree or disagree in a pleasant way.

A. Use two adjectives of the group's choice to describe each noun below. Then have the group choose a person, place, or thing that fits the description.

EXAMPLE: athlete
ANSWER: outstanding female athlete — Wilma Rudolph

1. _____ guitarist
2. _____ story
3. _____ hamburger
4. _____ town
5. _____ rabbit
6. _____ lake
7. _____ movie
8. _____ building
9. _____ song
10. _____ beach
11. _____ hair
12. _____ fruit

B. Expand each sentence by adding at least one adjective of the group's choice. The adjective must begin with the same sound as the noun it describes. Then make up more tongue twisters.

EXAMPLE: Tailors took tacks to Toytown.
ANSWER: Ten tall tailors took tiny tacks to tough Toytown.

13. Bruce brought back bread from the bakery.
14. Nora's niece nibbles noodles.
15. Oliver owns an owl and oysters.
16. Parrots polished pails of pineapples at the park.
17. A ram read riddles and rules on Roger's roof.

WRITERS' CORNER • Overused Adjectives

Using the same adjectives too many times can make your writing dull and boring. Avoid using words like *great* and *good* too often.

OVERUSED: The movie was good because the acting was good and the ending was especially good.
IMPROVED: The movie was delightful because the acting was superb and the ending was especially clever.

Read what you wrote for the Writer's Warm-up. Did you overuse any adjectives? Could you replace any overused adjective with a different descriptive word?

SPACIOUS SKIES *quilt by Charlotte Warr-Andersen, Kearns, Utah. Collection of the Museum of American Folk Art; Museum of American Folk Art: The Scotchgard Collection of Contemporary Quilts.*

USING LANGUAGE
TO
DESCRIBE

===== **PART TWO** =====

Literature   *Zeely* by Virginia Hamilton
A Reason for Writing Describing

CREATIVE
Writing

FINE ARTS ◆ Look at the images on the quilt at the left. The quilt seems to present images of America. Quilts can picture almost anything the designer wants. Imagine that you are designing a quilt. What would you like it to represent? Plan a quilt that shows images that are important to you. Write a description of your quilt. Tell what designs or pictures you would include.

CREATIVE THINKING ◆
A Strategy for Describing

A THOUGHT BALLOON

Describing is using details to paint word pictures. Authors use descriptive writing to make story characters come alive. After this lesson, you will read part of *Zeely* by Virginia Hamilton. It is a story with many interesting and well-described characters. Later you will describe someone when you write a character sketch.

What is a character description? It may be about the outside, how a person looks or acts. It may also be about the inside, how a person thinks and feels. In *Zeely*, Virginia Hamilton puts the reader right inside a young girl's mind. In this passage the girl, Geeder, is spending the night outdoors.

> She had closed her eyes again when she heard a rustling sound on Leadback Road. . . . Night travellers! She dove under the covers. But something's happening! she told herself, poking her head out again. It took all her courage to crawl out of the covers and the few feet over the wet grass up to the hedge. She trembled with fear but peeked through the hedge in spite of it. . . . Something tall and white was moving down the road. It didn't quite touch the ground.

How does Geeder feel when she hears strange sounds at night? Can you understand her point of view? How would *you* feel? Can you see how getting inside a character's mind can make a story interesting and exciting?

◆ Learning the Strategy

Understanding someone else's point of view is often useful. How can you do it? You can put yourself in that person's place. You can imagine how you would feel in the same situation. For example, suppose you have a younger cousin who is afraid to swim. Are you sympathetic? Why? Imagine that you are checking out of a store. You are in a hurry. An elderly person in front of you is moving slowly. Why might you be patient and polite even though you are in a hurry?

Making a thought balloon is one way to help imagine someone's point of view. Consider that cousin who is afraid to swim. The thought balloon below shows what that child might be thinking. What else might your cousin be thinking? What ideas can you add?

I won't be able to float. I'll sink. I'll get too tired.

cousin

Using the Strategy

A. Who is your favorite character from books, movies, or television? Imagine that that character has come to visit your community. How might he or she (or it!) feel about the place? What might that character want to do there? Make a thought balloon for that character about your community. You might want to use the balloon as the basis for a story.

B. Reread the passage from *Zeely* on page 248. What is the white shape coming down the road? Make a thought balloon for Geeder. Write what you think *she* thinks it is. Then read *Zeely* and decide if you—and Geeder—were right!

Applying the Strategy

- How does making a thought balloon help you imagine someone's point of view?
- When have you recently thought about someone else's point of view—and why?

AWARD
WINNING
AUTHOR

from
Zeely
by Virginia Hamilton

LITERATURE: Story

Elizabeth Perry was determined to make this a special summer on Uncle Ross's farm. She began by giving herself and her younger brother the new summer names of Geeder and Toeboy. During her first day on the farm, Geeder also made up names for the town and the road, but not for the huge razorback hogs that Mr. Nat Tayber and his daughter kept on Uncle Ross's land. That evening Geeder made up a story about night travellers.

Geeder told the frightening story as she and Toeboy were sleeping out behind the lilac bush on the farm's front lawn. Geeder could almost see these ghostly creatures, who walk along dark roads at night and scare anyone who dares to watch them. The thought of night travellers going by on Leadback Road kept Geeder and Toeboy awake for a long time. Then they finally fell asleep, hidden safely behind the hedge.

A long time passed. Geeder dozed and awoke with a start. The grass behind the tip of her toes was wet with dew. She pulled the blankets more tightly around her, tucking her feet safely inside. She had closed her eyes again when she heard a rustling sound on Leadback Road.

Some old animal, she thought. The sound grew louder and she could not think what it was. Suddenly, what she had told Toeboy flashed through her mind.

Night travellers! She dove under the covers.

But something's happening! she told herself, poking her head out again.

It took all her courage to crawl out of the covers and the few feet over the wet grass up to the hedge. She trembled with fear but peeked through the hedge in spite of it. What she saw made her bend low, hugging the ground for protection. Truthfully, she wasn't sure what she saw. The branches of the hedge didn't allow much of a view.

Something tall and white was moving down the road. It didn't quite touch the ground. Geeder could hear no sound of footsteps. She couldn't see its head or arms. Beside it and moving with it was something that squeaked ominously. The white, very long figure made a rustling sound when she held her breath. It passed by toward town.

Geeder watched, moving her head ever so slowly until she could no longer see it. After waiting for what seemed hours, quaking at each sound and murmur of the night, she crept back to bed, pulling the covers over her eyes. She lay, cold and scared, unable to think and afraid even to clear her dry throat. This way, she fell asleep. She awoke in the morning, refreshed but stiff in every muscle.

Geeder lay for a moment, watching mist rise from the pink, sweet clover that sprinkled the lawn. The air smelled clean and fresh and was not yet hot from the sun.

"I've got to decide," she whispered. In the stillness, the sound of her own voice startled her. She turned carefully around to see if Toeboy had stirred. The tangled bedding deep in the lilac bush did not move.

"If I tell Toeboy about the night traveller," she whispered, "he might not want to sleep outside any more. Just think of it! Not more than a few hours ago, an awful, spooky thing walked by here!"

Geeder wasn't at all sure she wanted to sleep outside again, herself.

"Goodness knows what a night traveller will do if it sees you watching! Maybe I'd better tell Uncle Ross . . . . Maybe I shouldn't."

Geeder knew it would take her a while to figure out what course to take. Almost any minute now, the people Uncle Ross rented land to would come down the road. Uncle Ross had said they came every morning as soon as the sun was well up in the sky. It was just about time, and watching them would be something to do.

When her dew-soaked blankets grew warm from the sun, Geeder whistled for Toeboy as softly as she could. Turning around, she saw one eye peek out from the lilac bush.

"Wake up, Toeboy!" she whispered loudly. "I think I hear them coming!"

Toeboy leaped up before he looked where he was going

and hit his head against a branch.
Leaves spilled dew all over him.
He was wet and still half asleep
when Geeder yanked him to the
ground before they could be seen.

They knelt low by the hedge. Trying
not to move or blink an eye, they
watched Mr. Tayber and his daughter
come into view along Leadback Road.
What they saw was no ordinary sight.
They watched, spellbound, for nothing
in the world could have prepared them
for the sight of Miss Zeely Tayber.

Zeely Tayber was more than six and
a half feet tall, thin and deeply dark as a
pole of Ceylon ebony. She wore a long
smock that reached to her ankles. Her
arms, hands and feet were bare, and her

thin, oblong head didn't seem to fit quite right on her shoulders.

She had very high cheekbones and her eyes seemed to turn inward on themselves. Geeder couldn't say what expression she saw on Zeely's face. She knew only that it was calm, that it had pride in it, and that the face was the most beautiful she had ever seen.

Zeely's long fingers looked exactly like bean pods left a long time in the sun.

Geeder wanted to make sure Toeboy noticed Zeely's hands but the Taybers were too close, and she was afraid they would hear her.

Mr. Tayber and Zeely carried feed pails, which made a grating sound. It was the only sound on the road besides that of Mr. Tayber's heavy footsteps. Zeely made no sound at all.

You would think she would, thought Geeder, she was so long and tall.

Geeder and Toeboy stayed quiet as the Taybers passed, and the Taybers gave no sign that they saw them hiding there. Uncle Ross had said that they were not known to speak much, even to one another. They had not lived in Crystal always, as Uncle Ross had.

Geeder and Toeboy watched the Taybers until they went out of sight. It was then that Toeboy said, "Let's go watch them in the field."

"No," said Geeder quietly, "no, Toeboy." She could not possibly have made him understand how stunned she had been at seeing Miss Zeely Tayber for the first time. Never in her life had she seen anyone quite like her.

Library Link ◆ *If you would like to read more about Geeder, Toeboy, and Zeely, read* Zeely *by Virginia Hamilton.*

 Reader's Response

Who was your favorite character in the story? Why?

Zeely

 ## Responding to Literature

1. Have you ever been as amazed by your first sight of someone as Geeder was by her first sight of Zeely? Explain.

2. Mr. Tayber and Zeely seem to be mysterious people. What makes a person "mysterious"?

3. Virginia Hamilton paints a word picture of Zeely. Draw a picture of how you think Zeely looks. Show details that make her a special person unlike any other. Underneath the picture write a sentence to tell classmates who or what Zeely reminds you of.

 ## Writing to Learn

Think and Imagine ◆ One way to learn about someone is to imagine what that person is thinking. In a thought balloon write words and phrases Geeder might have been thinking as Zeely and Mr. Tayber walked by her.

Thought Balloon

Write ◆ Write the entry that Geeder might have written in her journal that day.

GETTING STARTED

Choose an intriguing story character, such as Zeely. What questions would you like to ask that person?

SPEAKING and LISTENING ✦
Interviews

Are you interested in people? Do you enjoy talking to people? Do you like to find out what people do, and why? Most of us find people fascinating. That is why people make such good subjects for writers.

One of the best ways for a writer to collect accurate and lively details about a person is to conduct an interview. Before you begin an interview, it is important to prepare for it. Decide what main things you would like to find out about the person. Then develop a list of questions to use while you are interviewing. Write the questions on cards. They are easy to handle. Here are some guidelines to help you conduct an interview.

Asking Interview Questions	1. Avoid questions that can be answered by *yes* or *no*. They are conversation stoppers. 2. Ask questions that encourage your subject to talk—questions that begin with *who*, *what*, *when*, *where*, *why*, and *how*. 3. Keep the interview focused. 4. Take notes or ask permission to use a tape recorder. 5. Thank the person for the interview.
Being an Active Listener	1. *Really* listen, instead of thinking "What will I ask next?" 2. If the person makes a surprising remark, follow up on it. Be willing to leave your prepared list of questions. 3. Watch the person's body language. Watch for a raised eyebrow, a sudden grin, a frown, a glance at the clock. What does it show about the person's feelings? 4. Listen for good quotes and write them down. Later, have the person approve your written quotations.

Summary ✦ Writers interview people to observe and collect details about them. Before you interview someone, prepare a list of questions that focus on your main topics.

Guided Practice

Make up questions you might ask when interviewing each of the people below. Be sure to ask *who*, *what*, *when*, *why*, *where*, and *how* questions.

1. a popular TV star
2. the governor of your state
3. a computer programmer
4. a trapeze artist

Practice

A. Work with a partner. Take turns making up questions that you might ask when interviewing each of the people below. Ask questions that begin with *who*, *what*, *when*, *why*, *where*, and *how*.

    5. a forest ranger
    6. an airline pilot
    7. the owner of a movie theater
    8. an Olympic gymnast

B. Work with a partner. Take turns asking and answering questions you could use when interviewing each person below.

    9. the inventor of the vacuum cleaner
   10. the student who won a national science award

C. Prepare to interview your partner. Make a list of questions you will ask. Then follow the guidelines in this lesson as you interview each other in turn.

Apply ◆ Think and Write

Dictionary of Knowledge ◆ Read about Virginia Hamilton, author of *Zeely* and other award-winning books for young people. What else would you like to know about her? Write five questions you would ask if you could interview this author.

> ✎ **Remember**
> that an interview is a way to gather details about someone you wish to describe.

Choose one of your good friends. Tell three details you would include if you were describing your friend to a stranger. If the class knows your friend, see if they can guess who it is.

WRITING ♦
Organizing Descriptive Details

How could these details be organized into a description of a girl?

well-worn sneakers	space between front teeth	brown eyes
laughs a lot	mischievous eyes	new braces
writing on high tops	great sense of humor	large feet

> Alissa's mischievous brown eyes sparkle when she laughs. She laughs a lot, because she has a great sense of humor. She wears shiny new braces to correct the space between her front teeth. The metal glistens when she grins. The writing on her well-worn high tops distracts anyone who might notice her very large feet.

The details in this descriptive paragraph are organized in space order. Space order is the order in which objects are arranged in space. You can, for example, describe a person from top to bottom, as this writer did. You can also organize details in space order from front to back, left to right, near to far, or bottom to top.

Another way to organize details is by arranging them in their order of importance. You either state the most important detail first, or you build up to it last. For example, read the paragraph below that describes Zeely. (It is also on page 254.) Notice how the author leads up to the proud, serene beauty that Geeder sees in Zeely.

> She had very high cheekbones and her eyes seemed to turn inward on themselves. Geeder couldn't say what expression she saw on Zeely's face. She knew only that it was calm, that it had pride in it, and that the face was the most beautiful she had ever seen.

Summary ♦ **Space order** and **order of importance** are two ways to organize details in a paragraph. They are especially useful ways to organize descriptive writing.

Guided Practice

Tell in what order you would arrange details to describe each item below. Choose *top to bottom*, *bottom to top*, *left to right*, *near to far*, or *front to back*.

1. clothes on a rack
2. the Statue of Liberty
3. shoppers in a checkout line
4. your front door to the curb

Practice

A. Tell in what order you would arrange details to describe each item below. Choose *top to bottom*, *bottom to top*, *left to right*, *near to far*, or *front to back*.

5. the cars in a train
6. a ski slope
7. trophies on a shelf
8. a highway stretching ahead

B. Write the topic sentence below. Under it, write the five details in correct space order.

TOPIC SENTENCE: **Five cars were parked in the driveway.**

9. The station wagon was parked behind the taxicab.
10. The red convertible was parked at the head of the driveway.
11. The black limousine was parked at the end of the driveway.
12. In back of the convertible was the yellow taxicab.
13. The antique sedan was sandwiched between the station wagon and the black limousine.

C. Write the sentences below in the order of their importance. Put the most important detail first.

14. Sparks of color flashed from the fabric as she moved.
15. Threads of gold, red, and blue glimmered in the sun.
16. The robe was of shimmering, multicolored silk.
17. The fabric fell in graceful folds to her ankles.

Apply ◆ Think and Write

Organizing a Description ◆ Describe your favorite outfit—a sports uniform, party clothes, or something you wear to school. Use space order or order of importance to organize your description.

✎ **Remember**
to organize details to help the reader picture what you describe.

In one sentence, give your main impression of an important character in a book you have enjoyed. Can anyone guess who that character is?

WRITING •
A Descriptive Paragraph

Description starts with observation. You notice details that make your subject unique. You observe what a person looks like. You listen to the person's voice and the words he or she uses. When you have finished observing, you will have noticed many details. You will want to use some in your writing and discard others.

How will you decide which details to use and which to discard? You know that a paragraph focuses on one main idea, or topic. Often that topic is stated in a topic sentence. The other sentences give details that support the topic sentence. Details that do not support the topic sentence should be discarded.

How will you begin? Decide what impression you want to create. When you describe a person, think of one adjective that captures your main impression. Use that adjective in a topic sentence.

■ **Judd's manner is overwhelmingly <u>serious</u>.**

Then organize the details. Decide which support the topic and which do not. Decide which support the impression you want to create.

Support the Topic		Do Not Support the Topic	
gentle smile	solemn eyes	nervous laugh	not very tall
moves slowly	listens intently	taps feet	always late

Finally, decide on the best order for arranging the details. In this case, it might be order of importance. When your paragraph is written, the result should be a clearly organized description that creates the impression you want.

Summary ◆ A **descriptive paragraph** has a main idea and descriptive details. Choosing the appropriate details helps you create the desired impression.

Guided Practice

Give a detail that supports each of these topic sentences.

1. Brad looks unhappy today.
2. Anthony looks friendly.
3. Janine is very dignified.
4. Suzanne was really surprised.

Practice

A. Write a detail sentence for each topic sentence below.

    5. Kristen is dressed like a rock star.
    6. Tyrone looks calm and cool.
    7. Brenda appears to be annoyed.
    8. Mark's haircut suits his personality.
    9. Josh definitely looks angry.

B. Read the topic sentence below. Then read sentences **10–14.** Write *yes* if the sentence gives a detail that supports the topic sentence. Write *no* if it does not.

Topic Sentence: Anna is bold and outgoing.

10. When she meets you, she flashes a dazzling smile.
11. She sits in pale silver moonlight, reading poetry.
12. Her eyes sparkle as she talks "a mile a minute."
13. Her favorite outfit is fire-engine red.
14. Her voice is soft and soothing, a mere whisper.

C. Write a paragraph describing one thing about someone you know well.

Apply ◆ Think and Write

A Descriptive Paragraph ◆ Look at the people in the photographs on these two pages. Choose one person to describe. As you study the person, ask yourself, "What is my main impression?" Then write a paragraph that describes the person. Remember to choose details that support your main idea.

> ✎ **Remember**
> to use a main idea and suitable details to build a descriptive paragraph.

Focus on Sensory Words

A writer writes a description hoping that you, the reader, will picture just what he or she had in mind. To do this, the writer uses details. Details are exact bits of information. They are like the focus of a camera, giving a clear image.

In addition, the writer uses **sensory words**. Those are words that appeal to the senses. Sensory words help the reader *see, hear, feel* — and sometimes even *smell* or *taste* — what is being described.

Virginia Hamilton uses both details and sensory words in *Zeely*. You read part of the book earlier in the unit.

DETAILS: "awoke with a start"; "hit his head against a branch"; "carried feed pails"

SENSORY WORDS: "dew-soaked blankets"; "warm from the sun"; "thin and deeply dark"; "made a grating sound"

The details give a specific picture of what was happening —Geeder waking suddenly, Toeboy hitting his head against a branch, Mr. Tayber and Zeely carrying feed pails. The sensory words let you feel the dew-soaked blankets and warmth of the sun. They let you see the appearance of Zeely and hear the sound made by the feed pails.

The Writer's Voice ◆ Look back at the passage from *Zeely*. Find at least five details (in addition to the ones above) that show you what is happening in the story.

Find at least five sensory words in *Zeely* (in addition to the ones above). These words help readers see, hear, feel, smell, or taste.

Working Together

Well-chosen details and sensory words help a reader picture what is being described. Use details and sensory words to create clear descriptions as your group does activities **A** and **B**.

A. What sensory words would help create vivid and accurate pictures in the following sentences? Your group may wish to suggest two or three words for each sentence.

1. After ten minutes in the rain, my wool suit felt ____ .
2. The tall grass made a ____ sound in the gentle wind.
3. Through the trees we saw an abandoned house; its windows were ____ .
4. Church bells ____ cheerily in the small New England town.
5. The chili tasted almost ____ after the blazing hot salsa.

B. With your group, write five sentences like those in activity **A**. Each sentence should focus on a different sense. Leave blanks for the sensory words. Then choose the sensory word that your group feels is best for each blank.

THESAURUS CORNER · Word Choice

Each of the adjectives in dark type is a main entry in the Thesaurus. Replace it with a good synonym. After each sentence, write the name of the sense to which it appeals.

1. The hot soup had become **warm** before the girls returned.
2. On her finger was a **beautiful** and expensive diamond ring.
3. The cake is so **light** that it will barely support twelve candles.
4. The **exciting** odor of bacon frying awakened us in the morning.
5. Across the valley came the **clear** notes of a Swiss yodeler.

Writing a Character Sketch

"Zeely Tayber was more than six and a half feet tall, thin and deeply dark as a pole of Ceylon ebony." These words introduce the main character of the book *Zeely*. Geeder thinks Zeely looks like an African princess. Zeely, however, does not understand how special she is. She only feels different and shy. In the book, the

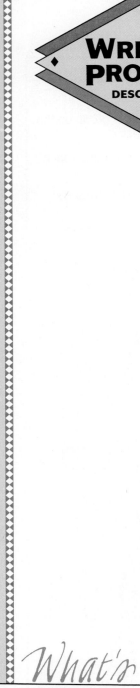

author Virginia Hamilton tells a great deal more about Geeder and Zeely. She tells her readers not only how her characters look, but also how they act and how they feel.

Know Your Purpose and Audience

What's
MY PURPOSE

Who's
MY AUDIENCE

In this lesson you will write a character sketch. Your purpose will be to write a vivid description of someone you know and admire.

Your audience will be your classmates. Later you can have a Who's Who Day to share character sketches. You might also make a gift card for the person you described.

1 Prewriting

First choose your topic—the person you will describe. Then use a strategy to gather details for your character sketch.

Choose Your Topic ♦ Start by listing the names of people who come to mind easily. Add to your list by giving it deeper thought. Then consider your list. Circle your best choice.

<table>
<tr><td>

Think About It

How will you narrow your list? Cross out the name of any person about whom you do not know many details. Visualize each name remaining. Whom can you see most clearly in your mind? Whose personality would be most interesting to describe? Circle that name.

</td><td>

Talk About It

Talk with a partner about people who are special to you. Is there someone that you know well or admire? Do you have a relative who is special to you? Tell your partner details about the characteristics and personality of each person.

</td></tr>
</table>

Topic Ideas

Aunt Libby—her pies
Mr. Wu—his store
Willy Miller—directs traffic
Sue Greene—her music
Mrs. Behan—librarian

Choose Your Strategy ♦ Here are two strategies for gathering details for your character sketch. Read both. Then decide which strategy you will use.

PREWRITING IDEAS

CHOICE ONE

A Character Map

Think about your person. What does the person look like? Do? Say? What are the person's interests? Hobbies? Talents? Does this person have a special outlook on life? If possible, interview him or her to find out more. Then make a simple sketch. Label it with details about the person.

Model

Willy Miller
big smile
directs traffic
as if conducting a symphony
blows his whistle with a musical beat
seems to dance as he directs cars

CHOICE TWO

A Thought Balloon

For a character sketch, don't consider only how your person looks and acts. Try to show that person's outlook on life, also.

If possible, interview your person. You might ask

- What do you most enjoy doing?
- Whom do you admire, and why?
- What do you think is a good rule to follow in life?

If you cannot interview your person, use what you know about him or her. Imagine his or her point of view. Then write a thought balloon to summarize what you believe is your person's view of life.

Model

Life is a symphony to be enjoyed and appreciated.

Willy Miller

2 Writing

How can you begin your character sketch? You might begin with an interesting fact. You might quote your person. You might tell why you chose that person. Here are some examples.

♦ Mr. Lopez was only eight years old the first time he _____.
♦ The first thing Lisa said when we met was, "_____."
♦ Would you like to meet a person who is the best _____?

Use your interview notes, character map, or thought balloon to help you continue. End by summing up why this person is so special.

Sample First Draft ♦

Willy Miller loves his job. Willy thinks all of life should be enjoyed. He told me, "Life is a symphony." He conducks his with style and spirit. That's just what Willy does when he works. He seems to dance as he directs traffic when I watch, I can almost hear the music. Willy has been a Police officer for ten years, directing traffic all that time. Willy is a lejund in our city. People go out of their way to drive through his intersection. They want to see his smile and join his symphony.

3 Revising

Now you have written your character sketch. Can you make it even better? This idea for revising may help you.

REVISING IDEA

FIRST   Read to Yourself

As you read, review your purpose. Did you write a vivid description of someone you know or admire? Consider your audience. Will your classmates enjoy your description?

Focus: Have you included sensory and other details to show what your person is like? Put a caret (^) to mark any places where you'd like to add a detail.

THEN   Share with a Partner

Ask a partner to be your first audience. These guidelines may help you work together on your character sketch.

The Writer

Guidelines: Ask your partner to read your character sketch silently, then respond.

Sample questions:
- Should I change the order of any details?
- **Focus question:** Do I need to add any details to show what this person is like?

The Writer's Partner

Guidelines: Be honest. Don't be afraid to give your opinion, but do it politely.

Sample responses:
- I think _____ is the most important detail. Maybe you should put it first.
- I could picture this person even better if you told _____.

Revising Model ◆ Here is a character sketch that is being revised. The marks show changes the writer wants to make.

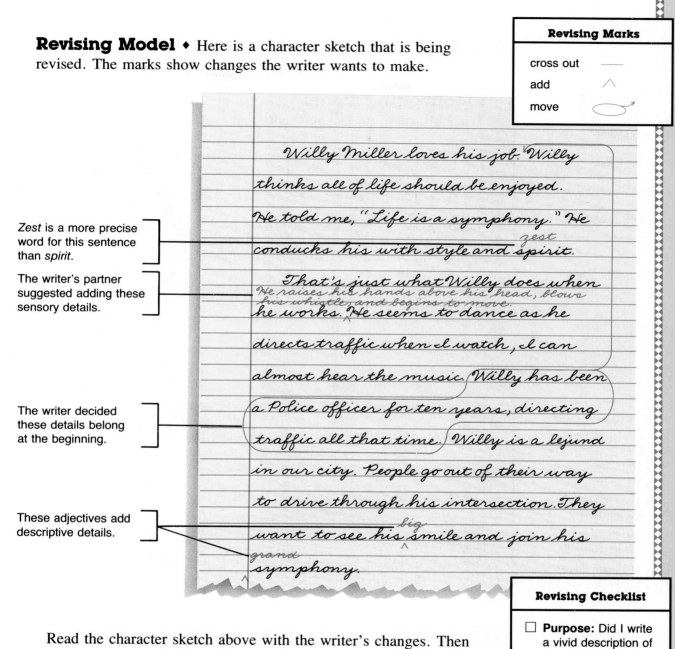

Zest is a more precise word for this sentence than *spirit*.

The writer's partner suggested adding these sensory details.

The writer decided these details belong at the beginning.

These adjectives add descriptive details.

Willy Miller loves his job. Willy thinks all of life should be enjoyed. He told me, "Life is a symphony." He conducts his with style and spirit. ^zest

That's just what Willy does when he works. *He raises his hands above his head, blows his whistle, and begins to move.* He seems to dance as he directs traffic when I watch, I can almost hear the music. Willy has been a Police officer for ten years, directing traffic all that time. Willy is a lejund in our city. People go out of their way to drive through his intersection. They want to see his ^big smile and join his grand symphony.

Read the character sketch above with the writer's changes. Then revise your own character sketch.

Grammar Check ◆ Adjectives add specific details to your writing.

Word Choice ◆ Do you want a more precise word for a word like *spirit*? A thesaurus is a good source of synonyms.

Revising Checklist

☐ **Purpose:** Did I write a vivid description of the person?

☐ **Audience:** Will my classmates enjoy my character sketch?

☐ **Focus:** Did I include details to show what this person is like?

4 Proofreading

Now correct any errors. A correct copy is easier to read.

Proofreading Model ♦ Here is the character sketch about Willy Miller. Proofreading changes appear in red.

Willy Miller loves his job. Willy thinks all of life should be enjoyed. He told me, "Life is a symphony." He *conducts* ~~conducks~~ his with style and ~~spirit~~ *zest*.

¶ That's just what Willy does when he works. *He raises his hands above his head, blows his whistle, and begins to move.* He seems to dance as he directs traffic. ~~when~~ I watch, I can almost hear the music. Willy has been a ~~Police~~ police officer for ten years, directing traffic all that time. Willy is a *legend* ~~lejund~~ in our city. People go out of their way to drive through his intersection. They want to see his *big* smile and join his *grand* symphony.

PROOFREADING IDEA

Punctuation Check

To catch spelling, punctuation, and other errors, read backwards from the end to the beginning. When you block out meaning, you can concentrate on finding mistakes.

Now proofread your character sketch, add a title, and make a neat copy.

5 Publishing

Try one of these ideas for sharing your character sketch.

> ### Willy Miller
>
> Willy Miller loves his job. Willy has been a police officer for ten years, directing traffic all that time. Willy thinks all of life should be enjoyed. He told me, "Life is a symphony." He conducts his with style and zest.
>
> That's just what Willy does when he works. He raises his hands above his head, blows his whistle, and begins to move. He seems to dance as he directs traffic. When I watch, I can almost hear the music.
>
> Willy is a legend in our city. People go out of their way to drive through his intersection. They want to see his big smile and join his grand symphony.

PUBLISHING IDEAS

Share Aloud	Share in Writing
Have a Who's Who Day. Form small groups and take turns reading your character sketches aloud. Ask each listener to tell what he or she found most admirable about your person.	Make a large gift card. Staple your character sketch between colorful covers. Illustrate the top cover. Sign the card and give it to the person you wrote about. Perhaps that person will respond in person or in writing.

CURRICULUM CONNECTION

◆ Writing Across the Curriculum   Health

In this unit you wrote a character sketch that gave your point of view about a person you admired. Many people admire the performance of athletes. To perform well in a sport, an athlete must exercise regularly and eat good foods.

Writing to Learn

Think and Imagine ◆ Picture your favorite athlete making a commercial about good health practices. Make a thought balloon showing what he or she might say.

Thought Balloon

Write ◆ What should you do to be healthy? Review your thought balloon. Then share your *own* point of view on the subject.

◆ Writing in Your Journal

In the Writer's Warm-up you wrote about qualities that make lasting impressions on people. Throughout this unit you learned about people who have made lasting impressions. Browse through the unit again. Choose one person. In your journal tell why many people admire this person. Then explain why you either agree or disagree with them.

BOOKS TO ENJOY

Read More About It

To Space and Back

by Sally Ride with Susan Okie

Sally Ride, the first American woman astronaut, writes about spaceflight. You will find out how astronauts manage some daily space chores, such as making a sandwich or brushing their teeth.

Ellis Island: Gateway to the New World

by Leonard Everett Fisher

Between 1890 and 1954, Ellis Island was the first stop in America for millions of arriving immigrants. Ellis Island is located in New York Harbor. Hopes and dreams got a start in the immigration buildings here.

U.S. Astronaut Sally Ride shares the adventure of outer space

TO SPACE & BACK
Sally Ride with Susan Okie

Book Report Idea Character Interview

Next time you share a book, interview a character.

Make Up a Character Interview ◆ Work alone or with a partner. Choose a main character in the book. Write some questions an interviewer might ask the character to learn more about his or her life. Use a tape recorder. Ask questions; then answer them as you think the character would. Change your voice so listeners can tell the interviewer from the character. If you work with a partner, be the character as your partner asks the questions you prepared.

Unit 5

Adjectives   *pages 234–241*

A. Write each of the following sentences. Underline each adjective. Include articles.

1. The smiling tourists admired the beautiful sunset.
2. In early America, families made homespun clothes.
3. The tallest building in town stands next to a vacant lot.
4. A small dog crept along the crooked path.
5. Clever people welcome a difficult challenge.
6. The shimmering green light suddenly vanished.
7. The weird creature from Planet X made strange hooting noises.
8. A little old man entered the haunted house.
9. I like sweet, ripe strawberries.
10. The beautiful painting stood in the dark hall.
11. The shy kitten hid behind the giant, flowery bush.
12. The cheerful guests danced and sang joyous songs.
13. Ms. Sanders is a dedicated and understanding teacher.
14. A lonely leaf fell to the cold ground.
15. A strong, bitter wind swooped down from the tall mountain.

B. Write each sentence. Underline the predicate adjective once. Underline twice the noun or pronoun it describes.

16. You look tired today.
17. Tony doesn't seem happy.
18. Robert E. Lee was brave in battle.
19. Martha is witty.
20. That giant yellow flower smells beautiful.
21. We are delighted to welcome you to our home.
22. The tacos tasted delicious.
23. Florence Nightingale was heroic.
24. The mother bear seemed angry.
25. The teenager looked impressed with himself.

C. Write each sentence. Use the correct form of the adjective in parentheses ( ).

26. My piece of spinach pie is (small) than yours.
27. Leon is the (tiny) member of our family.
28. Randy is the (intelligent) person I know.
29. No one is (brave) than Tanya.
30. You seem (cheerful) than I am.
31. This stamp is (valuable) than any other one in my collection.
32. Is your cat (swift) than my German shepherd?
33. That book is the (helpful) guide to woodcraft I have found.
34. Tom is the (bashful) person I know.
35. That is the (beautiful) painting in the entire museum.
36. Jill arrived (early) than Beverly.
37. Sam came (early) of all.

Suffixes   *pages 242–243*

D. Read each definition. Then write a word that has the same meaning by adding the suffix *-able, -ful, -less,* or *-y* to the underlined word.

38. being full of <u>mist</u>
39. with <u>skill</u>
40. having <u>honor</u>
41. without <u>speech</u>
42. full of <u>fear</u>
43. able to be <u>refilled</u>
44. without <u>harm</u>
45. worthy of <u>notice</u>

Organizing Details
pages 258–259

E. Read the topic sentence below. Then write the four details in bottom-to-top space order.

TOPIC SENTENCE: Chef Leo had created a beautiful salad.

46. Tasty leaves of romaine lettuce lay underneath the other vegetables.
47. Sprigs of parsley and strips of red pepper topped the salad.
48. Artichoke hearts and asparagus spears covered the cheese.
49. Fine cheese sat upon the lettuce.

F. Write the sentences below in the order of their importance. Put the most important detail first.

50. When Ed smiles, his face lights up.
51. His eyebrows arch a little.
52. His normally harsh features soften.
53. His cheeks dimple quite noticeably.

Describing   *pages 260–261*

G. Read the following paragraph. Then write answers to the questions.

Try as they might, Maria and Jared could not recall so cold a day. They were bundled from head to toe in heavy woolen caps, fluffy earmuffs, thick scarves, bulky coats, and fur-lined boots. Even so, the biting cold penetrated their clothing. Their legs were numb and felt almost frozen. Each leg seemed to weigh a ton. The crisp snow crackled under their feet as they trudged home. Their unprotected faces stung with the pain of the cold.

54. Which words and details indicate how cold it was?
55. Which words and details help you see how Maria and Jared looked?
56. Which words and details describe how Maria and Jared felt?
57. Which word describes the snow?
58. Which word indicates the sound they made as they walked?

H. Read the topic sentence below. Then read sentences 59–62. Write *yes* if a sentence gives a detail that supports the topic sentence. Write *no* if it does not.

It was an extremely hot summer day in the big city.

59. The bank sign said ninety degrees.
60. I wore a hat to keep my ears warm.
61. A street vendor was selling cups of ice-cold lemonade.
62. The pond was bustling with numerous skaters.

Impossible Possibility Rhymes

Write two-line Impossible Possibility rhymes like the ones below. The first line should contain a linking verb and a predicate adjective. The second line should contain an action verb.

The sweet rolls tasted sour.
I made the dough without flour.

The snow was hot in the sixth month of May
And sunshine was raining all night and all day.

The sun in the sky always is flat
When the bareheaded girl wears her top hat.

Arty Adjectives

Find the adjective in each box. You may check spellings in a dictionary.

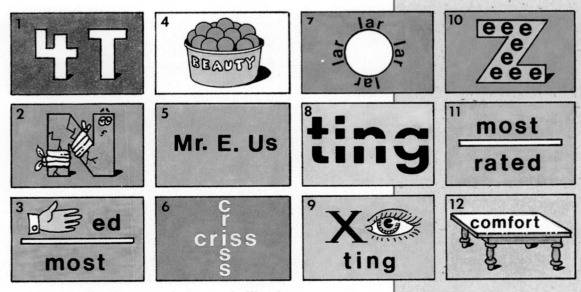

Use an adjective to make a puzzle like the ones above. Ask a classmate to solve your puzzle.

Unit 5 Extra Practice

1 Writing with Adjectives

p. 234

A. Write the adjectives in each sentence. Include articles.

1. Many people visit the historic sites in North Carolina.
2. The tourists enjoy the old mansions and villages.
3. One village is in an old section of Winston-Salem.
4. The colonial buildings and early clothing attract sightseers.
5. Some buildings are from 1766 and have interesting styles.
6. A popular event in North Carolina is a historical play.
7. It is staged at an old fort where early colonists lived.
8. The play shows the hard life the colonial settlers led.
9. The story tells about a lost colony and a strange word.
10. The colony was founded on an island called Roanoke thirty-three years before the Pilgrims landed.
11. Three years later all the colonists had vanished.
12. Some people searched for the lost colonists.
13. One word, *Croatoan*, was carved on a big post.
14. The mysterious disappearance has never been explained.

B. Write each sentence. Use *a* or *an* to complete it.

15. Pamela made _____ visit to Tryon Palace in New Bern.
16. It is _____ old North Carolina mansion.
17. The mansion was built by _____ colonial governor.
18. In 1774 _____ American revolutionary group met there.
19. The patriots made _____ pact against the British there.

C. Write each sentence. Underline the adjectives that tell *what kind* once. Underline the adjectives that tell *how many* twice. Do not include articles.

20. North Carolina's lovely capital, Raleigh, is an old city.
21. The original capitol was the big palace in New Bern.
22. The state flag has three colors and two dates.
23. Both dates stand for early declarations of independence.
24. It is a large state with a hundred counties.
25. We spent one vacation on the sandy beaches.

D. Write the adjectives in these sentences. Include articles.

26. North Carolina is a southern state with fertile farms, thick forests, a long coastline, and many industries.
27. Two products are furniture and cloth.
28. The wooden furniture in many homes in the United States is from North Carolina.
29. Textile production is an important industry, too.
30. North Carolina leads all states in textile manufacturing.

2 Adjectives After Linking Verbs *p. 236*

A. Write the predicate adjective in each sentence. Tell which noun or pronoun in the subject each adjective describes.

1. Washington was famous before the American Revolution.
2. The people felt secure with him as the President.
3. They were wise in their choice of a leader.
4. George Washington was successful at farming.
5. For a long while he was loyal to Great Britain.
6. Great Britain was harsh toward its colonies.
7. Then war seemed unavoidable.
8. The colonies were ready to fight for freedom.
9. They felt prepared for war.

B. Write each sentence. Underline the predicate adjective once. Underline twice the noun or pronoun it describes.

EXAMPLE: That cherry pie smells wonderful!
ANSWER: That cherry <u>pie</u> smells <u>wonderful!</u>

10. George Washington is famous for his honesty.
11. According to legend, he was careless cutting trees.
12. Young George was guilty of ruining the cherry tree.
13. His father probably looked angry.
14. However, Washington was honest about his mistake.
15. George Washington was brave, too.
16. During the long winters of the war, he seemed fearless.
17. He was sensitive to the hardships of the soldiers.
18. They were ready to follow him anywhere.
19. Later, Washington was also effective as President.

C. Write sentences using each of the following pairs of adjectives and nouns. Use a linking verb, and use the adjective as a predicate adjective.

EXAMPLE: brave soldiers
ANSWER: The soldiers were brave.

20. brilliant Thomas Jefferson
21. industrious John Adams
22. angry taxpayers
23. endless war
24. short supplies
25. weary colonists
26. delicious food
27. acceptable peace
28. independent country
29. happy people

D. Write the sentence. Underline the predicate adjective once and the noun or pronoun it describes twice.

30. Mexico is famous as the home of the Mayas.
31. These Indians were powerful a thousand years ago.
32. The Mayan cities are ancient.
33. Scientists were excited by their discovery.
34. Even today, the cities seem new.
35. Their condition is excellent.
36. The buildings are beautiful.
37. The Mayas were unknown to the outside world.
38. The land was rich and supplied all their needs.
39. They felt safe in their villages.
40. Astronomy was important to the Mayas.
41. The planets were special to them.
42. Mathematics seemed easy to these people.
43. The people were happy when it rained.

3 Adjectives That Compare   *p. 238*

A. Write the word in parentheses ( ) that correctly completes each sentence.

1. A duck egg is (smaller, smallest) than an ostrich egg.
2. A hummingbird egg is the (smaller, smallest) of all.
3. A giraffe is the (taller, tallest) animal in the world.
4. It is even (taller, tallest) than an elephant.
5. Is that the (bigger, biggest) animal you can think of?

B. Write each sentence. Use the form of the adjective shown in parentheses ( ).

6. The (early + -est) bridges were fallen trees.
7. (Late + -er) bridges were copies of this design.
8. (Flat + -er) pieces of wood were laid across streams.
9. In the (wet + -er) weather they were washed away.
10. People looked for ways to cross (wide + -er) rivers.
11. Bridge builders started using (heavy + -er) materials.
12. A special design was used for the (large + -est) bridge.
13. A bridge crosses Australia's (busy + -est) harbor.
14. Some modern bridges look like (early + -er) designs.
15. The (late + -est) idea is to make bridges of concrete.

C. Write each sentence. Use the correct form of the adjective in parentheses ( ).

16. Díaz is a (short) name than Fernández.
17. O is the (short) name in the world.
18. This tiger is the (big) cat in the zoo.
19. This leopard is (small) than that tiger.
20. The (long) worm of all is the bootlace worm.
21. It is (long) than 150 feet.
22. The cheetah is the (fast) animal on land.
23. The sailfish is even (fast) than the cheetah.
24. Is Mount Everest (high) than Mount McKinley?
25. Yes, it is the (high) mountain in the world.
26. Which is (long), the Mississippi or the Nile?
27. The Nile is the (long) river in the world.
28. Which is (heavy), an ounce or a gram?
29. An ounce is much (heavy) than a gram.
30. The world's (big) pizza was more than eight feet across.

4 Using *more* and *most* with Adjectives

p. 240

A. For each adjective below, write the two forms used to compare persons, places, or things.

1. long   **2.** admirable   **3.** bad   **4.** serious   **5.** polite

B. Write each sentence. Use the correct form of the adjective in parentheses.

   6. These track shoes are (comfortable) than those.
   7. The bar on the high jump is (low) now than it was before.
   8. Rosa is the (dependable) runner we have.
   9. I'm (breathless) after running than after swimming.
   10. Jim is a (careful) runner than Manuel.
   11. Nikki gave the (impressive) performance of her career.
   12. That high jumper was (nervous) than Nikki was.
   13. Pole vaulting is the (hard) event of the whole meet.
   14. Our team looked (cheerful) than their team.
   15. Tripping was the (awkward) way to start.
   16. Ours was the (high) score of the entire season.
   17. The high jump was the (difficult) event of all.
   18. The floor here is (slippery) than in our gym.
   19. A good warm-up is the (helpful) way to prepare.
   20. The coach's advice is (sensible) than Joe's.
   21. The Olympic Games are the (famous) of all sports events.
   22. To the ancient Greeks, nothing was (important) than the Games.
   23. They chose the (beautiful) spot in Greece for the Games.
   24. Only the (serious) athletes of all could take part in the events.
   25. They underwent (demanding) training than today's athletes.
   26. Winners received even (great) honors than war heroes.
   27. The Olympics still feature the (good) athletes of all.
   28. Some Olympic events are (recent) than others.
   29. Wrestling is an (old) event than volleyball.

C. Write the sentences. Use the correct form of *good* or *bad* to complete each sentence.

   30. Jim Thorpe was the (good) all-around Olympic athlete.
   31. His record was far (good) than anyone else's.
   32. This is the (good) score Howin ever had.
   33. Last season was (bad) than this one for us.
   34. This year we have done (good) than Hill School.
   35. Our (bad) event is the broad jump.
   36. Next year we plan to have an even (good) team than we have this year.
   37. Our (good) event is the 100-meter dash.

USING LANGUAGE
TO
RESEARCH

=== **PART ONE** ===

Unit Theme *Volcanoes*

Language Awareness Adverbs

=== **PART TWO** ===

Literature *Volcano* by Patricia Lauber

A Reason for Writing Researching

Writing
IN YOUR JOURNAL

WRITER'S WARM-UP ◆ What do you know about volcanoes? You may have heard of some famous volcanic eruptions of the past, such as the eruption of Mount Vesuvius. Have you ever built a model of a volcano in science class? Why is a volcano dangerous? What happens when a volcano erupts? Find out what you know by writing in your journal. Start by writing the word *volcano*, then just write whatever you know about volcanoes.

Complete the following sentences by replacing the word in each blank. How many sentences can you make?

Lightning flashes brightly.   *Thunder rumbles loudly.*

1 Writing with Adverbs

You have learned that every sentence contains a verb and that many verbs express action. When you write, you can use adverbs with verbs to make the action seem more real.

Read the sentences below. The underlined words in the sentences are adverbs. Each adverb describes a verb by telling *how*, *when*, or *where*.

Rita eagerly reads books about volcanoes. (reads how?)

She reported about volcanoes today. (reported when?)

A volcano erupted somewhere. (erupted where?)

Here are some common adverbs. Notice that many adverbs end in *-ly*, especially adverbs that tell *how*.

How? gladly, slowly, suddenly, quietly, well, badly, fast
When? always, often, lately, never, usually, now, today
Where? everywhere, here, there, forward, outside, nearby

Summary ◆ A word that describes a verb is an **adverb**. Use adverbs to add details to your writing.

Guided Practice

In the sentences below, the verbs are underlined. Name the adverbs that describe them.

1. Rita told us today about the eruption of Mount St. Helens.
2. She spoke excitedly about the burning lava.
3. The hot lava flowed everywhere.
4. I gave my report yesterday.
5. The class listened attentively.

Practice

A. In the sentences below, the verbs are underlined. Find the adverb in each sentence and write it.

6. Tourists frequently <u>visited</u> Mount St. Helens in Washington.
7. They gladly <u>camped</u> near this beautiful mountain.
8. Herds of elk and deer <u>lived</u> nearby.
9. Volcanoes often <u>erupt</u> after many years of stillness.
10. In the nineteenth century, Mount St. Helens <u>erupted</u> occasionally.
11. For over a hundred years, this volcano <u>slept</u> quietly.
12. In 1975, scientists correctly <u>predicted</u> another eruption.
13. On March 20, 1980, the mountain suddenly <u>shook</u>.
14. People fearfully <u>awaited</u> the volcano's eruption.
15. Some quickly <u>left</u> the area.

B. Write each sentence and underline the adverb. Write *how*, *when*, or *where* to show what the adverb tells about the verb.

16. On March 27, 1980, Mount St. Helens exploded violently.
17. Steam and ash flew skyward.
18. Smaller explosions frequently occurred through early May.
19. Ash soon covered the mountain peak.
20. Scientists traveled there to study this volcano.

C. Write each sentence. Use an adverb to complete it.

21. The herd of deer _____ fled the mountain.
22. The ash _____ covered the ground.
23. Scientists _____ studied the effects of the eruption.
24. They tried to determine if another eruption would _____ follow.
25. Clearly, Mount St. Helens had _____ awakened.

Apply ◆ Think and Write

From Your Writing ◆ Read what you wrote for the Writer's Warm-up. List the adverbs you used under these columns: *how*, *when*, *where*.

✎ **Remember**
that you can use adverbs to add strength to your images of action.

2 Adverbs That Compare

Adverbs can describe by making comparisons, just the way adjectives can. The *-er* form of an adverb is used to compare two actions. The *-est* form is used to compare three or more actions.

> Lava travels <u>fast</u>.
> Mud travels <u>faster</u> than lava.
> Water travels the <u>fastest</u> of all.

Many adverbs use *more* and *most* to show comparison.

> Linda watched <u>excitedly</u> as she neared the volcano.
> Linda watched <u>more excitedly</u> when hot steam hissed.
> Linda watched <u>most excitedly</u> when red lava gushed upward.

More and *most* are often used with adverbs that end in *-ly* and adverbs that have two or more syllables. Be careful not to use *more* with the *-er* form or *most* with the *-est* form of an adverb.

The adverbs *well* and *badly* use these forms for comparison.

> Huckleberries grow <u>well</u>.
> Trillium plants grow <u>better</u> than that.
> Fireweed grows <u>best</u> of all.

> The trees fared <u>badly</u>.
> The lake fared <u>worse</u> than the trees.
> The bridges fared <u>worst</u> of all.

> **Summary** ♦ Adverbs have forms that are used to compare actions. When you write comparisons with adverbs, use the *-er* and *-est* forms, or *more* and *most*, to compare actions.

Guided Practice

For each adverb, give the form that is used to compare two actions. Then give the form used to compare three or more actions.

1. early　　**2.** slowly　　**3.** neatly　　**4.** badly　　**5.** quickly

Practice

A. Write the sentences about Mount St. Helens. For each adverb in parentheses ( ), add *more* or use the *-er* form.

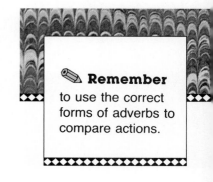

   6. Scientists study volcanoes (thoroughly) than other people do.

   7. Some scientists arrived at Mount St. Helens (early) than others.

   8. After the eruptions, life on the mountain reappeared (fast) than expected.

   9. Some burrowing animals, especially those living under the ground, survived (easily) than others.

 10. Chipmunks appeared (quickly) than deer and elk.

B. Write each sentence. For each adverb in parentheses ( ), add *most* or use the *-est* form.

 11. Plants that were buried under snow appeared (soon) of all.

 12. Ants and other tiny forms of life survived (hardily) of all.

 13. The tiny plants grew the (densely) of all the plants.

 14. Fungi are the plants we found (commonly) of all.

 15. They also grow the (fast) of all plants.

C. Write the sentences. Use the correct form of *well* or *badly* to complete each sentence.

 16. Rita read her report on Mount St. Helens (well) than I read mine on Krakatoa.

 17. I think the people near Krakatoa suffered (badly) than the people near Mount St. Helens.

 18. Rita gathered facts the (well) of all the students.

 19. Next time, I am determined to do (well) than this time.

 20. My report will not be prepared the (badly) of all.

Apply ♦ Think and Write

Dictionary of Knowledge ♦ Mount St. Helens is one of many famous volcanoes. Read about volcanoes in the Dictionary of Knowledge. Write some sentences comparing Mauna Loa, Mount Etna, and Cotopaxi. Use adverbs in your comparisons.

> ✎ **Remember**
> to use the correct forms of adverbs to compare actions.

Use words such as *extremely*, *slightly*, *completely*, and *terribly* to make word pairs that describe persons or places. Begin both words of a pair with the same letter. For example: *fairly famous*

3 Adverbs Before Adjectives and Other Adverbs

You have used adverbs to describe verbs.

■ Mount Fuji, an inactive volcano, rises <u>majestically</u> above the land.

Adverbs can also describe adjectives or other adverbs by telling *to what extent*.

1. A volcanic eruption is a <u>fairly</u> rare event.

2. The lava flowed <u>so</u> fast that people had no time to escape.

Notice that in sentence **1** the adverb *fairly* describes the adjective *rare*. In sentence **2** the adverb *so* describes the adverb *fast*.

Here are some adverbs you can use to describe adjectives and other adverbs.

rather	fairly	unusually	almost
certainly	slightly	quite	totally
incredibly	considerably	unbelievably	too
justly	very	terribly	so

Summary ◆ An adverb may describe a verb, an adjective, or another adverb. Use adverbs in your writing to make adjectives and other adverbs more exact.

Guided Practice

Name the adverb that describes each underlined adjective or adverb in the sentences below.

1. Mount Fuji is incredibly <u>beautiful</u>.
2. A volcanic eruption can occur quite <u>suddenly</u>.
3. People living near a volcano cannot be too <u>careful</u>.
4. I am rather <u>afraid</u> of volcanoes.
5. I wouldn't live very <u>close</u> to one.

Practice

A. Write each sentence. Then write the adverb that describes the underlined adjective or adverb.

6. A volcanic eruption is an unusually <u>interesting</u> phenomenon.
7. Magma, or melted rock, forms because the earth's interior is so <u>hot</u>.
8. The magma is considerably <u>lighter</u> than the rock around it.
9. Magma can rise terribly <u>quickly</u> to the top of a volcano.
10. The rising magma very <u>gradually</u> forms a magma chamber.
11. Magma that is completely <u>outside</u> is called lava.
12. Highly <u>fluid</u> lava flows down the sides of the mountain.
13. This lava forms extremely <u>smooth</u> sheets of rock.
14. Other fairly <u>thick</u> lava forms rough sheets of rock.
15. Flowing lava can be quite <u>destructive</u>.

B. Write each sentence. Use these adverbs to complete the sentences. Use each adverb only once.

extremely   **incredibly**   **too**   **significantly**   **very**

16. _____ much gas can make sticky magma blast into fragments.
17. The rock fragments differ _____ much in size.
18. Volcanic dust consists of _____ tiny particles.
19. _____ large fragments are called volcanic bombs.
20. Volcanic bombs may be _____ larger than basketballs.

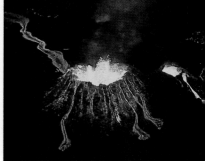

C. 21–25. Write five sentences that use adverbs to modify adjectives and other adverbs. Choose five of the adverbs below to use in your sentences.

extremely	**too**	**very**	**rather**
unusually	**slightly**	**fairly**	**almost**

Apply ◆ Think and Write

Riddle Paragraph ◆ Write a paragraph describing a common object that is behaving in a very strange way, but do not name the object. How about a vacuum cleaner that gobbles up carpets? Use adverbs that describe adjectives and other adverbs. Exchange papers with a classmate. Try to guess each other's object.

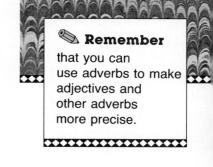

> ✎ **Remember**
> that you can use adverbs to make adjectives and other adverbs more precise.

4 Using Adverbs and Adjectives

In the sentences below, one underlined adjective describes a noun, and another describes a pronoun. The adjective *enormous* describes the noun *plume*. *Impressive* describes the pronoun *it*.

■ **The volcano's smoky plume seems <u>enormous</u>. It is <u>impressive</u>.**

While adjectives are used to describe nouns and pronouns, adverbs are used to describe verbs, adjectives, and other adverbs. In the sentences below, *violently* describes the verb *erupted*. *Unusually* describes the adjective *exciting*. *Very* describes the adverb *quickly*.

The volcano erupted <u>violently</u>.   It was <u>unusually</u> exciting.
The lava flowed <u>very</u> quickly.

The words *good*, *bad*, and *well* may be used as adjectives. *Well* is an adjective when it means "healthy." The adjective *well* usually follows a linking verb such as *is*, *seem*, *feel*, or *look*.

The tourists at Pompeii had a <u>good</u> time. The hotel food was <u>bad</u>.
After a day of rest, the tourists were <u>well</u> again.

Well and *badly* are often used as adverbs that tell *how*.

The youngest tourist behaved <u>well</u>.
The child acted <u>badly</u> in the restaurant.

Summary ◆ Use adjectives to describe nouns and pronouns. Use adverbs to describe verbs, adjectives, and other adverbs.

Guided Practice

Tell which word correctly completes each sentence.

1. Vesuvius in Italy looks (beautiful, beautifully).
2. Centuries ago, it (sudden, suddenly) erupted.
3. Scientists have studied this volcano (thorough, thoroughly).

Practice

A. Write the word in parentheses ( ) that correctly completes each sentence about the volcano Vesuvius.

  4. Vesuvius appears (high, highly) over the Bay of Naples.
  5. The soil around Vesuvius is (unusual, unusually) fertile.
  6. Its most (famous, famously) eruption occurred in A.D. 79.
  7. The volcano exploded (unexpected, unexpectedly).
  8. The city of Pompeii was (complete, completely) buried.
  9. Pompeii was not a (great, greatly) city.
  10. Today, however, this tourist spot is (popular, popularly).
  11. People (eager, eagerly) come to see how ancient Romans lived.
  12. Romans used Pompeii (main, mainly) as a vacation place.
  13. They built (large, largely) homes near the Mediterranean Sea.
  14. The people of Pompeii carried on a (rich, richly) trade in oil.
  15. The eruption (sudden, suddenly) changed all that.

B. Choose the word in parentheses ( ) that correctly completes each sentence. Write the sentence. Then write whether *good*, *well*, *bad*, or *badly* is an adjective or an adverb in the sentence.

  EXAMPLE: The ancient city of Pompeii is (well, good) preserved.
  ANSWER: The ancient city of Pompeii is well preserved. (adverb)

  16. The eruption of Vesuvius damaged Pompeii (bad, badly).
  17. Early excavations of the city were not done (good, well).
  18. A (good, well) method of digging began after 1860.
  19. Uncovered city blocks were not in (bad, badly) condition.
  20. Ancient buildings of Pompeii are (good, well) kept.

C. Use adjectives and adverbs to complete the sentences.

  21. The _____ townspeople fled _____ from the eruption.
  22. Today the volcano seems _____ .
  23. It might _____ erupt at any time.

Apply ◆ Think and Write

Travel Sentences ◆ Write sentences about a place you have visited or want to visit. Use the words *good*, *well*, *bad*, and *badly*.

> ✎ **Remember**
> to use adjectives and adverbs correctly to add important details.

◆ GETTING ◆
STARTED

Complete the following pair of incomplete thoughts with as many ideas as you can think of: *I don't* _____. *I won't* _____.

5 Using Negative Words

You use negative words to say or write *no*. Look at the following sentences. The underlined words are negative words.

Lien is <u>not</u> interested in volcanoes. She <u>never</u> reads about them.
"I <u>don't</u> feel that way," said Anita, "but I <u>won't</u> argue about it."

Here is a list of some other common negative words.

no   nobody   nothing   no one   nowhere   none

Often you express "no" by writing a contraction—a shortened form of two words. The contractions below are negatives. Each is formed from a verb and the adverb *not*.

isn't = is not	don't = do not	couldn't = could not
wasn't = was not	hasn't = has not	wouldn't = would not
doesn't = does not	haven't = have not	won't = will not

You need to use only one word to make a sentence negative. Avoid double negatives—two negatives in a sentence.

Wrong: Anita doesn't never stop talking about volcanoes.
Right: Anita never stops talking about volcanoes.
Right: Anita doesn't ever stop talking about volcanoes.

Summary ◆ Negative words mean "no." Avoid using two negative words in the same sentence.

Guided Practice

Name the negative word in each sentence. Tell which are contractions.

1. No one in class knows more about volcanoes than Maria.
2. She can't hide her enthusiasm.
3. Isn't a volcanic eruption an incredible event?

Practice

A. Write the sentences. Underline the negative words.

 4. No one knows when the first volcanic eruptions happened.
 5. Scientists can't tell when a volcano near Crete exploded.
 6. They aren't certain it happened in 1500 B.C.
 7. The mountain on the island of Thera was not ordinary.
 8. People on the island couldn't escape the flowing lava.
 9. Nobody expected the volcano to erupt.
 10. Nowhere on the island did people survive the blast.
 11. Some ancient people thought an eruption occurred because a god wasn't happy.
 12. Others didn't accept this idea.
 13. None were sure of the facts.

B. Write the word in parentheses ( ) that correctly completes each sentence. Avoid double negatives.

 14. Perhaps ancient people didn't (ever, never) realize how dangerous a volcano could be.
 15. The volcanic area (was, wasn't) no place for a home.
 16. There really (was, wasn't) any hope for survival.
 17. Probably nothing (could, couldn't) have saved the people.
 18. I wouldn't live (nowhere, anywhere) near a volcano.

C. Rewrite the following sentences. Correct each double negative.

 EXAMPLE: Anita won't never lose interest in volcanoes.
 ANSWER: Anita will never lose interest in volcanoes. *or*
     Anita won't ever lose interest in volcanoes.

 19. I haven't no interest in volcanoes.
 20. They don't never bore Mary Ellen.
 21. Doesn't nothing about volcanoes never interest Michael?
 22. Nancy won't never stop talking about them.
 23. No one here hasn't never seen a volcano.

Apply ♦ Think and Write

Negative Sentences ♦ Listen to what people around you say. Write five sentences you hear that contain negatives.

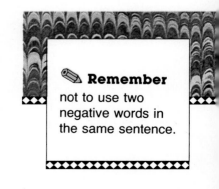

✎ **Remember** not to use two negative words in the same sentence.

How many words can you form by combining two or more of the following words?

up down in out side run walk roar door way stair

VOCABULARY ◆
Compounds

James is a big baseball fan. He likes to watch the pitcher's windup and to see the batter hit a grand slam. He enjoys eating hot dogs and watermelon. He wants to play big-league ball someday.

The underlined words above are called compounds. A **compound** is a word formed from two or more words. Many words in English are compounds.

Notice that compounds can be written in different ways. Some compounds, such as *baseball* and *watermelon*, are written as a single word. Some, such as *hot dog* and *grand slam*, are written as separate words. Other compounds, such as *big-league*, are written with a hyphen (-). More examples of these three kinds of compounds are shown below.

Ways to Form Compounds
One word: birthday, handbag, fireplace, cupcake, rowboat
Separate words: air conditioner, comic strip, ice cream, alley cat
With hyphens: good-by, merry-go-round, cross-eyed, high-rise

Building Your Vocabulary

Find the compounds in these sentences.

1. We found driftwood on the beach near the Coast Guard station.
2. The sailor watched the half-moon from the crow's nest.
3. Sally sold seashells by the seashore sometimes.
4. Dan made a flying saucer with a paper plate and a flashlight.
5. Her baby-sitter goes to high school.

Practice

A. Later in this unit, you will read about Mount St. Helens. This volcano in Washington State erupted in 1980. Join words in column **A** with words in column **B** to form single-word compounds from the story. Then use the compounds in sentences.

	A	**B**		**A**	**B**
1.	earth	blasted	**6.**	up	shoe
2.	side	heated	**7.**	mountain	land
3.	super	side	**8.**	horse	rooted
4.	sand	quake	**9.**	land	top
5.	country	ways	**10.**	waste	scape

B. Compounds sometimes make funny pictures if you look at the meaning of each word they are made from. A "nosedive" might look like this.

Write a compound for each picture below.

11. **13.** **15.**

12. **14.** **16.**

C. Draw pictures of other compounds to share with your classmates.

LANGUAGE CORNER · Coining Words

One way to coin, or invent, a new word is to combine two old words. For example, a fish that swims belly-up could be called a *bellyfish*. What would you call a bull that looks like a dog? Coin some new compounds of your own.

How to Expand Sentences with Adverbs

You know that adverbs are used to describe verbs, adjectives, and other adverbs. Verbs alone don't always give sentences as much detail as a writer would like. Adding adverbs can supply details and add information to your writing. Read the two sentences below. Which one gives you more detail? Which one seems to describe a more dangerous volcanic eruption?

■ **1. A volcano erupted in Hawaii.**

■ **2. A volcano erupted violently in Hawaii.**

Sentence **1** is a perfectly fine sentence. However, adding the adverb *violently* in sentence **2** gives more detail. The adverb tells you *how* the volcano erupted. Now read sentence **3** to see how adding another adverb can add even more detail to the sentence.

■ **3. Yesterday a volcano erupted violently in Hawaii.**

Like adjectives, different adverbs can paint different pictures in a reader's mind. Read sentence **4** to see how changing one adverb can turn the picture of a destructive volcano into a less dangerous one.

■ **4. Yesterday a volcano erupted quietly in Hawaii.**

The Grammar Game ◆ Concentrate on adverbs! Choose six verbs from the list below. Quickly write as many adverbs as you can to describe each one.

draw	drive	snore	end
jump	leave	cheer	discuss
tiptoe	chew	play	touch

Now that you're warmed up, do the same with the rest of the verbs. How many adverbs did you write in all?

Working Together

As your group works on activities **A** and **B**, use adverbs to give detail and information to your writing.

A. Each group member should add an adverb to expand each sentence below. Choose the most exact word possible to tell *how, when,* or *where*. Then mix up the papers and try as a group to guess who's who.

1. I dance.	**7.** I work.	**13.** I study.
2. I sing.	**8.** I read.	**14.** I draw.
3. I laugh.	**9.** I talk.	**15.** I argue.
4. I run.	**10.** I play.	**16.** I smile.
5. I frown.	**11.** I wait.	**17.** I eat.
6. I rest.	**12.** I travel.	**18.** I walk.

B. Find the verbs in the paragraph below. Write the paragraph, adding adverbs of the group's choice to describe each verb. Then write the paragraph again, using different adverbs to change the story of the baseball game.

The baseball game begins at noon. The players arrive and form teams. Aunt Sally walks toward home plate. She chooses a bat and holds it in place. She looks at little Tommy, the pitcher. We all smile. Tommy throws the first ball and Aunt Sally swings. The game gets underway. Aunt Sally hits a fly ball to center field. The center fielder catches the ball for the first out.

WRITERS' CORNER ◆ Precise Adverbs

Be sure that your adverbs are actually describing the words you want them to describe. Read the sample sentence below. Think about it. Can a letter be "full of hope"? Can it *arrive hopefully*?

EXAMPLE: Hopefully the letter will arrive.
IMPROVED: I waited hopefully for the letter to arrive.

Read what you wrote for the Writer's Warm-up. Did you use adverbs in your writing? Do they describe verbs correctly? If they do not, can you improve the sentences?

ERUPTION OF VESUVIUS
painting by Volaire
Virginia Museum of Fine Arts, Richmond, Virginia
Giraudon/Art Resource.

UNIT SIX

USING LANGUAGE
TO
RESEARCH

PART TWO

Literature *Volcano* **by Patricia Lauber**

A Reason for Writing Researching

CREATIVE
Writing

FINE ARTS ◆ At the left you can see a painting of a volcano erupting. Can you imagine what would happen if a volcano were to erupt near your town? What news bulletins would you hear? What would they advise you to do? Write a radio news bulletin. Warn your friends and neighbors about the volcano.

CRITICAL THINKING ◆
A Strategy for Researching

AN ORDER CIRCLE

Researching is gathering information. Writers often do research about unusual events. Information may be gathered from observations, interviews, reports, newspaper files, and many other sources. Then the writer organizes all this information, or puts it in order. After this lesson, you will read part of a research-based book, *Volcano*. Later you will write a research report of your own.

Here is a passage from *Volcano*. How has the author organized her material? In what order does she present the facts?

> Meanwhile the avalanche had hit a ridge and split. One part of it poured into Spirit Lake, adding a 180-foot layer of rock and dirt to the bottom of the lake. . . . The main part of the avalanche swept down the valley of the North Fork of the Toutle River. There, in the valley, most of the avalanche slowed and stopped.

In this passage, the author uses space order. She gives information in an order that shows the path of the avalanche. Information that is given in order is easier to understand.

◆ Learning the Strategy

You can put things in order in many different ways. Suppose you are listing what you want to do this weekend. You might list those things in order of importance, most important first. In what other kind of order might you write your list? Suppose you are following a recipe for pizza. In what order would the steps be listed? Would any other order work as well? Imagine you are writing a letter describing your cousin's birthday. In what order would you tell what happened? In what order would you tell the details about the party decorations? Imagine you are making a book of your friends' names and phone numbers. In what order would you arrange the names?

An order circle can help you put things in order. Inside the circle write what you want to put in order. On the arrows write some kinds of order. Decide which kind of order works best for what you plan to organize.

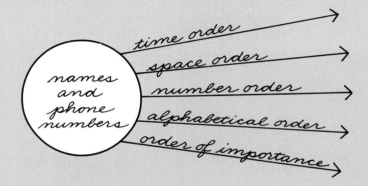

 ## Using the Strategy

A. Suppose you have been chosen to keep track of the birthdays in your family. In what kind of order should you list them? Write *family birthdays* inside an order circle. Write some kinds of order on the arrows. Make a birthday list for your family in the kind of order you decide is best.

B. *Volcano* is about the eruption of a famous volcano. Write the title inside an order circle. Write some kinds of order on the arrows. In what kind of order do you think most of the information in *Volcano* will be given? As you read *Volcano*, decide if you were right.

Applying the Strategy

♦ What kinds of ordering do you have to or like to do most often?

♦ When might you find it helpful to use an order circle?

from

VOLCANO

The Eruption and Healing of Mount St. Helens

"The Big Blast"

by Patricia Lauber

For many years, Mount St. Helens in southern Washington seemed to be only a big, beautiful mountain. It was thought to be one of the most beautiful mountains in the Cascade Range. Yet Mount St. Helens was really a still, sleeping volcano. At any time, it could have awakened and erupted with hot melted rock from inside the earth.

Mount St. Helens had erupted many times over thousands of years. Each time, the volcano had grown bigger. It had grown by being built up from the materials of its own eruptions—melted rock called lava, bits of rock called ash, and gas-filled rock called pumice. Together, the lava, ash, and pumice had built Mount St. Helens into a mountain more than nine thousand feet high.

On March 20, 1980, a strong earthquake shook Mount St. Helens. The earthquake was a sign that the volcano was waking after a long sleep of 123 years. On March 27, the volcano exploded, with smaller explosions coming in April and May. But the big blast, the most destructive one of all, came on May 18. Here is the true account, just as it happened.

The May 18 eruption began with an earthquake that triggered an avalanche. At 8:32 A.M. instruments that were miles away registered a strong earthquake. The pilot and passengers of a small plane saw the north side of the mountain rippling and churning. Shaken by the quake, the bulge was tearing loose. It began to slide, in a huge avalanche that carried along rock ripped from deep inside Mount St. Helens.

The avalanche tore open the mountain. A scalding blast shot sideways out of the opening. It was a blast of steam, from water heated by rising magma.

Normally water cannot be heated beyond its boiling point, which is 212 degrees Fahrenheit at sea level. At boiling point, water turns to a gas, which we call steam. But if water is kept under pressure, it can be heated far beyond its boiling point and still stay liquid. (That is how a pressure cooker works.) If the pressure is removed, this superheated water suddenly turns, or flashes, to steam. As steam it

takes up much more room—it expands. The sudden change to steam can cause an explosion.

Before the eruption Mount St. Helens was like a giant pressure cooker. The rock inside it held superheated water. The water stayed liquid because it was under great pressure, sealed in the mountain. When the mountain was torn open, the pressure was suddenly relieved. The superheated water flashed to steam. Expanding violently, it shattered rock inside the mountain and exploded out the opening, traveling at speeds of up to 200 miles an hour.

The blast flattened whole forests of 180-foot-high firs. It snapped off or uprooted the trees, scattering the trunks as if they were straws. At first, this damage was puzzling. A wind of 200 miles an hour is not strong enough to level forests of giant trees. The explanation, geologists later discovered, was that the wind carried rocks ranging in size from grains of sand to blocks as big as cars. As the blast roared out of the volcano, it swept up and carried along the rock it had shattered.

The result was what one geologist described as "a stone wind." It was a wind of steam and rocks, traveling at high speed. The rocks gave the blast its great force. Before it, trees snapped and fell. Their stumps looked as if they had been sandblasted. The wind of stone rushed on. It stripped bark and branches from trees and uprooted them, leveling 150 square miles of countryside. At the edge of this area other trees were left standing, but the heat of the blast scorched and killed them.

The stone wind was traveling so fast that it overtook and passed the avalanche. On its path was Spirit Lake, one of the most beautiful lakes in the Cascades. The blast stripped the trees from the slopes surrounding the lake and moved on.

Meanwhile the avalanche had hit a ridge and split. One part of it poured into Spirit Lake, adding a 180-foot layer of rock and dirt to the bottom of the lake. The slide of avalanche into the lake forced the water out. The water sloshed up the slopes, then fell back into the lake. With it came thousands of trees felled by the blast.

The main part of the avalanche swept down the valley of the North Fork of the Toutle River. There, in the valley, most of the

LITERATURE: Nonfiction

avalanche slowed and stopped. It covered 24 square miles and averaged 150 feet thick.

The blast itself continued for 10 to 15 minutes, then stopped. Minutes later Mount St. Helens began to erupt upwards. A dark column of ash and ground-up rock rose miles into the sky. Winds blew the ash eastward. Lightning flashed in the ash cloud and started forest fires. In Yakima, Washington, some 80 miles away, the sky turned so dark that street lights went on at noon. Ash fell like snow that would not melt. This eruption continued for nine hours.

Shortly after noon the color of the ash column changed. It became lighter, a sign that the volcano was now throwing out mostly new magma. Until then much of the ash had been made of old rock.

At the same time the volcano began giving off huge flows of pumice and ash. The material was very hot, with temperatures of about 1,000 degrees Fahrenheit, and it traveled down the mountain at speeds of 100 miles an hour. The flows went on until 5:30 in the afternoon. They formed a wedge-shaped plain of pumice on the side of the mountain. Two weeks later temperatures in the pumice were still 780 degrees.

Finally, there were the mudflows, which started when heat from the blast melted ice and snow on the mountaintop. The water mixed with ash, pumice, ground-up rock, and dirt and rocks of the avalanche. The result was a thick mixture that was like wet concrete, a mudflow. The mudflows traveled fast, scouring the landscape and sweeping down the slopes into river valleys. Together their speed and thickness did great damage.

The largest mudflow was made of avalanche material from the valley of the North Fork of the Toutle River. It churned down the river valley, tearing out steel bridges, ripping houses apart, picking up boulders and trucks and carrying them along. Miles away it choked the Cowlitz River and blocked shipping channels in the Columbia River.

When the sun rose on May 19, it showed a greatly changed St. Helens. The mountain was 1,200 feet shorter than it had been the morning before. Most of the old top had slid down the mountain in the avalanche. The rest had erupted out as shattered rock. Geologists

later figured that the volcano had lost three quarters of a cubic mile of old rock.

The north side of the mountain had changed from a green and lovely slope to a fan-shaped wasteland.

At the top of Mount St. Helens was a big, new crater with the shape of a horseshoe. Inside the crater was the vent, the opening through which rock and gases erupted from time to time over the next few years.

In 1980 St. Helens erupted six more times. Most of these eruptions were explosive—ash soared into the air, pumice swept down the north side of the mountain. In the eruptions of June and August, thick pasty lava oozed out of the vent and built a dome. But both domes were destroyed by the next eruptions. In October the pattern changed. The explosions stopped, and thick lava built a dome that was not destroyed. Later eruptions added to the dome, making it bigger and bigger.

During this time, geologists were learning to read the clues found before eruptions. They learned to predict what St. Helens was going to do. The predictions helped to protect people who were on and near the mountain.

Among these people were many natural scientists. They had come to look for survivors, for plants and animals that had lived through the eruption. They had come to look for colonizers, for plants and animals that would move in. Mount St. Helens had erupted many times before. Each time life had returned. Now scientists would have a chance to see how it did. They would see how nature healed itself.

Library Link ♦ *If you would like to learn more about Mount St. Helens, read* Volcano *by Patricia Lauber.*

 Reader's Response

Do you think Mount St. Helens will ever recover from the devastation? Why or why not?

VOLCANO

◆ Responding to Literature

1. You are high above Mount St. Helens. It is 8:32 A.M. on the morning of May 18, 1980. You are watching the explosion bursting beneath you. What are you thinking? What are you feeling? Write a page in your journal about the experience.

2. Scientists help us understand new information by making comparisons with things we do know. Patricia Lauber wrote that "Ash fell like snow that would not melt." What part of *Volcano* interested you? Write a comparison that you would use to explain that part to a younger person.

3. Scientists discovered that nature tried to heal itself after the Mount St. Helens blast. Will nature always be able to heal itself? Why or why not?

◆ Writing to Learn

Think and Order ◆ A scientist may tell how something happens by presenting information in a certain order. Prepare information for one paragraph about the Mount St. Helens eruption. How can you best arrange your information? Draw an order circle like the one below.

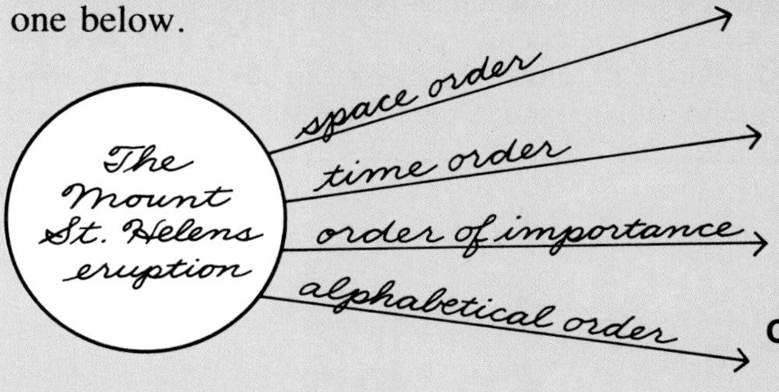

The Mount St. Helens eruption

- space order
- time order
- order of importance
- alphabetical order

Order Circle

Write ◆ Use the order you chose to write a one-paragraph summary about the eruption at Mount St. Helens.

SPEAKING and LISTENING ♦
An Oral Report

Oral reports are different from written reports in one important way. When you give an oral report, you face your audience directly. You must capture and hold their attention. You often start a written report with a topic sentence, but that kind of opening may not work with a "live" audience. You need to get the members of your audience interested in what you have to say. That is why speakers often start with an amusing statement or a fact that is startling or unusual.

Since you want to look at your audience as you speak, you do not want to read your report. Therefore, do not write it out word for word. Outline it on note cards to prompt yourself. Use only key words and phrases as reminders of what you want to say. Your listeners will expect you to be very familiar with your topic and the main ideas of your report. Use the guidelines below to give your report and to listen to the reports of others.

Giving a Report	**1.** Practice in front of a mirror. Know in advance what to say. **2.** Relax. Take a deep breath before you speak. **3.** Speak clearly and look at your audience. **4.** Use charts and illustrations if you wish.
Being a Critical Listener	**1.** Give the speaker your attention. Look at the speaker. **2.** Listen for main points and details. **3.** As you listen, form questions in your mind. Later ask any questions you had that the speaker's report did not answer.

Summary ♦ An effective speaker prepares an oral report in advance. An effective listener pays attention to the main points and supporting ideas.

Guided Practice

Turn each of these facts into an interesting opening sentence for an oral report. Try different kinds of sentences, such as statements, exclamations, and questions.

1. Mount St. Helens has erupted several times since 1980.
2. Many caverns are filled with oddly shaped rock formations.
3. Some of the highest waterfalls in North America are in Yosemite National Park.
4. Tokyo is the busiest and most populated city in Japan.
5. Tornado winds are first seen as a rotating funnel cloud.

Practice

A. Turn each fact below into an interesting opening sentence for an oral report. Try different kinds of sentences, such as statements, exclamations, and questions. Write your sentences.

> 6. Drifting icebergs in the ocean are dangerous to ships.
> 7. Some plants can survive the eruption of a volcano.
> 8. Insects are found all over the earth.
> 9. The production of iron has become essential to modern life.
> 10. Mount Rainier and Mount Hood are both inactive volcanoes.

B. Read the sentences you wrote for **Practice A.** Choose the one you like best. Read it aloud to your classmates. When it is your turn to listen, tell your classmates what you like about their opening sentences. Then offer any suggestions that you have.

C. Think of something you have recently learned in school. What would you like to tell about it? Make notes of key words and phrases you will use. Using the guidelines in this lesson, practice giving an oral report to a partner. When you are the listener, ask the speaker any questions that come to mind about what you hear.

Apply ◆ Think and Write

Strong Opening Sentences ◆ Write an opening sentence for an oral report on a subject that you would like to talk about.

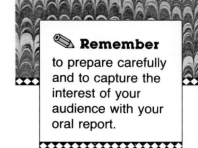

✎ **Remember**
to prepare carefully and to capture the interest of your audience with your oral report.

Everyone is good at something—music, a craft, a sport, household repairs, cooking. If your classmates were listed in an encyclopedia, in what articles would you find them and their talents described?

STUDY SKILLS •
Using an Encyclopedia

Jason wondered, "What makes a volcano erupt?" He decided to look in an encyclopedia for the answer.

An encyclopedia is a set of reference books with many volumes. Each volume contains articles about people, places, things, and ideas. Articles appear in alphabetical order. In an article about a person, of course, the last name is listed first.

To find information, Jason first identified the key word in his question. He decided to look up *volcano*. Then he found the volume that contains the key word. Jason saw that Volume 18 has articles for the letters *U* and *V*. The guide words at the top of each page helped him find the exact page of the article.

Jason could have found the key word in the index, Volume 20. The index alphabetically lists all the topics in the encyclopedia. It tells the volume and page number for each topic.

> **Summary** • Articles in an encyclopedia are arranged in alphabetical order.

Guided Practice

Name the key word in each of the following research questions.

1. What is a geologist?
2. What does the word *Fahrenheit* mean?
3. In what state is Mount St. Helens located?
4. How tall do fir trees usually grow?

Practice

A. Write the key word in each of these questions.

    5. How does an avalanche cause damage?
    6. What are the highest peaks in the Cascade Mountains?
    7. How deep is Crater Lake?
    8. What is special about Mount Rainier?
    9. Where is magma found?

B. Write the key word in each question. Then write the volume number of the encyclopedia that has the article. Use the illustration on page 310 to find the number.

    10. What are some uses for pumice?
    11. How hot can steam get?
    12. How do scientists predict an earthquake?
    13. What different shapes can a crater have?
    14. How many times has Mount St. Helens erupted?
    15. What other volcanoes are in the United States?
    16. Are there different kinds of lava?
    17. What can scientists learn from a seismograph?
    18. Where is igneous rock found?

C. The questions below have two key words. Write both key words. Then give both volume numbers in which articles would appear.

    19. How are earthquakes and volcanoes related?
    20. What does the Richter scale tell about earthquakes?
    21. Which state has the bigger fishing industry, Alaska or Oregon?
    22. Why did George Vancouver pick the name *Mount St. Helens?*
    23. Do the Yakima Indians live in the state of Washington?

Apply ◆ Think and Write

Key Words in Questions ◆ Write three questions that you would like to know the answers to. Underline the key word in each question. If you can, use an encyclopedia to find the answer to one question.

✎ **Remember**
to use the key word in a question to select the correct encyclopedia volume.

◆ GETTING ◆
STARTED

Newspaper headlines summarize events.
Baby Elephant Born at City Zoo
Missouri River Overflows Banks   Tired Astronauts Land Safely
Think of headlines that summarize recent events at school.

WRITING ◆
Taking Notes in Your Own Words

Taking notes helps you recall what you have read by summarizing the most important facts and ideas. Notes can remind you of main ideas and supporting details for a report. Take notes in your own words. You don't have to use full sentences.

Derek read the following paragraph about volcanoes. He took notes on an index card. He wrote the main idea at the top. Supporting ideas were listed under it. Derek used his own words.

Early Roman myth explains volcanoes.
— Vulcan, god of fire and metals
— had great underground workshop
— sounds escaped through mountains
— Vulcan's name — volcano

Throughout history, people have wondered about volcanoes. The early Romans had a myth to explain the smoke and rumbling that came from the earth. They believed in Vulcan, the god of fire and metals. The Romans said that Vulcan lived below the earth. There he had a great blacksmith shop. Mountains were his giant chimneys. Noises from underground were Vulcan's hammer banging the anvil. Sparks proved his enormous power. Our word *volcano* is from Vulcan's name.

Summary ◆ Use your own words to take notes on what you read.

Guided Practice

Summarize each idea in your own words.

1. Throughout history, people have wondered about volcanoes.
2. The Romans said that Vulcan lived below the earth.
3. Sparks proved his enormous power.
4. Our word *volcano* is from Vulcan's name.

Practice

A. Write these statements in your own words.

5. Centuries ago, people realized there was heat inside the earth.

6. They observed the terrible destruction a volcano could cause.

7. A volcano is a particular kind of mountain.

8. Some volcanic mountains build themselves as they erupt.

9. Some volcanic eruptions destroy the mountain.

10. A volcano has a vent, or opening, from the inner earth.

11. A vent is like a vertical pipe, or tube.

12. If enough pressure builds, the vent explodes.

13. When lava comes to the surface, it is red hot.

14. Sometimes vents get blocked by hardened lava.

B. Read the paragraph below about Crater Lake in Oregon. Take notes, beginning with a main idea. Then add the supporting ideas.

Oregon's Crater Lake exists because of a violent volcanic eruption that occurred long ago. Mount Mazama was a volcano nearly twelve thousand feet high. A powerful eruption thousands of years ago caused its top to collapse. The cave-in formed a crater a half-mile deep. Rainwater eventually filled it, forming Crater Lake. At first there were no fish in Crater Lake. Eventually the lake was stocked with trout, and now fish are added every year.

Apply ✦ Think and Write

Dictionary of Knowledge ✦ How is a geyser like a volcano? Look up *geyser* to find out. Using your own words, take notes on what you read. Tell someone else what you have learned, using your notes for reference.

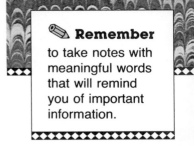

✎ **Remember**
to take notes with meaningful words that will remind you of important information.

WRITING ◆ An Outline

An outline is a written plan. It can help you organize a report by showing how information goes together. Your outline can tell you if you have enough details for each main idea. The outline below has an explanation beside it. The outline gives information for a report about a famous volcano.

The Paricutín Volcano
I. Description of location
   A. Small Mexican village
   B. 200 miles west of Mexico City
II. Farmer witnesses first blast
   A. Dionisio Pulido, corn farmer
   B. Notices unusual ground heat
   C. Hears strange noises
   D. Suddenly sees ground cave in
III. Mountain grows overnight
   A. Explosion breaks land open
   B. Steam, ash, rock, lava fly
   C. Forms hill 120 feet high

An outline begins with a title, centered at the top, which can become your report title. Each main idea becomes a main topic. Main topics are listed in logical order. Each is labeled with a Roman numeral with a period.

Details become subtopics. They are grouped under the proper main topic. Subtopics are indented, and each is labeled with a capital letter followed by a period.

Notice that the first word on each line is capitalized.

Summary ◆ An **outline** organizes information into main ideas and supporting details.

Guided Practice

Use the outline above to answer the questions.

1. What is the title of the outline?
2. How many main topics does the outline have?
3. How many subtopics support the first main idea?

Practice

A. 4–13. Copy the outline below about a new island. Beside each line, write *title, main topic,* or *subtopic.*

An Island Is Born

I. Surtsey becomes an island
   A. In Atlantic Ocean near Iceland
   B. Underwater volcano erupted
   C. Lava reached surface, May 14, 1963
II. Surtsey continues to grow
   A. Eruption went on for two years
   B. Island grew 568 feet high
   C. Area of one-and-a-half square miles
   D. Now considered part of Iceland

B. Use the topics below to form an outline titled ''After Mount St. Helens.'' Identify the two main topics. Then group the subtopics under them. Remember Roman numerals and capital letters.

   Problems for fish
   Water lacked oxygen
   Trees damaged
   Nesting areas lost
   Plants and berries destroyed
   Birds also suffer
   Rivers clogged with mud
   Ash-coated wings

C. Prepare an outline from the Dictionary of Knowledge entry on geysers. Identify one main topic from each paragraph in the entry. Add as many subtopics as you need. Don't forget to give your outline a title.

Apply ◆ Think and Write

An Informational Paragraph ◆ Write a paragraph using information from the outline you wrote for **Practice C.** Choose one of the main topics and its subtopics as the basis of your paragraph.

✎ **Remember**
that an outline is a good way to organize information.

Focus on Topic Choice

To write a good report, you must choose the right topic. That means, first of all, choosing a topic that interests you and is likely to interest your readers. It also means choosing a topic that is narrow enough to cover in your report. A topic like "Volcanoes of the World," for example, is too broad to cover in a short report. It could easily be the subject of a whole book.

But suppose you want to write a short report about volcanoes. Can you do it? Yes, you can do it by narrowing the broad topic of volcanoes to one of a workable size. Look at the five topics below. Notice the steps by which the broad topic ''Volcanoes of the World'' becomes the narrowed topic of ''Erpution of Mount St. Helens: May 18, 1980.''

Volcanoes of the World
Kinds of Volcanoes: Cone and Shield
Active and Inactive Cone Volcanoes
Active Cone Volcanoes in the Cascade Range
Eruption of Mount St. Helens: May 18, 1980

The Writer's Voice ◆ "Eruption of Mount St. Helens: May 18, 1980" is a suitable topic for a short report. Would it also make a good subject for a whole book? Explain.

Could the broad topic "Volcanoes" possibly be covered in a few paragraphs? Explain.

Working Together

When you write a short report, you should begin by choosing a topic that interests you. Then narrow the topic so that it can be covered well in a limited number of paragraphs or pages. With your group, complete activities **A** and **B**.

A. All the topics below are too broad for a short report. With your group, narrow each one until it is suitable for a short report. Compare your narrowed topics with those of other groups.

1. Birds of North America
2. Heroes of the American Revolution
3. Volcanoes (not the Mount St. Helens eruption)
4. Tall Buildings of the World
5. Professional Sports

B. Choose a broad subject area, such as *science, health, geography, history, entertainment*. With your group, try to decide on five good topics for short reports within that one subject area. You might want to work individually at first. Then, when everyone has finished, the group can decide on the five most appealing topics. Finally, each group can share its list with the rest of the class.

In Your Group

- Contribute ideas.
- Be sure everyone understands what to do.
- Help the group reach agreement.
- Record the group's ideas.

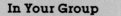

THESAURUS CORNER • Word Choice

Two of the main entry words in the Thesaurus are adverbs: *fast* and *well*. Write two original sentences about volcanoes. Use *fast* (or a synonym) as an adverb in one sentence. Use *well* (or a synonym) as an adverb in the other. Then write three more original sentences about volcanoes, using any of the words listed in the Thesaurus. The noun *energy* and the adjective *large* are possible choices. Underline the words you have chosen.

WRITING PROCESS
RESEARCHING

Writing a
Research Report

Volcano is a fascinating report of the eruption of Mount St. Helens. We do not know what kind of research its author, Patricia Lauber, did. We can imagine, however, that she might have interviewed witnesses. She might have read newspaper reports and studied scientific information about volcanoes. She probably gathered information from many sources.

Patricia Lauber arranged her facts in a logical order. She used time order to explain when the main events happened. She used space order to describe the scene of the volcano blast.

Know Your Purpose and Audience

MY PURPOSE

In this lesson you will write your own research report. Your purpose will be to write about an unusual natural event.

MY AUDIENCE

Your audience will be your classmates. Later you can give an oral report based on your research. You can also help to create a collection of ''Amazing But True'' reports.

1 Prewriting

Before you write, you need to choose and narrow a topic. Then you need to find and organize information on your topic.

Choose Your Topic ◆ Browse through the library, looking for ideas. Look at science books, encyclopedias, and science magazines. Write down every topic that sounds interesting. Find out a little about each.

Think About It

Make a list of possible topics. Which topic makes you most curious? Circle the topic you want to research. If your topic is too broad to write about, narrow it. Instead of writing about hurricanes, for example, write about one hurricane.

Talk About It

Find out what topics your classmates are choosing. Ask them how they made their choices. You could work with a partner to look through library books for topic ideas. Working with a partner often helps ideas come to you more easily.

Topic Ideas

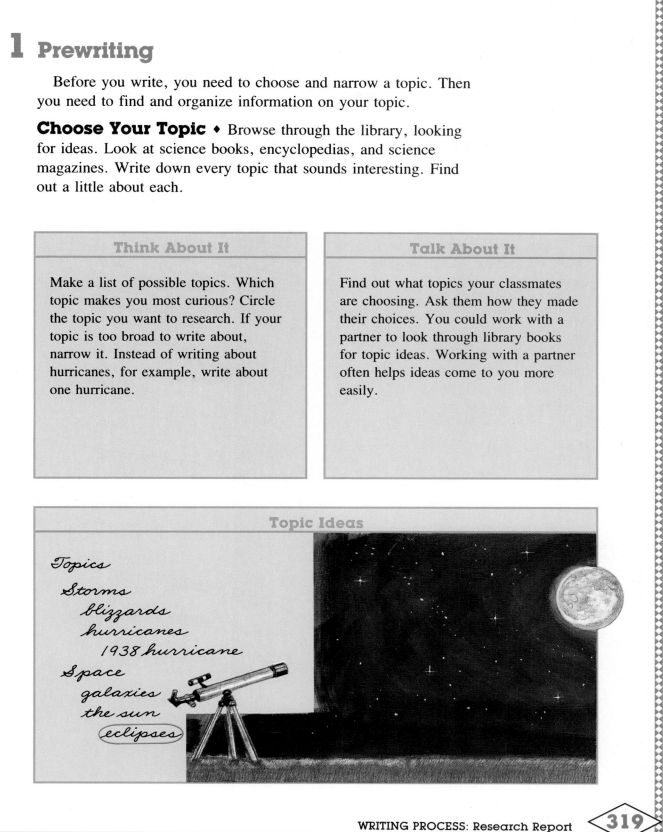

Topics
Storms
  blizzards
  hurricanes
    1938 hurricane
Space
  galaxies
  the sun
  eclipses

Choose Your Strategy ◆ Here are two fact-gathering strategies. Read both. Then use the strategy you think will help you more to prepare to write.

PREWRITING IDEAS

CHOICE ONE

Taking Notes

As you do your research, take notes on what you discover. Make a separate group of note cards for each main idea. The cards should contain supporting ideas. Be sure the notes are in your own words. Make source cards, too. Follow the examples shown for a book, a magazine, and an encyclopedia. Then make an outline to organize the information you found.

Model

Hahn, B. J. Eclipse! Morristown. Burdett 1986.

"Eclipses Rarely Seen." Space Report, March 9, 1987.

"Eclipse." Encyclopedia of Space.

Few people see eclipses.
— don't happen often
— last a short time
— touch a small spot

CHOICE TWO

An Order Circle

Write your topic inside an order circle. Write some kinds of order on arrows. How will you arrange your facts? Look at your order circle and decide which kind of order will work best.

You might try one of these kinds of order. Time order tells what happened first, next, last. Space order tells what happened in one place, then another. Size order starts or ends with the biggest or longest. Order of interest tells the most interesting fact first or last.

Model

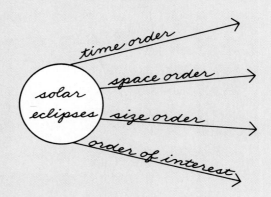

solar eclipses

time order
space order
size order
order of interest

2 Writing

Arrange your prewriting notes in the order you plan to use. Then begin to write. Be sure to state your topic in your first paragraph. You might begin with a dramatic, attention-getting fact. Here are two ideas.

- ♦ All hurricanes are bad, but some are worse than others. One of the worst was the hurricane of 1938.
- ♦ Solar eclipses do not happen very often. In an eclipse the moon moves between the sun and the earth.

Then keep writing in the order you chose. Include details that help the reader understand the event. End with a summary paragraph that includes a prediction for the future. Your prediction should be based on facts in your report.

Sample First Draft ♦

Few people ever see a total eclipse of the sun. An eclipse happens when the moon gets between the sun and the earth. When the moon hides the sun completly, the eclipse is total. Eclipses of the moon also happen. When an eclipse starts, an edge of the sun dissappears. It looks like a bite out of the sun that keeps growing. When the eclipse is Total, the sky is dark you can even see the stars. Minutes later, the sun starts to reapear. It soon grows to its full size again. An eclipse is total for only a few minutes.

You probably won't never see a total eclipse. Such an event is very rare. also, it lasts a short time.

3 Revising

You have written your report. Now would you like to make it clearer or more interesting? This idea may help you.

REVISING IDEA

FIRST   Read to Yourself

As you read, ask yourself questions. Did you accomplish your purpose, writing a research report about a natural event? Will your audience understand it and find it interesting?

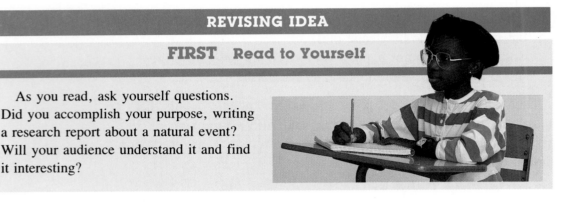

Focus: Did you choose a topic that was narrow enough for a short report? Are you trying to include too much information or cover too much material? Make a wavy line 〰〰 under parts you might like to remove.

THEN   Share with a Partner

Sit beside a partner. Read aloud as your partner reads along silently. Then ask your partner for comments. These guidelines may help you work together on your report.

The Writer

Guidelines: Ask your partner to tell you what is unclear.

Sample questions:
- What was the most interesting part?
- Did you understand my summary paragraph?
- **Focus question:** Is my topic narrow enough? Should I take anything out?

The Writer's Partner

Guidelines: Be honest but helpful. Tell which parts you liked and which parts confused you.

Sample questions:
- I didn't understand the part about ____.
- You could leave out these details about ____.

Revising Model ♦ This research report is being revised. The blue revising marks show changes the writer is making.

See is overused. *Witness* is more interesting.

The writer decided this was really about a broader topic.

This detail would make the summary paragraph stronger.

The writer's partner heard the double negative.

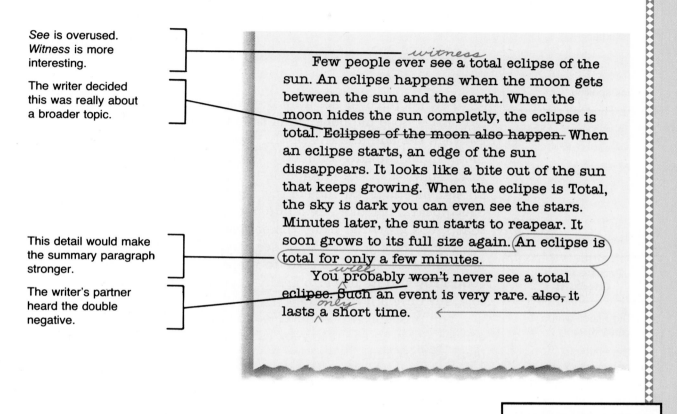

> *witness*
> Few people ever see a total eclipse of the sun. An eclipse happens when the moon gets between the sun and the earth. When the moon hides the sun completly, the eclipse is total. ~~Eclipses of the moon also happen.~~ When an eclipse starts, an edge of the sun dissapears. It looks like a bite out of the sun that keeps growing. When the eclipse is Total, the sky is dark you can even see the stars. Minutes later, the sun starts to reapear. It soon grows to its full size again. An eclipse is total for only a few minutes.
> *will*
> You probably ~~won't~~ never see a total eclipse. Such an event is very rare. ~~also,~~ it lasts a ∧*only* short time.

Read the above report the way the writer has decided it *should* be. Then revise your own research report.

Grammar Check ♦ Double negatives can make meaning unclear.

Word Choice ♦ Have you overused any words like *see* in your writing? A thesaurus can help you find more interesting words.

Revising Checklist

- ☐ **Purpose:** Did I write a research report about an unusual natural event?

- ☐ **Audience:** Will my classmates find my report understandable and interesting?

- ☐ **Focus:** Is my topic narrow enough to be covered well in a short report?

4 Proofreading

Be courteous to those who will read your writing. Now is the time to make sure that your report is neat and correct.

Proofreading Model ◆ Here is a draft of the report on solar eclipses. Proofreading changes in red have been added.

Proofreading Marks

capital letter =

small letter /

indent paragraph ¶

check spelling ⬭

Few people ever *witness* ~~see~~ a total eclipse of the sun. An eclipse happens when the moon gets between the sun and the earth. When the moon hides the sun ⬭completly⬭ *completely*, the eclipse is total. ~~Eclipses of the moon also happen.~~ ¶When an eclipse starts, an edge of the sun *disappears* ⬭dissappears⬭. It looks like a bite out of the sun that keeps growing. When the eclipse is Total, the sky is dark. you can even see the stars. Minutes later, the sun starts to ⬭reapear⬭ *reappear*. It soon grows to its full size again. An eclipse is total for only a few minutes.

You probably ~~won't~~ *will* never see a total eclipse. Such an event is very rare. ~~also,~~ it lasts *only* a short time.

Proofreading Checklist

☐ Did I spell words correctly?

☐ Did I indent paragraphs?

☐ Did I use capital letters correctly?

☐ Did I use correct marks at the end of sentences?

☐ Did I use my best handwriting?

PROOFREADING IDEA

Using a Ruler

A ruler can help you proofread. Place the ruler under the first line. Proofread that line carefully. Then do the same on each of the following lines. Reading one line at a time makes it easier to find mistakes.

Now proofread your research report, add a title, and make a neat copy.

5 Publishing

It is now time to share your report with others. Try one of the ideas below.

A Total Eclipse

Few people ever witness a total eclipse of the sun. An eclipse happens when the moon gets between the sun and the earth. When the moon hides the sun completely, the eclipse is total.

When an eclipse starts, an edge of the sun disappears. It looks like a bite out of the sun that keeps growing. When the eclipse is total, the sky is dark. You can even see the stars. Minutes later, the sun starts to reappear. It soon grows to its full size again.

You will probably never see a total eclipse. Such an event is very rare. It lasts only a short time. An eclipse is total for only a few minutes.

EARTH

PUBLISHING IDEAS

Share Aloud	Share in Writing
Read your report aloud to your classmates. Ask them to note facts about your topic. Later ask your audience to tell you which facts they found most interesting.	Help to make a file of ''Amazing But True'' reports. Place each report in its own folder and file alphabetically by title. The file should include a sheet titled ''Readers' Comments.''

CURRICULUM ·CONNECTION·

Writing Across the Curriculum

Social Studies

Recently you wrote a research report about an unusual natural event. You may have used an order circle to help organize the information. You can also put in order the facts you learn in social studies. For example, you can arrange facts to show time order or order of importance.

Writing to Learn

Think and Decide ◆ Many books have been written about volcanic eruptions. Some people spend their lives studying volcanoes. What do you think are the most important things we can learn about volcanoes? Use an order circle to help sort your ideas.

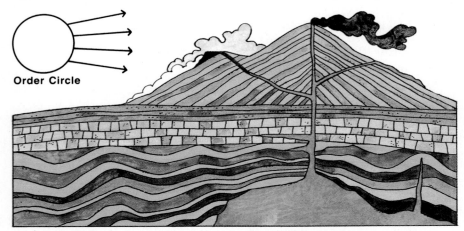

Order Circle

Write ◆ Make a list of important things to learn about volcanoes. Tell which you think is most important and why.

Writing in Your Journal

In the Writer's Warm-up you wrote about volcanoes. Throughout this unit you learned much about volcanic eruptions. Browse through the pages. What is the most startling thing you learned? Write about it in your journal.

BOOKS TO ENJOY

Read More About It

How Did We Find Out About Volcanoes?

by Isaac Asimov

You can learn about volcanoes because scientists share information. Isaac Asimov explains some of the mysteries of volcano study.

Pompeii: Exploring a Roman Ghost Town

by Ron and Nancy Goor

When Mount Vesuvius erupted in 79 A.D., lava and mudslides buried Pompeii. This book explains how scientists have pieced together a story of life in Pompeii before the terrible eruption.

Geology *by Dougal Dixon*

Geology is the study of the physical features of the earth. Geologists want to learn about what lies deep inside the earth. They examine ores, rocks, and minerals. Volcanoes give geologists a kind of window to the inner earth.

Book Report Idea — Scientist's Log Report

When scientists do experiments, they write down the steps they follow and what they find. For your next book report, try giving facts and details in the form of a scientist's report.

Create a Scientist's Log

Make up a form similar to the one shown here. Fill in information about your book. Give facts and details in a clear, exact way.

NAME OF BOOK: *A Shovelful of Earth*

AUTHOR OF BOOK: *L. J. and M. Milne*

THEME OF BOOK: *exploring earth layers*

MAIN CHARACTERS: *geologists, the earth*

UNEXPECTED EVENTS: _____

NEW FACTS: _____

CONCLUSIONS: _____

RECOMMENDATIONS: _____

SKETCH: _____

UNIT REVIEW

Unit 6

Adverbs and Adjectives
pages 284–291

A. Write each sentence. Underline the adverb.

1. The carpenter worked carefully.
2. She accurately measured everything.
3. She easily finished sawing the wood.
4. She accidentally hit her thumb with the hammer.
5. She groaned loudly.
6. She went back to work immediately.
7. Soon the cabinet was completed.
8. She smiled contentedly at her work.
9. Then she rested happily in a chair.

B. Write the correct form of the adverb in parentheses ( ).

10. Ron's essay is (neatly) written than Judy's.
11. Maggie rises (early) than Fran.
12. My box is the (densely) packed of all.
13. Terri runs (fast) than Charles.
14. Andrew chopped the vegetables (quickly) than Steven.
15. The (hard) I work, the more I learn.
16. I go to the library (often) on Thursday than on any other day.
17. Jeanne trains (energetically) than any other team member.
18. Pablo rides the (skillfully) of all the cowboys.

C. Write the adverb that describes each underlined adjective or adverb.

19. This is a rather difficult problem.
20. Quite suddenly the rain stopped.
21. That is an incredibly hard riddle.
22. Helga is unbelievably brilliant.
23. I am totally amazed by your reply.
24. It is an unusually cool evening.
25. Mr. Otis drives fairly skillfully.
26. The reward was justly deserved.
27. The band played extremely loudly.
28. The door was partially open.
29. A very tiny mouse darted by us.
30. We chased quite frantically after it.

D. Write each sentence. Choose the word in parentheses ( ) that correctly completes the sentence.

31. I whistle (bad, badly).
32. I feel (bad, badly) about my lack of skill.
33. Jenna whistles (good, well).
34. She has always been a (good, well) whistler.
35. She (proud, proudly) shows her skill.
36. I make a (terrible, terribly) noise when I try.
37. I know I sound (awful, awfully).
38. When my dog hears me, it howls (mournful, mournfully).
39. It (complete, completely) covers its ears with its paws.
40. I feel (terrible, terribly) about the whole thing.
41. My brother (thoughtful, thoughtfully) tries to console me.
42. I am (fortunate, fortunately) to have a brother who understands.

Negative Words *pages 292–293*

E. Write each sentence. Choose the word in parentheses ( ) that correctly completes the sentence.

43. Marc and Tammy don't have (no, any) homework to do.
44. No one can (ever, never) surpass Tina's skills on the diving board.
45. Doesn't (anybody, nobody) know the answer?
46. There (was, wasn't) no one at the park when I arrived.
47. I (won't, will) never go back to that place again.
48. None of your solutions (are, aren't) correct.
49. Sue hasn't done (any, none) of her homework.
50. There (is, isn't) nowhere Ms. Townsend hasn't visited.
51. Can't (anybody, nobody) help me?
52. I don't (ever, never) want to go through that again!

Compounds *pages 294–295*

F. Write the following sentences. Underline the compounds.

53. My uncle is a police officer.
54. His sister-in-law is a doctor.
55. The next bus goes downtown.
56. The afternoon sun made us squint.
57. The children were playing outdoors.
58. That noise is giving me a headache.
59. Have you seen the new high school?
60. I love my new beanbag chair.
61. The other car has the right-of-way.
62. This tablecloth is easy to clean.

Using an Encyclopedia
pages 310–311

G. Write the key word in each question. Then write the number of the encyclopedia that has the article. Use the illustration on page 310 to find the number.

63. What are some uses for sand?
64. Who invented the game of baseball?
65. What causes a tornado?
66. How many automobiles and trucks are there in Iceland?
67. What state is the leading producer of peaches?
68. Are there different kinds of algae?
69. What is the nickname for Wichita, Kansas?
70. How many bones are there in an adult human body?
71. Where was the final battle of the Revolutionary War fought?
72. What famous musical piece did Johann Strauss, Jr., write?

Outlining *pages 314–315*

H. Copy the outline below about yeast bread. Beside each line, write *title, main topic,* or *subtopic.*

73.   Yeast Bread
74. I. Kinds of yeast bread
75.   A. Pan bread
76.   B. Hearth bread
77. II. How yeast bread is made
78.   A. Commercial bakeries
79.   B. Home bakeries
80.   C. Conventional bread making
81.   D. Continuous bread making

CUMULATIVE REVIEW

UNIT 1: Sentences   pages 6–15

A. Write the complete subject of each sentence. Underline the simple subject. Write *(You)* if the simple subject is understood.

1. The circus came to town yesterday.
2. Tell me all about it!
3. A group of elephants marched in the parade.
4. A baby elephant was very appealing.
5. Look at those fantastic acrobats!
6. The clowns in tramp costumes did funny tricks.
7. Let me have the souvenir booklet.
8. I will always remember this wonderful circus!
9. Come to the show with me next year.

B. Write the complete predicate of each of the following sentences. Underline the simple predicate.

10. Helene is training for the swimming and diving meet.
11. She swims for two hours every day.
12. She is doing the backstroke now.
13. My friend Gary has practiced a daring new dive.
14. He performs it from a high platform.
15. He will perform at the sports meet next week.
16. All his friends will attend.
17. Many fine divers will compete.
18. Donna competed in last year's meet.

UNIT 2: Capital Letters and Periods   pages 66–69

C. Write the sentences. Capitalize the proper nouns. Write the abbreviations correctly.

19. Take wilson ave to rte 56 and then turn left.
20. Our family is going to orono, maine, on aug 15.
21. I read a newspaper article by phil cole, jr., my uncle harry's friend.
22. The committee will meet again on tues at 6 p m sharp.
23. I am going to a lecture by prof eric broudy.
24. My uncle's family will arrive from new mexico on fri aug 2.
25. My mother and mrs fay linden often play tennis together.
26. The traffic on thompson blvd during rush hour has gotten worse.

UNIT 2: Commas   pages 90–91

D. Write the sentences. Add commas where they are needed.

27. Jason please hand me the camera.
28. Yes I am the one who wrote the letter.
29. Peter Mary and Steve went to the softball game.
30. We are grateful Dennis for your assistance.
31. The library card catalog lists the author's name as McKenzie Ellen.
32. This Korean dish includes meat vegetables noodles and spices.
33. No we are not going to the game.
34. Well Jim you certainly made a mess!

Unit 3: Verbs   *pages 116–133*

E. Write each sentence. Choose the verb in parentheses ( ) that correctly completes the sentence.

35. Mr. Sherman (work, works) in the new office building.
36. The dog has (come, came) home.
37. We (did, done) our chores.
38. Tara and Lori (practices, practice) their duets every day.
39. I have (grew, grown) an inch since last summer.
40. Who (wrote, written) this note?
41. Sally has (wore, worn) this dress before.
42. I shall (give, gives) the letter to my sister.
43. John will (take, took) a seat in the back row.

Unit 4: Pronouns   *pages 176–185*

F. Write each sentence. Choose the pronoun in parentheses ( ) that correctly completes the sentences.

44. Will (they, them) follow directions carefully?
45. Denise and (I, me) like salads.
46. Ms. Greene asked (they, them) to be quiet.
47. Will Jackie and Mike bring (their, theirs) parents?
48. The victory is (their, theirs).
49. Alison told (we, us) a funny story.
50. (We, Us) couldn't stop laughing.
51. Give the paintbrush to (I, me).
52. Richard and (she, her) tied for first place.

Units 5 and 6: Adjectives and Adverbs   *pages 234–241, 284–291*

G. Write each sentence. Choose the word in parentheses ( ) that correctly completes the sentence. Then write whether the word is an adjective or an adverb.

53. Mr. Chao is a (proud, proudly) man.
54. This is a (real, really) good song.
55. Davy Crockett was a (real, really) person.
56. Sam ate his (usual, usually) lunch.
57. Martha (usual, usually) does her homework before dinner.
58. The (energetic, energetically) child cleaned the bicycle.
59. The child behaved (bad, badly).
60. I have a (bad, badly) headache.

Unit 6: Negative Words   *pages 292–293*

H. Write each sentence. Use the correct word in parentheses.

61. No person has (ever, never) run a mile in less than three minutes.
62. Can't (anyone, no one) help me carry this box upstairs?
63. There (is, isn't) no reason to be afraid.
64. Nothing (will, won't) happen unless you make it happen.
65. I couldn't find my pet rabbit (anywhere, nowhere).
66. None of this has (anything, nothing) to do with the subject.
67. We (have, haven't) no reason to doubt his word.
68. You (won't, will) never finish your homework by watching television.

LANGUAGE PUZZLERS

Tom Swifties

Tom Swifties are puns that are based on adverbs. Using different adverbs, write some Tom Swifties like the following.

1. "It hasn't rained in a month," said Tom dryly.
2. "You're late. It's already ten after ten," said Tom tensely.
3. "I think I have chickenpox," said Tom infectiously.
4. "May I have a spaniel for my birthday?" asked Tom doggedly.
5. "I didn't mean to break the window," said Tom fragilely.

Pig-Latin Puzzler

Pig Latin is a secret way of talking. In pig Latin the first consonant sound of each word is moved to the end and -*ay* is added. Figure out these messages. Then write your own message in pig Latin. Use some adverbs in your message.

Susan: E-way ent-way o-tay the ovies-may esterday-yay.

Joanne: At-whay id-day ou-yay ee-say?

Susan: E-way aw-say *ambi-Bay* again, or-fay the ird-thay ime-tay.

Joanne: Ow-hay as-way it?

Susan: Onderful-way! I ied-cray ietly-quay at the ad-say arts-pay and aughed-lay o-say oudly-lay at the unny-fay ones.

Unit 6 Extra Practice

1 Writing with Adverbs

p. 284

A. In the sentences below, the verbs are underlined. Find the adverb in each sentence and write it.

1. The group accidentally <u>found</u> a cave.
2. They <u>searched</u> inside.
3. The explorers quietly <u>admired</u> the cavern.
4. The tunnel <u>sloped</u> downward.
5. Tourists frequently <u>visit</u> Carlsbad Caverns.
6. Three children <u>approached</u> the cave cautiously.
7. Caves sometimes <u>contain</u> lakes.
8. Cave explorers <u>test</u> their equipment carefully.
9. Swarms of bats <u>flew</u> overhead.
10. Explorers ordinarily <u>carry</u> flashlight batteries.
11. She <u>marked</u> her trail clearly.
12. We <u>started</u> our journey early.
13. Water continually <u>follows</u> cracks in the rocks.
14. The water slowly <u>carves</u> the rock.
15. The cave's size always <u>amazes</u> tourists.
16. Beautiful rock formations <u>rise</u> upward.

B. Write each sentence and underline the adverb. Write *how*, *when*, or *where* to show what the adverb tells about the verb.

EXAMPLE: We never found the mysterious crystal cave.

ANSWER: We <u>never</u> found the mysterious crystal cave. (when)

17. Miki often brings a compass.
18. Ali studied the map closely.
19. The underground river flowed nearby.
20. Our voices echoed strangely.
21. Cave explorers usually wear sturdy boots.
22. The walls of the cave plunged downward.
23. They gladly gave her a hand.
24. My favorite rock formation will appear soon.
25. We finally reached the end of the tunnel.
26. Our friends were waiting for us outside.

2 Adverbs That Compare

p. 286

A. For each adverb below, write the form that is used to compare two actions. Then write the form that is used to compare three or more actions.

1. often **2.** well **3.** densely **4.** hard **5.** neatly

B. Write the sentences. For each adverb in parentheses ( ), add *more* or use the *-er* form.

6. The Sacramento River flows (gently) in late spring.
7. The river valley opens (wide) between the Coast Ranges.
8. Flowers grow (thickly) during the rainy season.
9. The river overflows (frequently) in that season than now.
10. The valley turns green (soon) than the mountaintop.
11. Moist chinook winds over the Sierra Nevada mountains blow (dry) on the eastern slopes.

C. Write each sentence. For each adverb in parentheses ( ), add *most* or use the *-est* form.

12. Trappers arrived (early) of all the explorers.
13. That area grew (fast) because gold was discovered there.
14. Which peak rises (high) in this range?
15. Mount Shasta rises (high) in the Cascade Range.
16. The mountains slope the (gradually) on the east side.
17. The elevation drops (low) at Death Valley.
18. These are the (commonly) grown flowers in warm weather.
19. The breeze blows (pleasantly) on the mountain slopes.

D. Write the sentences. Use the correct form of *well* or *badly* to complete each sentence.

20. This guide followed the trail (well) than that one.
21. Our party rode the (badly) of the three groups.
22. The horses managed (badly) than the mules on this trail.
23. We understood the map (well) than the scout did.
24. Ramon enjoyed hiking even (well) than riding.
25. Who remembers this trip the (well) of all?
26. Last year's vacation ended (badly) than this year's.
27. Could next year's be the (well) of all?

3 Adverbs Before Adjectives and Other Adverbs

p. 288

A. Write each sentence. Then write the adverb that describes the underlined adjective or adverb.

1. The Rockies are incredibly <u>beautiful</u> mountains.
2. The temperature feels slightly <u>cooler</u> as you climb higher.
3. Even in early summer, snowstorms occur quite <u>suddenly</u>.
4. Unusually <u>cold</u> weather can be dangerous.
5. You can't be too <u>careful</u> in the mountains.
6. The Rocky Mountains rise so <u>dramatically</u> above the plain.
7. The bighorn sheep is a very <u>rare</u> animal.
8. The sheep jumps so <u>fast</u> it is hard to see.
9. Idaho is justly <u>famous</u> for its sheep ranches.
10. Sheep are very <u>hardy</u> animals.
11. They can survive remarkably <u>cold</u> weather.
12. In summer the shepherds move their flocks rather <u>quickly</u>.
13. Fairly <u>often</u> they go from hot valleys to cool mountains.
14. These herders almost <u>always</u> use horses to move the sheep.
15. Cattle also graze in the unusually <u>lush</u> meadows.
16. Potato farms are certainly <u>common</u> in southern Idaho.
17. An incredibly <u>small</u> amount of the crop is eaten fresh.
18. Quite <u>often</u> the potatoes become frozen french fries.
19. Totally <u>vacant</u> towns dot the state's mining country.
20. Silver City was unbelievably <u>wealthy</u> at one time.
21. Now wind blows through the completely <u>empty</u> streets.
22. Skiing attracts a considerably <u>large</u> number of tourists.
23. Idahoans like their extremely <u>varied</u> way of life.

B. Write each sentence. Use the adverbs below to complete the sentences.

quite   so   extremely   too   incredibly   wildly

24. Good weather is ____ important to a potato farmer.
25. ____ much rain in early spring can ruin the crop.
26. Tourism has become ____ successful in Idaho.
27. Rafting trips on the Snake River can be ____ exciting.
28. Stretches of ____ rolling white water are scary and fun.
29. Mountain climbing is hard work but ____ rewarding.

4 Using Adverbs and Adjectives   *p. 290*

A. Write the word in parentheses ( ) that correctly completes each sentence.

1. Koko is a (remarkable, remarkably) clever gorilla.
2. Koko's teacher is (extreme, extremely) patient.
3. Koko (gradual, gradually) learns the Ameslan language.
4. Ameslan, or American Sign Language, is the hand speech (common, commonly) used by about 200,000 deaf Americans.
5. At first Koko made the signs (bad, badly).
6. Now she uses her fingers (good, well).
7. Koko's fingers move (quick, quickly) to make the signs.
8. She is extremely (smart, smartly).
9. She (occasional, occasionally) signs two words at once.
10. Koko often is (playful, playfully).
11. Sometimes she gestures (angry, angrily).
12. She is distracted (fair, fairly) easily.
13. She cleans things with a (slight, slightly) damp sponge.
14. Afterwards she (usual, usually) rips up the sponge.
15. Koko has never seen a (real, really) alligator.
16. But toy alligators frighten her (terrible, terribly).
17. Koko likes sandwiches that are (thick, thickly).
18. She brushes her teeth (careful, carefully).
19. She often smiles (happy, happily) in the mirror.
20. The teacher is (proud, proudly) of Koko's success.
21. Koko refers to herself as a (fine, finely) gorilla.

B. Choose the word in parentheses ( ) that correctly completes each sentence. Write the sentence. Then write whether *good*, *well*, *bad*, or *badly* is an adjective or an adverb in the sentence.

EXAMPLE: Koko needs a (good, well) night's sleep.
ANSWER: Koko needs a good night's sleep. (adjective)

22. Koko stays (good, well) by getting plenty of sleep.
23. A substitute teacher does a (good, well) job.
24. Unfortunately Koko performs (bad, badly) for him.
25. They do not work (good, well) together.
26. The substitute teacher feels (bad, badly).

5 Using Negative Words

p. 292

A. Write the negative word in each sentence. Tell which negatives are contractions.

1. In science, Mandy never gets lower than an A.
2. Mandy will not delay her science experiment.
3. "No extra equipment is needed," she said.
4. Didn't anyone know what to do first?
5. Nobody answered Mandy's question.
6. She put salt in the water till no more dissolved.
7. Now she doesn't know where to put the container.
8. Nothing will happen unless she heats it up.

B. Write the sentences. Underline the negative words.

9. Couldn't anyone guess what would happen next?
10. We haven't seen anything in the glass.
11. Perhaps none of the water has evaporated.
12. Actually I have never seen crystals form.
13. You surely need no help with this!
14. Nobody could understand the directions.
15. Doesn't anyone know how to solve the problem?
16. No one can fold a piece of paper in this shape.
17. Hasn't anybody tried yet?
18. I could find nothing to use as a funnel.

C. Write the word in parentheses ( ) that correctly completes each sentence. Avoid double negatives.

19. There is no tubing (nowhere, anywhere).
20. No one will (never, ever) be able to put this together.
21. There (was, wasn't) no place to work on my project.
22. Nothing (won't, will) happen if you change the water in the fish bowl.
23. Hasn't (no one, anyone) fed the fish yet?
24. None of this (isn't, is) visible without a microscope.
25. Couldn't (anyone, no one) see the blood vessels?
26. We haven't written down (any, none) of the steps.
27. We (won't, will) never be able to do this again.
28. There (was, wasn't) no need to check the results.

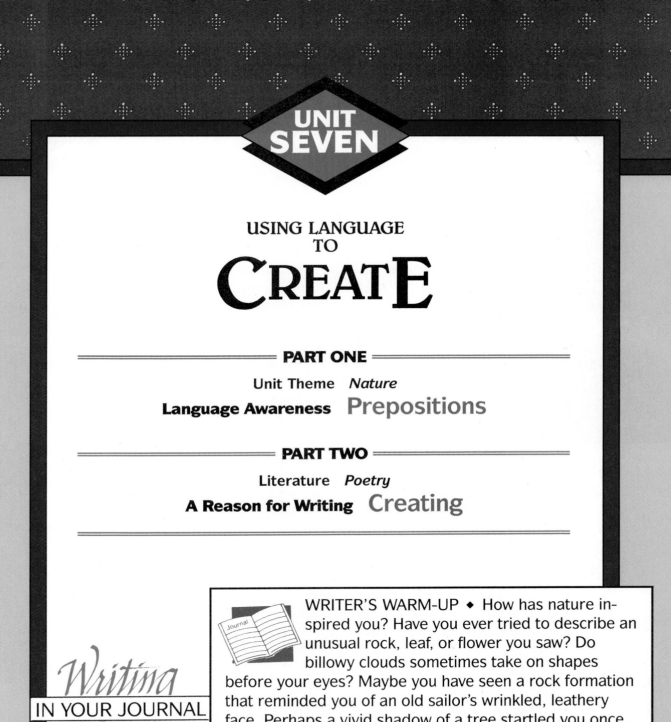

UNIT SEVEN

USING LANGUAGE TO CREATE

=== PART ONE ===

Unit Theme *Nature*
Language Awareness Prepositions

=== PART TWO ===

Literature *Poetry*
A Reason for Writing Creating

Writing
IN YOUR JOURNAL

WRITER'S WARM-UP ◆ How has nature in-spired you? Have you ever tried to describe an unusual rock, leaf, or flower you saw? Do billowy clouds sometimes take on shapes before your eyes? Maybe you have seen a rock formation that reminded you of an old sailor's wrinkled, leathery face. Perhaps a vivid shadow of a tree startled you once. Think about all the aspects of nature that puzzle you. Then write in your journal. Write about nature and what it means to you.

◆ GETTING STARTED ◆

You are going to have a picnic in the park. Tell how to locate the picnic spot. For example: *Walk over the bridge. Turn after the grove of pine trees.*

1 Writing with Prepositions

In the following sentences the underlined words are prepositions.

- The sun was <u>near</u> the horizon.
- Fiery flares shot <u>between</u> the clouds.

When you speak or write, you often use prepositions. A **preposition** relates the noun or pronoun that follows it to another word in the sentence. The noun or pronoun that follows the preposition is called the **object of the preposition**. In the sentence below, for example, the preposition *with* relates *gold* to *blazed*. *Gold* is the object of the preposition.

- Soon the trees blazed <u>with</u> <u>gold</u>.

Thirty Common Prepositions					
about	at	by	in	on	to
above	before	down	inside	out	under
across	behind	during	near	outside	up
after	below	for	of	over	with
around	beside	from	off	through	without

Summary ◆ A **preposition** relates a noun or a pronoun to another word in the sentence.

Guided Practice

Name the preposition in each sentence. The object of the preposition is underlined.

1. Poets see beauty in the <u>world</u>.
2. They write about many <u>subjects</u>.
3. Of all <u>subjects</u>, nature is a favorite.
4. Below a clear <u>sky</u>, the writer begins a poem.
5. A poem can come from a gentle <u>breeze</u>.

Practice

A. Write each sentence. Underline the preposition.

6. Poets are inspired by nature.
7. The splendor of a blue sky thrills many.
8. A poet may write a poem beside a rushing brook.
9. She may write about a fragrant rose.
10. Poets see much beauty around them.
11. Some poets live near beautiful lakes.
12. Others see colorful flowers under their windows.
13. Poets search for beauty.
14. The search is often satisfied by a glorious sunset.
15. Other poets might gaze at the starry heavens.

B. Write each sentence. Underline the preposition once. Underline the object of the preposition twice.

EXAMPLE: Taro wrote a poem about nature's beauty.
ANSWER: Taro wrote a poem <u>about</u> <u>nature's beauty</u>.

16. He described the flowers in the garden.
17. He read the poem to the class.
18. After class the students discussed the poem.
19. Eve said that Taro's poem filled her with pleasure.
20. Later, Taro gave the poem to her.

C. Write a sentence for each of the following prepositions.

21. above	**23.** behind	**25.** over
22. across	**24.** from	**26.** inside

Apply ◆ Think and Write

From Your Writing ◆ Read what you wrote for the Writer's Warm-up. Did you use any prepositions? Try to add some prepositions and objects to your sentences to make your writing more complete.

◆ GETTING STARTED ◆

Play "Where Can You Find It?" Ask questions such as "Where can you find a swing?" The answer must contain one of these words: *on*, *in*, *above*, *under*, *inside*, or *over*. For example: *I can find a swing in the park.*

2 Prepositional Phrases

Read the sentences below. Then read just the words in the boxes. Remember that the noun or pronoun that follows a preposition is the object of that preposition.

Many poets write about the seasons.
Each season of the year has its own special charm.
With every passing day nature shows its beauty.

Every prepositional phrase starts with a preposition and ends with its object. The phrase also includes any words that come between. The chart below gives examples from the sentences above.

Prepositional Phrases		
Prepositions	**Words Between**	**Objects**
about	the	seasons
of	the	year
with	every passing	day

Summary ◆ A **prepositional phrase** includes the preposition, the object, and any words that come between them.

Guided Practice

Name each prepositional phrase. The prepositions are underlined.

1. Summer is a wonderful time <u>of</u> the year.
2. The flowers are alive <u>with</u> color.
3. <u>Inside</u> the deep woods the birds chatter happily.
4. Winter displays other wonders <u>from</u> nature.
5. The snow drifts <u>across</u> the frozen meadows.

Practice

A. Write each sentence. Underline the prepositional phrase.

6. The seasons show the continuing cycle of nature.
7. During each year we have spring, summer, fall, and winter.
8. We wonder about the seasonal changes.
9. Poets are inspired by them.
10. Winter often arrives with heavy snow.
11. Icicles, like spears, hang from frozen rooftops.
12. In other areas, winters are quite mild.
13. Warm winters have appeal for the poet.
14. A breeze through the palm trees whispers softly.
15. Nature's magic is outside your own window.

B. Write the prepositional phrase in each sentence. Underline the preposition once. Underline the object of the preposition twice.

EXAMPLE: I read a poem built around the twelve months.
ANSWER: <u>around</u> the twelve <u><u>months</u></u>

16. The poem was written by Christina Rossetti.
17. It describes each of the twelve months.
18. Rossetti describes January with icy words.
19. The lines about May are my favorites.
20. She mentions the birds singing to the lovely flowers.

C. Write a sentence for each prepositional phrase below.

21. after the fierce storm
22. below the dark clouds
23. over the rainbow
24. before the sunset
25. at sunset
26. during the day

Apply • Think and Write

Creating a Verse • Write a Prepositional Phrase Verse. Try using a verse pattern. Study the example at the right. Then write your own verse.

> In the frozen forest,
> Near the icy creek,
> On soft, new snow,
> A startled deer leaps.

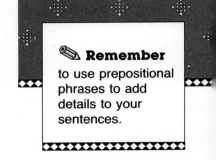

✎ **Remember**
to use prepositional phrases to add details to your sentences.

You are planning a hike in the mountains. Explain exactly where you will go. Use the words *up*, *down*, and *around* in your directions.

3 Prepositions and Adverbs

When you speak or write, you can use some words, such as *inside* and *up*, as either prepositions or adverbs. There is an easy way to tell how you are using such words. You are using the word as a preposition if it begins a prepositional phrase and has an object. You are using the word as an adverb if it describes a verb and stands alone, without an object.

Prepositions	Adverbs
We went <u>inside</u> the cavern.	We went <u>inside</u>.
John climbed <u>up</u> the steps.	John climbed <u>up</u>.

There are many words that can be used as prepositions or as adverbs. Here are twelve common ones.

along	below	in	near	out	under
around	down	inside	off	outside	up

Summary ◆ Some words can be either prepositions or adverbs.

Guided Practice

For each sentence below, tell whether the underlined word is a preposition or an adverb.

1. When we hiked, my friend came <u>along</u>.
2. We walked <u>along</u> a babbling brook.
3. Two noisy chipmunks came <u>near</u>.
4. Soon we stood <u>near</u> a stately oak tree.

Practice

A. Write each sentence. Then write whether the underlined word is a preposition or an adverb.

    5. In the summertime nature's beauty surrounds us.
    6. Flowers are blooming outside.
    7. Butterflies are fluttering in the gentle breeze.
    8. I watch as one quietly flies near me.
    9. I walk up the steep hill.
  10. Beside a giant tree I sit down.
  11. Colorful flowers are all around me.
  12. They are so beautiful that I will not go inside.
  13. I stay under the tree and open my notebook.
  14. My thoughts pour out as I write.

B. Write each sentence. If the underlined part is an adverb, change it to a prepositional phrase. If it is a prepositional phrase, change it to an adverb.

EXAMPLE: After writing my poem, I go inside the house.
ANSWER: After writing my poem, I go inside.

  15. I walk up the stairs.
  16. I put the poem inside.
  17. Then I go out the door again.
  18. I stroll around the garden.
  19. I wander along.

C. 20–29. Write two sentences for each word. Use the word once as a preposition and once as an adverb.

EXAMPLE: out
ANSWER: The bird flew out of the nest. The bird flew out.

  along   below   inside   outside   off

Apply • Think and Write

Dictionary of Knowledge ♦ Read about the praying mantis in the Dictionary of Knowledge. Using prepositions and adverbs, write about what makes this insect interesting.

✎ **Remember**
to choose prepositions and adverbs carefully to make your meaning clear.

4 Using Prepositional Phrases

When the object of a preposition is a pronoun, you need to use an object pronoun. The following are the object pronouns.

me   you   him   her   it   us   them

In these sentences, the prepositional phrases are underlined.

1. Show the book <u>to me</u>.
2. Will you share the poems <u>with us</u>?
3. <u>With Luisa and her</u> I read the nature poems.

In sentence **3,** the preposition has two objects, a noun and a pronoun.

The prepositions *between* and *among* are sometimes confused. In the sentences below, these prepositions are underlined.

The poetry books are <u>between</u> the two dictionaries.
Divide the poetry books <u>among</u> Carlos, Rachel, and Dave.

Use the preposition *between* when you refer to <u>two</u> persons, places, or things. Use the preposition *among* when you refer to <u>three or more</u> persons, places, or things.

> **Summary** ◆ When you speak or write, use object pronouns in prepositional phrases. Use the prepositions *between* and *among* correctly.

Guided Practice

Name the word that correctly completes each sentence.

1. Mr. Albeniz brought a book of poems with (he, him).
2. He read the first poem aloud to Pat and (I, me).
3. It told of ten geese flying (between, among) two mountains.
4. (Between, Among) the ten geese, one was the leader.
5. That poem was special to the students and (he, him).

Practice

A. Write each sentence. Choose the pronoun in parentheses ( ) that correctly completes the sentence.

6. Mr. Albeniz often read nature poems with (we, us).

7. Many of the poems enjoyed by Jason and (me, I) were written by Christina Rossetti.

8. To children and (she, her) some clouds look like sheep.

9. I found clouds like animals with my cousin and (he, him).

10. For (me, I) Rossetti's poem about colors was fun.

11. To (she, her) only an orange is orange.

12. To Kim and (I, me) many flowers are orange.

13. Rossetti loves cherry trees with blossoms on (they, them).

14. Such sights are a treat for Maria and (me, I).

15. Petals fall like pink snow near (we, us) and (they, them).

B. Write each sentence. Complete the sentence correctly with *among* or *between*.

16. Have you heard the wind blow (between, among) many leafy trees?

17. Have you felt the wind blow (between, among) two houses?

18. (Between, Among) you and me have you ever seen the wind?

19. A Rossetti poem asks who, (between, among) all people, has seen the wind.

20. Yet when the wind passes (between, among) two trees, we see them bow their heads.

C. Complete each prepositional phrase with an object pronoun. Then write a sentence for each phrase.

21. to Ana and _____
22. for _____ and me
23. by them and _____
24. from Lou and _____

Apply • Think and Write

Creating Phrases ◆ The poet Robert Frost wrote about stopping to rest "between the woods and frozen lake." Make a list of phrases beginning with *between* and *among* that you might use in a poem.

> ✎ **Remember**
> to use object pronouns in prepositional phrases.

How many different words can you think of to replace *furious* in this sentence? *The double-crossed wolf was furious.*

VOCABULARY ◆
Synonyms and Antonyms

Synonyms are words with similar meanings. **Antonyms** are words with opposite meanings. *Fast* and *quick* are synonyms. *Fast* and *slow* are antonyms.

Knowing synonyms and antonyms of words or knowing where to find them is helpful in making your writing more interesting. A thesaurus is one important tool that can help you.

Building Your Vocabulary

Replace the underlined words in the paragraph below with synonyms.

Tom talked on the phone for nearly an hour. He discussed an assortment of topics—current events, the fair weather, and the latest trends in fashion. As he chatted, Tom kept active. He wiped the counter, put away the plates and mugs, and shined the spigot.

Antonyms give opposite meanings to sentences. Make the sentences below opposite in meaning by replacing each underlined word with an antonym.

1. Brad bought his bike for thirty dollars.
2. Tammy shouted something in Elma's ear.
3. Susie likes swimming in cool water.

Practice

A. Write each pair of words below. Then write *S* after each pair of synonyms. Write *A* after each pair of antonyms.

1. accident, mishap
2. find, discover
3. exciting, dull
4. courage, daring
5. rare, unusual
6. joy, delight
7. ask, answer
8. arrive, depart

B. Find synonyms in the Thesaurus to replace the underlined words in the sentences below.

9. Niagara Falls has an <u>exciting</u> view.
10. "What a <u>beautiful</u> day for a picnic," Pepita declared.
11. Thelma often <u>thinks</u> about visiting the Grand Canyon.
12. Ian <u>wants</u> roasted almonds; they are his favorite snack.
13. Nelda always keeps her bedroom <u>neat</u>.

C. Find antonyms in the Thesaurus to replace the underlined words in the sentences below.

14. We searched all day but only found some <u>rare</u> rocks.
15. The night sky was <u>clear</u>, so we couldn't see any stars.
16. You will <u>find</u> your watch if you leave it lying around.
17. The <u>large</u> insect could only be seen under a microscope.

D. Use *un-* or *dis-* to make antonyms of the words below.

18. afraid
19. bend
20. please
21. likely
22. honest
23. trust
24. comfortable
25. friendly

How to Expand Sentences with Prepositions

In this unit you have been learning about prepositions and how to use them in sentences. Prepositions can add a great deal of information to your writing. Do you know, though, how important it is to choose your prepositions carefully? Read the following sentences to discover the difference prepositions can make.

1. Joe found the hidden treasure.
2. Joe found the hidden treasure inside the oak tree.
3. Joe found the hidden treasure behind the oak tree.

Sentence **1** gives us information. Sentence **2** tells us even more because it tells *where* the treasure was found. In sentence **3**, however, a single preposition completely changes the information.

Choose prepositions carefully when you write. Prepositions can make the information in your sentences exact.

The Grammar Game ◆ Focus on phrases! Unscramble the puzzles below to form prepositional phrases. Choose a piece from puzzle **A**. Then match the preposition with a piece from puzzle **B** to form a phrase. Write as many prepositional phrases as possible in three minutes.

A		
under	for	on
by	above	near
about	over	to
in	across	from

B	
a bridge	the summer
the library	a river
some people	an hour
two dollars	our class

Now trade lists with a classmate. Write sentences using your partner's prepositional phrases. Your sentences must make sense!

Working Together

Using exact prepositions will add specific information to your writing. Use them to complete activities **A** and **B** with your group.

A. Do the song lyrics below sound familiar? Write them, adding the missing prepositions. If you aren't sure of the correct word, use a preposition that makes sense. Can your group add other lyrics that include prepositional phrases?

 1. Row, row, row your boat, gently _____ the stream.
 2. _____ top _____ old Smokey, all covered _____ snow...
 3. _____ the river and _____ the woods _____ Grandmother's house we go.
 4. Oh beautiful, _____ spacious skies, _____ amber waves _____ grain, _____ purple mountain majesties, _____ the fruited plain...

B. Write a set of detailed directions that explains how to get from your classroom to another place in your school. Include at least ten prepositions or prepositional phrases. Some common prepositions are supplied here, but use any prepositions that the group agrees are necessary.

around	behind	into	against	after
before	past	upon	without	down
along	toward	through	over	during

When your group is finished, exchange the written directions with those of another group. Try to follow the directions. Can your group get to the right place?

WRITERS' CORNER ♦ Positioning Phrases

Be sure your prepositional phrases are correctly placed, or your sentences may sound confusing or silly. Can you explain what is wrong with the example sentence below?

EXAMPLE: I hummed a tune about elephants in the shower.
IMPROVED: In the shower I hummed a tune about elephants.

Read what you wrote for the Writer's Warm-up. Look carefully at the prepositional phrases you used. Are they correctly placed?

THE PARC MONCEAU
painting by Claude Oscar Monet
© The Metropolitan Museum of Art,
Bequest of Loula D. Lasker, New York City, 1961. (59.206).

USING LANGUAGE TO
CREATE

PART TWO

Literature *Poetry*

A Reason for Writing Creating

CREATIVE
Writing

FINE ARTS ◆ Poems, stories, songs, and legends have been created about trees. Look at the painting at the left. Monet painted this lovely scene of a park in France. The trees will be preserved forever in his painting. What is your favorite tree? Is it the tree you swing from in your backyard? Is it the tree in front of the town hall that was planted by early settlers? Picture your favorite tree. Then write either a poem, a song, a story, or a legend about your tree.

CREATIVE THINKING ◆
A Strategy for Creating

ANSWERING "WHAT IF?"

Creating is making up or expressing something new. Poetry is one kind of creative writing. Poets often see things in new, fresh ways. For example, sometimes a poet will describe a thing as if it were a person. This is called personification. After this lesson, you will read some poems that use personification. Later you will use personification to write a poem.

For example, suppose *night* were a person. Read these lines from the poem "Four Glimpses of Night" by Frank Marshall Davis.

> Peddling
> From door to door
> Night sells
> Black bags of peppermint stars. . . .

How do poets think of ideas like this? One way is to ask "what if" questions. You could ask, "What if night were a person? What kind of person would it be? What would it do?" How does Frank Marshall Davis's poem answer those questions?

◆ Learning the Strategy

Asking "what if" is a way of supposing or imagining. When you answer a "what if" question, you can imagine many possibilities. For example, what if a storm knocked out electrical power in your school? What might happen? What if America builds a space colony on Mars? What do you think life there might be like?

Sometimes "what if" questions can be about a make-believe situation. What if a horse you were drawing came to life? What answers might you give to that question? How would you think of your answers?

CREATIVE THINKING: Supposing

How can you think up possibilities in answer to a "what if" question? One way is to think of follow-up questions to your original "what if" question. Asking and answering these questions can help you develop your ideas. For example, think of that storm that might knock out electrical power. Here is a chart with a "what if" question and follow-up questions. What follow-up questions could you add? What answers could you add?

What if a storm knocked out electrical power in the school?	
What would the teachers do?	Try to keep teaching.
What would the kids do?	Start giggling.
What physical things would happen?	Clocks would stop.

Using the Strategy

A. Write "What if I won a trip to anywhere I wanted to go?" Consider the question. Then write two or three good follow-up questions and answer them. Find out what your classmates wrote. Find out what your teacher would write!

B. Later you will read some poems. They are about school, fog, night, the sun, the moon, clouds, tomatoes, and the wind. In each poem the poet writes about the thing as if it were a person. Before you read the poems, choose one of the things. Write "What if (the thing you chose) were a person? What would it do?" Then read to see what ideas the poets had.

Applying the Strategy

♦ Why were the follow-up questions important for **A** and **B**?
♦ What "what if" questions might you ask and answer about one of your school subjects?

LITERATURE

Like many of us, poets often look at the world and imagine it differently. Sometimes they imagine that ordinary objects can come to life and act like people. A school, clouds, the sun, and the moon once came to life in these poets' imaginations. Read the poets' stories about each one.

What They Say

"Hooray, ray, ray"
  says the sun at noon

"It's been so lovely"
  says the setting sun

"If only, my darling"
  says the rising moon

"Don't lose hope"
  say the white clouds floating by.
          — Lillian Morrison

Definitions

Fog: a cloud
That no matter how hard it tried
Couldn't get off the ground.

Cloud: a fog
That finally got tired
Lying around, a lot of useless weather.

So now it walks the sky
Trying to bunch a rain-bouquet together.
          — X. J. Kennedy

Four Glimpses of Night

III.

Peddling
From door to door
Night sells
Black bags of peppermint stars
Heaping cones of vanilla moon
Until
His wares are gone
Then shuffles homeward
Jingling the gray coins
Of daybreak.

— *Frank Marshall Davis*

Again and again,
The wind wipes away the clouds
And shines up the moon.

— *Kazue Mizumura*

Walking Past the School at Night

It lies
solid   stretched out
eyes blank   a blind
beast
dozing in the glare
of moonlight.

Under the dusty hide
heartbeats echo
in the hollow chest   pulse
has slowed to
nothing   the clanging bell
around its neck
is still.

We hurry past   staring at
each other   something
is moving!   A shadow?
Did you see an eye
blink?
A hot wind blows—breath of
the mammoth!
Run!

— *Barbara Juster Esbensen*

from

Ode to the Tomato

. . .

In December
the tomato
cuts loose,
invades
kitchens,
takes over lunches,
settles
at rest
on sideboards,
with the glasses,
butter dishes,
blue salt-cellars.
It has
its own radiance,
a goodly majesty. . . .
— _Pablo Neruda_

Reader's Response

Which poem was your favorite? What did you like about it?

Poetry

◆ Responding to Literature

1. X. J. Kennedy defined fog and a cloud. He gave them personalities. What aspect of weather puzzles you? Work with a partner to choose and define one aspect of weather. Start by listing types of weather, and then choose one to define. Discuss whether it might be sad or joyful. Then show that personality through your definition. Share your definition with the class.

2. Barbara Juster Esbensen passes a school at night and it becomes a mammoth. Look through a poet's eyes. Imagine one other thing that a school at night could be.

3. The tomato in Pablo Neruda's poem invades the kitchen. What would a potato, an onion, an ear of corn, or a squash do? Draw a picture that shows your vegetable at work.

◆ Writing to Learn

Think and Create ♦ Use a ''what if'' question to help you create. Look at the questions below. Then create three of your own.

What if stars were eyes?
What if clouds had arms?
What if trees were soldiers?

What if clouds had arms?	
How many arms would they have?	ten each
Would they have hands?	feet instead of hands
How would they use their arms?	to throw rainbows

What-if Chart

Write ♦ Choose your favorite question. Build on your ''what if'' idea, and answer the question that it asks.

Say this tongue twister different ways. Try being curious, sad, light-hearted, and surprised. *Betty Botter bought some butter. But, she said, this butter's bitter.*

SPEAKING and LISTENING ◆
Reading Poetry Aloud

Every poem ever written was meant for reading aloud. Poems have sounds and rhythms that are meant to be heard. Hearing poetry also helps people imagine their own pictures as they listen. Reading poetry aloud engages our imaginations as well as our ears.

With a little practice and some imagination, you can learn to read poetry aloud and to be an active listener. Here are some guides to help you.

Reading a Poem Aloud	1. Choose a poem you like and would enjoy reading for others. 2. Practice reading it aloud until you are comfortable with the words and rhythms. 3. Notice the poet's clues to understanding the poem. Look for complete thoughts and brief pauses, like the spaces between verses. The poem's shape and the length of its lines are also visual clues. Be alert to them all. 4. Think about how you can read the poem with expression. Make your own copy of the poem to mark for reading. You might underline words to emphasize, add a brief pause or two, or note where to lower your voice. 5. Imagine your own pictures for the poem as you say it. 6. Speak clearly in a natural, but expressive, voice.
Being an Active Listener	1. Use your imagination to create pictures for the poem. 2. Listen for repeated words, rhymes, and other clues that will help you remember what you heard.

Summary ◆ Choose a poem you like and practice reading it. Pay attention to the poet's clues to sound, rhythm, and meaning. Speak clearly, with expression.

Guided Practice

Read aloud these sentences, expressing a feeling of mystery and mounting suspense. Notice the end marks, the words that are underlined, and the spaces between words that indicate pauses.

1. Something is coming!

2. Who is it? Who's <u>there</u>?

3. Don't   come   any   <u>closer</u>!

4. <u>Where</u> could they be?

Practice

A. Make your own copy of the last verse of the poem "Walking Past the School at Night," on page 357. On your copy, add notes and marks that will prepare you for reading this verse aloud.

- Note complete thoughts and pauses. How will you mark them?
- Are there words that you would like to emphasize by underlining?
- Look at the word *blink*. Why do you think it is on a line all by itself? How will you say it?
- Look at the word *Run!* at the end of the verse. Why is it printed in italic, or slanted, type? How will you say it?
- What mood or feeling does this poem have?

B. With a partner, take turns reading "Walking Past the School at Night." Sketch the pictures you imagine as you listen.

C. With a small group, prepare a choral reading of "What They Say," on page 356. Decide which lines could be said by solo, or single, voices and which ones could be said by everyone.

Apply ◆ Think and Write

Dictionary of Knowledge ◆ Read about the poet X. J. Kennedy in the Dictionary of Knowledge. Read the poem in the article to a friend or relative.

> ✎ **Remember**
> to look for clues in a poem that will help you read it aloud.

Do you know the song "Row, Row, Row Your Boat"? Sing it with your classmates. What words are repeated? Think of another familiar song with repeated words or phrases. Sing it together and clap the repeated patterns.

WRITING ◆
Repetition in Poetry

Sound is one of the ways in which poetry appeals to our senses. Many poets use rhyme or rhythm to produce pleasing sound patterns. Other poets create sound patterns by using repetition, the repeating of a word or phrase. Listen to the repetition in these two poems. What beginning words do these poets repeat?

Direction

I was directed by my grandfather
To the East,
  so I might have the power of the bear;
To the South,
  so I might have the courage of the eagle;
To the West,
  so I might have the wisdom of the owl;
To the North,
  so I might have the craftiness of the fox;
To the Earth,
  so I might receive her fruit;
To the Sky,
  so I might lead a life of innocence.

—Alonzo Lopez

Night
—from The Windy City

Night gathers itself into a ball of dark yarn,
Night loosens the ball and it spreads.
The lookouts from the shores of Lake Michigan
  find the night follows day,
  and ping! ping! across the sheet gray
  the boat lights put their signals.
Night lets the dark yarn unravel,
Night speaks and the yarns change
  to fog and blue strands.

—Carl Sandburg

Alonzo Lopez repeats the phrase *so I might* six times in "Direction." What words does Carl Sandburg repeat in "Night"? How does he use repetition to describe a particular sound?

In "River," Locke repeats beginning words and phrases to add to the sound pattern. How many kinds of repetition can you find?

River

The river moans.
The river sings.

Listen to the Fox, the Menominee,
The Susquehanna, Colorado, Platte,
The Ottawa, Snake, Bear,
And the Delaware.

Listen to the river.
The river moans.
The river sings.

The river is always going home.

—*Lawrence Locke*

Summary ◆ **Repetition** is the repeating of a word or phrase. Poets use repetition as a way of bringing sound to poetry.

Responding to Poetry

A. To poet Lawrence Locke, the river moans and sings. What else have you heard in nature that seems to be crying or singing?

B. Lopez's grandfather wanted the poet to be like many animals. What are the characteristics you would most like to have?

C. Carl Sandburg uses the words *ping! ping!* to describe the signals sent by boat lights. Make a list of some repetitive words or phrases that *you* often use to describe things.

Apply ◆ Think and Write

Creative Writing ◆ Choose a subject you might like to write a poem about. Make a list of words and phrases you might like to use. Then underline two words or phrases you would like to repeat.

✏️ **Remember**
to listen for rhyme or repetition in poetry.

Picture in your mind something that happened to you today. Then, in the fewest possible words, describe it as though it were happening this minute.

WRITING ◆
Haiku

The haiku is a Japanese verse form that presents a picture to its readers. Long ago, the haiku was the beginning part of a longer poem. So the word *haiku* literally means "beginning phrase." Today, the haiku is still very much like the beginning of a story, but its readers must continue the story for themselves. Here is a haiku by the poet Meisetsu.

> A river leaping,
> tumbling over rocks roars on . . .
> as the mountain smiles.
> —*Meisetsu*

Meisetsu's haiku gives us a picture of a leaping river. Close your eyes and imagine that you, too, are watching the river tumble and roar over rocks. Can you add something to this image? Can you picture how far the river goes?

Haiku has many strict rules that give this form its special character. A haiku is usually written in three lines and seventeen syllables. The first and third lines each have five syllables. The second line has seven. In addition, a haiku should always contain a nature or a season word, or use words that suggest a particular season. A haiku should be about only one thing, just as Meisetsu's haiku is about a leaping river. Every haiku should picture what is happening in the present tense, as if it is happening now.

Boncho's haiku follows many rules of the haiku form. Read this haiku. How does it follow the rules you have learned?

> 1 2 3   4 5
> The ragged phantom
> 1 2 3   4 5 6 7
> of a cloud ambles after
> 1 2 3 4   5
> a slim dancing moon.
> —*Boncho*

These two haiku about the rain seem to suggest two different seasons. What season does each haiku seem to picture? What words that suggest a season helped you answer the question?

> All day in gray rain
> hollyhocks follow the sun's
> invisible road.
> —*Basho*

> Slanting, windy rain . . .
> umbrella, raincoat, and rain
> talking together . . .
> —*Buson*

Because a haiku is so brief, each word must be carefully chosen. Haiku poets seldom use repetition unless it is necessary. Haiku poets never use rhyme. Instead, they give us an image of a moment. The best haiku give us an image that leads us to make our own pictures to carry away in our minds.

Summary ♦ **Haiku** is a Japanese verse form that presents a picture to which we add our own thoughts and images.

Responding to Poetry

A. All the haiku on these two pages use personification. Human qualities and movement are given to such nonhuman things as a river, a mountain, a cloud, hollyhocks, rain, an umbrella, and a raincoat. What other things around you might leap, or amble, or talk together?

B. In Basho's haiku, *hollyhocks* and *sun's* are season words for summer. What other season words could you use for summer? Make lists of season words for spring, autumn, and winter.

C. Choose one haiku that you have read. What else do you see that is not pictured by the words? Draw a picture showing how you would complete this haiku image.

Apply ♦ Think and Write

Creative Writing ♦ Think of something you have seen happening that might make a good haiku. Write down the subject for your haiku. Then note the important words you might use in your poem.

> ✎ **Remember**
> that poets write haiku to present one image as if it were happening now.

Focus on the Poet's Voice

A poet may show something that is not human behaving in a human or lifelike way. If so, the poet is using **personification**. Poets often use personification to give life to what they see around them. Notice in these poems how balloons and clouds seem to act like animals or people.

Balloons

A balloon
is a wild
space animal,

restless pet
who bumps and butts
its head
on the cage walls
of a room —
bursts
with a bellow,
or escapes slowly
with sighs
leaving a limp skin

Balloons
on the street
fidget
in fresh air
strain
at their string
leashes.

If you loose
a balloon,
it bolts home
for the moon.

— *Judith Thurman*

Garment

The clouds weave a shawl
Of downy plaid
For the sky to put on
When the weather's bad.

— *Langston Hughes*

The Writer's Voice ◆ What actions do balloons and clouds have in common with animals or people?

What different personalities do the poets give to balloons and clouds? How well do these personalities fit? Why?

Working Together

Give human or lifelike qualities to things that are not alive as your group works on activities **A** and **B**.

In Your Group

♦ Encourage everyone to share ideas.

♦ Record the group's ideas.

♦ Remind group members to listen carefully.

♦ Help the group reach agreement.

A. Volunteers in the group read aloud the poems containing personification, on pages 356–358. Choose one of the poems to act out with pantomime, or body movement. Different people may act out different parts. Decide who will do each part. Then plan the actions and work together practicing them. Finally, present the pantomime to the rest of the class. Have the audience try to guess what is being portrayed.

B. Choose three things to personify from the following list of objects. Discuss what each object has in common with people. For example, a pencil sharpener *moves* its *arm* and *teeth* to *eat* the pencils put in its *mouth*. Decide which object can be most successfully presented as a human being. With your group, write three original sentences personifying the object.

1. Venetian blinds   **3.** wastebasket   **5.** bulldozer
2. airplane   **4.** windmill   **6.** weathervane

THESAURUS CORNER ♦ Word Choice

Look up these five words in the Thesaurus. For each word, choose a synonym that will help you personify a kite. Use each synonym in a sentence that brings the kite to life.

find   fly   make   turn   wait

Writing a Poem

Have you ever been greeted by the morning sun? Have you listened to the wind howl or the rain tap at your window? Our everyday speech is filled with personifications like these. We speak as if things can behave like people.

Poets also use personification. Poets like Esbensen, Davis, and Mizumura delight and amuse us with their fresh images. Did you ever imagine your school dozing like an unfriendly beast in the night? Can you picture the night peddling candy stars from door to door? How funny to think of the wind as the sky's housekeeper!

Know Your Purpose and Audience

MY PURPOSE

MY AUDIENCE

In this lesson you will write a poem. Your purpose will be to express a fresh image or idea through personification.

Your audience will be a friend you choose. The friend can be older, younger, or your own age. Later you can create a poetry gift card for your friend. You can also take part in a poetry festival.

1 Prewriting

First choose a topic for your poem. Then gather ideas.

Choose Your Topic ♦ Start by making a list of possible topics for a personification poem. Look at your list carefully, then circle your favorite topic.

Think About It

You are surrounded by possible topics for a personification poem. Look around your classroom and out the window. Maybe you notice a dancing curtain or a sleeping pair of shoes. Which item would be the most fun to write about? Circle your choice.

Talk About It

Discuss your topic ideas with a partner. Try to name two things each object could do if it were a person. You might give your object a name and then describe its personality. You might try talking to your object. Call it by name. What answers would it give?

Topic Ideas

tree	bus
flower	apple
cloud	wind
moon	highway
desk	taxi

Choose Your Strategy ♦ Here are two idea-gathering strategies. Read both. Use the one that appeals to you more.

PREWRITING IDEAS

CHOICE ONE

Playing a Role

Work with a partner. Act the part of the object you have chosen. Move around. Talk. Tell your partner what you are doing. Tell what you are thinking. Then ask your partner to help you make notes about what your object did and said. Use these as ideas for your poem.

Model

CHOICE TWO

Answering "What If?"

Write "What if ___ were a person?" Then write some follow-up questions, such as "What would it do?" Think of as many follow-up questions as you can. Write as many answers as you can to each question. Use your questions and answers as ideas for your poem.

Model

> What if a daffodil were a person?
>
> What would it do? — smile, curtsy, wave
> What would it say? — good morning
> What would it wear? — a yellow sunbonnet
> How would it feel? — cheerful but shy

2 Writing

Look over your role-playing notes or your "what if" answers. Recall the first idea you had about your object acting like a person. Did you imagine it bowing to you? Was it whispering in the wind? Was it just thinking about something? Your first idea might be the one you could use to begin your poem. Use other ideas from your prewriting notes or answers to help you develop your poem. Here are some sample beginnings.

- ◆ The daffodil wears a yellow sunbonnet.
- ◆ The cloud runs around the sky.
- ◆ The wind whistles a friendly tune.

As you write, try repeating a line or a word. This can help give your poem a special sound and meaning. You may wish to rhyme your poem, but it is not necessary. Look back at the poems in this unit for ideas.

Sample First Draft ◆

> The young daffodil
> wears a yellow sunbonnet.
> Shyly she razes her head
> to say good morning
> her voice is just a whisper
> just a whisper in the garden.
> Cheerfully the daffodil smiles
> at the warm Summer breezes
> that play at her feet.
> Her green stem makes a gentle curtsy
> to the wind, a gentle curtsy.

3 Revising

Now you have finished writing your poem. Would you like to make it even better? This idea for revising may help you.

REVISING IDEA

FIRST   Read to Yourself

As you read, think of your purpose. Did you write a poem that expresses a fresh image or idea? Consider your audience, the friend you are writing this poem for. Will your friend enjoy it? Decide what part *you* like best, and why.

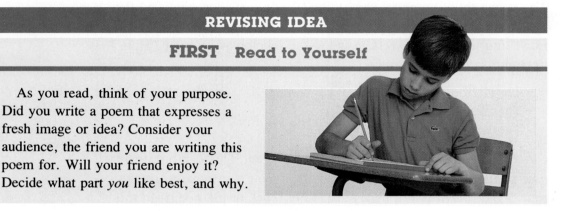

Focus: Did you use personification? Did you show your object behaving like a person?

THEN   Share with a Partner

Ask a partner to be your first audience. Read your poem aloud. Then ask for suggestions. These guidelines may help.

The Writer

Guidelines: Read slowly and with expression. Welcome your partner's ideas, but make only the changes *you* want to make.

Sample questions:
- Are there any words or lines I might repeat?
- **Focus question:** How else could this object behave like a person?

The Writer's Partner

Guidelines: Listen carefully. Help the writer think how the object can be like a person.

Sample responses:
- Why don't you try repeating the words _____?
- You've really made this object seem alive. Maybe you can add a personification by saying _____.

Revising Model ♦ This poem is being revised. Notice how the writer's changes are marked in blue.

The writer decided that *budding* is more poetic than *young*.

The prepositional phrase makes the image clearer.

The repeated words were moved for a different poetic effect.

The writer's partner suggested adding this personification.

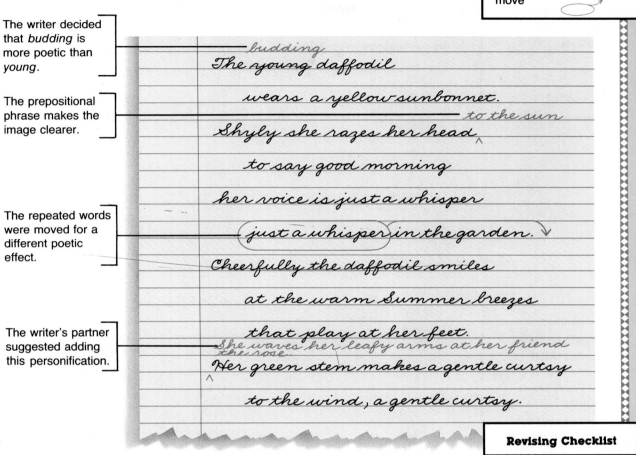

budding
~~The~~ young daffodil

wears a yellow sunbonnet.

to the sun
Shyly she raises her head∧

to say good morning

her voice is just a whisper

just a whisper in the garden.

Cheerfully the daffodil smiles

at the warm Summer breezes

that play at her feet.

~~She waves her leafy arms at her friend the rose.~~
∧Her green stem makes a gentle curtsy

to the wind, a gentle curtsy.

Read the poem above the way the writer has decided it *should* be. Then revise your own poem.

Grammar Check ♦ A preposition or prepositional phrase can clarify the relationship between one thing and another.

Word Choice ♦ Are you searching for a poetic word? A thesaurus is a good place to look.

Revising Checklist

☐ **Purpose:** Did I write a poem that expresses a fresh image or idea?

☐ **Audience:** Will my friend enjoy the poem I wrote for him or her?

☐ **Focus:** Did I use personification? Did I show my object behaving like a person?

4 Proofreading

Poets do not always follow normal indenting, punctuation, and capitalization rules. Use the poems in this book as models. Check your poem for correct spelling and readable handwriting.

Proofreading Model ♦ Here is the poem about the daffodil. The writer has made proofreading changes in red.

Proofreading Marks	
capital letter	=
small letter	/
check spelling	⬯

budding
The young daffodil

wears a yellow sunbonnet.

raises *to the sun*
Shyly she (razes) her head

to say good morning.

her voice is just a whisper

(just a whisper) in the garden,

Cheerfully the daffodil smiles

at the warm Summer breezes

that play at her feet.

She waves her leafy arms at her friend
the rose.
Her green stem makes a gentle curtsy

to the wind, a gentle curtsy.

Proofreading Checklist

☐ Did I spell words correctly?

☐ Did I use capital letters correctly?

☐ Did I use correct marks at the end of sentences?

☐ Did I use my best handwriting?

PROOFREADING IDEA

Spelling Check

Here is a trick for finding spelling mistakes. Check every other word the first time you read. Check the other words on your second reading. This way you will forget about meaning and concentrate on spelling.

Now proofread your poem, add a title, and make a neat copy.

5 Publishing

Try these ways of sharing your poem with others.

Daffodil

The budding daffodil
wears a yellow sunbonnet.
Shyly she raises her head to the sun
to say good morning.
Her voice is just a whisper
in the garden, just a whisper.
Cheerfully the daffodil smiles
at the warm summer breezes
that play at her feet.
She waves her leafy arms
at her friend the rose.
Her green stem makes a gentle curtsy
to the wind, a gentle curtsy.

PUBLISHING IDEAS

Share Aloud

Have a poetry festival with your classmates. Memorize your poems. Then invite another class to the festival. Take turns reciting your poems. When you finish, ask listeners to try to act out lines from your poem.

Share in Writing

Make a poetry gift card for a friend. Make a neat copy of your poem. Mount it on a sheet of paper at least twice as big. Fold the paper in half like a greeting card with the poem inside. Illustrate the cover with pictures about your poem. Send or deliver your card to your friend. Perhaps your friend will tell you what he or she liked about your poem.

CURRICULUM
•CONNECTION•

◆ Writing Across the Curriculum   Music

During this unit you wrote a poem about something in nature. Poems are often set to music and become the words of a song.

Writing to Learn

Think and Suppose ◆ In 1814 America was at war with Britain. During a battle Francis Scott Key watched the American flag waving over Fort McHenry. He saw it by the light of exploding bombs during the night. In the morning it was still there. His poem about it became the words to our national anthem.

What if you were asked to write one new verse for "The Star-Spangled Banner"? You would not write about the flag in 1814. You would write about what the flag means today. Read the verse below and think about what *you* would write.

What-if Chart

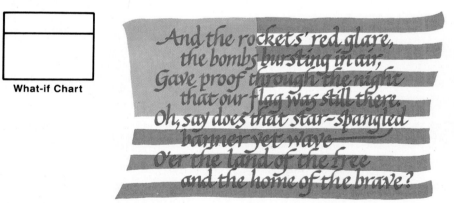

And the rockets' red glare, the bombs' bursting in air, Gave proof through the night that our flag was still there. Oh, say does that star-spangled banner yet wave O'er the land of the free and the home of the brave?

Write ◆ Think about the words to "The Star-Spangled Banner." Then write a new verse to add to our national anthem.

◆ Writing in Your Journal

In the Writer's Warm-up you wrote about nature. Then you read nature poems. Look through the unit. Notice what the poets wrote about. What things in nature might *you* choose to write about? Write your answers in your journal.

Read More About It

A Visit to William Blake's Inn

by Nancy Willard

William Blake was a poet who lived long ago. Nancy Willard was inspired by his poems to write this book. Each poem here tells about one of Blake's poetic characters.

**Newbery Award
Caldecott Honor Book**

River Winding *by Charlotte Zolotow*

Mrs. Zolotow is inspired by nature and the seasons. Each poem gives a glimpse of an image in nature.

Book Report Idea Book Jacket

A hardback book often has a paper cover called a book jacket. The book jacket may contain information about the story or author. It may give impressions of the book written by book reviewers. The next time you share a book, create an original book jacket for it.

Create a Book Jacket ◆ Look at some real book jackets for ideas about design and content. Use construction paper. Fold it like a real book jacket. Create a cover illustration that suits your book. Give the title and the names of the author and illustrator. On the back, give a brief summary of the book, but don't give away the ending.

A VISIT TO WILLIAM BLAKE'S INN

POEMS FOR INNOCENT AND EXPERIENCED TRAVELERS

BY NANCY WILLARD

ILLUSTRATED BY ALICE AND MARTIN PROVENSEN

"Delicate pen drawings go with these lovely poems about everyday objects."

Small Poems Again by Valerie Worth

Illustrated by Natalie Babbitt

UNIT REVIEW

Unit 7

Prepositions *pages 340–347*

A. Write each sentence. Underline the preposition once. Underline the object of the preposition twice.

1. The kitten with the black paws is mine.
2. He stood in the doorway.
3. Ian clambered onto the platform.
4. Joe received the news from Anna.
5. The wastebasket is near the desk.
6. During the evening we discuss the day's work.
7. The runners raced around the track.
8. Everyone was passed by Jill.
9. The thrill of victory was hers!
10. Philip hid behind the tree.
11. The policeman on the corner blew his whistle.
12. The little plane flew over the airport.
13. The black cap above the green coat is Roger's.
14. The salesperson from the store is here.
15. Ricky gave Jan his box of old toys.
16. The road to town is being repaired.
17. A small creek flows under the road.
18. That story was written by my aunt.
19. Yesterday afternoon we had a picnic in the park.
20. An enormous grasshopper appeared beside us.

B. Write each sentence. Underline the prepositional phrases.

21. Peggy and Aaron will work with the group.
22. This novel was written by Louisa May Alcott.
23. The ball soared through the air.
24. Behind the little boy stood a tall woman.
25. Yesterday we went to our grandparents' house.
26. The Knights of the Roundtable had many exciting adventures.
27. This poem by Marianne Moore delights me.
28. The horse with the brown spots jumped.
29. A huge tree swayed above the little log cabin.
30. We sat beside the cool, rippling stream.
31. Can I have one of your blueberry muffins?

C. Write *adverb* if the underlined word is an adverb. Write *preposition* if it is a preposition.

32. Mr. Austin went <u>down</u> the stairs.
33. Let's go <u>inside</u>.
34. Quiet <u>down</u>, please!
35. The worm crept <u>along</u> the roadside.
36. Debra stood <u>under</u> the big clock.
37. Put the coin <u>in</u> the collection box.
38. The fly buzzed <u>around</u> the room.
39. The mail carrier is <u>outside</u>.
40. Ms. Hayes got <u>off</u> the train.
41. Summer vacation is getting <u>near</u>.
42. Greg waited <u>outside</u> the store.

D. Write each sentence. Choose the word in parentheses ( ) that correctly completes the sentence.

43. Below (us, we), the waves dashed against the rocks.
44. The gifts are from Tom and (I, me).
45. Lee borrowed a book from (he, him).
46. Did you see the photo of (them, they)?
47. The scenery for our play was designed by Ms. Lee and (she, her).
48. Come with Kim and (me, I).

E. Write each sentence. Complete the sentence correctly with *among* or *between*.

49. (Between, Among) the three of us, she's the tallest.
50. A yellow line runs (between, among) the two sides of the road.
51. (Between, Among) you and me, I can't stand this heat!
52. How can anybody choose (between, among) all these flavors?

Synonyms and Antonyms
pages 348–349

F. Write the sentences. Find synonyms in the Thesaurus on pages 466–485 to replace the underlined words.

53. Belinda <u>came</u> before any of the other guests did.
54. <u>Find</u> the mouse in this picture.
55. I leaned against the <u>large</u> boulder.
56. The trip to Mexico was <u>exciting</u>.
57. The sculptor <u>made</u> a bronze statue.
58. Please <u>cut</u> me a piece of turkey.
59. She gave me a <u>definite</u> answer.

G. Write the sentences. Find antonyms in the Thesaurus on page 466–485 to replace the underlined words.

60. "What a <u>beautiful</u> dress!" exclaimed Helga.
61. This kind of metal is extremely <u>rare</u>.
62. The student gave the <u>wrong</u> answer.
63. Bill will <u>come</u> tomorrow.
64. This large piece of wood feels quite <u>rough</u>.
65. It's especially fun on a <u>warm</u> day.
66. My brother's room is very <u>neat</u>.

Proofreading

H. Proofread each sentence. Then write each sentence correctly.

67. Did you visit seattle?
68. "Wait for me, said Jennifer.
69. My uncles house is nearby.
70. I dont want to be late for school.
71. This is the clearer sky that I have ever seen.
72. The choice is between Susan, Jill, and Debbie.
73. Oaks, maples and, pines grow in this area.
74. Mr Buford's classroom is on the second floor.
75. How many countrys are in North America?
76. Let's walk to the Bus terminal.
77. That building is immense?
78. Tommys' bicycle has red reflectors.
79. There is a fountain among the two buildings.
80. The bus stoped at the corner.
81. Lisa said "You can do it."

An Animal Twister

Find the seven prepositional phrases in the following tongue twister.

An aging African aardvark
Ate an apple on an April afternoon
As it ambled across an ancient archway
Above an abandoned ark of aluminum.

Asked an ant of the awkward animal
"Are any ant-eating ant bears on the ark?"
"Approach and ask again about anteaters,"
Anxiously answered the ant-eating aardvark.

Write a third part for the tongue twister. In it tell how the ant escaped or was saved. Include as many prepositional phrases as you can.

Choose another letter of the alphabet, and write a tongue twister on another topic. Include as many prepositional phrases as possible.

Preposition Crossword

Draw the crossword graph on a sheet of paper. Then complete the puzzle. (Hint: The answers are all prepositions.)

Across
1. on top of; over
4. *cat* without a *c*
5. opposite of *without*
8. opposite of *off*
9. *mine* without *me*
10. next to

Down
2. in the middle
3. opposite of *up*
6. sounds like *two*
7. not outside

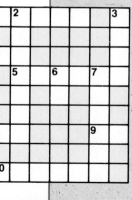

Unit 7 Extra Practice

1 Writing with Prepositions

p. 340

A. Write each sentence. Underline the preposition.

1. April Fool's Day falls on April 1.
2. This was once the date of New Year's Day.
3. The date changed, but some people forgot about it.
4. Each April 1 they still exchanged gifts with their friends.
5. Only now they gave joke gifts placed in pretty boxes.
6. April Fool's Day is celebrated in many countries.
7. Many tricks are played on this day.
8. Three hundred years ago it began in France.
9. The holiday soon spread across Europe.
10. The French call it "The Day of the Fish."
11. Children surprise each other with paper fish.
12. "April fish" is the French name for an April fool.
13. Friends learn each other's tricks over the years.
14. Most pranks are planned before April 1.
15. Few people can spend the whole day without a smile.

B. Write each sentence. Underline the preposition once. Underline the object of the preposition twice.

EXAMPLE: She plays jokes on her friends.

ANSWER: She plays jokes <u>on</u> her <u>friends</u>.

16. People play practical jokes during this day.
17. You might find a dollar by a tree.
18. Someone is hiding behind a bush.
19. He holds a long thread in his hand.
20. The other end is attached to the dollar.
21. He pulls on the thread.
22. The dollar disappears when you reach for it.
23. Don't be angry about the joke.
24. Get back at him.
25. Tell him a spider is crawling up his back.
26. Keep your practical jokes in the spirit of fun.
27. No one should be harmed by any practical joke.

C. Write the sentence. Underline each preposition once.
Underline the object of the preposition twice.

28. The eagle has long been a symbol of power.
29. This symbol has been used around the world.
30. It was stamped on Roman coins.
31. Eagles decorated the palaces of the emperors.
32. The eagle means certain things to certain countries.
33. Some countries have used eagles for national symbols.
34. The Austrian flag has an eagle on it.
35. Russian rulers' uniforms had them before the revolution.
36. Our founding fathers needed a symbol for the country.
37. People had many different ideas about it.
38. Once these great birds flew over America.
39. Now not even 3,000 eagles remain across this country.
40. Lately people have been paying more attention to the problem.
41. Without special protection all eagles could die.
42. Now laws protect eagles from hunters.
43. DDT in streams no longer poisons the eagles' food supply.
44. At one time many feared that eagles would die out completely.
45. The number of eagles is now increasing.

2 Prepositional Phrases

p. 342

A. Write each sentence. Underline the prepositional phrase.

1. Kate was reading about some humorous poets.
2. She found some poems by the famous Edward Lear.
3. Kate read his poems at the public library.
4. She showed them to her friend Gerald.
5. Gerald and Kate had smiles on their faces.
6. They were both reading a poem by Edward Lear.
7. It was a limerick, a poem in a special form.
8. The name *limerick* comes from Ireland.
9. Supposedly it is named after an Irish city.
10. Lear wrote poems about silly subjects.
11. His poems are filled with wonderful nonsense.
12. People enjoyed his sense of humor.
13. Sometimes his writing poked fun at other poets.
14. Friends sometimes recited his poems through the night.

B. Write the prepositional phrase in each sentence. Underline the preposition once. Underline the object of the preposition twice.

EXAMPLE: We read poems from a large book.
ANSWER: <u>from</u> a large <u>book</u>

15. Kate and Gerald read Lear's nonsense poems for fun.
16. There is often a serious message behind the nonsense.
17. He loved writing about people's habits.
18. One book had funny drawings above the limericks.
19. Gerald paused after his favorite poems.
20. He copied these poems in his notebook.
21. Kate kept a poetry collection beside her bed.
22. Sometimes she memorized a poem at bedtime.
23. Their teacher read some limericks before lunch.
24. Their favorite began, ''We went to the animal fair.''

C. Write the prepositional phrase in each sentence. Then underline the preposition once and the object of the preposition twice.

EXAMPLE: The sleds are put into the garage.
ANSWER: <u>into</u> the <u>garage</u>

25. The dew is heavy on the grass.
26. The rays of the sun are still strong.
27. There are more hours of daylight every day.
28. The air and the ground are being warmed by the sun.
29. Buds are forming on the trees.
30. Soon they will open into leaves.
31. Dandelions sprout in the lawn.
32. Bulbs begin poking their heads through the warming earth.
33. Soon they will delight us with their beautiful flowers.
34. Birds are gathering twigs and vines for their nests.
35. Bikes, skates, and wagons are taken to the street again.
36. Sweaters take the place of parkas.
37. Rakes and brooms clear away the last of the dead leaves.
38. A hose washes the winter's dirt from the porch.
39. People begin working in their gardens.
40. They set tiny seedlings carefully in the ground.
41. Spring is a time for new beginnings.
42. It is a welcome relief from the long winter.

A. Write each sentence. Then write whether the underlined word is a preposition or an adverb.

1. We are <u>near</u> the Museum of Natural History.
2. Rachel was <u>in</u> the subway car.
3. Leo was still standing <u>outside</u>.
4. Just before the door closed, he stepped <u>in</u>.
5. It was their first ride <u>below</u> the ground.
6. Rachel looked <u>down</u> the subway tunnel.
7. No one seemed to mind being so far <u>under</u> the city.
8. The train seemed to fly <u>along</u>.
9. At Seventy-seventh Street, they got <u>out</u>.
10. They saw that the museum was just <u>outside</u> the subway.
11. The doors were opening as they hurried <u>up</u> the walk.
12. Let's walk <u>around</u>.
13. The animals <u>in</u> these displays are so lifelike!
14. Which is the way <u>to</u> the cafeteria?
15. Let's go <u>in</u>.
16. Are the dinosaur skeletons <u>in</u> that room?
17. Observe the dinosaurs and walk <u>around</u> them.
18. Shall we see the marine life <u>next</u>?
19. To see the blue whale, look <u>up</u>.

B. Write each sentence. If the underlined part is an adverb, change it to a prepositional phrase. If it is a prepositional phrase, change it to an adverb.

EXAMPLE: Their friends were waiting <u>inside</u>.
ANSWER: Their friends were waiting inside the door.

EXAMPLE: Please put a donation <u>in the box</u>.
ANSWER: Please put a donation in.

20. They took their coats <u>off the bench</u>.
21. A guard gave them directions as she came <u>near</u>.
22. To see the Eskimo masks, go <u>up one floor</u>.
23. Let's go <u>down</u> now.
24. Rachel looked <u>around the gift shop</u>.
25. She waited for me <u>inside</u>.
26. Are you ready to go <u>outside</u>?

4 Using Prepositional Phrases   *p. 346*

A. Choose the word in parentheses ( ) that correctly completes each sentence. Write the sentence.

1. Cassie showed the garden book to (they, them).
2. The community garden was started by Alice and (him, he).
3. I divided my time (among, between) digging and planting.
4. Delsin planted six kinds of fruit for Pam and (she, her).
5. The tools were shared (between, among) Pat, Mona, and Ed.
6. Carla went to the garden center with (we, us).
7. Joan dug a strawberry bed beside Todd and (I, me).
8. Ms. Florio gave some seedlings to (she, her).
9. We planted sweet corn for Jesse and (her, she).
10. I borrowed tools from the Carons and (they, them).
11. The wheelbarrow and hose belong to Carrie and (me, I).
12. Leave a space in the garden for Robbie and (he, him).
13. Did you share the parsley plants with Leo and (she, her)?
14. Will the biggest tomatoes be grown by Gerry or (us, we)?
15. This area was donated by the Florios and (they, them).
16. Give the rake and hoe to Alonzo and (he, him).
17. The weeding was done by Martha and (I, me).
18. Shira put in a fence with the Florios and (we, us).
19. We fertilized an area for (them, they).
20. Carrie sprayed water at Luana and (he, him).

B. Write the sentences. Complete each sentence correctly with *among* or *between.*

21. Walk carefully (among, between) the two rows of lettuce.
22. I must decide (between, among) melon and squash.
23. Divide the fruits (among, between) Pam, Chen, and Jo.
24. Choose your favorite vegetable (between, among) carrots, peas, string beans, and broccoli.
25. (Among, Between) Arlo and Edith, who works harder?
26. At the fair, judges decided (between, among) the prize vegetables.
27. Second prize was shared (among, between) four farmers.
28. Then the decision was (between, among) their melon and our tomato.
29. (Among, Between) the two, the judges chose our tomato.

UNIT EIGHT

USING LANGUAGE
TO

CLASSIFY

=== PART ONE ===

Unit Theme *Animal Habitats*

Language Awareness Sentences

=== PART TWO ===

Literature "Two of a Kind" by Ron Hirschi

A Reason for Writing Classifying

Writing
IN YOUR JOURNAL

WRITER'S WARM-UP ◆ Did you know that a habitat is a place where an animal naturally lives? You know that different kinds of animals are suited to live under different conditions. You may have seen exhibits at a natural history museum that explain how camels can survive in the desert or how polar bears manage in the frozen north. What special characteristics allow animals to live in places where survival is difficult? What do you know about special habitats for animals? Write about them in your journal.

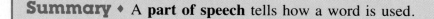

GETTING STARTED

They race to the finish line.   Lou came in one second later.
Pat won the race.   Lou took second place.

Make up other pairs of sentences in which the same word is used
as two different parts of speech.

1 Reviewing the Parts of Speech

The following chart reviews six parts of speech.

	Definition	Example
noun	A **noun** names a person, place, thing, or idea.	Prancer is a reindeer.
pronoun	A **pronoun** takes the place of a noun or nouns.	It lives in the Arctic.
verb	An **action verb** shows action. A **linking verb** shows being.	It eats plants. A reindeer is a strong animal.
adjective	An **adjective** describes a noun or a pronoun.	It thrives in cold climates. Its coat looks smooth.
adverb	An **adverb** describes a verb, an adjective, or another adverb.	A reindeer is very quick. It runs extremely fast.
preposition	A **preposition** relates a noun or pronoun to another word.	A reindeer is related to other hoofed animals.

A noun can follow a linking verb: *A fawn is a young reindeer*. A
noun that follows a linking verb renames or identifies the subject.

> **Summary** ◆ A **part of speech** tells how a word is used.

Guided Practice

Tell whether each underlined word is a noun, a pronoun, a verb,
an adjective, an adverb, or a preposition.

1. Reindeer have thick coats.

2. Reindeer usually travel in herds.

3. They roam across the tundra.

4. The tundra has no trees.

Practice

A. Write each sentence. Draw a line under the noun that follows the linking verb. Draw two lines under the subject that the noun renames or identifies.

EXAMPLE: A caribou is a reindeer.
ANSWER: A caribou is a reindeer.

  5. Reindeer are mammals.
  6. They are sturdy animals.
  7. These animals are strong swimmers.

B. Write each underlined word. After the word, write *noun*, *pronoun*, *verb*, *adjective*, *adverb*, or *preposition*.

  8. The reindeer has some long, hollow hairs.
  9. They serve as a kind of life jacket for the animal.
10. Reindeer have very large feet.
11. The feet act as snowshoes.
12. Reindeer move gracefully.
13. In the summer, reindeer are uncomfortable creatures.
14. Mosquitoes and blackflies bite them constantly.
15. The reindeer run into cold streams.
16. These animals are well adapted for survival in the cold parts of North America.
17. They feed on small plants under the snow.
18. Their speed enables them to outrun wolves.
19. Their antlers also protect them.

C. Study the sentence triangle on the right. Identify the part of speech of each word. Then write your own triangle.

> Reindeer
> Reindeer sprint.
> Speedy reindeer sprint.
> Speedy reindeer often sprint.
> Speedy reindeer often sprint in snow.

Apply • Think and Write

From Your Writing • List the words you used in the Writer's Warm-up. Use these six categories: nouns, pronouns, verbs, adjectives, adverbs, and prepositions.

> ✎ **Remember**
> to use a variety of parts of speech to add interest to your sentences.

The sentence below is about one person.
Jenny petted the goat.
How can you change it to make it tell about two people?

2 Compound Subjects

The simple subject is the main word in the complete subject of a sentence. In each of the following sentences, the complete subject is shown in blue. The simple subject is underlined.

| The <u>supervisor</u> of the zoo will tell us about animals.
| Her <u>assistant</u> at the zoo will tell us about animals.

Some sentences have more than one simple subject. In the following sentences, notice how the two simple subjects are combined to avoid repeating the predicate.

| The <u>supervisor</u> and her <u>assistant</u> will tell us about animals.
| <u>Ms. Juarez</u> and <u>Mr. Clayton</u> will tell us about animals.

Two or more simple subjects that have the same predicate are called a compound subject. Here are some more sentences that have compound subjects.

| <u>Forests</u>, <u>mountains</u>, and <u>deserts</u> are animal habitats.
| <u>Leon</u> and <u>I</u> will enjoy the talk.

Notice that the simple subjects are joined by the conjunction *and* or *or*. A **conjunction** joins words.

> **Summary** ◆ A **compound subject** is two or more simple subjects that have the same predicate. Using compound subjects can make your writing less repetitious.

Guided Practice

Each sentence below has a compound subject. Name the simple subjects in each compound subject.

1. Sheep, deer, and goats are animals with hoofs.
2. Camels and antelopes eat only plants.
3. Many children and adults enjoy the petting zoo.

Practice

A. Write the complete subject of each sentence. If the subject is compound, write *compound*.

4. Animals with hoofs are important.
5. They provide food for people in many parts of the world.
6. Mr. Clayton looks after the hoofed animals in the zoo.
7. Ms. Juarez and he studied them in native habitats.
8. Asia, Europe, and South America have many kinds of deer.
9. Caribou and reindeer can run faster than their enemies.
10. The powerful hippopotamus is not as swift.
11. Many creatures run faster than the hippopotamus.
12. Buffalo and antelopes band together in herds.
13. The herds move to different areas to find food.

B. Write each sentence. Underline the compound subject.

EXAMPLE: Lou and another student are reading about animals.
ANSWER: <u>Lou</u> and another <u>student</u> are reading about animals.

14. Hoofed animals and other creatures depend upon their habitats for survival.
15. Berries and leaves provide a diet for the gazelle.
16. Amy and Lou showed us pictures of antelopes.
17. Gazelles and impalas are antelopes that run fast.
18. Ellen and I admire the impala's gracefulness.

C. 19–23. Write five sentences of your own that have compound subjects. You may want to write about animals and their habitats.

Apply ♦ Think and Write

Dictionary of Knowledge ♦ Read about the moose in the Dictionary of Knowledge. Write a paragraph about these animals, using compound subjects in several sentences.

> ✎ **Remember**
> that you can use compound subjects to avoid repeating the same idea in different sentences.

3 Using Subjects and Verbs That Agree

The correct verb form must be used in a sentence in order for the subject and verb to agree. The singular form of a verb is used with a singular subject. The plural form of a verb is used with a plural subject. Study the chart below.

	Singular	**Plural**
action verbs	Danny raises goats.	They raise goats.
linking verbs	I am busy. He is a farmer.	They are busy. The goats are tame.

You know that a compound subject is two or more simple subjects that have the same verb. When the parts of a compound subject are joined by *and*, the verb is plural.

> Fran and Louise live on a farm.
> Their cows and their goat win prizes at the county fair.
> The Moffetts and the Garcias raise cattle.
> Cattle, goats, and sheep are domestic animals.

Summary ◆ Compound subjects joined by *and* use the form of a verb that is used with a plural noun. When a sentence has a compound subject, use the correct verb form.

Guided Practice

Name the verb in parentheses ( ) that completes each sentence.

1. Bill, Nancy, and Liu (visit, visits) Fran's farm.
2. Fran and her friend (watches, watch) the pigs.
3. Cows and goats (give, gives) milk.

Practice

A. Write the verb in parentheses ( ) that correctly completes each sentence.

4. The domestic hog and the wild boar (are, is) cousins.
5. Asia and Africa (have, has) wild boar habitats.
6. Roots and grain (serve, serves) as food for the animal.
7. Chinese and Americans (raises, raise) hogs.
8. Hogs and cattle (thrive, thrives) on farms.
9. The hog and the steer (provides, provide) meat.
10. Cow's milk and goat's milk (are, is) sources of cheese.
11. Wild goats and wild sheep (lives, live) on mountains.
12. Sheep and goats (resemble, resembles) each other.

B. Read the sentences below. If the subject and verb of a sentence agree, write *correct*. If the subject and verb do not agree, rewrite the sentence so that it is correct.

13. Mountains and plateaus was the first homes of wild sheep.
14. The ibex and the markhor are kinds of wild goats.
15. Juan and his parents has domestic goats on their farm.
16. Scots and Australians raise domestic sheep.
17. Both fine-wooled sheep and long-wooled sheep produces excellent wool.

C. Complete each sentence below. Remember that the form of the verb you use needs to agree with the subject of the sentence.

18. Farmers and ranchers ____ .
19. Sheep and goats ____ .
20. Horses and cattle ____ .
21. The cowhands and clowns at the rodeo ____ .
22. From the bleachers my friends and I ____ .

Apply • Think and Write

A Friendly Letter • Imagine that you are visiting a farm or ranch. Write a letter telling a friend about the animals you see. Use compound subjects in some of your sentences.

> ✎ **Remember**
> to use the plural form of a verb with a compound subject.

Turn these two sentences into one sentence: *The catcher caught the ball. She threw it to the pitcher.* Do the same thing with other sentences naming positions on a baseball team.

4 Compound Predicates

The simple predicate is the main word in the complete predicate of a sentence. It is the verb. In the following examples the words in green are the complete predicate of each sentence. The underlined word is the simple predicate, or verb.

- Carla opened the book.   Carla read the book.

Some sentences contain two or more verbs in the complete predicate.

- Carla opened and read the book.

Notice that *Carla* is the subject of both *opened* and *read*. The ideas of the sentences are combined, and the two verbs are joined by *and*.

A predicate with two or more verbs that have the same subject is called a compound predicate. Here are two more sentences with compound predicates.

She searched the index and found the word *llama*.
She smiled, stretched, and turned the pages.

> **Summary** ◆ A **compound predicate** is two or more verbs that have the same subject. You can use sentences with two or more verbs to add variety to your writing.

Guided Practice

Name the verbs in the complete predicate of each sentence.

1. We went to the zoo and watched the llamas.
2. One llama stared at us and walked by.
3. Another bared its teeth and tossed its head.
4. Carla sat nearby and opened her book.

Practice

A. Write the complete predicate of each sentence. If the predicate is compound, write *compound*.

5. Llamas live in the Andes Mountains of South America.
6. Llamas belong to the camel family.
7. A llama resembles a camel and has an unusual expression.
8. Its large teeth bite and chew tough grasses.
9. An angry llama glares and sometimes bites.
10. This animal adapted to the high altitudes of the Andes.
11. It endures cold and survives long dry periods.
12. Its fleece protects it and provides warmth.
13. Llamas rarely descend below eight thousand feet.
14. Their unusual behavior interests, amuses, and delights me.

B. Write each sentence. Underline the compound predicate.

EXAMPLE: Llamas carry heavy loads and travel many miles.

ANSWER: Llamas <u>carry</u> heavy loads and <u>travel</u> many miles.

15. The Indians of Bolivia raise llamas and use them as pack animals.
16. Pack llamas transport grain and work at high altitudes.
17. They graze during the day and sleep at night.
18. A llama caravan moves slowly and stops often for food.
19. The first llama wears a bell and walks ahead of the others.
20. The driver talks to the llamas and encourages them.

C. 21-25. Write five sentences of your own that have compound predicates. You may want to write about unusual animals.

Apply ◆ Think and Write

A Story ◆ Write a story about a herd of animals that is pursued by an enemy. Tell how the herd escapes danger. Use compound predicates in your story.

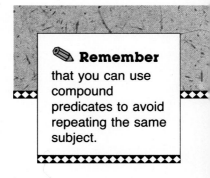

✎ **Remember**
that you can use compound predicates to avoid repeating the same subject.

Imagine that you have two pets, a dragon and a dinosaur. You have taught each one a special trick. Take turns making up sentences that tell the special tricks that both pets do. For example: *The dragon can roll over, and the dinosaur can shake hands.*

5 Compound Sentences

A simple sentence expresses one complete thought. It has one complete subject and one complete predicate.

> **Llamas lived in the Andes.**
> **The Indians tamed the llamas.**

A compound sentence contains two or more simple sentences. The simple sentences are joined by *and*, *or*, or *but*.

> **Llamas lived in the Andes, and the Indians tamed the llamas.**
> **Cynthia likes camels, but I prefer llamas.**
> **We will go to the zoo, or Ms. Shaw will take us on a hike.**

Notice that a compound sentence has at least two complete subjects and two complete predicates. It is not the same as a simple sentence that has a compound subject or a compound predicate.

Compound Sentence: Llamas are tame, but guanacos are wild.
Compound Subject: Llamas and guanacos live in South America.
Compound Predicate: Guanacos live in bands and are social animals.

> **Summary** ◆ A **compound sentence** contains two or more simple sentences joined by a conjunction. When you write, you can use compound sentences to combine related ideas.

Guided Practice

Tell whether each sentence is simple or compound.

1. A guanaco is a kind of llama.
2. A band acts as a family, and it stays together.
3. A guanaco band has about ten members.
4. The male in the band leads it and assures its safety.
5. Guanacos are found in Peru, and camels live in Arabia.

Practice

A. Write *simple* or *compound* for each sentence.

   6. The Arabian camel has one hump, and the Bactrian camel has two humps.

   7. The Arabian camel and the Bactrian camel are the chief kinds of camels.

   8. The dromedary is a special camel and is bred for racing.

   9. Once camels were wild, but today most of them are tame.

  10. Several hundred wild camels still live in Mongolia.

  11. I have never been on a camel, but Cynthia rode one once.

  12. The camel was friendly and gave her a smooth ride.

B. Write the sentences below. Then underline the two simple sentences in each.

  13. Camels once lived in North America, but they disappeared.

  14. Camels carry a large load, and they are called ''ships of the desert.''

  15. The camel's long hair provides wool, and the skin provides leather.

  16. Its hump stores fat, and its hair gives protection against hot weather.

  17. A camel can go without water for days, but its food provides some moisture.

  18. The animal can live without any water in winter, and some camels have refused offers of water.

  19. Llamas are well adapted to the mountains, and camels are suited to the desert.

  20. A camel can be pleasant, or it can be hostile.

C. 21–25. Write five compound sentences of your own. You may want to write about animals that people can ride.

Apply ✦ Think and Write

Creative Writing ✦ Imagine that you took a trip across a vast desert. Write some compound sentences telling what happened on your trip.

> ✎ **Remember**
> that compound sentences express two or more connected thoughts.

Play "One Word at a Time" with your classmates. One person says the first word of a sentence. Others in turn add a word to build a sentence. The player who adds the word that completes the sentence may suggest a word to begin a new sentence.

6 Avoiding Run-on Sentences

Remember that a compound sentence consists of two or more simple sentences joined by a conjunction. The conjunction can be *and*, *but*, or *or*. Notice that a comma is used before the conjunction in the following sentence.

> **Hoofed animals live in many different places, and these places have different climates.**

A run-on sentence strings sentences together incorrectly. The following is a run-on sentence.

> Reindeer live in the Arctic camels live in the desert.

You can correct a run-on sentence in two ways. You can make two simple sentences. You can also make a compound sentence by adding a comma and a conjunction.

> **Reindeer live in the Arctic. Camels live in the desert.**
> **Reindeer live in the Arctic, and camels live in the desert.**

Summary ◆ A **run-on sentence** is two or more sentences not separated by correct punctuation or connecting words. Avoid run-on sentences in your writing.

Guided Practice

Tell whether each is a compound sentence or a run-on sentence.

1. Some hoofed animals live in flat country, but others prefer mountains.
2. The chital deer avoids steep slopes the guanaco prefers them.
3. The camel flourishes in dry country, and the hippopotamus spends much of its time in water.
4. Chevrotains also live close to water they feed on soft plants.
5. Most antelopes live in Africa some are found in Asia.

Practice

A. Write each sentence. Add a comma before the conjunction.

  6. The dik-dik is the smallest kind of antelope and the eland is the largest.
  7. Antelopes live on grassy plains but the plains are dangerous.
  8. A leopard might catch an antelope or the antelope might outrun the cat.
  9. Antelopes are known for their speed and the adults can run up to fifty miles per hour.
  10. They are extremely graceful animals and a herd of racing antelopes is a thrilling sight.

B. Correct these run-on sentences. Write each as a compound sentence by adding a comma and a conjunction.

  11. The giraffe is the tallest animal an adult can be eighteen feet tall.
  12. Giraffes live in Africa they inhabit grasslands called savannas.
  13. A giraffe's coat has brownish markings this color pattern protects the animal.
  14. The giraffe's long neck helps it reach food in treetops its long legs help it outrun enemies.
  15. Lions attack giraffes the giraffes defend themselves by kicking.
  16. The giraffe can lie down it usually sleeps standing up.

C. Write compound sentences based on each idea below. Use the word in parentheses ( ).

  17. an animal you like and an animal you dislike (but)
  18. what you know and want to know about animals (and)
  19. a wild animal and a tame animal (but)
  20. an animal that either sits still or runs (or)

Apply • Think and Write

Observing Animals • Observe the behavior of an animal. Write compound sentences telling how the animal behaves.

> ✎ **Remember**
> to express your ideas clearly and to avoid run-on sentences.

GETTING
STARTED

Can you answer these riddles: Why was the river rich? Why did the fish have a low voice?

VOCABULARY •
Homographs

Have you seen a *bow bow*? Can a *shed shed*? These nonsense sentences illustrate special kinds of words called homographs. **Homographs** are words that are spelled the same but have different meanings and origins.

Homograph comes from Greek and means "written alike." Some homographs, such as the ones below, look and sound alike but have different meanings.

■ **Donna <u>rose</u> early in the morning.**   **She went tc pick a <u>rose</u>.**

Other homographs look alike but have different pronunciations as well as different meanings. Notice the different ways that *close* is pronounced in the sentences below.

■ **The great bicycle race was very <u>close</u>. (klōs)**

■ **We asked him to <u>close</u> the door. (klōz)**

Building Your Vocabulary

Homographs have separate entries in the dictionary because they are truly different words, with different meanings and origins. *Rear* appears twice in the dictionary, with these meanings.

Rhonda sat in the <u>rear</u> (the back) of the room.
Animals <u>rear</u> (raise) their young.

Find the homographs *hide* and *quiver* in the Dictionary of Knowledge. Use each word in two sentences to show the two different meanings.

The words below are familiar homographs. Make up two sentences for each word to show the two different meanings.

light   lean   lead   wind   bow

Which of these words have different pronunciations for each different meaning?

400   VOCABULARY: Homographs

Practice

A. Choose homographs from the list below to complete the sentences.

bill	lead	sow	row
live	dove	light	tear

  1. The _____ sat in the mud as the farmer began to _____ the seed.

  2. The _____ _____ off the branch and into the air.

  3. The vet gave us a _____ for fixing our bird's _____ .

  4. A _____ in my shirt caused a _____ on my face.

  5. John and I had a big _____ over who should _____ the boat.

  6. I _____ in the country and catch _____ lightning bugs.

  7. The _____ bullet was the only _____ the detectives had.

  8. "This _____ is not very _____ ," I complained as I carried it up the stairs.

B. Write each underlined homograph. Then use your own words to write its meaning.

   EXAMPLE: The tools were kept in the <u>shed</u>.
   ANSWER: a building used for storage

  9. The bear tried to <u>hide</u> in its cave.

 10. Its <u>hide</u> is thick and furry.

 11. His <u>pen</u> was made of gold and wrote in purple ink.

 12. The sheep were kept in a small, fenced-in <u>pen</u>.

 13. The mother bird would not <u>desert</u> its nest.

 14. The iguana lizard lives in the <u>desert</u>

LANGUAGE CORNER ◆ Word Histories

Loaf is a homograph with an interesting history. Long ago, you might have asked for a "bread of loaf"! *Loaf* originally was used to name what we now call *bread*, and *bread* meant "a piece of something."

What is another meaning of "loaf"?

How to Combine Sentences

You can combine two short sentences with ideas that go together to form one compound sentence. Combining sentences can add variety to your writing and show relationships between ideas. For example, what two facts about Jesse's class are expressed in example **1** below?

1. Jesse's class is studying sea animals. On Friday the students will visit the aquarium.

2. Jesse's class is studying sea animals, and on Friday the students will visit the aquarium.

Both examples tell us the same facts, but example **2** uses a comma and the word *and* to combine the facts in both sentences into one strong compound sentence.

Some short sentences can go together in a different way. Sometimes two sentences are about the same idea, but the second sentence gives an unexpected fact that contrasts, or goes against, the fact in the first sentence. The contrasting sentence can be joined with the first sentence by using a comma and the word *but*.

3. Ann had a cold. She went on the trip anyway.

4. Ann had a cold, but she went on the trip anyway.

Sometimes two sentences give two possible choices. These sentences can be combined with a comma and the word *or*.

5. Will you bring a lunch? Are you planning to buy a sandwich?

6. Will you bring a lunch, or are you planning to buy a sandwich?

The Grammar Game ◆ Create your own sentence examples! Write at least three pairs of sentences that can be combined with commas and the words *and*, *but*, or *or*. Then exchange papers with a classmate and combine each other's sentences.

Working Together

As your group works on activities **A** and **B**, combine sentences to add variety and strength to your writing.

In Your Group

♦ Ask questions to encourage discussion.

♦ Listen carefully to each other.

♦ Build on other people's ideas.

♦ Agree or disagree in a pleasant way.

A. Complete the pairs of sentences with words of the group's choice. Then combine each pair, using a comma and the word *and, but,* or *or*. Compare your results with those of other groups.

1. We looked in the _____ . Your _____ wasn't there.
2. Did Gail's team win the _____ ? Was it a tie?
3. We _____ for a long time. We didn't find the _____ .
4. Mark cooked delicious _____ . Karen made some _____ .
5. I really must study tonight. I will _____ the _____ test.

B. Find at least one pair of sentences to combine in the paragraph below. Think about how ideas in the sentences could go together. Can you write the paragraph again, combining four pairs of sentences?

Six of my friends and I play in a jazz band. We call ourselves "Sound System." Ellen is the best piano player. Joe also plays keyboards. We try to practice every Saturday afternoon. Sometimes we get together in the morning. Come to hear us practice this week. Drop in on any Saturday.

WRITERS' CORNER • Sentence Variety

Mixing kinds of sentences and varying sentence length can change a boring paragraph into an interesting one. Can you identify the kinds of sentences in the paragraph below? Can you find any combined sentences?

Give me your attention, pet owners. Are you taking a vacation this summer, or do you have to stay home with your pet? You can hire a Pet Pal, and your troubles will be over. Our motto is "We sit when you split." Call us, and ask for a caring pet. Pet Pals is the purr-fect solution for you.

Read what you wrote for the Writer's Warm-up. Did you vary the kinds of sentences you wrote? Did you use any combined sentences?

PRAIRIE DOG VILLAGE
painting by W.J. Hays
Courtesy of Kennedy Galleries, Inc. New York.

USING LANGUAGE
TO
CLASSIFY

PART TWO

Literature   "Two of a Kind" by Ron Hirschi
A Reason for Writing   Classifying

CREATIVE
Writing

FINE ARTS ◆ Look at the painting, "Prairie Dog Village," at the left. The prairie dogs all seem to be watching for something. What are they expecting? What will they do when it arrives? What sounds will they make? Will they run to the newcomer or run away? Write a story about this scene. Tell what the animals are waiting for and what will happen.

CRITICAL THINKING ♦
A Strategy for Classifying

AN OBSERVATION CHART

Classifying means sorting things into groups. It means putting together things that belong together. One way to classify is to compare, or notice how things are alike. Another way is to contrast, or notice how things are different. After this lesson, you will read part of "Two of a Kind." It is an article that compares and contrasts kinds of deer. Later you will write some comparisons and contrasts.

In this paragraph from "Two of a Kind," the author contrasts headgear. What is headgear? Read to find out.

> . . . did you know there are two species of deer native to North America? Headgear shape is one good way to tell one from the other. The mule deer's antlers rise abruptly, treelike. Each time a branch is formed, the branches fork in pairs. This is much different from the white-tailed buck's antlers. The single, main beams of his antlers arch forward. . . . Branches rise from the main beam, but they don't fork like those of the mule deer.

How does the author know so much about deer? He has observed them carefully. When you observe, you pay attention to details.

◆ Learning the Strategy

Observations are often useful. Suppose you are at the beach with your family. You want to go swimming. How would observation help you find your way back through the crowds? Imagine you have to decide which bike to buy to use on your paper route. How could observing help you choose? Suppose you are writing to a friend about your new cat. How could observations make your letter interesting?

How can you remember details you observe? One way is to make an observation chart. A chart about a cat might look like this.

Topic —

My Cat	
Appearance	*tiger stripes* *green eyes* *chubby*
Personality	*playful* *affectionate* *shy with strangers*
Activities	*plays hide-and-seek* *chases butterflies*

Subtopics —   — Details

Using the Strategy

A. Observe your classroom and make an observation chart. Write "My Classroom" as the topic. Write several subtopics, such as "What I See." Record details for each heading. If you like, write an article contrasting your classroom on a weekday and on Saturday.

B. "Two of a Kind" tells about headgear. What do you already know about antlers? Make an observation chart. Decide on headings for your chart. Record the facts you know. Then read "Two of a Kind" and see what more you can find out.

Applying the Strategy

♦ Did you choose the same headings and details for your charts as your classmates? Why might your choices differ?
♦ When might you need to observe something carefully?

LITERATURE

TWO of a KIND
from Headgear

by Ron Hirschi

The fragrant scent of ponderosa pine drifts on a gentle breeze. The light wind stirs overhead branches, bends golden stems of grass, and sets the tapered tips of shrubs in motion. But some of the branches tucked behind the shrubs do not move. These "branches" are attached to a deer.

The deer's branched antlers, spread behind the shrubs, help camouflage the buck. He naps in the late afternoon, chewing his cud as he keeps a watchful eye on the open hillside. Should the scent of a predator mingle with the odor of pine, he will be ready.

Like elk and moose, only male deer wear headgear. Their antlers are covered with velvet while growing and secrete an oily substance thought to act as sunburn protection or insect repellent. The antlers harden in the fall and drop each winter.

Perhaps the most familiar of all animals that wear headgear, deer are widespread in North America. You could probably describe a deer or draw its picture without looking at photographs. You may have even seen a deer bounding through the woods.

But did you know there are two species of deer native to North America? Headgear shape is one good way to tell one from the other.

The mule deer's antlers rise abruptly, treelike. Each time a branch is formed, the branches fork in pairs.

This is much different from the white-tailed buck's antlers. The single, main beams of his antlers arch forward as though bent by a constant breeze. Branches rise from the main beam, but they don't fork like those of the mule deer.

Mule deer can be distinguished from whitetails in many other ways. Like their namesakes, mule deer generally have large ears. White-tailed deer have longer, bushier tails with white edges and underparts. The mule deer's black-tipped tails led some North American Indians to call them black-tailed deer. This name persists in the Pacific Northwest where a darker and somewhat smaller mule deer inhabits wet, coastal forests.

Watch closely the next time you see a deer. Its tail will be one clue to its identity. If a buck, its headgear will point to the answer. But remember that no two deer are ever the same. Like people and other animals, each mule deer and each white-tailed deer is an individual. Try as you might, you will never find two alike.

Library Link ♦ *If you would like to learn more about animals with antlers, read* Headgear *by Ron Hirschi.*

◆ Reader's Response

Have you ever seen a deer in its natural surroundings? How did you feel? What did you think?

TWO of a KIND

Responding to Literature

1. Of all the facts that you have learned about deer, which piece of information was the most interesting? Why?

2. Make a survey of the wild animals that your classmates have seen in natural habitats. Show the information on a chart.

3. ''Two of a Kind'' compared two kinds of deer. With a partner, compare two species of dogs or other animal. Then in one sentence, tell the most striking likeness and the most noticeable difference.

4. People think deer are beautiful animals. What animal do you think is beautiful? Draw a picture of your animal. Tell why you think it is beautiful.

Writing to Learn

Think and Observe ◆ Make an observation chart like this one. Note differences between the mule deer and the whitetail deer.

Differences:	mule deer	whitetail deer
ears:		
tails:		
headgear:		

Observation Chart

Write ◆ Write a paragraph. Tell how the two deer are different.

LITERATURE: Nonfiction 411

Do you think it is important to protect all wild animals from extinction? State your opinion and the reasons for it. Ask others to state their opinions, too.

SPEAKING and LISTENING ◆
Group Discussions

What is the difference between ordinary conversation and a discussion? A discussion has a purpose. The purpose may be to solve a problem or to exchange ideas or information. Here are some possible topics for a classroom discussion.

What should we do for the assembly program on conservation?
What kinds of plants in our area are food for wildlife?
Should we take a class trip to a conservation center?
Are wildlife preserves a good idea?

As you can see, discussions enable us to share ideas and information and to solve problems. Here are guidelines to help you hold good discussions.

Speaking in a Discussion	1. Prepare for the discussion if possible. Find out the facts about a topic. 2. Contribute to the discussion. Your ideas count! 3. Use gestures, body movements, and facial expressions to emphasize what you say. 4. If you disagree with someone, politely explain why. 5. Stick to the topic of the discussion.
Being an Active Listener	1. Let others speak, and listen carefully to their ideas. 2. Do not interrupt the speaker. 3. While you listen, prepare to support or disagree with ideas that you hear. 4. If you do not understand something, prepare to ask questions.

Summary ◆ A **discussion** provides an opportunity to share ideas and information and to solve problems.

Guided Practice

Tell whether or not each of the examples agrees with the discussion guidelines. Explain why or why not.

1. Jan, what do you mean by "endangered species"?
2. Ralph: The deer in our area . . .
   Fran: If you want to see deer, just go to Bowman's Hill.
3. You're wrong, Steve. That's a terrible idea.
4. I disagree with you on that point. Let me explain why.
5. Speaking of wildlife conservation, did I ever tell you about the time I went on a camping trip to the Rockies?

Practice

A. Decide if each example agrees with the discussion guidelines. Write *agrees* or *disagrees*. Then write a sentence explaining your answer.

6. We must protect our wildlife heritage. Once an endangered species is lost, it is gone forever.
7. Your idea is ridiculous! How could anyone believe something like that?
8. Yes, we should help wildlife survive. By the way, did anyone see that movie last night about racing car drivers?
9. Wildlife preserves are important, but I disagree with one point you made.
10. Beth: I would like to say two things about wildlife conservation. First . . .
    Michael: I know what you're going to say.

B. With three or four of your classmates, hold a group discussion about a topic that interests you. Follow the discussion guidelines given in this lesson.

Apply ◆ Think and Write

Discussion Topics ◆ Write three topics that you think would be interesting to discuss as a class.

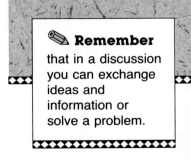

🖉 **Remember**
that in a discussion you can exchange ideas and information or solve a problem.

Compare a butterfly and a kite. Tell how they are alike. How many likenesses can you discover?

WRITING ◆
A Paragraph That Compares

Scientists often compare things and describe how they are *alike*. That is how scientists classify plants and animals. Writers also use comparisons to describe or explain how things are alike. For example, a writer might compare an anthill with a small city or note that a cloud looks like a castle in the sky.

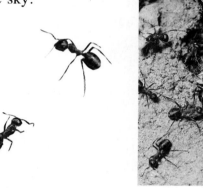

Here is a paragraph that compares a deer's antlers with a tree. Notice how the paragraph is organized.

Topic Sentence

Details That Give Likenesses

> The male deer's antlers are much like a growing tree. First of all, they look like a tree, with their forked branches. In fact, the antlers look so much like a tree that they help to camouflage the buck. Like the branches of a tree, the deer's antlers grow. Also, somewhat like the leaves that are shed by a tree, the antlers are shed by the buck each winter.

Summary ◆ A **paragraph of comparison** tells how one thing is *like* another. It begins with a topic sentence that tells what things are being compared.

Guided Practice

How are these two things alike? Think of as many likenesses as you can. Make a list of them.

Practice

A. Write two ways in which each pair of things is alike.

1. a deer and a moose
2. a bear and a football player
3. a student your age and a puppy
4. a rabbit and an indoor TV antenna
5. a spider and a weaver

B. Write a paragraph of comparison. Compare any two things you choose. Choose an idea from **Practice A**, for example, or compare yourself with something else. You might choose an animal, a flower, a car, or a famous person to compare with yourself.

Apply ◆ Think and Write

Listing Likenesses ◆ Think of a pair of twins or brothers or sisters that you know well. How are they alike? Write a list of the ways in which they are like one another.

✎ **Remember**
that in a paragraph of comparison you show how things are alike.

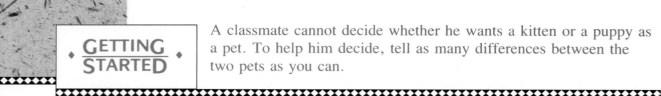

GETTING STARTED

A classmate cannot decide whether he wants a kitten or a puppy as a pet. To help him decide, tell as many differences between the two pets as you can.

WRITING •
A Paragraph That Contrasts

In the preceding lesson you made comparisons. You compared two things to find out how they were alike. Now you will make contrasts. You will take two similar things and find out how they are *different*. Differences are important. They are what make each and every thing unique.

In the following paragraph from "Two of a Kind," the author contrasts two kinds of deer, mule deer and white-tailed deer. They are very similar. When you need to tell one from the other, however, the differences are what count. Notice how the author organizes this paragraph of contrast.

Topic Sentence

Details That Give Differences

Mule deer can be distinguished from whitetails in many other ways. Like their namesakes, mule deer generally have large ears. White-tailed deer have longer, bushier tails with white edges and underparts. The mule deer's black-tipped tails led some North American Indians to call them black-tailed deer. This name persists in the Pacific Northwest where a darker and somewhat smaller mule deer inhabits wet, coastal forests.

> **Summary** • A **paragraph of contrast** tells about *differences* between two similar things. It often begins with a topic sentence that tells what things are being contrasted.

Guided Practice

Study these photographs of two similar animals, a hamster (left) and a gerbil (right). How are they different? Contrast them. Make a list of their differences.

Practice

A. Take any two books that you have. Place them side by side. Examine them carefully to contrast them. Then copy this chart. Fill in the information.

	Book 1	**Book 2**
1. Title 2. Size 3. Appearance of cover 4. Number of pages 5. Kinds of illustrations 6. Subject		

B. Write a paragraph of contrast. Choose a pair of similar things to contrast. Here are some ideas: two pets, two movies, two sports, two kinds of music, two kinds of storms. Begin your paragraph with a topic sentence. Then give detail sentences that tell how the two things are different.

Apply ◆ Think and Write

Dictionary of Knowledge ◆ Look up the entry for Lewis and Clark. Then contrast the two explorers. Tell in what ways they were different.

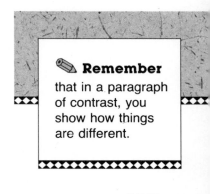

✏ **Remember**
that in a paragraph of contrast, you show how things are different.

Focus on Likenesses and Differences

People classify, or organize, information according to likenesses and differences. That is why teachers so often ask you to find likenesses and differences when you study science, social studies, or even literature.

Finding and pointing out likenesses and differences is also important when you write. It is an excellent way to organize certain information. It helps the reader understand what you are saying.

The author of "Two of a Kind," which you read earlier, makes effective use of this organizing method.

LIKENESSES: Both white-tailed deer and mule deer have antlers. The antlers of both species are grown by male deer only. The antlers are covered with velvet while growing and secrete an oily substance.

DIFFERENCES: The mule deer's antlers rise abruptly and fork in pairs. The white-tailed deer's antlers arch forward and don't fork. Mule deer have larger ears than white-tailed deer. White-tailed deer have longer, bushier tails, which are white. Mule deer have black-tipped tails.

The Writer's Voice ✦ You have seen an author use likenesses and differences to explain the "headgear" of deer. Now try the same thing for human "footgear." In your mind, select one shoe from two different students. Do not tell whose shoes you are choosing. List the likenesses and differences of the shoes. Then read your lists aloud and see who can identify the two students whose shoes you have described.

Working Together

Pay close attention to likenesses and differences and point them out as your group works on activities **A** and **B**.

A. Discuss what you see in the picture below of an old-time classroom. Compare it with your own classroom. What are the likenesses? What are the differences? Make a list of each.

B. With your group, write a paragraph comparing the old schoolroom with your classroom. Begin with a topic sentence. Use your lists from activity **A** to tell how the rooms are alike and different. When you have finished, share your paragraph with other groups. Compare your observations with theirs.

In Your Group

♦ Contribute ideas.

♦ Encourage others to share ideas.

♦ Keep the group on the subject.

♦ Record the group's ideas.

THESAURUS CORNER ♦ Word Choice

Look up the entry for *same* in the Thesaurus. Choose five of the synonyms given for *same* and write a sentence for each one. In each sentence, compare two similar things. Underline the synonym. Be sure that each synonym fits the meaning of the sentence.

WRITING PROCESS
CLASSIFYING

Writing an Article That Compares

When we classify, we group items that belong together. The items share similar qualities. For example, apples and oranges can both be classified as fruit. Like all fruit, they both contain seeds. Both also have a skin. Both grow on trees.

To tell how two things are alike is to compare them. To tell how they are different is to contrast them. In "Two of a Kind," the author compares and contrasts two kinds of deer.

Know Your Purpose and Audience

In this lesson you will write an article that compares. Your purpose will be to describe how two things are alike.

Your audience will be your classmates. Later, you can have a team read-around or help to create a bulletin board display.

What's
MY PURPOSE

Who's
MY AUDIENCE

1 Prewriting

First you need to choose a pair of topics, two things to compare. Then you will need to gather details about them.

Choose Your Topic ♦ Think creatively. What two things are alike in some ways? You might compare a red rose and a brilliant red ruby. Make a list of topics, and circle your first choice.

Think About It	Talk About It
Think creatively. You might make a list of single topics, then go back and give each a mate. When you have your topic list, narrow your choice to one. You might choose the pair you know the most about. Which comparison would be most interesting?	With your classmates brainstorm possible pairs of topics to compare. Listen as others offer topics. For each one, think of something that would make an interesting comparison for it.

Topic Ideas

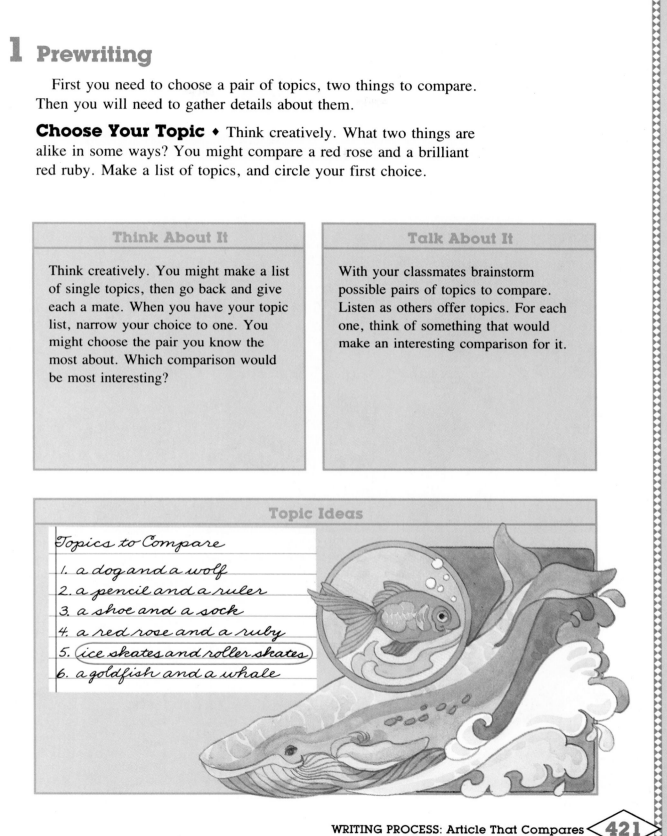

Topics to Compare

1. a dog and a wolf
2. a pencil and a ruler
3. a shoe and a sock
4. a red rose and a ruby
5. (ice skates and roller skates)
6. a goldfish and a whale

Choose Your Strategy ◆ The following strategies may help you plan your article. Read both. Then decide which strategy you will use.

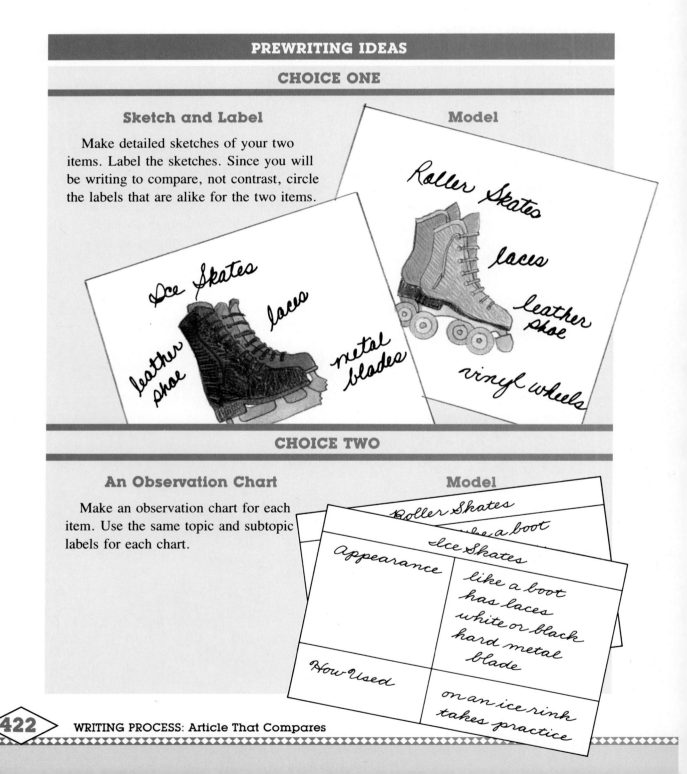

PREWRITING IDEAS

CHOICE ONE

Sketch and Label

Make detailed sketches of your two items. Label the sketches. Since you will be writing to compare, not contrast, circle the labels that are alike for the two items.

Model

Ice Skates

laces

leather shoe

metal blades

Roller Skates

laces

leather shoe

vinyl wheels

CHOICE TWO

An Observation Chart

Make an observation chart for each item. Use the same topic and subtopic labels for each chart.

Model

Roller Skates

like a boot

Ice Skates

Appearance	like a boot has laces white or black hard metal blade
How Used	on an ice rink takes practice

2 Writing

Follow the diagram to write a four-paragraph article. Begin by introducing your topics and comparing them. For example:

- ◆ Gerbils and hamsters are very similar animals.
- ◆ Roses and rubies are different but surprisingly alike.

Write a paragraph telling how the items are alike on one point, such as appearance. Then write a paragraph telling how they are alike on another point. In the last paragraph, sum up the likenesses.

Sample First Draft ◆

Look carefully at ice skates and roller skates. They seem different, but they are realy a lot alike.

For one thing, they look very similar. Many roller skates have lace-up boots, just like ice skates also both ice skates and roller skates are usually white or black. One has blades and the other has wheels.

Ice skates and roller skates is used similarly, too. Both carry you fast over a hard surface. Once you lace on skates and step onto the Rink, you can really zoom! The trick is to stay on your feet.

Introduction
Name the items.
Say they are alike.

Paragraph 1
Compare the items on one point, such as appearance.

Paragraph 2
Compare the items on another point, such as uses.

Conclusion
Sum up the likenesses.

3 Revising

Now that you have written your comparison article, would you like to improve it? Here is an idea that may help you.

REVISING IDEA

FIRST Read to Yourself

As you read, think about your purpose. Have you written an article that compares two things? Think about your audience. Will your classmates understand your article? Circle any unclear parts that you would like to go back and improve.

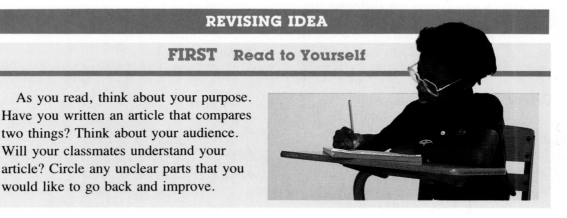

Focus: Have you clearly described the likenesses of two items? Have you omitted details about their differences?

THEN Share with a Partner

Sit next to a partner. Ask your partner to read along silently as you read aloud. Then discuss your article. These guidelines may help you work together.

The Writer

Guidelines: Read aloud slowly and clearly. Listen to your partner's suggestions. Make the changes *you* want to make.

Sample questions:
- Are there any details that don't belong?
- **Focus question:** Can you think of other ways these items are alike?

The Writer's Partner

Guidelines: Read along with the writer. Make comments that are honest but polite.

Sample responses:
- You might take out this detail about differences.
- Another way they are alike is _____.

Revising Model ♦ The comparison article below is being revised. The revising marks show the writer's changes.

Revising Marks

cross out —————

add ∧

move ⟲

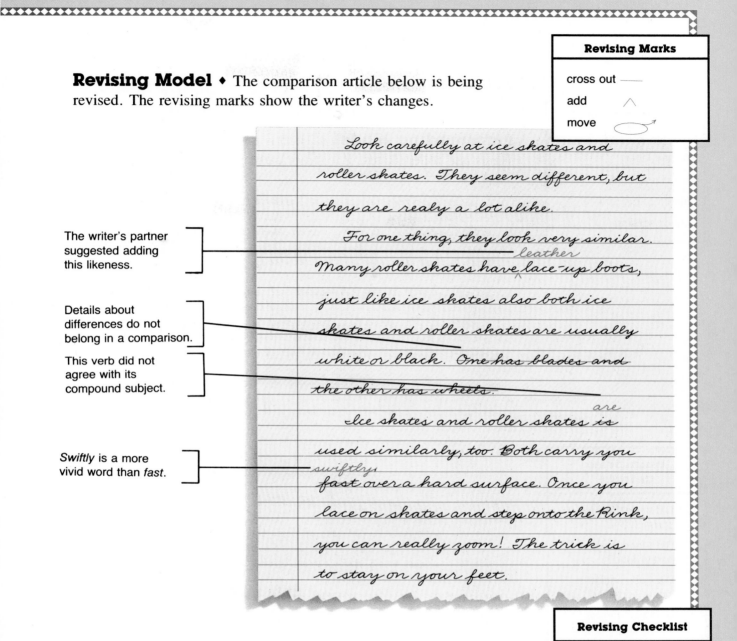

The writer's partner suggested adding this likeness.

Details about differences do not belong in a comparison.

This verb did not agree with its compound subject.

Swiftly is a more vivid word than *fast*.

Look carefully at ice skates and roller skates. They seem different, but they are realy a lot alike. For one thing, they look very similar. Many roller skates have lace-up boots, ^leather^ just like ice skates ~~also both ice skates and roller skates are usually white or black. One has blades and the other has wheels.~~ Ice skates and roller skates ~~is~~ ^are^ used similarly, too. Both carry you ~~fast~~ ^swiftly^ over a hard surface. Once you lace on skates and step onto the Rink, you can really zoom! The trick is to stay on your feet.

Read the comparison article above with the writer's changes. Then revise your own comparison article.

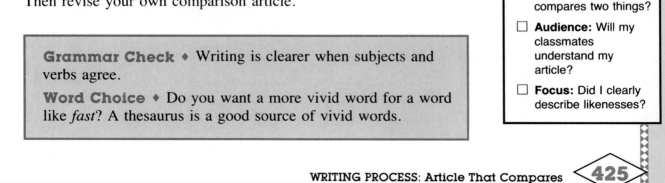

Grammar Check ♦ Writing is clearer when subjects and verbs agree.

Word Choice ♦ Do you want a more vivid word for a word like *fast*? A thesaurus is a good source of vivid words.

Revising Checklist

☐ **Purpose:** Did I write an article that compares two things?

☐ **Audience:** Will my classmates understand my article?

☐ **Focus:** Did I clearly describe likenesses?

4 Proofreading

Be courteous to your readers by correcting your errors.

Proofreading Model ◆ Here is the article comparing ice skates and roller skates. Red proofreading marks have been added.

Proofreading Marks	
capital letter	=
small letter	/
indent paragraph	¶
check spelling	⬭

> Look carefully at ice skates and
> roller skates. They seem different, but
> they are ⟨reaty⟩ *really* a lot alike.
> For one thing, they look very similar.
> Many roller skates have ∧*leather* lace-up boots,
> just like ice skates also both ice
> ∧= skates and roller skates are usually
> white or black. One has blades and
> the other has wheels.
> Ice skates and roller skates is *are*
> used similarly, too. Both carry you
> *swiftly* fast over a hard surface. ¶∧ Once you
> lace on skates and step onto the Rink,
> you can really zoom! The trick is
> to stay on your feet.

Proofreading Checklist

☐ Did I spell words correctly?

☐ Did I indent paragraphs?

☐ Did I use capital letters correctly?

☐ Did I use correct marks at the end of sentences?

☐ Did I use my best handwriting?

PROOFREADING IDEA

Handwriting Check

Check for crowded words that are hard to read. Then check for crowded letters.

Proofread your comparison article, add a title, and make a neat copy.

5 Publishing

You have written and polished your comparison article. Now it's time to share it. Here are two ideas you can try.

> ## Ice Skates and Roller Skates
>
> Look carefully at ice skates and roller skates. They seem different, but they are really a lot alike.
>
> For one thing, they look very similar. Many roller skates have leather lace-up boots, just like ice skates. Also, both ice skates and roller skates are usually white or black.
>
> Ice skates and roller skates are used similarly, too. Both carry you swiftly over a hard surface. Once you lace on skates and step onto the rink, you can really zoom! The trick is to stay on your feet.

PUBLISHING IDEAS

Share Aloud

Have a team read-around. Form small groups. Take turns reading your articles aloud. Have each writer challenge teammates to name one more likeness. If they do, score a point for that person!

Share in Writing

Illustrate a cover for your article. Include the names of your two items. Display the articles with your classmates' articles. Look at each cover and try to guess how the items are alike. Then read the article to find out if you and the writer had the same ideas.

CURRICULUM CONNECTION

Writing Across the Curriculum   Science

In this unit you wrote an article describing how two things were alike. You used an observation chart to gather information and help you make comparisons. Scientists, too, gather information on observation charts. They make careful observations about the world around us.

Writing to Learn

Think and Observe ◆ What would the world be like if there were no domesticated animals? Make an observation chart for a domesticated animal, such as a chicken, cow, or dog. Show where the animal lives, how it gets food, and how it is useful to us. Then make another observation chart for a wild animal, such as a wild goose, deer, or wolf.

Observation Chart

Write ◆ Compare your two charts and list the differences between a domesticated and a wild animal. You may wish to discuss how life would be different if there were no domesticated animals.

Writing in Your Journal

In the Writer's Warm-up you wrote about animals and their habitats. Throughout this unit you learned how and where different animals live. Did any facts or passages puzzle you? In your journal write about an animal habitat that you would like to learn more about.

BOOKS TO ENJOY

Read More About It

Do Animals Dream? *by Joyce Pope*

This fascinating book answers 85 questions children most often ask at natural history museums. Perhaps you, too, have wondered if crocodiles really cry. How do animals find their way? The answers to these questions are waiting for you to read.

Misty of Chincoteague

by Marguerite Henry

Chincoteague Island is part of Virginia. Wild ponies have roamed there for many years. This is a classic story of a wild pony and the children who love her.

DO ANIMALS DREAM?
Children's questions about animals most often asked of the Natural History Museum answered by Joyce Pope

Book Report Idea Mask

Share your next book by making a mask to represent an animal, character, or theme.

Make a mask ◆ You can use a variety of materials to make masks. You might try papier-mâché, fabric, cardboard, or large brown paper shopping bags. Be creative! Make your mask colorful, dramatic, funny, or scary, depending on your book. Hang your completed mask on a bulletin board. Make a written report to go with the mask. In it, explain how the mask relates to the book. Describe in writing the details that the mask cannot convey.

UNIT REVIEW

Unit 8

Sentences *pages 388–399*

A. Write each underlined word or words below. After the word or words write *noun, pronoun, verb, adjective, adverb,* or *preposition.*

1. Darryl <u>walks</u> to school every day.
2. <u>Ms. Payne</u> teaches mathematics.
3. Trudy ran <u>quickly</u> to the library.
4. The cat sat quietly <u>in</u> the corner.
5. The <u>ferocious</u> lion growled.
6. Tell <u>me</u> what happened.
7. Sid gave <u>them</u> clear directions.
8. You are <u>very</u> intelligent.
9. The committee <u>will meet</u> again soon.
10. I never watch television <u>on</u> Monday.
11. <u>Tall</u> oaks grow from small acorns.
12. The blacksmith <u>whistled</u> loudly.
13. The meeting was <u>unusually</u> brief.
14. Jacob <u>had risen</u> early that morning.
15. The chores were finished <u>surprisingly</u> quickly.
16. The lion's <u>cub</u> is adorable.
17. This orange juice tastes <u>sour</u>.
18. She works <u>from</u> sunrise to sundown.
19. I <u>shall study</u> harder.
20. The leopard sprung <u>suddenly</u>.
21. <u>It</u> chased after the wild antelope.
22. The <u>frightened</u> antelope fled.
23. The animals ran <u>across</u> the plain.
24. A tour group observed <u>the</u> chase.
25. A <u>photographer</u> filmed the event.

B. Write each sentence below. Underline the compound subject or the compound predicate.

26. The woman and her son enjoyed a good laugh.
27. The two spaniels barked and growled.
28. Bob, Sally, and Marjorie are very close friends.
29. The hikers walked, rested, and walked again.
30. The supermarket and the department store are having sales this week.
31. Mr. Rosen and Dr. Orontes have offices next to each other.
32. Danielle or Megan will play the lead in the play.
33. The audience became bored and walked out.
34. Mr. Davis and Mrs. Perry are writing a cookbook together.
35. New hats and dresses were displayed in the shop window.

C. Write each sentence. Choose the verb in parentheses ( ) that correctly completes the sentence.

36. Bob and I (is, are) in the same class.
37. Jill and Rodney (make, makes) the party decorations.
38. Lisa and her mother (is training, are training) for the race.
39. The muffins and the rolls (was baked, were baked) by Mr. Semple.
40. The soup and the salad (taste, tastes) delicious.
41. The Clausens (lives, live) in the yellow house across the street.

D. Write each sentence. Underline the two simple sentences in each.

42. Some people prefer to play golf, but some prefer tennis.
43. Will you wrap the party favors, or will Dorothy do it?
44. Jim pitched the ball, and Betty batted it over the fence.
45. The sun rises, and the day begins.
46. Troy has learned to ice skate, but he can't do a figure eight yet.
47. The Tigers might win the game, or they might lose it.
48. The guinea pig almost got away, but Ms. Weng caught it.
49. The fox crept up on the chickens, but the farmer chased it away.
50. A strong wind gusted, and the pine trees swayed.

E. Write *compound* or *run-on* for each sentence.

51. I like Ann she is pleasant company.
52. The train may arrive on time, or it may be late.
53. Molly Pitcher was a hero her real name was Mary Ludwig Hays.
54. Steve is afraid of raccoons, and he doesn't like skunks either.
55. The owl hooted the coyote howled.
56. Mrs. Bates teaches science her husband teaches history.
57. E. B. White is my favorite writer, and I have read many of his books.
58. Yesterday was cold and rainy, but the day before that was pleasant.
59. Jennie Cartwright is a fine singer her mother also sings.

Homographs *pages 400–401*

F. Write each pair of sentences. Underline the two homographs.

60. Turn on the light. This package is very light.
61. Some snakes shed their skins. The shed stands next to the old house.
62. Help me wind this toy. A cold wind is coming from the north.
63. The fleet deer jumped over the fence. A fleet of ships set sail.
64. Will you lead us out of here? The lead in this pencil is almost gone.
65. The sink dripped all night. We watched the sun sink in the west.
66. The desert is covered with sand dunes. Please do not desert us!
67. The actors took a deep bow. Suzie put a yellow bow in her hair.
68. The ink in this pen is gone. The squealing pigs wrestled in the pen.

Comparison and Contrast *pages 414–417*

G. Write two ways in which each of the following are alike.

69. two friends of yours
70. an automobile and an airplane
71. a gerbil and a rabbit
72. a tennis ball and a basketball

H. Write two ways in which each of the following are different.

73. a dog and a cat
74. two relatives of yours
75. swimming and jogging
76. a microscope and a telescope

·CUMULATIVE· REVIEW

UNITS 1 and 8: Sentences
pages 6–15, 388–399

A. Write the complete subject of each sentence. Underline the simple subject. Write *(You)* if the subject is understood.

1. My mother has gone back to college.
2. Come with me to Stacy's party next Saturday.
3. The hawk flew over the plain.
4. The running shoes with the yellow stripes are mine.
5. Close your books now.
6. Put down your pencils.
7. Ms. Matsu is a fine sculptor.
8. Kenny's dog is very frisky today.
9. Take this note to Annette.
10. The man in the sports car waved.

B. Write the complete predicate of each sentence. Underline the simple predicate.

11. My sister is writing a new story.
12. She gets her inspiration from everyday events.
13. Many reviewers have praised her work.
14. I shall ask her about her stories.
15. She also composes beautiful songs.
16. Many singers have performed them.
17. She will appear on a television program next Monday night.
18. My parents take great pride in her.
19. I have spoken about her often.
20. She is a very talented person.

C. Write each sentence. Underline the compound subject or the compound predicate.

21. Sam and Tina play on our team.
22. Tina bats and pitches well.
23. The shortstop and the catcher are members of the same family.
24. Coach Buckner has trained us and improved our batting averages.
25. He played professional baseball for ten years and then retired.
26. My collie and Tina's doberman like to watch us practice.
27. Coach Buckner pats them and gives them dog biscuits.
28. Ms. Cohen and Mrs. Soroba are the team's sponsors.
29. They attend our games and cheer.

D. Choose the verb in parentheses ( ) that correctly completes each sentence.

30. Rabbits and hamsters (makes, make) good pets.
31. Thunder and lightning (frightens, frighten) our cats.
32. Sandy and Sue (play, plays) tennis.
33. Tourists and sightseers rarely (travel, travels) this route.
34. Hamburgers and chili (is, are) my favorite foods.
35. Joe, Frank, and Beverly (practices, practice) their juggling act daily.
36. The Hayes brothers and Phil (performs, perform) jazz music.
37. Mr. Lee and Ms. Lang (manage, manages) our theater group.
38. Two deer and one rabbit (has come, have come) this way.

E. Write *simple* or *compound* for each sentence.

39. The mechanic took off the old tire and put on a new one.

40. Brian smiled, and Cheryl took his picture.

41. Charles likes spinach, but I hate that vegetable!

42. Marie, Sam, and George told stories around the campfire.

43. We might go to the shoe store today, or we might go Tuesday.

44. We finished our homework and went to a movie.

45. You can argue with Alice, but you cannot convince her.

46. Steve and Harry came home completely soaked.

UNIT 2: Capital Letters and Periods   *pages 66–69*

F. Write the sentence. Capitalize the proper nouns. Write the abbreviations correctly.

47. You can find dr cooper's office on kamen st near rte 85.

48. Nathan shaw, jr, will give a piano recital on tues, apr 17.

49. Next mon, ms flores will become chairperson of our committee.

50. Meet me on jan 29 at 2 p m promptly.

51. Author j c pierce, sr, will speak about his new book.

52. The new store on madison ave is always crowded.

53. Last sept our family went to new hampshire.

UNIT 2: Commas   *pages 90–91*

G. Write the sentences. Add the commas where they are needed.

54. Jeff Elise and their parents have moved into a new house.

55. No Donald you may not have another dollar!

56. Shari don't go outdoors without your overcoat.

57. You know perfectly well Brad that you are not allowed in that room.

58. The eagle swooped down fed its young and flew away.

59. These cups saucers and plates are beautiful.

60. Well I'm fairly sure I know the answer.

61. Please tell us a story Denise.

62. Michael where have you been?

UNIT 3: Verbs   *pages 116–133*

H. Write each sentence. Underline the verb. Then write whether it is an action verb or a linking verb.

63. This apple tastes sour.

64. The squirrel scooped the nut off the ground.

65. I gave the book to David.

66. This weather is delightful.

67. That towel feels rather damp.

68. The tour group followed the guide.

69. Maria tells scary ghost stories.

70. Ned seems frightened by the tales.

71. Those two girls are best friends.

72. The robin flew around Paula's head.

73. Paula watched the bird carefully.

74. The movie was long and boring.

I. Write each sentence. Draw one line under the main verb. Draw two lines under the helping verb.

75. The bird is making a nest for its young.
76. Jeff will visit some interesting places this summer.
77. Carol has written a lovely poem.
78. Penny and Sam have sung together often.
79. Marcia and Luis had read that story before.
80. Our band is practicing for the concert.
81. Now the Smiths are waving goodbye to us.
82. I shall remember your kind words always.

J. Write the past-tense form of each verb.

83. cry
84. do
85. go
86. see
87. eat
88. fall
89. run
90. wear
91. like
92. hop
93. ride
94. give
95. take
96. worry
97. sip
98. think

Unit 4: Pronouns *pages 176–185*

K. Write whether each pronoun is a subject pronoun or an object pronoun.

99. I
100. him
101. us
102. they
103. me
104. we
105. her
106. he
107. them
108. she

L. Write each sentence below. Choose the correct pronoun in parentheses ( ).

109. Give me (my, mine) pencil.
110. (Their, Theirs) is the fifth house on the block.
111. Florence practiced (her, hers) scales.
112. Is that painting above the dresser (your, yours)?
113. We went to (our, ours) history class together.
114. (My, Mine) brother walks with me to school.
115. Kathy and Norman saw (their, theirs) cousin at the mall.
116. That outfit of (her, hers) is certainly colorful!

Units 5 and 6: Adjectives and Adverbs *pages 234–241, 284–291*

M. Write each sentence. Underline the predicate adjective once. Underline twice the noun or pronoun it describes.

117. Georgia O'Keeffe's paintings are famous.
118. This ladder seems shaky.
119. The work was difficult.
120. The popcorn tasted salty.
121. The bull looked angry as it paced across the corral.
122. I feel comfortable in your company.
123. We were exhausted after the very long race.
124. The woman seems restless as she waits in line.
125. Herman was ready for anything!
126. The little boy felt pleased by the compliment.

N. For each adjective write the two forms used to compare persons, places, or things.

127. bright
128. happy
129. good
130. long
131. quick
132. sturdy
133. brave
134. special
135. strong
136. serious
137. bad
138. big
139. helpful
140. comfortable

O. For each adverb write the form used to compare two actions. Then write the form used to compare three or more actions.

141. early
142. often
143. quickly
144. fast
145. gently
146. well
147. hard
148. slowly
149. badly
150. remarkably

P. Write each sentence. Use the correct word in parentheses ( ).

151. The rehearsal went (fair, fairly) quickly.
152. Ms. Perelli is certainly a (fair, fairly) person.
153. Earl has been (extreme, extremely) patient with his new puppy.
154. Most of the time, you write very (good, well).
155. This is a very (good, well) book.
156. Mr. Stein has a very (low, lowly) singing voice.
157. The bear (careful, carefully) walked around the trap.
158. Carol raised her hand (impatient, impatiently).

UNIT 7: Prepositions
pages 340–347

Q. Write each sentence. Then write whether the underlined word is a preposition or an adverb.

159. When the train stopped, Laurie got off.
160. Get off the couch, please.
161. I shall be waiting outside.
162. Janie lives near the subway.
163. Step inside this cave.
164. As the door slowly opened, we went inside.
165. To see our fancy ceiling, look up.
166. I see my uncle coming up the walk.
167. Wearing a suit, he is coming near.
168. He shops at a store near us.

R. Write each sentence. Underline the preposition once. Underline the object of the preposition twice.

169. Old clothes were piled in one corner.
170. After a rainstorm the air smells fresh.
171. She comes from a distant land.
172. The dog with the floppy ears hung its head.
173. The train raced across the bridge.
174. I am pleased with my report.
175. Jake told Glen about the test.
176. Rosie accepted the bouquet from Herbert.
177. She handed him a glass of juice.
178. They sat together on the porch.
179. Between them was a plump cat named Irving.
180. Herbert handed a toy to Irving.

Presidential Pairings

Play this game about United States Presidents. Match a subject in **Column A** with the correct predicate in **Column B**. Write each sentence.

Column A

1. Our first President
2. Theodore and Franklin D.
3. Thomas Jefferson
4. President Lincoln's face
5. Franklin D. Roosevelt's face
6. President Johnson and President Kennedy
7. The White House and Camp David
8. The Oval Office

Column B

appears on a five-dollar bill.
have space centers named for them.
have the same last name.
wrote the Declaration of Independence.
has a state named for him.
are places where Presidents stay.
is where the President works.
is on a dime.

Coded Communication

Figure out the following message. (Hint: Each sentence contains either a compound subject or a compound predicate.)

Dear LN,

U N MLE R Nvited 40 2morrO. After T we can plA 10S or go 2 a moV. J N I wrote this in code TT U. We wrote 1 4 K 2 N ¢ it 2 her. B a friend N come 2 R parT. We will plA NE games U like N have a gr8 time!

Your friend,
KT LS

Write a coded message like the one above for a classmate. Include some compound subjects and compound predicates.

Unit 8 Extra Practice

1 Reviewing the Parts of Speech

p. 388

A. Write whether each underlined word is a noun, a pronoun, a verb, an adjective, an adverb, or a preposition.

1. The <u>Romans</u> picked flowers.
2. They <u>made</u> lovely bouquets.
3. The flowers were <u>for</u> Flora.
4. <u>They</u> decorated her statue.
5. Everyone danced <u>merrily</u>.
6. It <u>was</u> her holiday.

B. Write each sentence. Draw a line under the noun that follows a linking verb. Draw two lines under the subject that it renames or identifies.

EXAMPLE: On May Day in Sweden, actors are warriors.
ANSWER: On May Day in Sweden, <u>actors</u> are <u>warriors</u>.

7. One fighter is Summer.
8. The other is Winter.
9. Of course, Summer is always the winner.

C. Write each underlined word. After the word, write *noun*, *pronoun*, *verb*, *adjective*, *adverb*, or *preposition*.

10. The <u>ancient</u> Celts <u>believed</u> in a sun god.
11. During the <u>winter</u> the sun god <u>disappeared</u>.
12. <u>They</u> <u>thought</u> he was a prisoner.
13. <u>Evil</u> spirits had captured <u>him</u>.
14. They lit <u>fires</u> to chase the spirits <u>away</u>.
15. Some <u>ancient</u> peoples <u>were</u> believers in tree gods.
16. The people got up <u>early</u> <u>on</u> May Day.
17. They went <u>into</u> the <u>woods</u> to cut tree branches.
18. The <u>branches</u> were supposed to bring <u>good</u> luck.
19. In <u>England</u>, May Day <u>became</u> a big holiday.
20. People were always glad to see <u>warm</u> days <u>again</u>.
21. <u>They</u> cut down a <u>tall</u> tree.
22. Then they decorated <u>it</u> to make a Maypole.
23. Everyone <u>danced</u> <u>around</u> the Maypole.
24. <u>Colorful</u> <u>Maypoles</u> can still be seen on this holiday.

2 Compound Subjects

p. 390

A. Write the complete subject of each sentence. If the subject is compound, write *compound*.

1. The principal and our teacher announced a cleanup contest.
2. Mrs. Colucci or my father will be our block captain.
3. Our school and the newspaper will print advertisements.
4. The police and firefighters will help us.
5. Sidewalks and steps will be swept clean.
6. You and Jonathan can collect the fallen branches.
7. One of the cleanest streets in our town is Davis Avenue.
8. A cousin of mine lives there.
9. Her family and my family planted trees there last spring.
10. We put up fences to protect the young trees.
11. Lew, Ira, or I will care for the trees.
12. Davis Avenue doesn't need a contest to look neat.
13. Sonja and I hope our street will look as nice.
14. Mrs. Colucci and my father made a work plan.

B. Write each sentence. Underline the compound subject.

EXAMPLE: Asheville and our town tied for the award.
ANSWER: Asheville and our town tied for the award.

15. The mayor and the governor will award the prizes.
16. Antonia and she have painted their front door.
17. Carl or you should win a special award.
18. The drugstore and the supermarket displayed posters.
19. Friday and Saturday were the busiest cleanup days.

3 Using Subjects and Verbs That Agree

p. 392

A. Write the verb in parentheses ( ) that correctly completes each sentence.

1. Nancy and Oliver (make, makes) posters.
2. The races and the games (was, were) fun last year.
3. The students, parents, and teachers (sell, sells) tickets.
4. The adults and the children (like, likes) fairs.

B. Write the verb in parentheses ( ) that correctly completes each sentence.

5. Juice and peanuts (is, are) popular snacks at the fair.
6. Mr. Ching and his daughter (cook, cooks) the chicken.
7. The Boy Scouts and Girl Scouts (serve, serves) the food.
8. The corn, fruit, and potatoes (taste, tastes) great.
9. Coleslaw and salads (completes, complete) the meal.
10. After lunch the blue team and the gold team (plays, play) tug-of-war.
11. Masao and Serena (are, is) captains of their teams.
12. Parents and teachers (cheers, cheer) both sides.
13. Serena and her team (pull, pulls) Masao over the line.
14. The winning team and the losing team (looks, look) tired.

C. Write each sentence. Use the correct form of the verb in parentheses ( ).

15. Boris and Heather (make, makes) kites for the fair.
16. Two students and Boris (plans, plan) a kite contest.
17. The kite contest and the soccer game (begin, begins).
18. The Blues and the Golds (play, plays) for the soccer cup.
19. All the soccer players and kite fliers (run, runs) onto the field.
20. Boris and the Blues (crash, crashes) into each other.
21. The Golds and Heather (are, is) a tangle of string.
22. The principal and the coaches (come, comes) to help.
23. Other students and parents (helps, help), too.
24. Boris, Heather, and the soccer players (laughs, laugh) at themselves.

4 Compound Predicates

p. 394

A. Write the verbs in the complete predicate of each sentence.

1. The class planned and wrote a class newspaper.
2. The students chose and edited the articles.
3. Ms. Doyle read and approved each story.
4. Mr. Cortes typed and proofread everything.
5. Sandra photocopied, sorted, and stapled the pages.

B. Write the complete predicate of each sentence. If the predicate is compound, write *compound.*

6. Everyone helped with the newspaper.
7. Juan sat and thought of ideas.
8. Elena revised and corrected articles.
9. Ms. Doyle stayed after school every day.
10. She explained things and answered questions.
11. Matt planned and designed the front page.
12. He arranged all the articles and pictures.
13. He pasted everything into place.
14. The newspaper surprised and pleased the other classes.
15. Everyone read and enjoyed it.

C. Write each sentence. Underline the compound predicate.

16. We stopped, rested, and talked.
17. The auditorium sparkled and shone.
18. The curtain opened and closed.
19. We danced and sang.
20. The audience cheered and clapped.

5 Compound Sentences

p. 396

A. Write the sentences below. Then underline the two simple sentences in each.

1. We see stars and planets at night, and we see other bright lights, too.
2. Some lights are comets, and some are meteors.
3. Meteors are often seen, but comets are rare.
4. Comets are balls of frozen gas, and they orbit the sun.
5. Meteors are called shooting stars, and they travel fast.
6. Meteors burn up in space, or they fall to Earth as meteorites.
7. Sometimes very large meteorites hit Earth, and they make big holes in the ground.
8. The largest meteorite was found in Africa, and the second largest was found in Greenland.
9. People sometimes find meteorite holes, but the meteorites are usually gone.

B. Write *simple* or *compound* for each sentence.

10. Mercury is a small planet, and Jupiter is a large planet.
11. Jupiter is very far away, but you can often see it.
12. Mercury is nearest the sun, and Venus is second closest.
13. Each planet moves around the sun.
14. Mercury's year lasts 88 days, but Mars's year is 687 days.
15. The sun is a star, and it supplies heat for Earth.
16. Our sun and the other stars are giant balls of gas.
17. The sun is very bright, but it has some dark spots.
18. Scientists call these areas sunspots and study them closely.

6 Avoiding Run-on Sentences   *p. 398*

A. Write each sentence. Add a comma before the conjunction.

1. Flag Day was first officially celebrated in 1877 and it became a national holiday in 1916.
2. Before the Revolution colonists flew the British flag but later they had their own flag.
3. It was called the Grand Union and it had thirteen stripes with the British flag in the corner.
4. The Grand Union flag flew over Boston and it could be seen for miles.
5. After July 4, 1776, the colonists needed a new flag but they had trouble deciding on one.
6. Each colony had its own flag and each thought its flag was best.
7. Virginia's flag had a rattlesnake and it had the words ''Don't Tread on Me.''

B. Correct these run-on sentences. Write each as a compound sentence by adding a comma and a conjunction.

8. A flag was chosen on June 14, 1777 it was soon flown.
9. In 1814, Francis Scott Key wrote a poem about the flag he called it ''The Star-Spangled Banner.''
10. He saw a flag with fifteen stars it had fifteen stripes.
11. Stripes were added for new states the flag got too large.
12. Today's flag has fifty stars it has only thirteen stripes.

Acknowledgments continued from page ii.

Permissions: We wish to thank the following authors, publishers, agents, corporations, and individuals for their permission to reprint copyrighted materials. Page 24: Excerpt from *The Midnight Fox* by Betsy Byars. Copyright © 1968 by Betsy Byars. All rights reserved. Reprinted by permission of Viking Penguin, Inc., NY, NY, and Faber & Faber, Ltd., London. Page 80: Excerpt from ''Handicrafts'' by Patricia Fent Ross from *Mexico* © 1982 Courtesy of Gateway Press, Inc. Page 142: Excerpt from ''Paul Bunyan'' from *American Tall Tales* by Adrien Stoutenburg. Copyright © 1966 by Adrien Stoutenburg. Reprinted by permission of the publisher Viking Penguin, Inc., and Curtis Brown, Ltd. All rights reserved. Page 196: "The Littlest Sculptor" Copyright © 1986 Joan T. Zeier. Used with permission. Page 250: Excerpt from *Zeely* by Virginia Hamilton. Copyright © 1971 by Virginia Hamilton. Reprinted with permission of Macmillan Publishing Co. and McIntosh & Otis, Inc. Page 302: "The Big Blast" by Patricia Lauber. Reprinted by permission of Bradbury Press, an affiliate of Macmillan, Inc., from *Volcano, The Eruption and Healing of Mount St. Helens* by Patricia Lauber. Copyright © 1986 by Patricia Lauber. Page 356: "Definitions" from *The Forgetful Wishing Well* by X.J. Kennedy. Reprinted with permission of Margaret K. McElderry Books, an imprint of Macmillan Publishing Co. Copyright © 1985 by X.J. Kennedy. "What They Say" from *Who Would Marry a Mineral?* by Lillian Morrison. Copyright © 1978 by Lillian Morrison. Used by permission. Page 357: "Again and Again" plus illustration from *Flower, Moon, Snow* by Kazue Mizimura (Thomas Y. Crowell). Text copyright © 1977 by Kazue Mizimura. Reprinted by permission of Harper & Row, Publishers, Inc. The poem "Walking Past the School at Night" from *Cold Stars and Fireflies* by Barbara Juster Esbensen (Thomas Y. Crowell). Copyright © 1984 by Barbara Juster Esbensen. Page 358: "Ode to the Tomato" by Pablo Neruda. From *Selected Poems*. © 1972 by Dell Publishing Co. Used by permission of Delacorte Press/Seymour Lawrence. Page 362: "Direction" by Alonzo Lopez from *The Whispering Wind* edited by Terry Allen. Copyright © 1972 by the Institute of American Indian Arts. Reprinted by permission of Doubleday, a division of Bantam, Doubleday, Dell Publishing Group, Inc. "Night," nine lines from "The Windy City" in *Slabs of the Sunburnt West* by Carl Sandburg. Copyright 1922 by Harcourt Brace Jovanovich, Inc. Renewed 1950 by Carl Sandburg. Reprinted by permission of Harcourt Brace Jovanovich, Inc. "River" by Lawrence Locke. © 1981 by Lawrence Locke. Reprinted by permission of the author. Page 364: "The ragged phantom..." by Boncho. From *More Cricket Songs* Japanese haiku translated by Harry Behn. Copyright © 1971 by Harry Behn. All rights reserved. Reprinted by permission of Marian Reiner. "A river leaping..." by Meisetsu. From *Cricket Songs* Japanese haiku translated by Harry Behn. © 1964 by Harry Behn. All rights reserved. Reprinted by permission of Marian Reiner. Page 365: "All day in gray rain..." From *Cricket Songs* Japanese haiku translated by Harry Behn. © 1964 by Harry Behn. All rights reserved. Reprinted by permission of Marian Reiner. "Slanting, windy rain..." by Buson. From *More Cricket Songs* Japanese haiku translated by Harry Behn. Copyright © 1971 by Harry Behn. All rights reserved. Reprinted by permission of Marian Reiner. Page 366: "Balloons!" From *Flashlight and Other Poems* by Judith Thurman. Copyright © 1976 by Judith Thurman. All rights reserved. Reprinted by permission of Marian Reiner for the author. "Garment" by Langston Hughes. © 1941 Harper & Bros. Reprinted by permission of Harold Ober Associates. Page 408: "Two of a Kind" from *Headgear* by Ron Hirschi. Reprinted by permission of The Putnam & Grosset Group. Text copyright © 1986 by Ron Hirschi. Every effort has been made to locate the authors. If any errors have occurred, the publisher can be notified and corrections will be made.

Study Skills Lessons

Study Habits

1. **Listen in class.** Make sure that you understand exactly what your teacher wants you to do for homework. Write each homework assignment in a notebook.

2. **Have your homework materials ready.** You will need such items as textbooks, pens, pencils, erasers, rulers, and your notebook.

3. **Study in the same place every day.** Try to find a quiet and comfortable place where other people will not interrupt you. There should be good lighting, a comfortable chair, and a desk or table. Do not have the television or radio on while you are studying. The fewer distractions you have, the better you will study.

4. **Plan your study time.** Develop a daily study schedule. First decide on the best time of the day for studying. Then plan exactly when you will study each of your subjects. Also plan time for chores, or household tasks, and recreation. Use the study schedule below as a guide.

Study Schedule
3:30 to 4:00 P.M. — chores
4:00 to 5:00 P.M. — sports, play
5:00 to 5:30 P.M. — study science
5:30 to 6:00 P.M. — study math
6:00 to 7:00 P.M. — dinner and free time
7:00 to 7:30 P.M. — study English
7:30 to 9:00 P.M. — hobbies, reading, TV

5. **Set a goal or purpose each time you study.** Keep that goal in mind while you study. If you do, you will concentrate better.

Practice

Answer the following questions about study habits.

1. Which of the study tips above would most help you improve your study habits? Why?
2. Write a study schedule that would help you use your time wisely.

Test-Taking Tips

1. **Be prepared.** Have several sharp pencils and an eraser.

2. **Read or listen to the directions carefully.** Be sure you know what you are to do and where and how you are to mark your answers.

3. **Answer the easy questions first.** Quickly read all the questions on the page. Then go back to the beginning and answer the questions you are sure you know.

4. **Next, try to answer the questions you are not sure you know.** You may have a choice of answers. If so, narrow your choice. First eliminate all the answers you know are wrong. Try to narrow your selection to two answers. Then mark the answer you think is right.

5. **Answer the hardest questions last.** If you can't answer a question at all, don't waste time worrying about it. Skip the question and go on to the next.

6. **Think about analogy questions.** Some tests you take may include analogy questions. An analogy is a way of showing relationships between things. To complete an analogy question, figure out the relationship between the first two items. Then complete the analogy so that the second pair has the same relationship.

   EXAMPLE: cat : kitten :: bear : <u>cub</u>

7. **Plan your time.** Don't spend too much time on just one question. Check your watch or a clock from time to time as you take the test.

8. **Check your answers when you have finished.** Make sure you have marked your answers correctly. Unless you're sure you made a mistake, you probably should not change an answer.

Practice

1. How can you best prepare for a test?
2. In what order should you answer the questions on a test?
3. What should you do when you have answered all the questions?

Parts of a Book

Certain parts of a book give important information about the book. These parts have special names.

In the front of the book is the **title page**. It shows the title, author, and publisher of the book. The **copyright page** is on the back of the title page. It tells the year in which the book was published. The copyright date can help to tell you how up-to-date the facts in the book are.

The **table of contents** usually comes next. It shows the major divisions of the book and lists each chapter. Use the table of contents to find out what broad topics a book covers.

Nonfiction books often have an **index** at the back. It alphabetically lists the topics covered in the book. Use the index to see if a book has the specific information you need.

TABLE OF CONTENTS

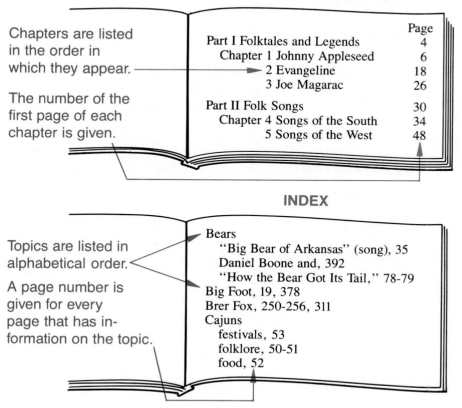

Chapters are listed in the order in which they appear.

The number of the first page of each chapter is given.

INDEX

Topics are listed in alphabetical order.

A page number is given for every page that has information on the topic.

Practice

A. Tell whether you would use the title page, copyright page, table of contents, or index to answer each of these questions about a book. Write each answer.

    1. Who is the author?

    2. Does the book have any information on the folklore of Georgia?

    3. On what page does Chapter 2 begin?

    4. How up-to-date is the information in the book?

    5. Which pages tell about Barbara Frietchie?

B. Use the sample table of contents and index on the opposite page to answer the following questions.

    6. How is the book organized?

    7. In which chapter would you expect to find cowboy songs?

    8. Which pages tell about the folklore of the Cajuns?

    9. Which page tells about Daniel Boone and bears?

  10. On which pages would you look to find out who wrote tales about Brer Fox?

C. Use the copyright page, table of contents, and index of this book to answer the following questions.

  11. When was this book published?

  12. On what page does the Dictionary of Knowledge begin?

  13. In which unit will you learn about prepositions?

  14. On which pages will you find information on prefixes?

  15. On which pages will you find information about using an encyclopedia?

Using the Library

Once you have chosen a topic for a report, where can you find information about it? For information on most topics, the first place to look is in the library. In the library, books are divided into two main categories; fiction and nonfiction. Fiction books contain made-up stories. They are arranged alphabetically by the author's last name. Nonfiction books are books that give facts. They are arranged numerically. Each nonfiction book has a number printed on its spine. This is the **call number** of the book. The books are numbered in such a way that books about the same subject are grouped together.

When you want to find a book in the library, check the card catalog or computer listing. These sources list every book in the library by its title, its author, and its subject. Catalog cards are arranged in alphabetical order. Study the information given on each kind of card.

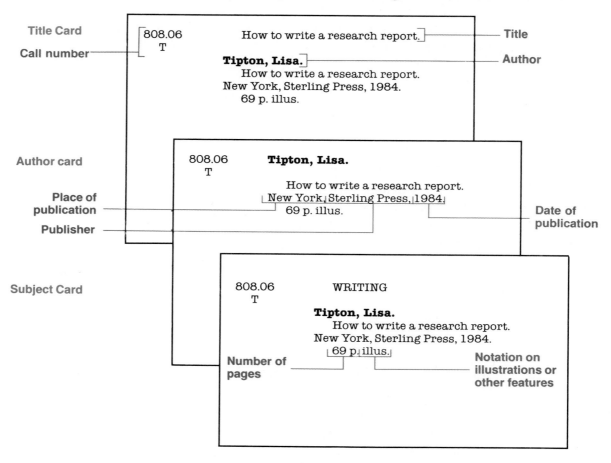

Title Card

Call number

808.06
T

How to write a research report.

Title

Tipton, Lisa.
How to write a research report.
New York, Sterling Press, 1984.
69 p. illus.

Author

Author card

Place of publication

Publisher

808.06
T

Tipton, Lisa.

How to write a research report.
New York, Sterling Press, 1984.
69 p. illus.

Date of publication

Subject Card

Number of pages

808.06
T

WRITING

Tipton, Lisa.
How to write a research report.
New York, Sterling Press, 1984.
69 p. illus.

Notation on illustrations or other features

Practice

A. Use the catalog cards on the opposite page to answer these questions.

1. What is the title of the book listed?
2. Who is the author?
3. Where and when was the book published?
4. Is this book illustrated?
5. What is the book's call number?

B. Write the word or words you would look up in the card catalog or computer listing to find the following items.

6. a book by Margery Sharp
7. the call number of the book *Westward by Canal*
8. the title of a book about eating good foods
9. the call numbers of books about volcanoes
10. the title of a book by P.L. Travers

C. Write *title, author,* or *subject* to tell what kind of catalog card you would use to answer each of these questions.

11. Who wrote *Kingdom of the Sun*?
12. What children's book did Ian Fleming write?
13. Does the library have any books about termites?
14. Did Isaac Asimov write any novels?
15. Did the same author write *This is the Texas Panhandle* and *A Tree Grows in Brooklyn*?

Using Reference Materials

Libraries contain many kinds of reference materials besides encyclopedias. By using different kinds of reference materials, you can gather a wide variety of information on a topic.

Atlas   An **atlas** is a book of maps. A **key**, or **legend**, tells us what the symbols mean. A **physical map** gives facts about the natural surface of the earth. It shows rivers, mountains, and seas. A **political map** shows such items as cities and boundaries between countries. The map of Alaska below has both physical and political features. Notice in the map key, labeled *ALASKA*, that different colors stand for different elevations, or heights above sea level.

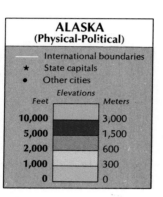

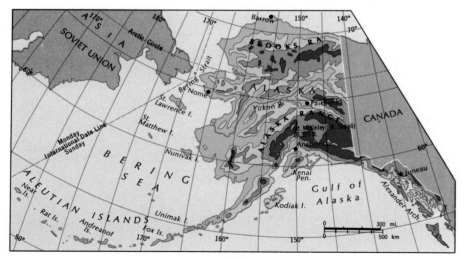

Practice

A. Use the map of Alaska above to answer the following question.

  1. What is the capital of Alaska?
  2. What country borders Alaska on the east?
  3. At about what elevation are most of the Aleutian Islands?
  4. What is the name of the river that is shown on this map of Alaska?
  5. What is the highest peak in the Alaska Range?

Almanac   An almanac specializes in up-to-date information and is usually published every year. The information in an almanac is often given in the form of a chart or table. An almanac does not devote as much space to background information as an encyclopedia does.

High Peaks in United States, Canada, Mexico

Name	Place	Feet	Name	Place	Feet
McKinley	Alas	20,320	South Buttress	Alas	15,885
Logan	Can	19,850	Wood	Can	15,885
Citlaltepec (Orizaba)	Mexico	18,700	Vancouver	Alas-Can	15,700
St. Elias	Alas-Can	18,008	Churchill	Alas	15,638
Popocatepetl	Mexico	17,400	Fairweather	Alas-Can	15,300
Foraker	Alas	17,400	Zinantecatl (Toluca)	Mexico	15,016
Iztacchuatl	Mexico	17,343	Hubbard	Alas-Can	15,015
Lucania	Can	17,147	Bear	Alas	14,831
King	Can	16,971	Walsh	Can	14,780
Steele	Can	16,644	East Buttress	Alas	14,730
Bona	Alas	16,550	Matlalcueyetl	Mexico	14,636
Blackburn	Alas	16,390	Hunter	Alas	14,573
Kennedy	Alas	16,286	Alverstone	Alas-Can	14,565
Sanford	Alas	16,237	Browne Tower	Alas	14,530

Other Reference Materials   Newspapers and magazines are periodicals. You can find them in libraries. Many libraries also have records, films, and videotapes.

Practice

B. Use the almanac entry above to answer these questions.

   6. In what state is Mount Kennedy located?
   7. What is the highest peak in the United States?
   8. Which mountain is higher—Mount Blackburn or Mount Steele?

C. Decide where you would look for answers to the questions below. Write *atlas, almanac,* or *periodical* for each.

   9. Where is Lake Tahoe?
   10. What cities were hit by last month's hurricane?
   11. Is Switzerland a coastal country?
   12. Who won gold medals in the most recent Olympic Games?
   13. What is the tallest building in the United States?

Using a Dictionary

A dictionary contains thousands of words in alphabetical order. Each word that is defined is called an **entry word**. How can you find the word you want? Luckily, there are some shortcuts to help you.

The first shortcut is to think of the dictionary in three parts: the front, *a–g;* the middle, *h–p;* and the back, *q–z.*

Front: a, b, c, d, e, f, g
Middle: h, i, j, k, l, m, n, o, p
Back: q, r, s, t, u, v, w, x, y, z

When you need to look up a word, decide in which part of the dictionary it appears. Then open to that part, trying to open to the first letter of the word you want.

The second shortcut is to use the guide words. The **guide words** show the first and last entry words on the page. All the other entry words on the page fall between the guide words in alphabetical order.

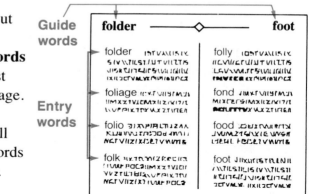

Practice

A. Write each word. Then write *front, middle,* or *back* to show in which part of a dictionary it appears.

1. tradition	**5.** hive	**9.** primitive
2. ballot	**6.** mole	**10.** culture
3. fantasy	**7.** suburb	**11.** villain
4. rhyme	**8.** ancient	**12.** hero

B. Follow the directions below. Write the words you choose in alphabetical order.

> **Hint:** Remember that words are put into alphabetical order by the first letter that is different.
>
> game, sport   rate, rent
> chin, chunk   blue, blush

13. Write five words that name animals.
14. Write the first names of five classmates.
15. Write five words that name articles of clothing.

C. Guide words for imaginary dictionary pages 218–221 are shown at the right. Write words **16–27**. Then write the page number for each entry word.

bunt	**218**	burro

burrow	**219**	butterfly

buttermilk	**220**	cabbage

cabin	**221**	calcium

16. bushel
17. bygone
18. cactus
19. burlap
20. buttercup
21. cafeteria
22. cadet
23. buzzard
24. burnt
25. cabbage
26. caboose
27. burr

D. Write each set of guide words below. After each set, write three words that could be entry words on that page. You may use a dictionary if you wish.

28. guide words: chant—clash
29. guide words: plum—point
30. guide words: royal—sack

E. Write five words from the Dictionary of Knowledge, which begins on page 456. Scramble the alphabetical order of the words. Then exchange papers with a classmate. See how quickly you can find each other's words. Repeat this activity with other words, and try to improve your time.

The answers to all the questions at the right can be found in one book, the dictionary. Of all reference books, the dictionary is probably the most useful. To find out why, study the entry below. It is from the Dictionary of Knowledge.

How is chasm pronounced?

Do you write on stationary or stationery?

Did I spell yield right?

What does leonine mean?

Entry word — **cam•ou•flage** (kam′ə fläzh) *n*. **1.** the act of hiding soldiers and things from an enemy by making them blend in with the landscape.

Pronunciation

Part of Speech

The soldiers used a camouflage of twigs and leaves in the jungle. **2.** a disguise of this kind in nature, as the green color of insects that live on leaves. —*v.* **camouflaged, camouflaging**. to hide by blending in. *The insect's green color camouflages it from enemies.* [from Italian *camuffare* to disguise] — *Syn.* **disguise**.

— Meanings

— Verb forms

— Etymology
— Synonym

Entry word   This shows how to spell the word. The dots between syllables show how to divide it at the end of a line of writing.

Pronunciation   This tells how to say the word. It is given in symbols that stand for certain sounds. For example, the symbol **ä** stands for the vowel sound heard in *father* and *march*. The Pronunciation Key on page 456 tells the sound for each symbol.

Part of speech   This label is abbreviated, such as *v.* for *verb*.

Meaning   The different meanings of the word are numbered.

Example sentence   This helps to make a meaning clear.

Verb forms or plural forms   These are shown when the spelling of the base word changes.

Etymology   This is a word history, and it appears in brackets.

Synonym   This is a word that has a meaning similar to that of the entry word. Its label is abbreviated *Syn.*

Practice

F. Write the answer to each question. Use the dictionary entry on page 454.

   31. How many syllables does the entry word contain?
   32. How many meanings are given for *camouflage* as a noun?
   33. How many meanings are given for *camouflage* as a verb?
   34. How many example sentences are included in the entry?

G. Use the dictionary entries below for questions **35–38.**

buoy (bɔi) *n.* **1.** a floating object kept in a certain place on the water to show safe areas or dangerous areas. **2.** a life buoy; something used to keep a person afloat in the water.

leg•end (lej′ ənd) *n.* **1.** a story handed down through the years, which many people have believed. **2.** such stories as a group. **3.** what is written on a coin or medal. *The legend on a dime is "IN GOD WE TRUST."* **4.** a remarkable person, much talked about while still alive.

   35. What is the number of the meaning that *buoy* has in the following sentence? *Throw a buoy to the weakest swimmer.*
   36. For which meaning of *legend* could the following be an example sentence? *Hank Aaron is a baseball legend.*
   37. Which entry word rhymes with *annoy*?
   38. What part of speech is each entry word?

H. Use the Dictionary of Knowledge to answer the questions below.

   39. What does a geologist study?
   40. Which word is spelled incorrectly, and how should it be spelled: *creditable, ebony, laquer, repellent*?
   41. What is pumice used for?
   42. What does the word *quiver* mean in the following sentence? *Is the quiver made of leather?*

I. Use the Dictionary of Knowledge to write a word quiz for your classmates. Write three questions like those in **Practice H.** Then see who can answer the questions in the shortest time.

Dictionary of Knowledge

This Dictionary of Knowledge has two kinds of entries, **word entries** and **encyclopedic entries.** Many of the word entries in this dictionary are taken from the literature pieces found throughout this book. You might use these entries to help you understand the meanings of words. You will use the encyclopedic entries in two ''Apply'' sections in each unit.

Word Entries ♦ These entries are just like the ones found in the ordinary dictionaries you are familiar with. Each entry includes such elements as pronunciation respellings, definitions, and example sentences.

Encyclopedic Entries ♦ These entries resemble encyclopedia articles. Each entry provides interesting information about a particular topic or person.

Abbreviations Used in this Dictionary			
adj.	adjective	pl.	plural
adv.	adverb	prep.	preposition
Ant.	Antonym	pron.	pronoun
conj.	conjunction	Syn.	Synonym
n.	noun	v.	verb

Full pronunciation key* The pronunciation of each word is shown just after the word, in this way: **abbreviate** (ə brē′ vē āt).
The letters and signs used are pronounced as in the words below.
The mark ′ is placed after a syllable with a primary or heavy accent as in the example above.
The mark ′ after a syllable shows a secondary or lighter accent, as in **abbreviation** (ə brē′vē ā′shən).

SYMBOL	KEY WORDS	SYMBOL	KEY WORDS	SYMBOL	KEY WORDS	SYMBOL	KEY WORDS
a	ask, fat	o͝o	look, pull	b	bed, dub	v	vat, have
ā	ape, date	o͞o	ooze, tool	d	did, had	w	will, always
ä	car, father	yo͝o	unite, cure	f	fall, off	y	yet, yard
		yo͞o	cute, few	g	get, dog	z	zebra, haze
e	elf, ten	ou	out, crowd	h	he, ahead		
er	berry, care			j	joy, jump	ch	chin, arch
ē	even, meet	u	up, cut	k	kill, bake	ŋ	ring, singer
		ʉr	fur, fern	l	let, ball	sh	she, dash
i	is, hit			m	met, trim	th	thin, truth
ir	mirror, here	ə	a in ago	n	not, ton	*th*	then, father
ī	ice, fire		e in agent	p	put, tap	zh	s in pleasure
			e in father	r	red, dear		
o	lot, pond		i in unity	s	sell, pass	′	as in (ā′b'l)
ō	open, go		o in collect	t	top, hat		
ô	law, horn		u in focus				
oi	oil, point						

*Pronunciation key adapted from *Webster's New World Dictionary; Basic School Edition*,
Copyright © 1983 by Simon & Schuster, Inc. Reprinted by permission.

— A —

Ad·ams, An·sel (ad′əmz, an′səl) 1902–1984

Ansel Adams was an American photographer. He took pictures of the wilderness areas of the West. He loved nature, and he was an active conservationist.

Adams believed in a straight style of photography. His photographs are simple and direct. Some photographers believe in a misty, out-of-focus style. Adams took detailed, sharply focused photographs.

Most of Adams's photographs are of landscapes. His pictures feature rivers, mountains, and forests. The pictures are quite beautiful.

Adams helped establish the Department of Photography at New York's Museum of Modern Art. He also founded a photography department at the California School of Fine Arts. It was the first such department of study at any college in the United States. Adams also wrote several books on photography.

— B —

Boone, Dan·iel (bo͞on, dan′ yəl) 1734–1820

Daniel Boone was a real-life American hero. He explored unknown regions of Kentucky. He marked trails and led settlers there. He blazed the Wilderness Road, which became the main roadway for families moving west. Boone was the most famous pioneer of the Colonial period.

Boone was captured by Native Americans several times. The Shawnee developed such respect for him that they adopted him into their tribe. Boone was made a full-fledged Shawnee brave. He pretended to love his life with the Shawnee. He finally escaped to warn his friends in Boonesborough that the Shawnee were about to attack them. By the time of his death, Daniel Boone had become one of the most famous and well-respected men in American history.

— C —

cam·ou·flage (kam′ə fläzh) *n.* **1.** the act of hiding soldiers and things from an enemy by making them blend in with the landscape. *The soldiers used a camouflage of twigs and leaves in the jungle.* **2.** a disguise of this kind in nature, as the green color of insects that live on leaves. — *v.* **camouflaged, camouflaging.** to hide by blending in. *The insect's green color camouflages it from enemies.* [from Italian *camuffare* to disguise] — *Syn.* **disguise.**

a fat	er care	ī bite, fire	oi oil	u up	th thin	ə = a *in* ago
ā ape	ē even	o lot	o͞o look	ur fur	th then	e *in* agent
ä car, father	i hit	ō go	o͞o tool	ch chin	zh leisure	i *in* unity
e ten	ir here	ô law, horn	ou out	sh she	ṅg ring	o *in* collect
						u *in* focus

Car·ver, George Wash·ing·ton (kär′vər, jôrj wôsh′ing tən *or* wosh′ing tən) 1864–1943

George Washington Carver was an American scientist who developed products from different plants, such as sweet potatoes and pecans. He is best known for his work with peanuts. Carver produced more than three hundred products, including soap and ink, from this one crop. Carver was born in Missouri of slave parents. As a youngster, he always showed interest in plants. He graduated from Iowa State College in 1894 and became an assistant botanist there. In 1896, Carver became an instructor at Tuskegee

Portrait of George Washington Carver, Mary Randolph Witmer, 1935 National Portrait Gallery, Smithsonian Institution, Washington, D.C.

Institute in Alabama. He spent the rest of his life there, later becoming the head of the agricultural department. Carver did a lot of research on soil conservation and on ways to grow bigger and better crops. He wrote much helpful material for farmers. Carver received many awards for his valuable contributions to science.

col·o·niz·er (kol′ə nīz ′ər) *n.* **1.** a person or group of persons that settles in a distant land and establishes a colony or settlement. *The English were colonizers of America.* **2.** a group of animals or plants that begins to live or grow in an area. *Tiny flowers were colonizers of the mountain slope.*

cred·it·a·ble (kred′it ə b′l) *adj.* deserving praise or credit for something. *Sam did a creditable job on his report.—syn.* **honorable.—creditably** *adv.*

Crock·ett, Da·vy (krok′it, dā′vē) 1786–1836

Few frontiersmen in America were ever as famous as Davy Crockett. He was an expert marksman, a member of Congress, a scout, a humorist, and a real hero.

Crockett started school at age thirteen. His education lasted only four days. He got into a fight with another student and ran away for three years to avoid punishment.

As a humorist, Crockett told many tall tales about himself. Writers exaggerated Crockett's stories even more. Because of this, Crockett became a famous folk hero during his lifetime. He settled in a wild area of Tennessee where he claimed to have killed 105 bears in seven months. Later he became a Tennessee congressman.

Davy Crockett is best known for trying to defend the Alamo against Mexican troops in 1836, during the war for Texas independence. All of the defenders of the San Antonio mission, including Crockett, were killed during that famous battle. The name Davy Crockett remains one of the first names in American folklore.

Portrait of David Crockett, William Henry Huddle (painted 1889) State Preservation Board, Texas State Capitol. Photo courtesy of the Archives Division, Texas State Library.

────────── **D** ──────────

de·mol·ish (di mol′ish) *v.* to tear down; to smash or ruin. *The wrecking crew demolished the old building.* [from Latin *de-* down + *moliri* to build, to construct] — *Syn.* **destroy.** — *Ant.* **construct.**

────────── **E** ──────────

eb·on·y (eb′ə nē) *n.* the black, hard wood of certain tropical trees. — *adj.* **1.** made of ebony. **2.** black or dark. *The ebony statue gleamed in the display case.*

⎯⎯⎯⎯⎯⎯ **G** ⎯⎯⎯⎯⎯⎯

ge•ol•o•gist   (jē ol′ə jist) *n.* one who studies the earth's crust and the ways in which its layers were formed. *The geologist gave a speech about rocks and fossils.*

gey•ser   (gī′zər)

A geyser is a spring that shoots hot water with great force. Among the most famous geysers is Old Faithful, in Yellowstone National Park.

Geysers are formed deep below the earth's surface. Cold water seeps into a channel until it reaches very hot rocks. The water is heated by the rocks. It cannot boil, however, because of the weight of other water on it. The heat at the bottom of the channel continues to rise, and steam begins to form. A small amount of water bubbles over the earth's surface, leaving more room for deep water to turn into steam. Suddenly the water at the bottom expands and forces out the rest of the steam in an explosion.

In some ways, geysers are similar to volcanoes. They both shoot forth with explosive force. Volcanoes, however, shoot molten rock; geysers shoot water with mineral matter in it. Volcanoes and geysers both usually erupt at irregular time periods. Old Faithful is an exception to this. It erupts about once in every sixty-five minutes.

gourd   (gôrd *or* gŏŏrd) *n.* **1.** a vine with large fruit containing many seeds. *Gourds and pumpkins belong to the same family of plants.* **2.** the fruit of this vine, not fit for eating but often dried and used for cups, bowls, and decorations. *The basket filled with gourds makes a charming decoration.*

⎯⎯⎯⎯⎯⎯ **H** ⎯⎯⎯⎯⎯⎯

Ham•il•ton, Vir•gin•ia   (ham′ əl t'n, vər jin′yə) 1936–

Virginia Hamilton is an American writer of children's books. The subjects of her books reflect the dignity of the black American heritage.

Hamilton has won several important awards in children's literature. She won the Newbery Medal and the National Book Award for the book *M.C. Higgins, the Great,* published in 1974. This is a story about a mountain family.

Hamilton was born in Yellow Springs, Ohio. Some of her other books are *Zeely, The House of Dies Drear, The Time-Ago Tales of Jahdu,* and *The Planet of Junior Brown.*

hide[1]   (hīd) *v.* **hid, hidden** or **hid, hiding. 1.** to keep or put out of sight. **2.** to keep others from knowing about. *He tried to hide the birthday present in the closet.* — *Syn.* **conceal.**

hide[2]   (hīd) *n.* the skin of an animal, either raw or tanned. *Some belts and shoes are made from the hides of animals.*

a fat	**er** care	**ī** bite, fire	**oi** oil	**u** up	**th** thin	ə = a *in* ago
ā ape	**ē** even	**o** lot	**ŏŏ** look	**ur** fur	**th** then	e *in* agent
ä car, father	**i** hit	**ō** go	**ōō** tool	**ch** chin	**zh** leisure	i *in* unity
e ten	**ir** here	**ô** law, horn	**ou** out	**sh** she	**ŋ** ring	o *in* collect
						u *in* focus

Dictionary of Knowledge

I

in•dig•nant (in dig′ nənt) *adj.* angry about something that seems unfair or mean. *She was indignant when he criticized her work.* [from Latin *in-* not + *dignari* to deem worthy]—*Syn.* **angry.** —**indignantly** *adv.*

K

Ken•ne•dy, X.J. (ken′ə dē, eks jā) 1929–

X.J. Kennedy is a poet and writer. Many of his works were written for children. Kennedy has won several awards for his writing. He has also taught English at numerous colleges and universities.

Kennedy was born in Dover, New Jersey. His real name is Joseph Charles Kennedy. He chose the initial *X* so he would not be confused with other well-known Kennedys.

Kennedy became seriously interested in writing during childhood. He has not stopped writing since then. Among his publications for children are a collection of poetry called *The Phantom Ice Cream Man* and a novel named *The Owlstone Crown.* Here is one of his poems.

Exploding Gravy

My mother's big green gravy boat
Once thought he was a navy boat.

I poured him over my mashed potatoes
And out swam seven swift torpedoes.

Torpedoes whizzed and whirred, and—WHAM!
One bumped smack into my hunk of ham

And blew up with an awful roar,
Flinging my carrots on the floor.

Exploding gravy! That's so silly!
Now all I ever eat is chili.

L

lac•quer (lak′ər) *n.* a varnish made of shellac and other substances. **2.** a natural varnish obtained from certain trees in Asia. — *v.* to coat with lacquer. *We lacquered the table to give it a waterproof finish.*

Lew•is, Mer•i•weth•er (loo′ is, mer′ē we*th*′ər) 1774–1809 **and Clark, Wil•liam** (klärk, wil′yəm) 1770–1838

Together, Meriwether Lewis and William Clark explored the northwestern wilderness of America during the early nineteenth century. The most important result of their work was that the United States was able to claim the Oregon region for itself.

Lewis was a private secretary to President Thomas Jefferson, who commissioned him to lead the expedition. Lewis had been an army captain and seemed a good choice for the hard job. The expedition, which included about forty-five persons, was filled with many great adventures. Lewis spent a lot of time talking with Native Americans and learning about their lives. On the return journey, Lewis took part of the group down the Marias River. Clark took the other part down the Yellowstone River. Later on, Lewis became governor of the Louisiana Territory.

Lewis and Clark at Three Forks (Detail), E.S. Paxson, Completed 1912
Courtesy of the Montana Historical Society

Before the expedition, Clark had been a retired soldier. He rejoined the army to go west with Lewis, as the second in command. Clark trained men for the dangerous journey. He was a fine mapmaker and drew routes for the expedition. He also drew the animals he saw along the way. After the expedition, Clark became superintendent of Indian affairs and governor of the Missouri Territory.

—————————— **M** ——————————

mag·ma (mag′mə) *n.* **1.** molten rock deep in the earth from which igneous rock is formed. *The magma inside a volcano is extremely hot.* **2.** a pasty mixture of mineral or organic matter.

mire (mīr) *n.* **1.** an area of wet, soft ground; a bog. **2.** deep mud. *The rock sank in the mire.* —*v.* **mired, miring.** to sink or get sunk in mire. *The animal was mired in the swamp.*—*Syn.* **swamp.**

moose (mo͞os) *n.*
The moose is the largest member of the deer family. The animal lives in most of the northern parts of the world. The moose has long legs and high, humplike shoulders. It also has an unusual hair-covered growth, called a bell, under its throat. It has heavy, flat antlers. Each year the moose sheds its antlers and grows new ones. It polishes these great weapons against trees.

Moose like to live in forests with swamps and lakes nearby. In summer, moose live alone. In winter they stay together in bands. They try to find warmth in the swamps and woods. Their long legs help them walk easily in the snow. Moose feed on water plants, leaves, and young shoots of trees.
At one time, hunters almost destroyed the entire moose population of our country. Today, moose are protected by law.

—————————— **N** ——————————

name·sake (nām′sāk) *n.* one that has the same name as another; especially, one named after another. *Jeff is my uncle's namesake.*

—————————— **O** ——————————

o·blige (ə blīj′) *v.* **obliged, obliging. 1.** to force to do something because the law, conscience, or something else demands it. **2.** to make feel as if something is owed because of a favor or kindness received. *I am obliged to return the favor.* **3.** to do a favor for. *I'll oblige you and rake the leaves.* [from Latin *obligare* to bind] —*Syn.* **force.**

ob·long (ob′lôn̂g) *adj.* different from a square or circular form through elongation. *That long, rounded swimming pool is oblong in shape.* —*n.* an oblong figure.

om·i·nous (om′ə nəs) *adj.* threatening, like a bad sign or omen. *There were ominous clouds overhead.* [from Latin *ominiosus*] — **ominously** *adv.*

—————————— **P** ——————————

pot·ter·y (pot′ ər ē) *n.*
Pottery is a kind of ware made from baked clay. Some pottery is very valuable and unique. Some of it is inexpensive. Pottery can be made in a factory or by a potter at home.
There are three main kinds of pottery. One kind, earthenware, is made mostly from mixed

						ə = a *in* ago
a fat	**er** care	**ī** bite, fire	**oi** oil	**u** up	**th** thin	e *in* agent
ā ape	**ē** even	**o** lot	**o͞o** look	**ur** fur	*th* then	i *in* unity
ä car, father	**i** hit	**ō** go	**o͞o** tool	**ch** chin	**zh** leisure	o *in* collect
e ten	**ir** here	**ô** law, horn	**ou** out	**sh** she	**n̂g** ring	u *in* focus

earthenware clays. It usually has colorful glazes, but it breaks more easily than other kinds of pottery. Earthenware is fired at a low temperature.

Stoneware, a second kind of pottery, is hard and heavy. It is made from a mixture of stoneware clays and is fired at a very high temperature. It often becomes shiny when fired, so many potters don't glaze it. Stoneware is stronger and heavier than earthenware.

Porcelain is the most delicate kind of pottery. Porcelain can be fired at high or low temperatures. Light can shine through a thin piece of porcelain.

The four steps in making pottery are preparing the clay, shaping the clay, decorating and glazing the clay, and firing it.

Potters prepare clay by pressing it with their hands. This softens the clay.

There are many methods of shaping the clay. One method makes use of a potter's wheel. This device consists of a flat, round surface that turns while the potter shapes clay on it.

Potters decorate pottery by scratching lines into it. A colorful glaze is often brushed on.

Firing makes pottery strong. Pottery is fired in an oven called a kiln.

poul•tice (pōl′ tis) *n.* a soft, hot, wet mixture, as of flour or mustard and water, put on a sore or inflamed part of the body.

pov•er•ty (pov′ər tē) *n.* **1.** the condition of being poor, or not having enough to live on. **2.** the condition of being poor in quality or lacking in something. *The poverty of this writer's imagination is disgraceful.*

praise•wor•thy (prāz′wʉr′ *th*ē) *adj.* deserving praise; that should be admired.

pray•ing man•tis (prā′ iɪŋ man′ tis)

This insect got its name because it often lifts its front legs as if it were praying. It takes this position when hunting. Praying mantises, or mantids, are among the greediest of all insects. They feed on other kinds of insects and on their own kind as well. They usually eat their prey alive.

The praying mantis is an example of nature's camouflage. In shape and color, it looks very much like the plants on which it stays.

The forelegs of a praying mantis look like arms. They have sharp hooks that hold the victims. Human beings benefit from the praying mantis because it eats harmful insects.

pred•a•tor (pred′ə tər) *n.* an animal that lives by killing and eating other animals. *The shark is a predator of the sea.*

prov•erb (prov′ərb)

A proverb is a saying that tells something useful or wise. Only sayings that have been used for a long time and are fairly well known are proverbs.

Proverbs exist in all languages. In fact, the same proverb can often be found in several different languages.

Some frequently used proverbs are
* A bird in the hand is worth two in the bush.
* Don't put off till tomorrow what you can do today.

- Smile, and the world smiles with you. Weep, and you weep alone.
- A place for everything, and everything in its place.

Many proverbs can be found in Benjamin Franklin's *Poor Richard's Almanac.*

pulse (puls) *n.* **1.** the regular beating in the arteries, caused by the movements of the heart in pumping the blood. *A person's pulse can be felt in the wrist.* **2.** any regular beat. *I can hear the pulse of the drum.* [from Latin *pulsus* beating]

pum•ice (pum′is) *n.* a light, spongy rock sometimes formed when lava from a volcano hardens. It is often used for polishing, smoothing, or cleaning. *This piece of pumice is as light as a feather.*

———————————— **Q** ————————————

quiv•er[1] (kwiv′ər) *v.* to shake with little, trembling movements. *The delicate flowers quivered in the gentle breeze.* — *Syn.* **shake.**

quiv•er[2] (kwiv′ər) *n.* a case for holding arrows. *How many arrows are in that quiver?*

———————————— **R** ————————————

ra•di•ance (rā′dē əns) *n.* **1.** bright shininess. **2.** an appearance of joy or good health.

Radiance shone in her sparkling eyes and her cheery smile.

re•pel•lent (ri pel′ənt) *adj.* that drives back in various ways. *The spoiled milk had a repellent smell.* — *n.* something that repels, or makes stay away. *I hope that the insect repellent will keep the mosquitoes away.* — *Ant.* **attractive.**

———————————— **S** ————————————

salt•cel•lar (sôlt′sel′ər) *n.* a small dish for salt at the table; a saltshaker. *All of the saltcellars need refilling.* [from Latin *sal* salt]

sand•blast (sand′blast) *n.* a strong stream of air carrying sand, used to etch glass or clean the surface of stone. — *v.* to etch or clean with a sandblast. *The workers sandblasted the walls of the building in two days.*

se•crete (si krēt′) *v.* **secreted, secreting. 1.** to put in a secret place; to hide. **2.** to make in or give off into or out of the body. *Our salivary glands secrete a substance that helps us digest food.*

side•board (sīd′bôrd) *n.* a piece of furniture with drawers and shelves for holding dishes, silverware, linen, and other things. *Please get more dishes from the sideboard.*

slurp (slʉrp) *v.* to drink or eat in a noisy way. *It is not polite to slurp food.* — *n.* a loud sucking or sipping sound.

speechmaking technique
(spēch′ māk′iṅg tek nēk′)

There are many opportunities both in school and outside of school to make speeches. A good speechmaker considers the following points: the subject of the speech, the audience, him- or herself as the speaker, and the occasion.

Speakers must know their subjects well. It is best to have firsthand information about a subject. There are usually three kinds of subjects to choose from: those that persuade, those that inform, and those that entertain.

Speakers must know their audience. They should determine what the audience already

a fat	**er** care	**ī** bite, fire	**oi** oil	**u** up	**th** thin	ə = a *in* ago
ā ape	**ē** even	**o** lot	**oo** look	**ʉr** fur	**th** then	e *in* agent
ä car, father	**i** hit	**ō** go	**o͞o** tool	**ch** chin	**zh** leisure	i *in* unity
e ten	**ir** here	**ô** law, horn	**ou** out	**sh** she	**ṅg** ring	o *in* collect
						u *in* focus

knows about the subject of the speech and, if possible, what their opinions are. If a speaker knows that the audience is already against something, then he or she will have to use strong or charming techniques to win the audience over.

A speaker's best tool is his or her personality. Speakers should look at themselves carefully to discover their own strengths and weaknesses.

When a speaker is a natural storyteller, he or she should include an anecdote — a brief amusing story — in a speech. A speaker should always stand straight and speak loudly and slowly enough to be heard by everyone.

A speaker should understand the occasion at which a speech is to be given. Is the subject of the speech appropriate? A speech about great baseball players might not impress the local gardening club.

A speech should always have an interesting introduction, a clear main idea, a lot of supporting material, and a strong conclusion.

sprad•dle (sprad′′l) *v.* **spraddled, spraddling**. to stand or sit with legs spread apart as on a horse. *The child spraddled the log fence.* [a blend of the words *spread* and *straddle*]

sta•tion•ar•y (stā′shə ner′ē) *adj.* **1.** not to be moved; fixed. *That stationary bicycle is attached to the floor.* **2.** not changing in condition or value. *How long has the price of fuel remained stationary?*

sta•tion•er•y (stā′shə ner′ē) *n.* paper and envelopes for writing letters. *My stationery has a small picture of a flower on it.*

T

team•ster (tēm′stər) *n.* a person whose work is hauling goods with a team or truck. *He works as a teamster hauling paper products in his truck.*

U

Ur•sa Ma•jor (ur′ sə mā′jər)

Ursa Major is the constellation, or group of stars, known as the Great Bear. This constellation includes the Big Dipper. The two stars in the front of the dipper's cup point to the North Star. The dipper's cup marks the hindquarters of the bear. The handle shows the bear's tail. Other stars make up the head and legs.

On winter evenings the handle of the Big Dipper points down. On summer evenings its handle points up. By morning, the Big Dipper's position changes because of the rotation of the earth.

To find Ursa Major, simply look for the Big Dipper. Then use your knowledge and imagination.

V

vol•ca•no (vol kā′nō)

A volcano is an opening in the earth's surface through which lava, hot gases, and rock fragments are ejected from the earth's interior. Most volcanoes are atop cone-shaped mountains. In fact, the mountains themselves are also called volcanoes. Erupting volcanoes can be quite beautiful, but many have caused a great deal of death and destruction.

Dictionary of Knowledge

Perhaps the most famous volcano is Vesuvius, located in Italy. In A.D. 79 a huge eruption of this volcano destroyed three towns and many thousands of lives.

Mauna Loa, in Hawaii, is the world's largest volcano. It rises almost 30,000 feet from the ocean floor and has a 60-mile-wide base.

In 1912, Mount Katmai, in Alaska, created a glowing flood of hot ash. The ash traveled 15 miles, forming the Valley of Ten Thousand Smokes.

Cotopaxi, in Ecuador, is 19,347 feet above sea level. It erupted in 1877, producing a mudflow that traveled 150 miles. About one thousand people were killed.

At 22,831 feet above sea level, Aconcagua, in Argentina, is the highest mountain in the Western Hemisphere. Its volcano is now extinct.

Mount Etna, in Italy, is 11,122 feet above sea level. In 1669 its eruption killed about twenty thousand people.

———————————— **W** ————————————

ware (wer) *n.* **1.** a thing or things for sale. *The store sells unusual wares such as corn cob holders.* **2.** pottery or earthenware.—*Syn.* **goods.**

Wil•der, Lau•ra In•galls (wīl′ dər, lôr′ə iṅg′ gəlz) 1867–1957

Laura Ingalls Wilder was an American author of children's books. She is best known for her *Little House* books. The books were based on her childhood in the pioneer Midwest. They tell about the hardships of prairie life and the importance of a close family. The books are filled with warmth and the spirit of the American frontier.

Imagine what it would be like to travel to a rugged, unpopulated place and to establish a home there. This is the experience Wilder lived through.

Today the Laura Ingalls Wilder award is given every three years to an outstanding author of children's literature. Wilder herself received the first award in 1954. During the 1970s, a successful television series based on the *Little House* books was created.

a	fat	er	care	ī	bite, fire	oi	oil	u	up	th	thin	ə = a *in* ago
ā	ape	ē	even	o	lot	o͝o	look	ur	fur	th	then	e *in* agent
ä	car, father	i	hit	ō	go	o͞o	tool	ch	chin	zh	leisure	i *in* unity
e	ten	ir	here	ô	law, horn	ou	out	sh	she	ṅg	ring	o *in* collect
												u *in* focus

THESAURUS

A thesaurus contains lists of synonyms and antonyms. You will use this Thesaurus for the thesaurus lesson in Unit 1 and for the Thesaurus Corner in each Reading-Writing Connection in this book. You can also use the Thesaurus to find synonyms to make your writing more interesting.

Sample Entry

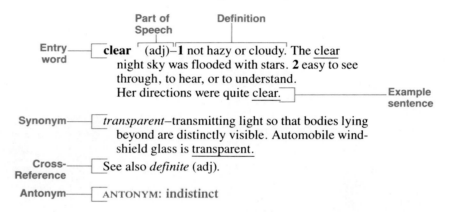

clear (adj)–**1** not hazy or cloudy. The <u>clear</u> night sky was flooded with stars. **2** easy to see through, to hear, or to understand. Her directions were quite <u>clear</u>.

transparent–transmitting light so that bodies lying beyond are distinctly visible. Automobile windshield glass is <u>transparent</u>.

See also *definite* (adj).

ANTONYM: indistinct

Entry word — Part of Speech — Definition — Example sentence — Synonym — Cross-Reference — Antonym

How to Use the Thesaurus Index

To find a word, use the Thesaurus Index on pages 467–471. All entry words, synonyms, and antonyms are listed alphabetically in the index. Words in dark type are entry words, words in italic type are synonyms, and words in blue type are antonyms. A cross-reference (marked "See also") lists an entry that gives additional synonyms, related words, and antonyms. The page numbers tell you where to find the word you are looking for.

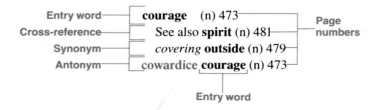

Entry word — **courage** (n) 473

Cross-reference — See also **spirit** (n) 481

Synonym — covering **outside** (n) 479

Antonym — cowardice **courage** (n) 473

Page numbers

Entry word

THESAURUS INDEX
A list of all the words in this thesaurus

A

accident (n)–An unfortunate event that happens by chance and that results in loss, injury, or death. There is an automobile accident almost every month at that dangerous intersection.

calamity–an extremely grave event or misfortune marked by great loss and lasting distress; a disaster. The fire was a calamity to the family whose home was destroyed.

catastrophe–a sudden or widespread tragic event or disaster; a great calamity. The earthquake that devastated most of the city is a catastrophe that will not be easily forgotten.

disaster–a sudden event that causes much damage, suffering, or loss. The train wreck was a disaster that fortunately took no lives.

misadventure–an unfortunate accident; a piece of bad luck. I knew that our vacation trip was a misadventure when it began to rain on the very first day.

misfortune–bad luck; adverse fortune. By misfortune I arrived on the island just ahead of the typhoon.

mishap–an unfortunate accident. Falling from her bicycle was a mishap that left Kim badly bruised.

ask (v)–**1** to question; to call on to answer. I asked my brother questions about geography. **2** to make a request for something. I asked the waiter for more water.

inquire–to ask about someone or something. Have you inquired about the time that the game will be played?

interrogate–to question systematically. The police officer interrogated the woman who saw the accident.

question–to ask for the purpose of finding out. Mark questioned me about my science project.

quiz–to question carefully. Our teacher quizzed us on yesterday's homework assignment.

request–to ask for. I requested extra help in math after school.

ANTONYMS: **answer (v), reply (v), respond**

B

beautiful (adj)–very pleasing to see or hear; delighting the mind or the senses. That is a beautiful painting.

attractive–pleasing; winning attention and liking. You are wearing an attractive sweater.

dazzling–brilliantly shining; splendid. Dazzling gems sparkled in the jewelry store display cases.

glorious–having great beauty; splendid; magnificent. This crisp and clear autumn day is truly glorious.

handsome–pleasing or impressive in appearance. That limousine is certainly a handsome automobile.

lovely–beautiful in mind, appearance, or character; delightful. Having dinner at that new restaurant sounds like a lovely idea.

pretty–pleasing by delicacy or grace. Look at this pretty bouquet of daisies.

ANTONYMS: **ugly, unattractive**

before (prep)–**1** preceding in time; earlier than. Does Memorial Day come before Flag Day? **2** in the sight or presence of. Bill was standing before the principal. **3** in front of. There is a curtain before the window.

ahead of–in front of. I saw Berta ahead of me in line.

in advance of–prior to. The thunderstorms along the cold front should arrive in advance of the cooler air.

in the face of–in the presence of; confronting. In the face of danger, Susan remained calm and did not panic.

in the presence of–in front of; before. Was she ever in the presence of royalty?

prior to–earlier than. We had breakfast prior to our departure.

ANTONYMS: **after (prep), behind (prep)**

C

clear (adj)–**1** not hazy or cloudy. The clear night sky was flooded with stars. **2** easy to see through, to hear, or to understand. Her directions were quite clear.

audible–loud enough to be heard. The volume control is turned down so low that the sound is barely audible.

cloudless–free from clouds; clear. The full moon shone brilliantly in the cloudless winter sky.

distinct–easily heard, seen, or understood; plain. Cara drew the distinct outline of a jet airplane.

explicit–clearly expressed or distinctly stated. The auto manual had explicit instructions.

lucid–easy to understand or follow. He gave a lucid explanation of his whereabouts.

transparent–transmitting light so that bodies lying beyond are distinctly visible. Automobile windshield glass is transparent.

See also *definite* (adj).

ANTONYMS: **cloudy, hazy, indistinct, obscure, unclear, vague**

come (v)–**1** to move toward or approach. Come here as soon as you can. **2** to arrive at a certain place, end, or conclusion. We came to this town five years ago.

advance–to move forward. The long freight train is steadily advancing toward the tunnel.

approach–to come nearer to. Emilio approached the busy intersection with caution.

arrive–to reach the end or destination of a journey; to come to a place. The plane will arrive in Dallas at four o'clock.

attain–to arrive at or reach by living or by developing. That department store has attained a reputation for quality.

near–to come close to; to approach. When you begin to see skyscrapers in the distance, you will be nearing New York City.

reach–to arrive at; to get to. The mountain climbers reached the summit of Mt. Rainier on Wednesday.

ANTONYMS: **depart, go, leave (v), retreat (v), withdraw**

courage (n)–the strength of mind or will to face danger. Fire fighters showed courage in battling the blaze.

boldness–show of scorn for danger; daring. The boldness of the plan surprised us.

bravery–fearlessness in the face of danger or difficulty; courage. The bravery of the hostages was astounding.

heart–enthusiastic courage. It takes heart to persist.

heroism–willingness to take risks to help others; valor. Davy Crockett's heroism is admired.

valor–willingness to take risks to help others; heroism. Knights of old showed valor in battle.

See also *spirit* (n).

ANTONYMS: **cowardice, fear (n), timidity**

cut (v)–**1** to separate, divide, or remove with a knife or any tool that has a sharp edge. Cut the paper in two pieces with scissors. **2** to make by or as if by cutting. The sculptor will cut a human figure from that block of wood.

carve–**1** to cut into pieces or slices. When will you carve the Thanksgiving Day turkey? **2** to make by cutting. Which Presidents are carved on Mt. Rushmore?

cleave–to cut, split open, or divide. The construction crew will cleave those giant rocks by using jackhammers.

engrave–to form by cutting; to carve in an artistic manner. The jeweler will engrave your initials on the back of the ring.

prune–to cut undesirable twigs or branches from a bush, a tree, or a vine. I must prune some of the older branches from the forsythia bushes.

score–to cut, scratch, or line. Before baking the ham, score it by cutting shallow grooves into it with a knife.

slice–to cut into flat, broad pieces. Slice the roast beef very thin, please.

D

definite (adj)–**1** exact or clear; precise; not vague. The dark clouds and strong winds are definite signs that a thunderstorm is approaching. **2** having certain limits; restricted. There are definite procedures to follow in case of an emergency.

certain–without any doubt; sure. I am certain that the concert is at seven o'clock.

defined–having settled limits or boundaries. This fence forms a clearly defined property boundary between the two lots.

explicit–clearly expressed or distinctly stated. Carol's explicit remarks about the basketball game could hardly be misinterpreted.

specific–definite; particular; precise. Every pair of shoes has a specific size.

unequivocal–having no doubt or ambiguity; straightforward; blunt and plain. Toshio's unequivocal refusal to attend the meeting was a surprise to everyone.

unmistakable–not capable of being misunderstood or mistaken; clear. A 747 aircraft has an unmistakable shape.

See also *clear* (adj).

definite *(continued)*

Thesaurus

ANTONYMS: ambiguous, equivocal, imprecise, indefinite, undefined, vague

do   (v)–**1** to carry through to the end any action or piece of work; to perform; to complete. Juan did a report on conservation. **2** to produce or make. He does beautiful landscapes in watercolors.

construct–to make by combining parts; to put together; to build. The workers have already constructed a new bridge over the river.

execute–to carry out fully; to do. A plan of action is useless unless it is properly executed.

manufacture–to make by hand or by machinery; to make something that is useful. That corporation manufactures paper towels.

perform–to do or to carry out; to go through and finish; to accomplish. Since you must perform that difficult task, be sure to ask questions about what you do not understand.

practice–**1** to do something again and again to learn to do it well. Great violinists practice several hours a day. **2** to work at a profession or occupation. He has practiced law for over ten years.

produce–to bring into existence by labor; to create; to make from various materials; to manufacture. How many automobiles does that company produce in one year?

See also *make* (v).

E

energy   (n)–the ability for forceful action; the capacity for doing work. Toby had enough energy to run five miles.

liveliness–high spirits; the quality of being full of life and spirit. The liveliness of the kittens was evident in their spirited play.

power–force or strength; might; the ability to act or do. Does that railroad locomotive have enough power to pull one hundred freight cars?

stamina–power to resist that which weakens; endurance; staying power. Derrick has the stamina to run long distances.

strength–the condition or quality of being strong; force; power; vigor. I do not have the strength to move that heavy table.

vigor–strength or force; flourishing physical condition; intensity of action. Pam does push-ups and sit-ups with vigor.

vitality–vital force; the power to live and develop. My little sister is a happy and healthy young girl who is filled with vitality.

See also *vigor* (n).

ANTONYMS: fatigue, inertia, powerlessness, sluggishness, tiredness, weakness

exciting   (adj)–producing excitement or a feeling of agitation; arousing; stirring. Traveling by airplane is always an exciting and enjoyable experience for me.

breathtaking–thrilling; exciting. The view from the scenic overlook just off the interstate highway is breathtaking.

inflammatory–tending to arouse or excite; tending to excite anger or disorder. The manager of the baseball team made several inflammatory remarks regarding the umpires.

stimulating–rousing to action; inspiring; stirring. Cold, stimulating mornings in winter wake me up in a hurry.

stirring–exciting; rousing; inspiring. The mayor's stirring speech left everyone applauding and cheering.

suspenseful–characterized by or full of suspense; causing the condition of being mentally uncertain, especially such a condition induced by craft in order to hold the attention of an audience or reader. Alfred Hitchcock directed some of the most suspenseful and terrifying movies ever made.

thrilling–characterized by excitement, or causing a sudden sharp feeling of excitement. Riding a roller coaster is a thrilling experience for most people.

ANTONYMS: dull, monotonous, tedious, uneventful, unexciting.

F

famous   (adj)–well-known; much talked about or written about; celebrated; noted. The famous singer gladly signed autographs after the concert.

celebrated–well-known; much talked about. The celebrated ballet dancer will perform tomorrow evening.

eminent–above most or all others; outstanding; famous. The eminent scientist made a profound discovery that left most of her peers in awe.

illustrious–brilliantly outstanding because of

achievements or actions. His illustrious motion-picture career included several award-winning performances.

notable–remarkable; worth noticing; striking; important. Winning a gold medal in the Olympic Games is certainly a notable achievement.

notorious–generally known and talked about because of something bad; having a bad reputation. The notorious gang robbed many banks a long time ago.

popular–liked by most people; liked by associates or acquaintances. That toy is so popular that most stores do not have any left to sell.

ANTONYMS: **humble, inconspicuous, obscure, undistinguished, unknown**

fast (adv)–**1** in a rapid manner; quickly; swiftly. I walked fast in order to get to the bus stop in time. **2** in a fixed or firm manner, tightly. The window frame is stuck fast.

firmly–solidly or securely. Make sure that the handle on that pan is firmly attached.

hastily–in a hurried manner; in a rash or careless manner. It was obvious by the numerous errors in spelling and punctuation that the letter was written hastily.

quickly–with haste; rapidly; very soon. Go quickly to your room.

rapidly–in a manner marked by a high rate of motion, succession, or occurrence. The seasons seem to be rapidly flying by.

securely–firmly or solidly. The steel railing is bolted securely to the bridge.

swiftly–in a fast or speedy manner. A deer ran swiftly across the road.

ANTONYMS: **insecurely, loosely, slow (adv), slowly**

find (v)–to come upon by chance; to discover by searching. We could not find the glove that Lori had misplaced.

catch–to hold or capture, especially after a chase. After several days of detective work, the police finally caught the thief.

detect–to discover the presence, existence, or fact of. I detect the odor of gas near the kitchen stove.

discover–to see or learn of for the first time; to find out. Astronomers continually discover new stars in the universe.

encounter–to meet or come upon unexpectedly.

Tourists driving on narrow mountain roads often encounter dangerous hairpin turns.

locate–to seek out the exact position of. The forest rangers located the hungry deer and gave them food.

trace–to follow by means of tracks, signs, or other evidence. Scientists easily traced the source of the town's air pollution.

ANTONYMS: **lose, mislay, misplace, miss (v)**

fly (v)–to move through the air with wings; to travel in an airplane or a spacecraft; to wave or float in the air. We will fly to Chicago next week.

flutter–to wave back and forth lightly and quickly. The flag in front of our school fluttered in the breeze.

glide–to move along effortlessly, smoothly, and evenly. The bird calmly glided in a circular pattern high above the treetops.

hover–to remain in or near one place in the air; to hang suspended or fluttering in the air. The helicopter hovered above the traffic jam.

jet–to fly by jet airplane. You can jet across the country in a relatively short time.

soar–to fly in the air, often at a great height; to fly upward. The rocket soared into the sky and soon disappeared from view.

G

get (v)–to come to have; to gain possession of; to obtain. Allen will get a new pair of glasses tomorrow.

acquire–to get by one's own efforts; to come to have. Through years of work he acquired a large fortune.

contract–to get, usually without choice. Ellen contracted the flu last week.

earn–to get in return for service or work. I earned extra money by delivering newspapers.

inherit–to receive after someone dies. The Benson family inherited their beautiful house many years ago.

obtain–to get through effort or diligence; to come to have. Sharon obtained two tickets to the basketball game.

receive–to take into one's hands; to be given. I received a wonderful birthday present from my parents.

ANTONYMS: **give, lose, relinquish**

Thesaurus

good (adj)–**1** having high quality; superior. A <u>good</u> rocking chair lasts a long time. **2** as it ought to be; right; proper; agreeable. Doing what is <u>good</u> sometimes takes courage. **3** clever; skillful. He always tells a <u>good</u> joke.

beneficial–producing good; helpful. Proper exercise is <u>beneficial</u> to good health.

excellent–very good; better than others. The food in this restaurant is <u>excellent</u>.

honest–not lying, stealing, or cheating; truthful. An <u>honest</u> person does not cheat others.

just–fair; right; impartial. The judge made a <u>just</u> decision.

pleasant–giving pleasure; agreeable. A person with a <u>pleasant</u> disposition usually has a warm smile.

proficient–well advanced in an art, science, or subject; skilled. A <u>proficient</u> carpenter can do excellent work quickly.

ANTONYMS: **awful, bad, disagreeable, dishonest, incompetent, worthless**

H

have (v)–**1** to hold in one's possession or in one's keeping. Do you <u>have</u> a pencil I could borrow? **2** to experience. Henry <u>has</u> a terrible toothache.

command–to have power over; to be in authority over; to control by position. The fortress <u>commands</u> the harbor entrance.

endure–to put up with; to tolerate; to experience. I <u>endured</u> a terrible sore throat for about three days.

experience–to feel; to live through. That famous actress <u>experienced</u> many thrilling moments.

own–to have or hold as property; to possess. They <u>own</u> two automobiles.

possess–to have as a knowledge, an attribute, or a skill; to have as property. Gan <u>possesses</u> exceptional artistic ability.

undergo–to go through; to experience. The library will <u>undergo</u> a major renovation during the next couple of years.

ANTONYMS: **lack (v), need (v)**

J

joy (n)–a glad feeling; a strong feeling of pleasure; happiness. On a morning this beautiful, Marta felt <u>joy</u> at being alive.

bliss–great happiness or joy. Walking in the park on a warm morning in spring is sheer <u>bliss</u>.

delight–great pleasure or joy. The little boy ate his ice-cream cone with <u>delight</u>.

ecstasy–a feeling of very great joy; strong feeling that thrills or delights. The older man was filled with <u>ecstasy</u> when he saw his brother for the first time in many years.

glee–great delight or lively joy; merriment. We laughed with <u>glee</u> as we watched the monkeys at the zoo.

happiness–a state of contentment and well-being; joy; gladness. Sometimes <u>happiness</u> can be found in the simplest things.

hilarity–great mirth or enjoyment; boisterous or noisy merriment. My friends and I talked and laughed with <u>hilarity</u> at the party.

ANTONYMS: **despair (n), grief, misery, sadness, sorrow (n), unhappiness.**

L

large (adj)–of more than the usual amount, size, or number; big. The <u>large</u> tray was filled with delicious sandwiches.

considerable–in large quantity; much. A <u>considerable</u> number of people will take part in the Fourth of July parade.

enormous–extremely large; huge. That <u>enormous</u> tree must be over one hundred years old.

great–large in amount, extent, number, or size; big. Many <u>great</u> boulders line the shoulder of the road.

huge–very large; unusually large in bulk, dimensions, or size. A <u>huge</u> stalled tractor blocked the entrance to the freeway.

immense–very big; vast; huge. The state of Alaska covers an <u>immense</u> area.

massive–large and solid; big and heavy; huge. The <u>massive</u> wall was over four feet thick.

ANTONYMS: **little, minute (adj), slight (adj), small, tiny**

last (adj)–coming after all others; being at the end; final; conclusive. I know someone who likes to read the <u>last</u> page of a novel before reading the rest of it.

closing–being the final portion or last stage of an item. The <u>closing</u> chapter of the book was by far the most exciting.

conclusive–convincing; decisive; final. Those
　　X rays gave <u>conclusive</u> proof that the tennis
　　player had fractured her wrist.
farewell–parting; last; final. The <u>farewell</u> address
　　of our retiring principal was truly inspiring.
farthest–most distant in time or space. Are satel-
　　lites now exploring the <u>farthest</u> reaches of outer
　　space?
final–being the last; at the end. The <u>final</u> game
　　of the season takes place tomorrow afternoon
　　at two o'clock.
ultimate–most remote in time or space; farthest;
　　last in a series of steps; extreme. Her <u>ultimate</u>
　　goal is to win a gold medal in the Oympics.
ANTONYMS: beginning (adj), first (adj), in-
　　conclusive, initial (adj), introductory, opening
　　(adj)

light　　(adj)–**1** not heavy; having little weight.
　　Those suitcases are surprisingly <u>light</u> when
　　empty. **2** easy to do or bear. Ted has to do some
　　<u>light</u> chores. **3** of little importance. Sheila en-
　　joys <u>light</u> reading just before bedtime.
effortless–showing or requiring little use of energy;
　　easy. The gymnast performed with seemingly
　　<u>effortless</u> skill and grace.
feathery–light and delicate; almost weightless.
　　With a <u>feathery</u> touch the pianist produced deli-
　　cate tones that could hardly be heard.
simple–easy to do, understand, or solve. Assem-
　　bling that model airplane was <u>simple</u>.
superficial–of or on the surface; lying on or affect-
　　ing only the surface. Although she tripped on
　　the step, she received only a <u>superficial</u> scratch
　　on her knee.
trivial–not important; insignificant. We talked
　　about <u>trivial</u> things like the weather.
weightless–having little or no weight. Astronauts
　　experience <u>weightless</u> conditions when they
　　travel in space.
ANTONYMS: burdensome, cumbersome, diffi-
　　cult, heavy (adj), profound, strenuous

little　　(adj)–**1** not big or great; small. The dia-
　　mond stylus on a stereo phonograph is <u>little</u>.
　　2 small in amount, number, or importance.
　　There is <u>little</u> time remaining before the end of
　　this class.

insignificant–having little influence or importance;
　　too small to be important. An <u>insignificant</u>
　　amount of snow fell last night, so we were able
　　to get to school easily.
microscopic–unable to be seen without using a mi-
　　croscope; extremely small; minute; tiny. Those
　　<u>microscopic</u> dots on the leaves of the plant are
　　actually tiny insects.
minor–inferior in importance, size, or degree;
　　smaller. Get the job done without worrying
　　about <u>minor</u> details.
minute–very small. That restaurant served <u>minute</u>
　　portions of food.
slight–lacking in strength or importance; having
　　a slim build. The movie has a <u>slight</u> plot, but,
　　after all, it is a comedy.
small–not large; little in size; not large in com-
　　parison with other things of the same kind. Be
　　sure to buy only a <u>small</u> loaf of bread and a quart
　　of milk.
ANTONYMS: big (adj), great (adj), huge, im-
　　mense, important, large (adj)

M

make　　(v)–**1** to bring into being; to build, form,
　　put together, or shape. I can <u>make</u> a bowl from
　　this modeling clay. **2** to cause to; to force to.
　　Will you <u>make</u> us run three laps around the
　　entire track?
assemble–to put or fit together. Brian <u>assembled</u>
　　that model airplane in less than five days.
build–to make by putting materials together; to
　　construct. Did you <u>build</u> the shelves in this
　　closet?
compel–to urge or drive with force; to force. The
　　high-wind warnings <u>compelled</u> us to keep the
　　boat close to the shore.
create–to make something which has not been
　　made before; to bring into being. The florist
　　<u>created</u> a beautiful floral centerpiece for the
　　dinner party.
force–to make someone act against his or her will.
　　My sister <u>forced</u> me to wash all the dishes.
form–to make in a certain shape; to give shape to.
　　Take the three strips of cardboard and <u>form</u> a
　　triangle.
See also *do* (v).
ANTONYMS: destroy, wreck (v)

many (adj)–consisting of a large number; numerous. There are <u>many</u> new office buildings in this part of town.

abundant–more than enough; amply supplied. There was an <u>abundant</u> harvest of wheat this year.

frequent–happening often or every little while. We have <u>frequent</u> bus service to and from the city.

much–in great degree or amount. Try not to eat too <u>much</u> food at the picnic.

numerous–very many; consisting of great numbers of individuals or units. I have swum in that lake on <u>numerous</u> occasions.

plentiful–more than enough; ample. We are fortunate to live where food is <u>plentiful</u>.

several–more than two, but fewer than many. Michele was late for school <u>several</u> times last month.

ANTONYMS: few (adj), infrequent, rare, scant (adj), sole (adj)

N

neat (adj)–clean and in order; marked by tasteful simplicity. Diego keeps his room <u>neat</u>.

orderly–in order; with regular system, arrangement, or method. When the alarm sounds for the fire drill, proceed to the exits in an <u>orderly</u> fashion.

organized–arranged in some order or pattern; put into working order. He has the most <u>organized</u> loose-leaf binder in our class.

tidy–neat and in order; trim; orderly. He keeps the inside of his car as <u>tidy</u> as his home.

trim–in good order or condition; tidy; neat. Their <u>trim</u> apartment is obviously well taken care of.

uncluttered–not littered; in order; neat. This <u>uncluttered</u> living room appears very spacious.

well-groomed–well dressed and very neat; neat and trim. Even on extremely hot days, Kai always wears a tie and maintains a <u>well-groomed</u> appearance.

ANTONYMS: cluttered (adj), disorderly, disorganized (adj), messy, sloppy, untidy

need (n)–**1** the lack of a desired or useful thing; a want. There is a desperate <u>need</u> for more room in the overcrowded hospital. **2** something that

has to be; a requirement; a necessity. The reason for the <u>need</u> for quiet when working in a library is obvious.

absence–the state of being without; a lack. The <u>absence</u> of rainfall has geatly diminished the water supply in the reservoir.

deficiency–an absence or lack of something needed; incompleteness. Because of a <u>deficiency</u> of funds, a new municipal building could not be built.

must–something that is necessary; an obligation. Seeing that exciting new movie is a <u>must</u>.

necessity–that which cannot be done without; a needed thing. Good lighting is a <u>necessity</u> when you are reading.

requirement–something needed; a necessity. One <u>requirement</u> for that job is the completion of a special training course to handle medical emergencies.

shortage–too small an amount; a deficiency; a lack. During the water <u>shortage</u> the watering of lawns was prohibited.

ANTONYMS: abundance, adequacy, excess (n)

next (adj)–**1** nearest. The <u>next</u> town is Pleasantville. **2** immediately following. The <u>next</u> train will arrive at this station in about fifteen minutes.

adjacent–lying close or near, or touching; adjoining or neighboring. Do <u>adjacent</u> apartments usually have soundproof walls between them?

adjoining–being next to or in contact; adjacent; bordering. Those two <u>adjoining</u> buildings are connected to each other by a glass-enclosed pedestrian mall.

following–that immediately follows; next after. On the <u>following</u> day huge waves pounded the already-battered rocky shore as the storm grew even more fierce.

nearest–closest; least distant. The <u>nearest</u> service station must be at least ten or twelve miles from here.

neighboring–being or living near; adjacent; bordering. The <u>neighboring</u> county is almost entirely made up of rolling acres of rich productive farmland.

succeeding–following in time, place, or order. The mystery story will be continued in the next three <u>succeeding</u> issues of the magazine.

nice (adj)–pleasing or satisfying. It will be a nice afternoon if the sun comes out.

agreeable–suiting one's pleasure. We will do everything possible to be sure our guests have an agreeable stay.

blissful–full of great happiness or joy. The child spent a blissful afternoon playing with the new toy.

delightful–enjoyable and very pleasing. Most of the movie was delightful, but the ending made me cry.

fine–excellent; very good. The new community center has fine facilities, including an indoor ice-skating rink.

refreshing–pleasantly different or unusual. After you spend all day in the house, a long walk can be a refreshing activity.

splendid–grand; wonderful. Everyone is still talking about this year's splendid school carnival.

ANTONYMS: **awful** (adj), **disagreeable, dreadful, miserable, terrible, unpleasant**

O

outside (n)–the outer part of something. I would like to try on the jacket that has pockets on the outside.

coating–the layer that covers a surface. The table and chairs come in different colors of plastic coatings.

covering–the outer part of something, which protects or hides what is inside. It is difficult to tell what is in that package with the plain, paper covering.

exterior–the outside. They live in the new apartment building with the brick exterior.

face–the front, top, or outer side of something. The face of her watch has many dials that glow in the dark.

shell–a hard outer covering. I cannot crack the shell of this walnut with my fingers.

surface–the outer part of something solid; the top level of a liquid. I would use the paper with the shiny surface for the bulletin-board display.

ANTONYMS: **center (n), core (n), inside (n), interior (n)**

P

piece (n)–a part of a whole. Be careful not to step on a piece of glass from the broken window.

allotment–a person's share of the whole. Each band member was given an allotment of tickets to sell.

chunk–a short, thick piece. Would you like a chunk of cheese with your lunch?

fragment–a piece broken off something. They found a fragment from an antique pot near the ruins.

portion–a part that is divided or separated from the whole. Each person may take a small portion of mashed potatoes.

share–the part belonging to one person. Carolyn did more than her share of work on the project.

shred–a small strip that is torn or cut off. Maybe there is a shred of paper caught in the copying machine.

ANTONYMS: **all (n), entirety, whole (n)**

place (n)–the space occupied by or intended for a person or thing. The cross-country skiers looked for a place to stop and rest.

area–an open space used for a special purpose. There is a large area for parking behind the shopping center.

dwelling–a place where someone lives. This museum was originally a family dwelling.

habitat–the place where an animal or plant grows or lives. The photographer traveled to India to observe the animals in their natural habitat.

locale–the scene of an event or some action. Several reporters dashed to the locale of the blazing fire.

site–a particular place where something is, was or will be located. The site chosen for the monument is near the river.

territory–a section of land. The settlers claimed the undeveloped territory for farmland.

put (v)–to lay or cause to be in some place or position. At the end of the day, the librarian always puts the books back on the shelves.

arrange–to put in a proper or desirable order. Marcus arranged the name cards in alphabetical order.

deposit–to set down. We deposited items for the garage sale on a long table.

insert–to put into something. I'll try, but I don't think I can insert this bent key into the lock.

put (*continued*)

install–to put in position and fix for use. Someone from the store will install our new washing machine tomorrow.

position–to put in a particular place. Sandy carefully positioned the clock on the mantel.

rest–to place something to prevent it from falling. Michelle rested her bicycle against a tree while she waited for her friend.

ANTONYMS: **displace, remove, withdraw**

R

rare (adj)–**1** uncommonly found or happening. A snowstorm in April is rare here. **2** unusual in quality, often valuable. The rare gem is priceless.

exceptional–not like it usually is; not like others. The choir director was impressed by Christopher's exceptional voice.

infrequent–not occurring often. Our trips to the beach have been infrequent because of the poor weather.

uncustomary–not the usual way of acting or doing something. It is uncustomary for her to go to bed this early.

unique–being the only one of its kind. Katie's aunt made her a unique wooden jewelry box.

unusual–out of the ordinary; different. We tasted many unusual foods at the international bazaar. See also *unusual* (adj).

ANTONYMS: **common (adj), everyday (adj), ordinary (adj), regular (adj), routine (adj), usual (adj)**

report (n)–a written or spoken account of something. Before Steve wrote his report, he researched his topic carefully.

address–a formal speech. In his address, the senator said he would support the housing bill.

announcement–a report that is given to bring something to the public's attention. The principal sent out a newsletter to make several announcements about the new school year.

bulletin–a brief report of the latest news. The television program was interrupted to present an important news bulletin.

chronicle–a record of events in time sequence. The speaker showed slides to go with the chronicle she had written about her worldwide journey.

critique–a review of something in which personal judgment is expressed. The judges gave a critique of each drawing entered in the contest.

rumor–a story or report that is told to others, but has not been proven to be true. Did you hear the rumor that Joshua is moving to another state?

rough (adj)–not smooth, even, or level; bumpy. This floor is too rough to roller-skate on.

bristly–having a texture like that of short, stiff, coarse hairs. You will need strong soap and a bristly sponge to scrub those mud-caked tires.

coarse–rough in appearance or texture. The tent is made of a coarse material.

harsh–rough or unpleasant to the touch or other sense. The stiff towel felt harsh against my face.

irregular–uneven. The ceiling is irregular because some of the tiles have come loose.

jagged–having sharp points sticking out. Adam cut his foot on a piece of jagged glass.

rugged–having an irregular, broken surface. The northern part of the state has a cold climate and a rugged terrain.

ANTONYMS: **even (adj), flat (adj), level (adj), silky, smooth (adj), soft**

S

same (adj)–being alike or unchanged; not different. My brother and I listen to the same kind of music.

consistent–without changing one's way of thinking or acting. She believes in consistent exercise and good eating habits.

identical–exactly alike in every way. Pat and Kim laughed when they realized they were wearing identical coats.

indistinguishable–not able to be recognized by differences. The street signs are indistinguishable in this thick fog.

monotonous–not varying or changing; boring. Do we have to play that monotonous game again?

stable–not likely to change or move; steady. Barbara would like to have a stable job after she completes the training program.

uniform–like all others; all the same. The gardener planted the bushes so they would be a uniform height.

ANTONYMS: **contrasting (adj), different, dissimilar, distinct, inconsistent, variable (adj)**

save (v)–**1** to keep or make free from harm or danger. Lona saved the baby bird from falling out of its nest. **2** to lay aside; to have or hold on to. Should we save the empty cartons or throw them away?

conserve–to keep from being used up. You can conserve electricity by turning off the light when you leave a room.

economize–to keep from waste. The office workers are economizing their supplies so they do not run out before the end of the year.

preserve–to keep from change; to keep safe from harm. Matina preserves her favorite photographs in a picture album.

reserve–to hold back, usually for a brief period of time. The librarian said he would reserve the book for me until tomorrow.

salvage–to save from being ruined or wrecked. The citrus growers salvaged a part of the orange crop from the severe frost.

store–to put away for later use. We store old clothes and toys in the attic.

ANTONYMS: consume, discard (v), endanger, risk (v), spend, waste (v)

say (v)–to speak; to put into words. Carlotta did not say where she was going.

comment–to make a brief statement, giving a personal judgment about something. Many people commented on the colorful decorations we made for the party.

declare–to make known by publicly announcing. In the broadcast, the city official declared her acceptance of the job.

exclaim–to speak with force, usually when surprised or angry. "I can't believe that I really won!" exclaimed the tennis champion.

expound–to explain in detail in order to make something clear or understood. The famous doctor expounded the results of his latest research study.

mention–to speak about or refer to briefly. Did anyone mention what time the next train will be arriving?

reveal–to say what was not known before. At the next meeting, the club president will reveal her plans for a charity event.
See also *tell* (v).

see (v)–**1** to perceive by use of the eyes; to look at. Can you see that beautiful little bird in the dogwood tree? **2** to form a picture in the mind. I can still see the castle we visited two years ago.

glimpse–to catch a quick or brief view of. We glimpsed the express train as it sped through the station.

observe–to see and note; to notice; to carefully examine; to watch; to study. Peter observed the cooking demonstration with great interest.

picture–to form an image of in the mind. I pictured the hotel to be much larger than it actually is.

view–to look at; to see. As her mother drove the car, Teena viewed the majestic countryside of Montana.

visualize–to form a mental picture of. Try to visualize the store as it was the last time you were there.

witness–to observe; to see for oneself. Jonathan witnessed a landing of the space shuttle.

ANTONYMS: disregard (v), ignore

spirit (n)–liveliness; courage; vigor; enthusiasm. Her cheery smile shows that she has spirit.

enthusiasm–eager interest; zeal; strong excitement of feeling. The fans cheering loudly at the game were filled with enthusiasm.

fervor–intense enthusiasm, emotion, or earnestness. After she received some encouragement and helpful advice from her teacher, Patty continued working on her science project with renewed fervor.

grit–courage; endurance; pluck. Showing true grit, she finished running the marathon even though she was on the verge of total collapse.

liveliness–the quality or condition of being full of life and spirit; vigor. The liveliness of kittens at play is a joy to behold.

vitality–life force; the power to live. The bustling city has a vitality of its own.

zest–keen enjoyment; an exciting or pleasant quality. With a zest for the beauty of nature, he watched the sun slowly disappear beneath the motionless pines.
See also *courage* (n).

ANTONYMS: dullness, lifelessness, spiritlessness, timidity

Thesaurus

story (n)–an account of a happening or group of happenings. Do you enjoy reading adventure <u>stories</u> as much as I do?

biography–a written story of a person's life. Jeff has just read a <u>biography</u> of Abraham Lincoln.

history–a record or story of important events, usually including an explanation of their causes. Every day I learn more of the <u>history</u> of the United States.

legend–a story coming down from the past, especially one that many people have thought of as true. The stories about King Arthur are <u>legends</u>.

myth–a story or legend, usually one that tries to explain something in nature. Is there a <u>myth</u> that explains the causes of thunder and lighting?

narrative–an account or story; a tale. Who was the author of the funny <u>narrative</u> that our teacher read to us?

tale–a story of an incident or event, especially a fictional story. I just read an exciting <u>tale</u> about pirates.

T

tell (v)–to express in words; to say; to give an account of; to relate. <u>Tell</u> me what you think of it.

advise–to give advice to; to counsel; to offer an opinion to. Would you <u>advise</u> me about what to get my mother for a birthday present?

communicate–to give news or information by speaking or writing; to telephone; to write. Have you <u>communicated</u> recently with your sister in New Mexico?

inform–to supply with facts, knowledge, or news; to tell. I was not <u>informed</u> of the change in plans until today.

instruct–to teach; to train; to give knowledge to; to give orders or directions to. I was <u>instructed</u> to hand out the drawing materials.

narrate–to tell the story of; to relate. He will <u>narrate</u> the well-known story, which has been set to music.

report–to tell of something seen, done, heard, or read; to state or announce. Allison <u>reported</u> the results of her science experiment to us.

See also *say* (v).

ANTONYMS: listen

think (v)–**1** to exercise the powers of the mind; to have an idea or thought in mind. I <u>think</u> about many different things all of the time. **2** to have an opinion. I <u>think</u> the librarian is a very nice person.

believe–to think something is real or true. I <u>believe</u> that the rocky cliffs along the coastline are being slowly worn away by the pounding surf.

conclude–to reach certain decisions or opinions by reasoning; to infer. The jury <u>concluded</u> that the defendant was not guilty of the crime for which he was being tried.

dream–to think, see, hear, or feel while sleeping. Did you ever <u>dream</u> that you were trying to run but could not move?

imagine–to form a picture of something in the mind. Juan <u>imagined</u> that he was an astronaut floating in space.

judge–to make up one's mind about; to conclude; to think. Can you <u>judge</u> the distance from this side of the lake to the other?

suppose–to consider as possible; to assume; to consider as probably true. Do you <u>suppose</u> we could all fit in that little car?

trap (v)–to catch; to entrap. The police <u>trapped</u> the crafty criminal.

capture–to take captive; to take by force, skill, or trickery. The troops <u>captured</u> the enemy headquarters.

catch–to take and hold; to capture; to seize. The shortstop <u>caught</u> the hard-hit ground ball.

entrap–to catch in a trap; to bring into danger. The small boat was <u>entrapped</u> by the huge ice floes in the river.

lasso–to catch with a long rope that has a running noose at one end. The rancher <u>lassoed</u> the stray steer.

lure–to attract or tempt, as with a bait. When fishing, people often <u>lure</u> fish by using worms.

net–to catch in a net. Many fish were <u>netted</u> by the trawlers that day.

ANTONYMS: discharge (v), extricate, free (v), release (v), remove

true (adj)–**1** agreeing with fact; not false. The story about the adventures of the explorer was <u>true</u>. **2** genuine, real. The miners found <u>true</u> gold. **3** loyal, faithful. He was <u>true</u> to his word and returned as he had promised.

authentic–coming from the stated source; not copied; real; genuine. The signature on the document is <u>authentic</u>.

factual–concerned with something known to be true. The factual account of the admiral's visit to the South Pole was fascinating.

genuine–actually being what it seems or is claimed to be; true. How can you tell if that gemstone is a genuine diamond?

loyal–faithful and true to duty, promise, love, or other obligations. A loyal fan roots for the same team whether it wins or loses.

real–existing as a fact; not made up or imagined; true; actual; not artificial; genuine. The mountain scene depicted on the stage was so well made that the mountains looked real.

steadfast–loyal; firm of purpose; not changing; unwavering. Clarita remained steadfast in her desire to finish the fifty-mile hike.

ANTONYMS: artificial, counterfeit (adj), false, fictitious, untrue, untrustworthy

turn (v)–**1** to move around as a wheel does; to revolve; to move partway around in this manner. Please turn the handle counterclockwise. **2** to take the opposite direction or a new direction. After about two miles the road turns westward.

bend–to curve out of a straight position. The branches of white birch trees usually bend under the weight of heavy snow or ice.

circle–to move in or as if in a circle; to form a circle. The seagull circled above the fishing boat.

curve–to bend in a line that has no straight part; to move in the course of such a line. The rising tiers of seats curve gracefully around the center of the arena.

revolve–to move in a curve around a point; to move in a circle. The planets of the solar system revolve around the sun.

spin–to revolve or turn around rapidly. The pinwheel spins whenever a strong breeze blows.

twist–to turn around; to have a winding course or shape; to curve or wind. The steep trail twisted through the rugged terrain.

U

unusual (adj)–out of the ordinary; different; not commonly seen, used, or happening; uncommon. That unusual plant grows in the tropical areas of the world.

rare–uncommonly found or happening; unusual. Some species of birds are rare.

singular–unusual; extraordinary; strange. With singular devotion to duty, the soldier carried out the difficult assignment.

uncommon–unusual or rare; exceptional or remarkable. He had many uncommon minerals in his rock collection.

unexpected–not expected; not anticipated; unforeseen. The unexpected major snowfall caught everyone by surprise.

unfamiliar–not well-known; strange; unusual. While traveling in Europe, we sampled many unfamiliar foods.

unique–being the only one of its kind. This unique painting was done nearly a century ago.

See also *rare* (adj).

ANTONYMS: common (adj), commonplace (adj), customary, familiar, routine (adj), usual (adj)

use (v)–**1** to put into action or service; to utilize; to practice or employ actively; to exercise. Whenever I use tools, I keep safety in mind. **2** to consume or take regularly. That old automobile uses too much gasoline.

consume–to use up; to spend; to destroy. The forest fire consumed hundreds of acres of trees.

employ–to use; to use the services of. Chris employed a pair of tweezers to remove that tiny wire from the model.

exercise–to actively use to cause improvement or to give practice and training. If you exercise every day, you may actually begin to feel healthier.

exhaust–to empty completely; to drain. The campers exhausted their food supply within a week.

operate–to keep at work; to run or drive. May I operate the model train set?

utilize–to make use of; to put to a practical use. A good student utilizes his or her time wisely when studying.

ANTONYMS: conserve (v), preserve (v), save (v)

V

vigor (n)–strength or force; flourishing physical conditions; intensity of action. Lien begins each day with surprising vigor.

vigor *(continued)*

drive–initiative, energy, vigor. Being a person with drive, she pushed herself beyond the normal limits of endurance.

energy–the ability for forceful action; the capacity for doing work. Mowing the lawn takes a great deal of energy.

fervor–great warmth of feeling; intense earnestness, enthusiasm, or emotion. With fervor in his eyes, the artist gazed at his masterpiece.

intensity–vigorous activity or strong feeling; great strength. My parents said they never saw anyone play tennis with more intensity than Jimmy Connors.

vim–energy, force, vigor. The joggers began their daily run with vim.

vitality–vital force; the power to live and develop. I never saw anyone with as much vitality as that actress.

See also *energy* (n).

ANTONYMS: **apathy, feebleness, lethargy, slowness, sluggishness, weakness**

W

wait   (v)–to stop doing something or to stay until something happens or someone comes. Please wait here until I return.

dawdle–to waste time; to be idle; to dally. If you dawdle over your homework, you will never finish it.

delay–to put off until a later time. Severe thunderstorms delayed the departure of our plane for over an hour.

linger–to be slow in quitting something or in parting, as if unwilling to leave. Some of the guests lingered for quite some time after the wedding reception had ended.

remain–to continue in a place; to stay. We remained indoors through much of the sub-freezing weather.

stay–to continue in a place or condition; to remain. We will stay here until it is time to board the train.

tarry–to delay leaving; to stay, to remain. If you tarry any longer, you will not get to school on time.

ANTONYMS: **depart, go, leave (v)**

want   (v)–**1** to feel that one needs or would like to have; to wish for; to desire. I want to visit Hawaii someday. **2** to fail to possess, especially in the required or customary amount; to be without. The ballet dancer's performance was good, but at times it wanted gracefulness.

crave–to desire very much; to long for. The new student craved friendship.

desire–to long or to hope for; to wish earnestly for. Above all else he desired happiness.

hunger–to feel uncomfortable because of not having eaten; to be hungry. At about the same time every evening, Gene hungers for a snack.

lack–to be without; to not have enough; to need. Although she plays basketball well, she lacks the desire to become an outstanding player.

need–to be in want of; to be unable to do without; to require. This houseplant needs water right now.

wish–to have a desire for; to want. I wish I could go swimming today.

See also *wish* (v).

ANTONYMS: **decline (v), have, own (v), possess, refuse (v), reject (v)**

warm   (adj)–**1** more hot than cold; having or giving off heat to a moderate or adequate degree; having some heat. Is it warm outside today? **2** marked by or showing affection, gratitude, or sympathy. Being a warm person, he is always considerate of other people's feelings.

affectionate–having or showing fondness or tenderness. The new mother gave her baby an affectionate kiss.

compassionate–wishing to help those that suffer; sympathetic; pitying. The compassionate doctor comforted the seriously ill patient.

kind–doing good rather than harm; sympathetic; friendly; gentle. The kind woman gave her sweater to the shivering child.

mild–calm; warm; moderate; not severe or harsh. We had a mild winter with less snow than usual.

temperate–neither very hot nor very cold; moderate. Places with a temperate climate generally have summers that are not too hot and winters that are not too cold.

tepid–slightly or moderately warm; lukewarm. My hot tea had become tepid before I had a chance to drink it.

ANTONYMS: **coldhearted, cool (adj), cruel, uncaring, unfriendly, unsympathetic**

well (adv)–in a satisfactory, good, or proper manner; all right. She did her work well.

capably–in a competent manner; with ability; ably. During the captain's illness, the next officer in rank capably commanded the ship.

efficiently–ably producing the effect wanted without waste of energy or time. Working efficiently, I was able to finish my homework in much less time than it usually takes me.

excellently–in a manner better than others; very well; superiorly. Kim's teacher said that her composition was excellently done.

expertly–in a skillful or knowledgeable manner, adroitly. That diagram was expertly drawn.

ingeniously–in an inventive, resourceful, original, or clever manner. She solved that difficult puzzle ingeniously.

skillfully–with expert ability; expertly. The technician skillfully adjusted the equipment.

ANTONYMS: **badly, imperfectly, improperly, poorly, unsatisfactorily**

wish (v)–**1** to have a desire for; to express or feel a desire for; to desire something for someone. I wish we were going to the zoo today. **2** to command or request a person to do something. Mark wishes you to attend his birthday party.

ask–to make a request for something. He asked the movers to be careful with the large couch.

crave–to desire very much; to long for. The lonely child craved affection.

demand–to ask or call for, either as a right or with authority. My parents demand my respect.

desire–to long or hope for; to wish earnestly for. Francis desired to play on the team.

request–to ask for. Terry requested a map for the city.

want–to feel that one would like to have; to wish for; to desire. Tom wants a new bicycle for his birthday.

See also *want* (v).

wrong (adj)–**1** not right; unjust, bad. Cheating on a test is wrong. **2** not correct; not according to truth or facts; inaccurate. You gave a wrong answer to the question. **3** not proper or right according to a code or standard. A sweat suit is the wrong thing to wear to a wedding.

improper–not in accordance with accepted standards; not suitable; wrong. It is improper for spectators to shout when a tennis player is about to serve.

inappropriate–not right for an occasion; not suitable; not fitting. A tuxedo is inappropriate clothing for a camping trip.

incorrect–not correct; containing mistakes or errors; faulty; wrong. That clock keeps incorrect time.

unjust–characterized by the absence of justice; not fair. It is unjust to force one person to do the work of many.

unlawful–against the law; contrary to law; prohibited by law; illegal. It is unlawful to drive faster than the speed limit.

untrue–not true to the facts; incorrect; false. That story you heard about me is untrue.

ANTONYMS: **correct (adj), fair (adj), proper, right (adj), suitable, true**

Y

young (adj)–in the early part of life, growth, or development; not old; of, belonging to, or having to do with youth; having the vigor, freshness, looks, or other qualities of youth. That young woman graduated from college last year.

budding–being in an early stage of development; in the process of emergence. The budding astronomer made her visit to the planetarium.

fresh–newly arrived, gathered, or made; recent; looking young or heathly. I enjoy eating peaches that are fresh and not yet mushy.

immature -not full-grown; not completely developed; not ripe. These immature seedlings must be protected from extreme cold.

junior–**1** the younger (used chiefly to distinguish a son with the same given name as his father). William Dobbs, Junior, is on the phone. **2** of or for younger people; youthful. Do you sing in the junior chorus?

new–never having been before; now first made, heard of, or discovered; not old. Noriko is moving into a new house.

youthful–young; suitable for young people; having the qualities or looks of youth; vigorous; fresh. My grandfather, who jogs every morning, is a youthful person.

ANTONYMS: **adult (adj), ancient (adj), mature (adj), old (adj), ripe, senior (adj)**

Reports, Letters, Notes

Book Reports

A **book report** tells what a book is about and gives an opinion of the book. Read Jaime's book report. What does it tell about the book?

> *True Tall Tales of Stormalong*
> *by Harold W. Felton*
>
> This book tells the story of Alfred Bulltop Stormalong. It begins with his birth in the middle of a hurricane. Even as a baby, Stormalong was meant to be a sailor. His cradle was a whaleboat!
>
> When Stormy and his friend Jonathan sailed over a peninsula, I learned what a good sailor Stormy was. He had an answer for every problem. He solved each one with his imagination and strength. Stormy sailed the oceans all over the world.
>
> The story has exaggeration, suspense, and humor. I liked this exciting, fun-filled book.

Notice these things about the book report.

1. The title and author are named. The title of the book is underlined. In a book title the first word, the last word, and all important words are capitalized.
2. The report describes the book's characters, setting, and plot, but it does not tell the whole story.
3. The report gives an opinion about the book.

Practice

Write answers to these questions about the book report.

1. What is the title and author of the book?
2. What words are used to describe Stormalong?
3. Why does Jaime like the book?

Friendly Letters

- A **friendly letter** has five parts: the heading, the greeting, the body, the closing, and the signature.

- The **heading** shows the address of the writer and the date. Proper nouns are capitalized. A comma is used between the city and the state and between the day and the year.

- The first word of the **greeting**, as well as the proper noun, is capitalized. The greeting is followed by a comma.

- The **closing** is followed by a comma. Only the first word in the closing is capitalized.

- The **signature** tells who wrote the letter.

Heading	121 South Main Street Charlotte, NC 28204 July 17, 1991
Greeting	Dear Vicki,
Body	I'm so glad you're coming to visit us next Monday! Just let me know what train you're taking, and I'll be at the station to meet you. Don't forget your bathing suit!
Closing **Signature**	Your cousin, Dana

Practice

Using the form shown above, write a friendly letter to a friend or relative. Give that person some news about yourself. Tell what you have been doing lately. Use the form shown on page 489 to address the envelope correctly.

Thank-You Notes and Invitations

♦ A **thank-you note** is a short letter of thanks for a gift or favor. It follows the form of a friendly letter.

> 23 King Street
> Richmond, VA 23222
> June 4, 1991
>
> Dear Aunt Sara,
>   I really enjoyed the book you sent me for my birthday, _The Case of the Curious Computer_. It was fascinating, and it taught me a lot about computers, too!
>
>   Love,
>   Todd

♦ An **invitation** is a note or letter that invites someone to an event. It should name the event, tell where and when it is being held, and tell who sent the invitation.

> **You are invited to** _my Halloween party_
> **Place:** _423 Lincoln Avenue_
> **Date and Time:** _October 31, 2:00–4:00 P.M._
> **Held by:** _Scott Park_
>   _Wear a costume!_

Practice

A. Write an invitation to a party or other special event.

B. Write a thank-you note to a real person or someone you make up.

Addressing Envelopes

♦ When you address an envelope, you write the return address and the receiver's address.

♦ Write your name and address in the upper left-hand corner. This is the **return address**. It shows where to return the letter if it cannot be delivered.

♦ In the center of the envelope, write the **receiver's address**. This is the name of the person who will receive the letter. For business letters, the receiver's address is an exact copy of the inside address.

♦ You may use an abbreviation for the name of a state. There is an official two-letter abbreviation for each state name. You can get a list of the abbreviations from our local post office.

Return address
    Elena Sanchez
    6 Sunset St.
    El Paso, TX 77910

                                    [25¢]

Receiver's address
State abbreviation
    Dr. Joyce Chang
    11 South Street
    Muncie, IN 47302

Practice

Using a ruler, draw three envelopes like the sample above. Then address each one, using the information given below.

1. *Return address:* Robert Gula   418 Monroe St.   Oxford, CT 06483
Receiver's address: Ms. Theresa Kwon   4 Lake Rd.   Aztec, NM 87410

2. *Return address:* Jesse A. Stanton   31 Wayne Ave.   Lodi, NJ 07644
Receiver's address: Mrs. Ann Tully   28 Reed Rd.   Cody, WY 82414

3. *Return address:* Vincent Ricci   8 Budd Ave.   Barre, VT 05641
Receiver's address: Mr. Scott Macey   27 Cedar Dr.   Bristol, TN 37620

A Guide to Spelling

Some useful spelling rules are listed below. Learning them will help you to spell words easily. Remember to use these rules when you write.

1. The suffix -*s* can be added to most nouns and verbs. If the word ends in *s*, *ss*, *sh*, *ch*, *x*, or *zz*, add -*es*.

Nouns		**Verbs**	
gas	gases	hiss	hisses
bush	bushes	match	matches
fox	foxes	buzz	buzzes

2. If a word ends in a consonant and *y*, change the *y* to *i* when you add a suffix, unless the suffix begins with *i*.

Nouns		**Verbs**		
cherry	cherries	study	studies	studied
baby	babies	try	trying	

Adjectives		
muddy	muddier	muddiest

3. If a word ends in a vowel and *y*, keep the *y* when you add a suffix.

Nouns		**Verbs**	
turkey	turkeys	stay	stayed

4. If a one-syllable word ends in one vowel and one consonant, double the last consonant when you add a suffix that begins with a vowel.

Nouns		**Verbs**	
swim	swimmer	stop	stopping

Adjectives		
big	bigger	biggest

5. When you choose between *ie* and *ei*, use *ie* except after *c* or for the long *a* sound.
    (Exceptions: *leisure, neither, seize, weird*)

Nouns	**Verbs**	
field	shriek	
neighbors	receive	

6. If a word ends in a single *f* or *fe*, usually change the *f* to *v* when you add *-s* or *-es*.

NOUNS calf   calves   knife   knives

7. If a word ends in *e*, drop the *e* when you add a suffix that begins with a vowel. Keep the *e* when you add a suffix that begins with a consonant.

VERBS drive   driving   **ADVERBS** sure   surely

8. Add an apostrophe and *s* (**'s**) to a singular noun to show possession, but do not add them to a pronoun. Special pronouns show possession.

doctor   doctor's   Mary   Mary's
his   hers   its   ours   yours   theirs

9. The letter *q* is always followed by the letter *u* in English words. The letter *v* is always followed by another letter; it is never the last letter in a word.

question   give

10. Use an apostrophe (**'**) to show where a letter or letters have been left out in a contraction.

is not   isn't   we are   we're   you will   you'll

Another way to help improve your spelling is to keep a notebook of special words. Collect words you think are interesting or hard to spell. Write them carefully in your spelling notebook. You may wish to add a short meaning next to each word.

Your notebook should have a page for each letter of the alphabet. Keeping these words in alphabetical order will make your personal words easy to find when you need them. If you use a looseleaf binder, you can add pages as your spelling notebook grows.

Words Often Written

The words in the list below came from compositions that were written by students your age. They are the words the students used most often. Are they the words *you* use most often, too?

1. also	26. next
2. apple	27. night
3. around	28. no
4. asked	29. off
5. boy	30. old
6. dad	31. once
7. didn't	32. other
8. find	33. put
9. first	34. ran
10. found	35. really
11. friends	36. summer
12. girl	37. take
13. has	38. teacher
14. how	39. their
15. I'd	40. thing
16. I'm	41. think
17. it's	42. thought
18. looked	43. told
19. make	44. took
20. man	45. two
21. more	46. way
22. morning	47. well
23. name	48. where
24. named	49. who
25. never	50. why

Diagraming Guide

Subjects, Verbs, and Direct Objects

Whenever you assemble a model airplane, you use a diagram to see how the parts fit together. In the same way, a sentence diagram can help you see how all the words of a sentence fit together.

To begin a sentence diagram, draw a horizontal line. On this line, write the subject and the verb of the sentence you wish to diagram. Then draw a vertical line to separate the subject and the verb. This shows how you do it.

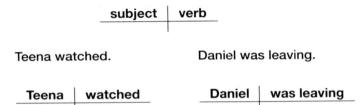

Teena watched.   Daniel was leaving.

The subject of an imperative sentence is usually understood to be *you*. In a diagram, write *you* in parentheses in the subject place, like this.

Walk.   Do continue.

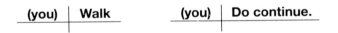

A direct object receives the action of a verb. (See pages 122–123.) To diagram a direct object, write it on the horizontal line after the verb. Separate the direct object from the verb by drawing a vertical line that does not cut through the horizontal line. These diagrams show you how.

Susan repairs bicycles.

Notice that a sentence diagram shows the capital letters of a sentence. Punctuation marks, however, are not shown.

Practice

A. Identify the subject and the verb in each sentence. Then diagram each sentence.

1. Children sing.
2. Listen.
3. Sharon is talking.
4. I was drawing.
5. Linda will try.
6. They forgot.
7. Mark was smiling.
8. Stand.
9. They understand.
10. Frank laughed.

B. Identify the subject, the verb, and the direct object of each sentence. Then diagram each sentence.

11. Joe carried boxes.
12. We moved them.
13. Juan is drinking milk.
14. Mr. Harrison opened windows.
15. They ate supper.
16. Ted cooked chicken.
17. Ann has planted flowers.
18. Judy is taking pictures.
19. Michelle told jokes.
20. I will make shelves.

C. Diagram each of the following sentences.

21. Amy is playing ball.
22. Stop.
23. Cindy was running.
24. We picked tomatoes.
25. Wait.
26. Jill shouted.
27. I bought bread.
28. She has seen Bill.
29. Michael is waving.
30. They sang songs.
31. We were working.
32. Julie painted pictures.
33. I enjoy movies.
34. Arnold is attaching streamers.

Every sentence part can be shown in a sentence diagram. An adjective is written on a slanting line connected to the noun or pronoun it describes. The articles *a, an*, and *the* are also diagramed in this way.

The big truck carries new cars.

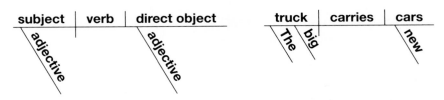

A predicate adjective follows a linking verb and describes the subject. (See pages 236–237.) Diagram a predicate adjective by placing it on the horizontal line after the verb. A line that slants backward separates the predicate adjective from the verb. This slanting line does not cross the horizontal line.

Pat seems happy.

Adverbs are diagramed on slanting lines. An adverb that describes a verb appears directly under the verb.

Trees were swaying slowly.

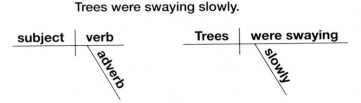

Diagram an adverb that modifies an adjective or another adverb by writing it on a slanting line connected to the word it describes.

Very young children are singing quite loudly.

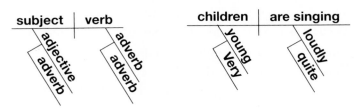

Practice

A. Diagram each sentence. Notice the adjectives and the predicate adjectives.

1. The tiny kitten played.
2. He appeared confident.
3. Pam threw the red ball.
4. Bob is tall.
5. We picked colorful flowers.
6. Many highways cross America.
7. You are ready.
8. Jill borrowed an interesting book.
9. Mountains are majestic.
10. Doris wore a pretty blue sweater.

B. Diagram each sentence. Notice the adverbs.

11. I walked quickly.
12. The very large elephant came near.
13. The noisy crowd watched excitedly.
14. Very warm weather continued.
15. The bird flew quite swiftly.
16. Heather slept soundly.
17. The powerful storm moved closer.
18. The extremely hungry birds ate noisily.
19. The overdue train finally arrived.
20. A very bright light blinked rapidly.

C. Diagram each of the following sentences.

21. The green grass is beautiful.
22. A very colorful butterfly fluttered silently.
23. The gate slowly closed.
24. The little dog barked quite noisily.
25. A new theater opened yesterday.
26. The temperature was falling quite rapidly.
27. Very dark clouds suddenly appeared.
28. The very tall boy bought a newspaper.
29. The little birds chirped softly.
30. Two young girls carefully planted a very small tree.

Glossary of Terms

Abbreviation   An abbreviation is a shortened form of a word. Many abbreviations begin with a capital letter and end with a period. *page 68.*

Action verb   An action verb shows action. *page 116.*

Adjective   An adjective describes a noun or a pronoun. *page 234.*

Adverb   An adverb describes a verb, an adjective, or another adverb. *pages 284, 288.*

Anecdote   An anecdote is a short, interesting story about someone. *page 30.*

Antonyms   Antonyms are words with opposite meanings. *page 348.*

Apostrophe   An apostrophe (') shows where a letter or letters have been left out. *page 186.*

Base word   A base word is the simplest form of a word. *page 134.*

Business letter   A business letter has six parts: the heading, inside address, greeting, body, closing, and signature. *page 206.*

Character   A character is a person, an animal, or an imaginary creature in a story. *page 32.*

Common noun   A common noun is the general name for a person, place, or thing. *page 64.*

Complete predicate   The complete predicate is all the words in the predicate part of a sentence. The predicate part tells what the subject is or does. *page 8.*

Complete subject   The complete subject is all the words in the subject part of a sentence. The subject part names someone or something. *page 8.*

Compound   A compound is a word formed from two or more words. *page 294.*

Compound predicate   A compound predicate is two or more verbs that have the same subject. *page 394.*

Compound sentence   A compound sentence contains two or more simple sentences joined by a conjunction. *page 396.*

Compound subject   A compound subject is two or more simple subjects that have the same predicate. *page 390.*

Conjunction   A word such as *and* or *or* that joins other words is a conjunction. *page 390.*

Context clue   A clue that helps a reader find the meaning of an unknown word is a context clue. *page 72.*

Contraction   A contraction is a shortened form of two words. *page 186.*

Declarative sentence   A declarative sentence makes a statement. It ends with a period. *page 6.*

Direct object   A direct object receives the action of the verb. *page 122.*

Encyclopedia   An encyclopedia is a set of reference books with articles about people, places, things, and ideas. The articles are arranged in alphabetical order. *page 310.*

Exaggeration   Exaggeration is the stretching of the truth. *page 146.*

Exclamatory sentence   An exclamatory sentence expresses strong feeling. It ends with an exclamation mark. *page 6.*

Fact   A fact is true information that can be checked. *page 202.*

Future tense   The future tense of a verb shows action that will happen in the future. *page 124.*

Haiku   Haiku is a Japanese verse form that presents a picture to which we add our own thoughts and images. *page 365.*

Helping verb   A helping verb works with the main verb. *page 120.*

Homographs   Homographs are words that are spelled the same but have different meanings and origins. *page 400.*

Homophones   Homophones are words that sound alike but have different meanings and spellings. *page 188.*

Imperative sentence   An imperative sentence gives a command or makes a request. It ends with a period. *page 6.*

Initial   An initial is the first letter of a name. It is written with a capital letter and followed by a period. *page 68.*

Interjection   An interjection is a word that expresses feeling or emotion. It is usually followed by an exclamation mark. *page 34.*

Interrogative sentence   An interrogative sentence asks a question. It ends with a question mark. *page 6.*

Irregular verb   An irregular verb does not form the past or past participle by adding *-ed*. *page 128.*

Linking verb   A linking verb shows being. It connects the subject of a sentence with a word or words in the predicate. *page 118.*

Main verb   The main verb is the most important verb in the predicate of a sentence. *page 120.*

Metaphor   A metaphor compares two things by saying one thing *is* the other. *page 148.*

Noun   A noun names a person, a place, a thing, or an idea. *page 60.*

Object of the preposition   An object of the preposition is the noun or pronoun that follows a preposition. *page 340.*

Object pronoun   The pronouns *me, you, him, her, it, us,* and *them* are object pronouns. *page 180.*

Opinion   An opinion is what someone *thinks* is true. *page 202.*

Order of importance   Order of importance is a way of organizing details, either by stating the most important first, or by building up to it last. *page 258.*

Outline   An outline organizes information into main ideas and supporting details. *page 314.*

Paragraph   A paragraph is a group of sentences that tell about one main idea. The first word of a paragraph is indented. *page 86.*

Paragraph of comparison   A paragraph of comparison tells how one thing is *like* another. *page 414.*

Paragraph of contrast   A paragraph of contrast tells about differences between two similar things. *page 416.*

Part of speech   A part of speech tells how a word is used in a sentence. *page 388.*

Past tense   The past tense of a verb shows action that already happened. *page 124.*

Persuasive paragraph   A persuasive paragraph gives the writer's opinion and reasons to support it. Reasons are often listed in the order of importance. *page 204.*

Plot   A plot is the series of events in a story in the order in which they happen. *page 32.*

Plural noun   A plural noun names more than one person, place, thing, or idea. *page 62.*

Possessive noun   A possessive noun shows ownership. *page 70.*

Possessive pronoun   The pronouns *my, your, his, her, its, our,* and *their* are possessive pronouns. They show ownership and replace possessive nouns. *page 182.*

Predicate adjective   A predicate adjective follows a linking verb and describes the subject of a sentence. *page 236.*

Prefix   A prefix is a word part added to the beginning of a word. It changes the meaning of the word. *page 134.*

Preposition   A preposition relates a noun or a pronoun to another word in the sentence. *page 340.*

Prepostional phrase   A prepositional phrase includes the preposition, its object, and any words that come between them. *page 342.*

Present tense   The present tense of a verb shows action that happens now. *page 124.*

Prewriting   Prewriting is the stage in which writers gather ideas and get ready to write. *page Introduction 4.*

Pronoun   A pronoun takes the place of a noun or nouns. *page 176.*

Proofreading   Proofreading is the stage in which writers look for and correct errors in their writing. *page Introduction 7.*

Proper noun   A proper noun names a particular person, place, or thing. Each important word in a proper noun is capitalized. *page 64.*

Publishing   Publishing is the stage in which writers share their writing with others. *page Introduction 7.*

Quotation marks   Quotation marks (" ") show the exact words of a speaker. *page 34.*

Repetition   Repetition is the repeating of a word or phrase as a way of bringing sound to poetry. *page 363.*

Revising   Revising is the stage in which writers make changes to improve their writing. *page Introduction 6.*

Run-on sentence   A run-on sentence is two or more sentences not separated by correct punctuation or connecting words. *page 398.*

Sentence   A sentence is a group of words that expresses a complete thought. *page 4.*

Setting   A setting is the time and the place of a story. *page 32.*

Simile   A simile uses the word *like* or *as* to compare two things. *page 148.*

Simple predicate   The simple predicate is the main word or words in the complete predicate of a sentence. *page 12.*

Simple subject   The simple subject is the main word in the complete subject of a sentence. *page 10.*

Singular noun   A singular noun names one person, place, thing, or idea. *page 62.*

Space order   Space order is the way things are arranged in space. *page 258.*

Subject pronoun   The pronouns *I*, *you*, *she*, *he*, *it*, *we*, and *they* are subject pronouns. They replace nouns that are the subjects of sentences. *page 178.*

Suffix   A suffix is a word part added to the end of a word. It changes the meaning of the word. *page 242.*

Supporting sentence   A supporting sentence develops the main idea of a paragraph. *page 88.*

Synonyms   Synonyms are words with similar meanings. *page 348.*

Tense   The tense of a verb shows the time of the action. *page 124.*

Thesaurus   A thesaurus is a book that lists entries in alphabetical order. It gives synonyms, or words with similar meanings, for each entry. Antonyms, or words with opposite meanings, are listed for many entries. *page 16.*

Topic sentence   The topic sentence states the main idea of a paragraph. *page 88.*

Verb   A word that shows action or being is a verb. *pages 116, 118.*

Writing   Writing is the stage in which writers put their ideas on paper. *page Introduction 5.*

Index

L M N – VH – 97 96 95